MARY AND THE FATHERS OF THE CHURCH

LUIGI GAMBERO, S.M.

MARY AND THE FATHERS
OF THE CHURCH

The Blessed Virgin Mary in Patristic Thought

Translated by Thomas Buffer

IGNATIUS PRESS   SAN FRANCISCO

Title of the Italian original:
Maria nel pensiero dei padri della Chiesa
© 1991 Edizione Paoline, s.r.l., Milan

Cover art:
Madonna and Child with Angels, detail
Duccio
Galleria Nazionale dell'Umbria, Perugia, Italy
Scala/Art Resource, NY

Cover design by Roxanne Mei Lum

© 1999 Ignatius Press, San Francisco
ISBN 978–0–89870–686–4
Library of Congress catalogue number 98–71259
Printed in the United States of America ∞

Contents

PART TWO

FROM THE COUNCIL OF NICAEA
TO THE COUNCIL OF EPHESUS (431)

PART FOUR

THE END OF THE PATRISTIC PERIOD
(SIXTH–EIGHTH CENTURY)

Abbreviations

AAS   *Acta apostolicae sedis* (Vatican City, 1909–)

ACO   *Acta conciliorum oecumenicorum*, ed. E. Schwartz and J. Straub (Berlin, 1914–)

CCL   *Corpus Christianorum*, Series Latina (Turnhout, 1953–)

CSCO   *Corpus scriptorum Christianorum orientalium* (Paris-Louvain, 1903–)

CSEL   *Corpus scriptorum ecclesiasticorum latinorum* (Vienna, 1865–)

CWS   *Classics of Western Spirituality* (New York: Paulist Press)

GCS   *Die griechischen christlichen Schriftsteller* (Leipzig-Berlin, 1897–)

MGH   *Monumenta germaniae historica* (Hanover-Berlin, 1826–)

PG   *Patrologiae cursus completus*, Series Graeca (Paris: Migne, 1857–1866)

PL   *Patrologiae cursus completus*, Series Latina (Paris: Migne, 1841–1864)

PLS   *Patrologiae latinae supplementum*, ed. A. Hamman (Paris, 1957–1971)

PO   *Patrologia orientalis* (Paris, 1903–)

SC   *Sources chrétiennes* (Paris, 1941–)

TU   *Texte und Untersuchungen zur Geschichte der altchristlichen Literatur* (Leipzig-Berlin, 1882–)

Introduction

The exploration of the very earliest history of Christianity, where the original roots of Christian faith and theology are buried, is an undertaking that has never ceased to arouse enthusiasm and curiosity. This is so despite the fact that this period remains enigmatic and mysterious in many ways. It poses various problems of a historical-critical nature, both for the student of Christian origins and for the theologian. Still, many find it truly fascinating to rediscover the beginnings of such an enormously important religious and historical phenomenon as Christianity.

In any case, the purpose of such research cannot be the search for a verification of our religious creed and our personal Christian life, or a quest to make sure that we are being faithful to the patrimony of faith (*depositum fidei*) entrusted by the Lord to his apostles and to the Church. The teaching of the Church, in every age of her history, is sufficient to guarantee this certainty, because it embraces the whole treasury of tradition, rendered present and alive by the faith and Christian action of the people of God.

Our interest in rediscovering the very beginning of the Christian tradition becomes more understandable if considered from a different perspective. For us, retrieving the origins of Christian doctrine can be like tasting the fresh waters of a spring, where the word of God is poured out by the pen of man under the illuminating and charismatic impulse of the Spirit, where the first Christian generations found nourishment for their faith, prayer, and life. We, too, know the wellsprings of this inspiration: Sacred Scripture and the apostolic tradition, the marvelous works of the Holy Spirit, acting in the lives of the scriptural authors and Fathers of the Church to make them authoritative witnesses and outstanding heralds of the good news of Jesus, through their preaching, writings, and living example.

The teaching of the Fathers boasts both evangelical simplicity and doctrinal riches. When we examine it today, it is easy to discover that this same spiritual patrimony has survived to our day as the treasure of today's Church. This treasure has been handed down to us in a long development, from generation to generation, and we will have to hand it on to future generations.[1] The study of the Fathers involves more than just admiring and recognizing what they accomplished in developing Christian thought; above all, it is a task carried out by today's believers on behalf of tomorrow's Christians. The Church makes her own the words of the apostle Paul, "I hand on to you what I received from the Lord" (1 Cor 11:23). The faith of the Fathers has to be handed down to successive generations, intact, yet enriched and updated by the Christian experience of present generations.

The Fathers of the Church were the first to put this divine mandate into practice. Blessed with a special charism, in most cases related to their role as bishops,[2] they nourished themselves on the word of God, profoundly assimilating its contents. They made it the object of their preaching and writing, but above all they witnessed to it by their lives, thus becoming the first models of Christian holiness. The Church recognizes these eminent persons as Fathers of the Church on the basis of two conditions: the authoritative teaching of revealed truth and the example of personal holiness. The time in which they lived (the first six or seven centuries) was still close enough to the historical period of New Testament revelation that their mentality and upbringing made them particularly attentive and open to the hermeneutical problems present from the beginning of Christianity. They felt the urgent need to provide an exact interpretation of God's word, which, inevitably, is expressed in human language.

In addition, their status within the Church makes them faithful and authoritative witnesses to the faith of the Christian people, and this is the most important aspect of the teaching they have left us. Cardinal Newman makes the point well, "We receive those doctrines which [the Fathers] thus teach, not merely because they teach them, but because they bear witness that all Christians everywhere

---

[1] Cf. J. P. Mackey, *The Modern Theology of Tradition* (New York, 1963), p. x.

[2] The hypothesis has been advanced that holding the episcopal office is one of the requirements for a man to be a Father of the Church. This would make it possible to distinguish between a Father of the Church and a simple early Christian writer. It appears that this distinction ought to be made in the case of an author who, knowingly or unknowingly, taught a heretical doctrine.

then held them."[3] And, in more recent times, Pius XII has emphasized the role the Fathers played as witnesses to the universal tradition of the Church.[4]

For all these reasons, it is not difficult to understand the importance of the doctrine that the Fathers of the Church taught about Mary. We can understand and evaluate the first steps taken by Christian tradition as it labors, sometimes with difficulty, to remain faithful to the Marian statements of the New Testament. During the first centuries, the Fathers and other Christian writers rarely speak of Mary apart from Christ. Allusions to the Virgin usually arise out of a christological and biblical context. The discussion of the mystery of the incarnate Word becomes clear and concrete when Mary and her role as mother are brought into it.

As the centuries passed, especially from the second half of the fourth century on, the Fathers and other Christian writers began to pay more attention to Mary, although we must grant that the quantity of Marian literature produced in that period is fairly modest. We also see ecclesiological discourse beginning to take an interest in the Mary–Church parallel. After the Councils of Ephesus (431) and Chalcedon (451), there is a sharp increase in the level of Marian doctrine and devotion. Mary's extraordinary role as Virgin Mother of the Savior had more and more influence on the faith of the Church. Christians began using the texts of Scripture to reflect on the mystery of this woman, in whom the Lord's extraordinary intervention was interwoven with her own faith and openness.

The homilies of the Church Fathers help to make even more room for the Blessed Virgin in the liturgical worship of the Christian people and in the personal devotion of the faithful. This devotion took on a life of its own, to the point that Mary's conduct became a model for Christian life. This influence became even more apparent in the Christian practice of consecrated virginity and in the monastic life in general. Then, under the influence of Western theology, the Mary–Church parallel took on considerable importance, which would influence future developments in Mariology and ecclesiology.

---

[3] John Henry Newman, *Discussion and Arguments on Various Subjects* (London: Longmans, Green, and Co., 1899), p. 45.

[4] *Munificentissimus Deus*, AAS 42 (1950), pp. 760–62, 767–69.

At the same time, the patristic age was already drawing to its conclusion, under the influence of the historical and cultural transformation of the Greco-Roman world. This period, from the end of the fifth century to the beginning of the seventh, saw an extraordinary flowering of Marian literature, especially in the field of homiletics. This was favorable soil for the development of panegyrics directing the attention of Christians toward the moral figure of the Mother of the Lord. She became, not only an object of admiration and exaltation, but also a model for imitation with regard to the Christian moral life and the practice of Gospel virtues.

Another interesting phenomenon of this period was the development of Marian hymns. At their best, these compositions wonderfully combined formal beauty of composition with richness of doctrinal content. Worship and devotion mingled in celebrations of the first Marian feast days. It was ever more apparent to the eyes of the faithful that the Virgin Mary, after accomplishing her essential function in the mystery of the redeeming Word incarnate, continues to carry out a mission. This mission binds her closely together with the people of God, who are called to receive the grace of salvation and bring it to every nation. The Fathers of the Church became the interpreters of the sentiments and convictions of the Christian faithful; in so doing, they worked out the Marian doctrinal patrimony that became the basis for all later Church tradition.

The witness of the Fathers might give the impression that Marian doctrine and piety passed through a rather long and slow process of evolution. We must, however, recall that the times of the Lord's grace are different from our own. The Lord knows how to adapt himself to the rhythms of the continual development of each individual and of humanity as a whole, and he awaits our answer with goodness and patience. Beneath the sobriety that veils the Marian doctrine of the earliest Fathers, the fertile seeds of future developments were planted, developments that profoundly influenced the Christian authors of the golden period of patristics as well as those of its closing years.

Reading the Fathers of the Church with an awareness of history, we become convinced that faith, devotion, and interest in the ineffable mystery of the Mother of the Lord were never lacking among the people of God,[5] even though the manifestations and expressions of faith and doctrine may vary in different historical periods. Recent trends in the Church's Magisterium and among theologians with regard to the mystery of Mary confirm that the teaching of the Fathers contains something indispensable, whose value the Church constantly recalls to us, so that we may build our Christian faith and Christian mentality upon the foundation left us by the Fathers.

READING

THE MARIAN TEACHING OF THE FATHERS OF THE CHURCH

For myself, hopeless as you consider it, I am not ashamed still to take my stand upon the Fathers, and do not mean to budge. The history of their times is not yet an old almanac to me. Of course I maintain the value and authority of the "Schola," as one of the *loci theologici*; nevertheless I sympathize with Petavius in preferring to the "contentious and subtle theology" of the middle age, that "more elegant and fruitful teaching which is moulded after the image of erudite Antiquity."

The Fathers made me a Catholic, and I am not going to kick down the ladder by which I ascended into the Church. It is a ladder quite as serviceable for that purpose now, as it was twenty years ago. Though I hold, as you know, a process of development in Apostolic truth as time goes on, such development does not supersede the Fathers, but explains and completes them. And, in particular, as regards our teaching concerning the Blessed Virgin, with the Fathers I am content;—and to the subject of that teaching I mean to address myself at once. I do so, because you say, as I myself have said in former years, that "That vast system as to the Blessed Virgin . . . to all of us has been the special *crux* of the Roman system."

Here, let me say, as on other points, the Fathers are enough for me. I do not wish to say more than they suggest to me, and will not

---

[5] Cf. Théodore Koehler, S.M., *Maria nei primi secoli*, Fons signatus, 10 (Vercelli: Centro Mariano Chaminade, 1971), p. 21.

say less. You, I know, will profess the same; and thus we can join issue on a clear and broad principle, and may hope to come to some intelligible result. We are to have a Treatise on the subject of our Lady soon from the pen of the Most Reverend Prelate; but that cannot interfere with such a mere argument from the Fathers as that to which I shall confine myself here. Nor indeed, as regards that argument itself, do I profess to be offering you any new matter, any facts which have not been used by others,—by great divines, as Petavius,—by living writers, nay, by myself on other occasions. I write fresh nevertheless, and that for three reasons; first, because I wish to contribute to the accurate statement and the full exposition of the argument in question; next, because I may gain a more patient hearing than has sometimes been granted to better men than myself; lastly, because there just now seems a call on me, under my circumstances, to avow plainly what I do and what I do not hold about the Blessed Virgin, that others may know, did they come to stand where I stand, what they would, and what they would not, be bound to hold concerning her.

—John Henry Newman, *A Letter Addressed to the Rev. E. B. Pusey, D.D., on His Recent Eirenicon*, London: Longmans, Green, Reader, and Dyer, 1866

PART ONE

*From the Apostolic Age
to the Council of Nicaea (325)*

Prologue

This is the period most directly influenced by the apostolic preaching. In style and content, it closely resembles the New Testament. Consequently, as the Sacred Scripture makes only rare and brief statements about the Mother of Jesus, the same thing happens in the Christian writings of this period. However, allusions to the holy Virgin are often put into the context of a profession of faith, so that they appear as clear and explicit testimonies of the Church's faith and traditional doctrine at that time.

Here it is helpful to remember that Christian theology began to be expressed in Christology; more precisely, with the primitive Church's concern to formulate a kerygmatic definition of the person of the Lord and of his earthly mission. At first, the Church focused her christological teaching on the mystery of the Lord's Resurrection. Quite early, however, the Church also turned her attention to the events of Jesus' birth. Though this initially happens only to a limited extent, we must recognize that the Church was less interested in the historical modalities of Christ's birth than in the mystery of his Incarnation, which was one of the principal objectives of the apostolic kerygma from the beginning. The ancient Christians held beyond a doubt both the divine origin of the person of Christ and his perfect humanity; but they likewise held that his actions would be incomprehensible if reduced to a scheme of purely human categories.

The first christological preoccupation of the Church was with the question of the relations between Christ's human nature and his divine nature, and between Christ, as Son, and his Father. Two attempts at a solution, diametrically opposed to one another but both denying the data of revelation, appeared quite early on the horizon of theological thought. The sect of the Ebionites, which originated as a group of Jewish Christians, denied both the divinity of Jesus and his virginal birth, considering him the mere natural son of Joseph and Mary. The Ebionites, however, accepted him as Messiah and awaited his return in glory. The opposite solution, that of the Docetists, denied instead the humanity of Christ, reducing it to mere appearance. The Docetists were a particular group within the religious and cultural movement known as *Gnosticism*. The Gnostics taught that Jesus did not have a real body; that it was only in appearance that he showed himself in the flesh, suffered, and died on the Cross. He was a completely spiritual being, and, therefore, his birth from Mary was not real either. He passed through her, without taking anything from her flesh.

These first christological heresies offered the earliest Fathers of the Church the occasion to assert the truth about Jesus with vigor. Rather than using theological arguments, they re-present, in a typically evangelical style, the message Christ announced about himself. It is this doctrine that constitutes the primitive apostolic kerygma, in which the following christological statements can be recognized: Jesus was born of the Virgin Mary by the power of the Holy Spirit; he died and rose; he was glorified at the Father's right hand; he will return at the end of time.[1] We observe, then, how the virginal birth of Jesus from Mary formed part of the central kerygma of primitive Christianity. On the other hand, this confirms that, in the first centuries, the Church did not know any mariological doctrine separated from christological doctrine.[2] Mary's role is presented as being strictly tied to the person of her Son.

---

[1] Adolf von Harnack, *History of Dogma*, trans. from the 3d German ed. by Neil Buchanan (New York: Dover Publications, 1961), vol. 2.

[2] Walter Delius, *Geschichte der Marienverehrung* (Munich: E. Reinhardt, 1963), p. 35.

I

THE APOSTOLIC FATHERS

At the beginning of the Church's tradition, we encounter certain writers called "Apostolic Fathers". Apparently, these men were personally acquainted with the apostles. Only some of the Apostolic Fathers and their works are known to us: Ignatius of Antioch, Polycarp of Smyrna, Clement of Rome, Papias of Hierapolis, the *Shepherd of Hermas*, the *Letter of Barnabas*, the *Letter to Diognetus*, and the *Didache*. The period in which these authors lived corresponds to the initial spread of the gospel in the Greco-Roman world. While the Christian religion was proving how effective and forceful it could be, it also sensed the urgent need to defend itself from the numerous religious and philosophical currents of that time, which threatened to empty Christianity of its content and transcendent values. In an environment permeated by eclecticism and Gnosticism, the necessity of announcing the Lord as true God and true man led preachers to formulate a gospel centered on the mystery of the Incarnation of the Son of God.

In such a context, perhaps, we should expect to meet the name of the Virgin Mother frequently; but if we put the problem purely in terms of quantity, we find ourselves mistaken: the name of Mary rarely appears in the writings of the Apostolic Fathers. This parallels the situation of Scripture, where the figure of Mary remains, at times, in a sort of *chiaroscuro*.[1] In the Old Testament, Mary appears in a veiled way, in enigmatic prophecies that signify different things simultaneously. In the New Testament, she is silently present in the so-called "infancy narratives"; she fades back into obscurity during the years of Jesus' public life; she reappears briefly under her Son's

---

[1] Cf. Hilda Graef, *Mary in Doctrine and Devotion*, 2 vols. (New York: Sheed and Ward, 1964).

Cross; her presence in the Christian community of Jerusalem is just touched upon in the Acts of the Apostles; she finishes by becoming mingled with the figure of the Church in the vision of Revelation. Likewise, in the writings of the Apostolic Fathers, silence about the person and life of Mary seems to be a constantly observed rule. And it is not difficult to isolate the reasons, the most obvious being of a pastoral nature.

Almost all of the Hellenistic religions of that time boasted of some feminine deity who had a considerable influence on the faithful. From this we can understand the spread of a cult dedicated to a kind of mother-goddess who took different names, according to the places in which she was honored and the different religions practiced there: for the Romans, she was *Magna Mater*; for the Phrygians, *Cybele*; for the Palestinians, *Astarte*; for the Egyptians, *Isis*; for the Ephesians, *Diana*. Still others could be found in religions outside the Greco-Roman world.

In announcing the gospel to people whose mentality was conditioned by belief in a cult of this kind of feminine deity, there was a risk that placing stress on the figure of Mary might provoke ambiguous or even erroneous interpretations of her person and her role in relation to Christ. Hence, the Church of that time preferred not to make her one of the usual themes of her evangelical preaching.

But perhaps this is not the only reason. There could also be an explanation of a "mystical" nature for the silence of Scripture and the ancient Fathers about Mary. Silence is part of the mystery of God. Ignatius of Antioch affirmed that Christ himself "came forth from silence"[2] and that "even those things he did in silence are worthy of the Father."[3] And he adds: "Whoever grasps the words of Jesus is able to hear his silence as well."[4] We could apply this arcane explanation to the primitive Church's silence about the holy Virgin. Indeed, in speaking of the bishop of Philadelphia, Ignatius makes the significant distinction, "He accomplishes more by his silence than others who speak in vain."[5] Apparently, the primitive Church remained faithful to this Ignatian principle. The few references to

---

[2] *To the Magnesians* 8, 2.
[3] *To the Ephesians* 15, 1.
[4] Ibid., 15, 2.
[5] *To the Philadelphians* 1, 1.

Mary in the writings of the earliest Fathers reveal a capacity to emphasize her mysterious maternal presence in the faith and life of the first Christians: a presence rendered even more intense and intriguing by silence.

Ignatius of Antioch

Tradition presents Ignatius as a most extraordinary character, gifted with a rich and fascinating personality and with an overwhelming faith. He was passionately devoted to Christ. St. Peter's second successor to the episcopal see of Antioch, in Syria, he was arrested during a persecution begun in that province around the end of the first century. He was brought to Rome under the escort of ten soldiers whom he called "leopards", apparently because of the fierce treatment they reserved for him. During the long and painful journey to the capital, where he was to be committed to the flames in the arena, Ignatius wrote seven beautiful letters to various Christian communities. These letters remain among the most precious and fascinating documents of primitive Christianity.[6] His letter to the Church of Rome is famous; his words arouse admiration and emotion as he begs the Christians not to use their good offices to save him from martyrdom:

> I am writing to all the Churches to tell them all that I die willingly for God, as long as you do not hinder me. I beseech you not to show me unseasonable kindness. Allow me to become the food of the wild beasts, for through them I will reach God. I am God's wheat; let me be ground by the teeth of the wild beasts, that I may be found Christ's

---

[6] Three editions of Ignatius' letters have been compiled: one long, one short, and one of medium length. In general, modern scholars exclude the first two as unauthentic and accept the authenticity of the medium-length version, which comprises seven letters: Ephesians, Magnesians, Trallians, Romans, Philadelphians, Smyrnaeans, and Polycarp. Joseph Barber Lightfoot, in *The Apostolic Fathers* (London, New York, 1889–1890), vol. 1, pt. 2, closed the controversy by demonstrating the authenticity of these seven letters. A recent publication by Josep Rius-Camps, *The Four Authentic Letters of Ignatius, the Martyr*, Orientalia Christiana Analecta, 213 (Rome: Pontificium Institutum Orientale, 1980), does not appear to discredit Lightfoot's conclusions.

pure bread. Better still, entice the wild beasts to become my tomb
and to leave no part of my body behind. Then, when I am dead, I will
no longer be a burden to anyone. Only then shall I truly be a disciple
of Jesus Christ, when the world will not see so much as my body.
Entreat Christ on my behalf that, through these instruments, I may
become [God's] sacrifice.[7]

As far as Mary is concerned, it appears that Ignatius was faithful to
his convictions concerning the mystical value of silence. His references to Mary are rare and brief; however, they witness to an extremely significant fact: the mystery of the birth of Jesus from the
Virgin Mary had entered into the most ancient liturgical tradition of
the Church. In fact, he hands down some of the most ancient professions of the Christian faith, which were doubtless used in liturgical
celebrations, especially during the rite of baptism, and in which there
is an explicit mention of the Virgin. In these texts, brief but incisive
and full of vigor, Mary is presented as Mother of Christ according to
his human nature, as the heavenly Father is his Father according to
his divine nature.[8] Mary's motherhood becomes part of God's plan of
salvation and is the fruit of the Holy Spirit's intervention.[9] To the
Christians of Tralles, Ignatius presents Mary as the woman who has
inserted Christ into the line of David's descendants and, thus, as the
instrument for the realization of the messianic prophecies.[10] In another passage, Mary is pointed out as the person who guarantees the
reality of the Savior's human nature: he was born of her in the same
way that every child is born of his own mother.[11]

From Ignatius' statements, it is clear how important the ancient
Christians considered it to express their faith in God made flesh by
explicitly mentioning his birth from the Virgin; and it does not seem
difficult to understand their motivation.

Among the threats against the Church, Docetism was especially
dangerous. It denied the reality of the Incarnation: Christ was not a
true man but a kind of human phantasm. Ignatius seems to be con-
testing this heresy when he insists that Jesus was truly born from

---

[7] *To the Romans* 4, 1–2.

[8] *To the Ephesians* 7, 2.

[9] Ibid., 18, 2.

[10] *To the Trallians* 9, 1.

[11] *To the Smyrnaeans* 1, 1.

Mary, testifying to the Church's faith in the reality of the Incarnation and, consequently, the value of Christ's redemptive action. Mary, then, truly engendered the flesh of Christ; she really carried him in her virginal womb, and his birth is the wondrous result of the Holy Spirit's direct action in her. This is God's plan of salvation, which Ignatius calls the "economy", a term that later became routine in the Christian tradition.

In his letter to the Ephesians, Ignatius stresses three mysteries that, in God's plan, had to be kept hidden from the prince of this world, namely, the devil: the virginity of Mary, the virginal birth of the Son of God, and his death on the Cross.[12] But Ignatius does not explain why or how these mysteries had to remain hidden from the devil. Other Fathers, after Ignatius, explained that Mary's marriage to Joseph was the means of hiding these three mysteries from the devil. God refrains from solemnly revealing them until the glorious manifestation of the Lord Jesus in his Resurrection.

The Marian testimony of Ignatius of Antioch, though extremely succinct, has great value. It echoes the gospel message; it refers to the Church's most ancient professions of faith; and it comes from a man who, as a bishop, was considered to be vested with teaching authority.

READINGS

IGNATIAN PROFESSIONS OF FAITH

There is only one Physician, having both flesh and spirit, born and unborn, God become man, true life in death, from Mary and from God, first passible and then impassible—Jesus Christ our Lord.

—Ignatius of Antioch, *To the Ephesians* 7, 2

For our God Jesus Christ, according to God's economy, was conceived by Mary of the seed of David (cf. Jn 7:42; Rom 3:27), but also

---

[12] *To the Ephesians* 19, 1.

by the Holy Spirit. He was born and baptized, that by his Passion he might purify the water.

—Ignatius of Antioch, *To the Ephesians* 18, 2

Stop your ears, therefore, when anyone speaks to you of anything except Jesus Christ, David's descendant and Mary's Son, who was truly born, and ate, and drank; who was truly persecuted under Pontius Pilate, truly crucified and died, in the sight of [beings in] heaven and earth and under the earth; who also truly rose from the dead, his Father raising him up—this same Father who will likewise raise us who believe in him as well, through Jesus Christ, apart from whom we do not have true life.

—Ignatius of Antioch, *To the Trallians* 9, 1–2

[The Lord] is truly descended from David according to the flesh (Rom 1:3, 4), and the Son of God by the will and power of God; he was truly born of a virgin and baptized by John in order to fulfill every command (Mt 3:15). Under Pontius Pilate and Herod the tetrarch, he was really and truly nailed [to the Cross] in the flesh for our sake.

—Ignatius of Antioch, *To the Smyrnaeans* 1, 1

2

THE NEW TESTAMENT APOCRYPHA

In every age, religious souls have yearned to know Jesus and the other important characters in the story of our salvation. The Virgin Mary has always had a privileged place in this kind of understandable and legitimate curiosity. The silence of the New Testament writings and the Apostolic Fathers concerning her person left a knowledge gap that Christians have been trying to fill since the first centuries. In response to this need, the so-called New Testament *apocrypha* proliferated—works that, with their sometimes fantastic and picturesque accounts, went overboard in making up for the extremely scarce information in the inspired books of Scripture.

Some of these writings come from the earliest Christian times. They cannot be considered a witness to the official teaching of the Church, but they can at least serve to give a certain idea of the religious interests and Marian piety of their time and of the questions that the faithful asked about the Lord's Mother. These writings note her mysterious presence and important role in the divine work of salvation, which is perpetuated in the time of the Church.

The anonymous authors of the apocryphal writings, therefore, are not pursuing objectives of a dogmatic or apologetic character, but they do offer some nourishment to the faith and devotion of the Christian people.[1]

The list of known apocrypha that are concerned more or less predominantly with the holy Virgin is quite long. Some are of Judeo-Christian origin, such as the *Ascension of Isaiah*, the oldest document that stresses Mary's virginity *in partu*,[2] and the *Odes of Solomon*, whose

---

[1] For an English translation of the New Testament apocrypha, see James Keith Elliott, *The Apocryphal New Testament* (Oxford: Clarendon Press, 1993).

[2] "And while they were alone, Mary looked up and saw a little child, and she was frightened. And at that very moment her womb was found as it had been

text dedicated to the Virgin, in the nineteenth ode, contains some very enigmatic statements.[3] Others make up the category of the so-called *apocrypha of the nativity and infancy of Jesus*. Still others give an extensive account of the Passion and Resurrection of Jesus, with lengthy references to his Mother. Then there is the series of so-called "acts", usually attributed to some apostle, and the series of "apocalypses". Among the apocrypha written in the Coptic language, we find two that speak extensively of Mary: the *Gospel of Philip*[4] and the *Gospel of Thomas*.[5] The anonymous authors of these writings do not always distinguish between real historical facts and imaginative exaggerations or fairy-tale touches. Origen suggests a useful criterion for evaluating this kind of literature:

> We are not unaware that many of these secret writings were produced by wicked men, famous for their iniquity. . . . We must therefore use caution in accepting all these secret writings that circulate under the name of saints . . . because some of them were written to destroy the truth of our Scripture and to impose a false teaching. On the other hand, we should not totally reject writings that might be useful in shedding light on the Scripture. It is a sign of a great man to hear and carry out the advice of Scripture: "Test everything; retain what is good" (1 Th 5:21).[6]

This criterion of common sense and balance allows us to recover precious information from a literary corpus that, from the point of view of its religious and historical value, is so copious and at the same time quite varied.

---

before she had conceived" (Robert Henry Charles, trans., rev. by J. N. T. Barton in H. F. D. Sparks, ed., *The Apocryphal Old Testament* [Oxford: Clarendon Press, 1984], pp. 809–10). This apocryphal text, which shows strong Gnostic influences, dates from the end of the first century or the beginning of the second century.

[3] English trans. in Sparks, *Apocryphal Old Testament*. This was written in the first half of the second century.

[4] English trans. by R. M. Wilson, *The Gospel of Philip* (London: A. R. Mowbray, 1962).

[5] Elliott, *Apocryphal New Testament*, pp. 123–47.

[6] *In Matth.* 28; PG 13, 1637.

The Protoevangelium of James

This work belongs to the group of infancy narratives and stories of Mary's life from her birth to the birth of Jesus. The original title was "The Nativity of Mary", but the title by which it is universally known and cited is the *Protoevangelium of James*, since it is attributed to the apostle James the Less. The earliest manuscript is contained in the Bodmer Papyrus V.[7] The Bollandist Emile de Strycker, comparing this text with other Greek manuscripts, the Syriac and Armenian editions, and the old edition of Tischendorf,[8] has furnished us with an excellent critical edition.[9]

It was probably written around the middle of the second century. Its author must have been a non-Jew or, at most, a Jew who lived outside of Palestine, since he seems to possess a limited knowledge of Palestinian geography and Jewish customs.

Notwithstanding the limits and shortcomings that a work of this genre exhibits, we must recognize that it cast an undeniable spell over the Christian mentality of the first centuries and that it has profoundly conditioned Christian liturgy, preaching, popular devotion, and art. It has a minimal value from the theological point of view; however, because of its popular character and extraordinarily wide distribution, even the Fathers of the Church referred to it, especially when writing and speaking to the people. Despite its minimal theological value, we may recognize that the *Protoevangelium* has great value because of its antiquity.[10]

The Virgin is presented as having been an extraordinary child since the beginning of her life, predestined to great things. This follows a well-known biblical structure that, among other things, would typically have a birth occurring within a series of paranormal events, marked by a direct intervention on the part of God. It is here that the names of the Virgin's parents are given for the first time.

---

[7] Michel Testuz, *Papyrus Bodmer V: Nativité de Marie* (Cologne-Geneva: Bibliotheca Bodmeriana, 1958).

[8] Constantin von Tischendorf, *Evangelia Apocrypha* (Leipzig: H. Mendelssohn, 1876), pp. 1–49.

[9] Emile de Strycker, *La Forme la plus ancienne du Protévangile de Jacques*, Subsidia Hagiographica, 33 (Brussels: Société des Bollandistes, 1961).

[10] See Elliott, *Apocryphal New Testament*, pp. 48–49.

They are called Joachim and Anna, a wealthy couple, not necessarily elderly, but afflicted by the problem of sterility, which led them to turn to the Lord with insistent and anguished supplications. One day, finally, their prayers were heard.

Obviously, the plot is stereotypical, as is its purpose, which is to prepare the earth for an extraordinary divine intervention. This illustrates how responsive the Lord is to those who pray with faith and perseverance and the exceptional mission to which he calls his creature who is born amid such extraordinary circumstances. There is even an angel of the Lord to announce the blessed event. Angels present themselves separately to the two spouses and bring them a joyful proclamation:

> Anna, Anna! The Lord has heard your prayer: you shall conceive and bear, and your offspring shall be spoken of in the whole world (4:1). . . .
>   Joachim, Joachim! The Lord has heard your prayer. Go down from here; behold, your wife Anna shall conceive (4:2).[11]

It appears that the slightly premature birth of the baby (in the seventh month) also underlines the exceptional character of her future life. She was given the name Mary, and she soon became the object of unusual care and attention on the part of her two happy parents.

A kind of official presentation of the baby to the people of Israel happened when she reached her first birthday. During a solemn banquet, to which the priests, the scribes, the elders, and all the people were invited, the chief priest pronounced a portentous blessing:

> O God of our fathers, bless this child and give her a name eternally renowned among all generations. . . . Look upon this child and bless her with a supreme blessing which cannot be superseded (6:2).[12]

Anna does not know how to conceal her joy and breaks out into a canticle in praise of the Lord that closely echoes similar canticles in the Old Testament:

---

[11] Ibid., p. 58.
[12] Ibid., p. 59.

> I will sing a praise to the Lord my God,
> for he has visited me and removed from me
>   the reproach of my enemies.
> And the Lord gave me the fruit of his righteousness,
>   unique yet manifold before him.
> Who will proclaim to the sons of Reuben
>   that Anna gives suck?
> Hearken, hearken, you twelve tribes of Israel:
>   Anna gives suck (6:3).[13]

At three years of age, Mary is presented in the Temple, in fulfillment of the promise made by her parents. A throng of young girls accompanies her with lighted lamps; she is received by the high priest, who, after embracing her, pronounces over her the prophetic words:

> The Lord has magnified your name among all generations; because of you the Lord at the end of the days will reveal his redemption to the sons of Israel (7:2).[14]

When Mary had completed her twelfth year, the Temple priests were faced with the problem of finding her a new place to live, since the onset of puberty in the woman, with its consequent phenomenon of menstruation, brought with it official periods of legal impurity, as defined in Scripture (cf. Lev 15:19ff.). During these times, therefore, the presence of Mary in the Temple would have been unacceptable. It was the angel of the Lord who indicated the proper solution to the high priest, Zechariah, future father of John the Baptist. Mary was to be entrusted to the custody of a husband. To this end, Zechariah called together all the widowers of Israel, commanding each of them to bring a staff with him; God would make known his will by a sign. Joseph was there among the widowers. Zechariah collected the staves and entered the sanctuary to pray. When he came back, he returned each staff to its owner. While nothing happened to all the other staves, a dove flew out of Joseph's staff and came to rest on his head. At this, the high priest proclaimed him the Lord's chosen one:

---

[13] Ibid.

[14] Ibid., p. 60.

You have been chosen by lot to receive the Virgin of the Lord as your
ward (9:1).[15]

Joseph wanted to excuse himself from this task, because he was old
and already a father. He feared becoming the laughingstock of the
people should he take such a young wife into his home. However,
after having been severely admonished by the high priest Zechariah,
he resigned himself to the will of God. First he took Mary into his
home; then he took leave of her:

I have received you from the temple of the Lord, and now I leave you
in my house and go away to build my buildings. I will return to you;
the Lord will guard you (9:3).[16]

During Joseph's absence, the great event occurred. One day, Mary
was about to set out to fetch water when she heard a voice:

Hail, highly favored one, the Lord is with you, you are blessed among
women (11:1).[17]

Mary looked around, deeply astonished, but saw no one. Only
when she went into her house did she discover an angel, who went
on to say:

Do not fear, Mary: for you have found grace before the Lord of all
things and shall conceive by His Word (11:2).[18]

The Virgin did not understand, and so she asked:

Shall I conceive by the Lord, the living God, and bear as every
woman bears? (11:2).[19]

Mary's reaction is very human. The anonymous author of the
Protoevangelium does not seem inclined to attribute to her a clear and
total knowledge of the mystery of salvation at the first moment of her
involvement in it. And so the angel has to define things more clearly
for her:

---

[15] Ibid., pp. 60–61.
[16] Ibid., p. 61.
[17] Ibid.
[18] Ibid.
[19] Ibid.

Not so, Mary; for the power of the Lord shall overshadow you; wherefore that holy one who is born of you shall be called the Son of the Most High. And you shall call his name Jesus; for he shall save his people from their sins (11:3).[20]

Then Mary gives her consent:

Behold, [I am] the handmaid of the Lord before Him: be it to me according to your word (11:3).[21]

While the description of the angel's announcement clearly retraces the steps of the account in Luke's Gospel, the apocryphal author distances himself strangely from Luke's account of Mary's visit to Elizabeth. After Elizabeth addresses her elegy to Mary, the author states that Mary had forgotten the mysteries about which the angel had spoken to her, so that her reaction to Elizabeth's words was one of complete surprise:

Who am I, Lord, that all generations of the earth count me blessed? (12:2).[22]

The Virgin stayed with her cousin for three months; then, seeing her own belly growing larger, she decided to go back to her house, where she hid out of fear. At this point the author states that Mary was sixteen years old; he seems to have skipped over a long time, from the day on which she went to live with Joseph as his wife until the moment when she conceived the Son of God.

In the sixth month of her pregnancy, Joseph finally came home and discovered her condition. The apocryphal gospel describes his decidedly hysterical initial reaction (cf. 13:1). But he soon recovers and interrogates his wife with an air of bitter reproach. Mary protests that she is completely innocent but does not know how to explain her pregnancy. The apocryphal gospel presents her as totally ignorant of the mystery, as if she had never received any message from the angel. Again, it will fall to the angel to reveal the truth of the situation and to free Joseph from his agonizing doubts.

---

[20] Ibid.

[21] Ibid.

[22] Ibid., p. 62.

At this point, the sudden visit of the scribe, Anna, complicates things. Having heard that Mary was pregnant, she went to the priests to denounce the spouses, accusing them of having consummated their marriage in a clandestine and unlawful manner. Notwithstanding Mary and Joseph's protestations of innocence, the two were submitted to the bitter water test, prescribed by the law for such cases (cf. Num 5:11–13). They had to drink water mixed with dust, which, in the case of guilt, would have caused physical symptoms and led to punishment. But since nothing happened to Mary and Joseph, they were acquitted and released.

When the emperor Augustus promulgated his edict, Joseph took his children and his pregnant wife and set out for Bethlehem to be registered in the census. During the journey, Mary gave birth to her Son in a cave, amid strange wonders, described with an abundance of details in the text. Then follows the account of the visit of the Magi, the slaughter of the infants in Bethlehem, the martyrdom of the high priest Zechariah, and the election of his successor, Simeon.

In order to understand and evaluate such a "storybook" text as the *Protoevangelium of James*, it is necessary to keep in mind that its principal objective is to demonstrate the virginal conception of Jesus and Mary's virginity before and during Jesus' birth. It is in this perspective that certain curious facts introduced into the account have to be understood. The bitter water test confirms Mary's virginity before giving birth. The absence of labor pains and the sometimes crudely realistic examinations carried out by the midwife and a woman named Salome, who was then punished for her unbelief,[23] confirm Mary's virginity in the act of giving birth. At the same time, the realism with which the Lord's birth is described leads one to think that the apocryphal gospel means to oppose the error of gnostic Docetism, which considered Christ's body to be a mere appearance or phantasm.

Obviously, works such as the *Protoevangelium* cannot claim the seal of divine inspiration. However, in some way they helped the first generations of Christians to intuit the truth of certain mysteries whose dogmatic formulation would later become more and more clear in the light of divine revelation.

---

[23] Here our text is obviously retracing the Gospel account of the unbelief of the apostle Thomas (cf. Jn 20:24–29).

These writings also traced an itinerary through which the believing people sought to draw near to the unfathomable mystery of a virgin mother. Such an arduous goal can justify a text in which varied and, at times, contradictory elements are mixed together, "where the search for edification is mixed with poetry; where the taste for the miraculous is united to a certain lack of taste".[24] The *Protoevangelium*'s author, as a collector of different stories and traditions, can be considered a very early and quite valid witness to the Christian people's faith in the complete holiness and virginity of the Mother of the Lord.[25]

READING

THE VIRGIN BIRTH ACCORDING TO
THE "PROTOEVANGELIUM OF JAMES"

(19:1) And behold, a woman came down from the hill-country and said to me, "Man, where are you going?" And I said, "I seek a Hebrew midwife." And she answered me, "Are you from Israel?" And I said to her, "Yes." And she said, "And who is she who brings forth in the cave?" And I said, "My betrothed." And she said to me, "Is she not your wife?" And I said to her, "She is Mary, who was brought up in the temple of the Lord, and I received her by lot as my wife, and she is not yet my wife, but she has conceived by the Holy Spirit." And the midwife said to him, "Is this true?" And Joseph said to her, "Come and see." And she went with him.

(19:2) And they stopped at the entrance to the cave, and behold, a bright cloud overshadowed the cave. And the midwife said, "My soul is magnified today, for my eyes have seen wonderful things; for

---

[24] Théodore Koehler, S.M., *Maria nei primi secoli*, Fons signatus, 10 (Vercelli: Centro Mariano Chaminade, 1971), p. 21.

[25] Cf. Licinio M. Peretto, *La Mariologia del Protovangelo di Giacomo* (Rome, 1955); idem, "La 'Natività di Maria' ", *Marianum* 22 (1960): 176–96; idem, "Recenti ricerche sul Protovangelo di Giacomo", *Marianum* 24 (1962): 129–57; Édouard Cothenet, "Marie dans les Apocryphes", in *Maria*, ed. Hubert Du Manoir, vol. 6 (Paris: Beauchesne, 1961), pp. 73–156.

salvation is born to Israel." And immediately the cloud disappeared from the cave and a great light appeared, so that our eyes could not bear it. A short time afterwards that light withdrew until the baby appeared, and it came and took the breast of its mother Mary. And the midwife cried, "This day is great for me, because I have seen this new sight."

(19:3) And the midwife came out of the cave, and Salome met her. And she said to her, "Salome, Salome, I have a new sight to tell you about; a virgin has brought forth, a thing which her condition does not allow." And Salome said, "As the Lord my God lives, unless I insert my finger and test her condition, I will not believe that a virgin has given birth."

(20:1) And the midwife went in and said to Mary, "Make yourself ready, for there is no small contention concerning you." And Salome inserted her finger to test her condition. And she cried out, saying, "Woe for my wickedness and unbelief; for I have tempted the living God, and behold, my hand falls away from me, consumed by fire!"

(20:2) And she bowed her knees before the Lord, saying, "O God of my fathers, remember me; for I am the seed of Abraham, Isaac, and Jacob; do not make me pilloried for the children of Israel, but restore me to the poor. For you know, Lord, that in your name I perform my duties and from you I have received my hire."

(20:3) And behold, an angel of the Lord appeared and said to her, "Salome, Salome, the Lord God has heard your prayer. Bring your hand to the child and touch him and salvation and joy will be yours."

(20:4) And Salome came near and touched him, saying, "I will worship him, for a great king has been born to Israel." And Salome was healed as she had requested, and she went out of the cave. And behold, an angel of the Lord cried, "Salome, Salome, do not report what marvels you have seen, until the child has come to Jerusalem."

—*The Protoevangelium of James*,
in Elliott, *Apocryphal New Testament*, pp. 64–65

3

THE SECOND-CENTURY APOLOGISTS

In general, the works of the Apostolic Fathers were written to proclaim or defend Christian faith and morals within the Christian community. The apologists of the second century will make the first attempt at openness and outreach to the outside world, especially the pagan and Jewish worlds, which had taken a hostile attitude toward Christianity. Consequently, the writings of these Christian authors took on an apologetical and polemical tone, but their content usually proves to be firmly grounded in Scripture. Despite the improvisatory character of their terminology and method, these writings could be considered the first attempts at a kind of theological reflection. For the most part, their style follows the rules of Greek dialectic and rhetoric.[1]

Two of these authors, Aristides and Justin, are usually mentioned in connection with Mariology.

The Greek philosopher and apologist Aristides was probably from Athens. He lived in the first half of the second century and wrote an *Apology*, which is mentioned both by Eusebius of Caesarea[2] and by Jerome.[3] After the publication of a fragment of the Armenian translation and of the entire Syriac version (in 1878 and 1889 respectively), Armitage Robinson managed to identify that the original Greek text had been partially inserted into the *Life of Balaam and Josaphat*, published by Migne among the spurious works of St. John Damascene.[4] In the Syriac version, we find a passage in which Mary is called "Hebrew virgin" and "daughter of man":

---

[1] The first critical edition of the works of these writers is J. C. Otto, *Corpus Apologetarum Christianorum saeculi secundi*, 9 vols. (Jena, 1847–1872).

[2] *Hist. Eccl.* 4, 3.

[3] *De viris illustribus* 20; *Epist.* 70, 4.

[4] PG 96, 1108–24.

> The Christians calculate the beginning of their religion from Jesus Christ, who is called Son of the Most High God; having come down from heaven, he took flesh from a Hebrew virgin and clothed himself therein, so that Son of God dwelt within a daughter of man.[5]

Aristides explicitly affirms the virginal nature of Mary's motherhood, while her divine motherhood appears as an implicit consequence of her Son's divinity. In its polemical context, this passage is meant to affirm that the virginal birth of Christ and the other wondrous events of his life are totally different from the mythological stories of pagan religion. The figure of the Virgin Mary appears almost as a challenge to the numerous pagan goddesses, created by human imagination and immorality. By contrast, the role played by Mary was made possible by the miraculous intervention of the Holy Spirit. The apologist contrasts the Christian faith to pagan fantasies.

Justin Martyr

Born in Palestine between 100 and 110, Justin began to study philosophy while still a youth. He followed the different philosophical schools of his day, one after the other; first he was a Stoic, then a Peripatetic, then Pythagorean, then Platonic. In his impassioned search for truth, he finally arrived at Christianity and converted. At first he continued his career as a wandering teacher; later, during the reign of the emperor Antoninus Pius (138–161), he opened a school at Rome. Among his disciples was Tatian, who later became an apologist himself. Justin was martyred around 165, under Marcus Aurelius. An authentic document about his death has survived: the *Martyrium S. Iustini et Sociorum* (the Martyrdom of St. Justin and companions).[6]

Although Justin was a prolific writer, only three of his works (along with some fragments) have survived: the two *Apologies* and the *Dialogue with Trypho*. They are contained in a single manuscript copy

---

[5] Ibid.

[6] English trans. in Alexander Roberts and James Donaldson, eds., *The Ante-Nicene Fathers,* vol. 1 (New York: Charles Scribner's Sons, 1926), pp. 305–6.

from the fourteenth century (Paris, gr. 450). Eusebius of Caesarea confirms their authenticity.[7]

The mystery of the Virgin Mother is treated in the first *Apology* and in the *Dialogue*. In the *Apology*, addressed to Antoninus Pius and Marcus Aurelius, the author rejects anti-Christian calumnies and shows the truth of the Christian faith and way of life. His discussion of the economy of salvation is located within the exposition of the doctrine about the virginal birth of Jesus. Considered in a superficial manner, this mystery might exhibit some analogies to certain pagan myths; in reality, it is nothing else than the final fulfillment of a precise divine plan. According to this plan, the only begotten Son of the Father, begotten by him before all things and existing from all eternity, came into this world in the time of the Roman Empire and was made man in the womb of the Virgin Mary, daughter of the ancient patriarchs Abraham, Isaac, and Jacob, descendant of the tribe of Judah and of the house of David. By her, Christ was conceived, brought to light in a cave, and laid in a manger. For this reason, he could claim, in all truth, to be the Son of Man.

Since he was born of a Virgin, one cannot say that he came into the world in the same way as all other men, that is, as the result of marital relations. He became incarnate by an exercise of God's power. Had it not been thus, the Virgin could not have remained a virgin. Therefore, the angel of the Lord came to bring her the glad tidings, and the power of God entered into her, rendering her a mother without taking away her virginity.

Her husband, Joseph, thinking that she had become pregnant as a consequence of adulterous relations, wanted to put her away; however, an angel stopped him from doing so, revealing to him the miracle wrought by God.

In presenting the Gospel account, Justin is more concerned with its apologetic potential than with its theological content. His objective was to establish the historical and messianic character of the text, especially in the eyes of the Jews, who were accusing the Christians of having imitated the stories of Greek mythology. Justin shows how the prophecies of the Old Testament serve only to confirm the

---

[7] *Hist. Eccl.* 4, 18.

historical truth of the facts narrated by the Gospels.[8] He particularly insists on Isaiah 7:14,[9] and explains why God had wanted to pre-announce the events of salvation; namely, to help men recognize and accept facts that seemed unbelievable, facts whose realization required an extraordinary intervention of divine omnipotence.[10]

Eve–Mary

Justin was probably the first author to use the Eve–Mary parallel. The theological value of this doctrine emerges clearly from its subsequent development in the history of Christian thought. In Holy Scripture, Eve is called mother of the living (Gen 3:20), but, to the Fathers, quite early on, there seemed to be a sharp contrast between this title and her role with regard to the destiny of her descendants. For it is true that Eve transmitted physical life to her descendants, yet (by her sin) she was also the cause of their ruin and death. For this reason, the prevalent tendency among Christian authors will be to see, in the title "mother of the living", attributed to the old Eve, the prophetic type of a new Eve, who would become the mother of the living in a truer and fuller sense of the word. This "new Eve" could only be the Virgin Mary.

From this intuition arose the famous Eve–Mary parallel, which led to the formulation of a doctrine that represents the first attempt at theological reflection about the Mother of Jesus. By means of this comparison, the early Fathers achieved an important measure of clarity about the Blessed Virgin's function in the divine plan for our salvation. The parallel has a properly soteriological content and demonstrates that the primary concern of the earliest theological reflection about Mary was focused less on her person than on her role in relation to Christ. Mary has a role in relation to Christ, the second Adam, just as the first Eve had a role in relation to the first Adam. The soteriological perspective arouses interest in Mary's personal condition, so that some of her more proper prerogatives (for

---

[8] *Apologia I*, 12; PG 6, 345.
[9] Ibid., 33; PG 6, 380.
[10] Ibid.

example, her divine motherhood and her virginity) could be brought out. Indeed, these are the two Marian prerogatives directly suggested by the Eve–Mary parallel, because both women were virgins up until receiving the divine proposal, and then both became mothers.

Cardinal John Henry Newman rightly asserts that the truth about Mary as new Eve constitutes a rudimentary but extremely important Marian doctrine left to us by Christian antiquity. It is the first meditation on her and on her mission, the fullest profile of her, the view of her that has been handed down to us in the patristic writings.[11]

The Eve–Mary parallel has its scriptural foundation in the Pauline doctrine of the second Adam: "Since by man came death . . . in Christ shall all be made alive" (1 Cor 15:21–22). It was not difficult for the Fathers to perceive the profound connection between the concept of Christ as new Adam and the concept of Mary as new Eve.

In his *Dialogue with Trypho*, Justin proposes this doctrine, which appears to have been present in the earliest tradition of the Church. He wants to show how the Lord had decided to accomplish the salvation of man by following the same procedure by which sin had been committed and the ruin and death of the human race perpetrated.

Justin locates the parallel within the christological context of the double generation of the Redeemer:

> [The Son of God] became man through a Virgin, so that the disobedience caused by the serpent might be destroyed in the same way it had begun. For Eve, who was virgin and undefiled, gave birth to disobedience and death after listening to the serpent's words. But the Virgin Mary conceived faith and joy; for when the angel Gabriel brought her the glad tidings that the Holy Spirit would come upon her and that the power of the Most High would overshadow her, so that the Holy One born of her would be the Son of God, she answered, "Let it be done to me according to your word" (Lk 1:38). Thus was born of her the [Child] about whom so many Scriptures speak, as we have shown. Through him, God crushed the serpent, along with those angels and men who had become like the serpent.[12]

---

[11] John Henry Newman, *A Letter to the Rev. E. B. Pusey on His Recent Eirenicon* (London: Longmans, Green, Reader, and Dyer, 1866).

[12] *Dialogue with Trypho* 100; PG 6, 709–12.

Here it is interesting to note how Justin already presents Mary's role in salvation as the consequence of a free and conscious choice in response to the angel's message. However, just as the harmful action of Eve was subordinate to that of Adam, on whom fell the primary responsibility for sin, in the same way the action of Mary, in the order of human salvation, remains absolutely subordinate to the necessary and essential action of Christ, the only Redeemer.

Only a few decades separate the letters of Ignatius of Antioch from the writings of Justin; nevertheless, in that short span of time, the image of Mary acquired a clearer and more detailed profile. We find ourselves in the presence of an embryonic Marian theology. However, if Justin feels the need to dedicate more energy to studying the person of the Mother of Jesus, clearly he does so in order to cast more light on the mystery of her Son. His testimony is all the more precious inasmuch as it is the work of a simple Christian layman who does not see himself as offering his own teaching but who intends to reinforce the traditional teaching of the Church and to defend it against the calumnious insinuations of pagans and Jews. Finally, Justin's testimony can be related to the faith of the whole Church of his time, since, as an itinerant philosopher, he was undoubtedly familiar with both Eastern and Western Christianity.

Melito of Sardis

He is considered an apologist because, around 170, he addressed an apology on behalf of the Christians to the emperor, Marcus Aurelius. We know this document only from a few citations in the writings of Eusebius of Caesarea and in the *Paschal Chronicle*. Melito was bishop of Sardis, in Asia Minor, and appears to have been involved in the controversy that arose between the Eastern and Western Churches over the celebration of Easter. Recently, the entire text of one of his Easter homilies was discovered, in which he mentions the holy Virgin. The homily was composed in the style of an Easter proclamation; its content is predominantly christological.[13] The saving work

---

[13] A critical edition of this homily and of fragments of Melito's other writings is by Othmar Perler, *Méliton de Sardes: Sur la Pâque et fragments,* SC 123 (Paris: Éditions du Cerf, 1966).

of Christ is presented in three inseparable phases: Incarnation, Passion-death, and glorification. The mystery of Mary's maternity finds its obvious reference in the Incarnation and earthly birth of the Son of God. Mary's virginity is an essential part of this mystery. Melito calls her "fair ewe", by way of analogy with Jesus, whom the Gospel calls the "Lamb of God" (cf. Jn 1:29).

READING

MELITO OF SARDIS, "EASTER HOMILY"

He it is, who came from heaven to earth
for the sake of suffering man;
he clothed himself in man's flesh
in the womb of a Virgin from whom he came forth as man
and took upon himself the sufferings of him who suffered,
by means of a body capable of suffering,
and destroyed the sufferings of the flesh
and slew death-dealing death
by his spirit which cannot die. . . .

It is he who became incarnate in a Virgin,
who was hung upon the wood,
who was buried in the earth,
who was raised from among the dead,
who was lifted up to the heights of heaven.
He is the mute lamb,
he is the slain lamb,
he is born of Mary, the fair ewe,
he is taken from the flock
and delivered over to immolation
and slain in the evening
and buried in the night;
who was broken on the wood,
was not corrupted in the earth,
he rose from the dead,
and raised man from the depths of the tomb. . . .

He it is who made heaven and earth,
who formed man in the beginning,
who was announced by the law and the prophets,
who became incarnate in a Virgin,
who was hung upon the wood,
who in the earth was buried,
who rose from the dead
and ascended into the heights of the heavens.

—Melito of Sardis, *Easter Homily*, SC 123

4

IRENAEUS OF LYONS

Among the second-century Fathers of the Church, Irenaeus is certainly the most prominent character as well as the first theologian in the proper sense of the word. He is rightly considered the father of Catholic dogmatic theology.

We have a very meager and unwritten record of his life. He was born in Smyrna between 140 and 160, where he knew the bishop, Polycarp. For reasons we do not know, he left Asia Minor and moved to Gaul. There, he was ordained priest of the Church of Lyons and, as such, was invited to Rome to be a mediator in a controversy regarding Montanism. Upon his return to Lyons, he succeeded the bishop, Pothinus, who had been martyred in the meantime. Once again, we see Irenaeus as mediator in the controversy between Pope Victorius I and the Asian bishops over the celebration of Easter, exhorting the two parties to a peaceful understanding. This is why Eusebius of Caesarea attests that the bishop of Lyons lived and acted according to the meaning of his name, for, in Greek, Irenaeus means "man of peace".[1] We do not know the year of his death, but it probably occurred in the year 202. Gregory of Tours wrote that Irenaeus died a martyr's death,[2] but this information is too late (sixth century) to be fully credible.

The testimony of Irenaeus is very precious, because in his youth he had been in contact with Polycarp and with other important Christians who had known the apostles directly.[3] Hence, he must

---

[1] *Hist. Eccl.* 5, 24.

[2] *Historia Francorum* 1, 27.

[3] Irenaeus himself emphasizes this: "As I heard from a certain presbyter, who had heard it from men who had seen the apostles, and from others who had heard them" (*Adv. haer.* 4, 27; PG 7, 1056).

have been well-informed about the apostolic tradition, as is also apparent from his writings.

As bishop, Irenaeus took his pastoral responsibilities very seriously. He considered it one of his pressing duties to defend the faith and knowledge of his faithful from the dangers of the Gnostic heresy, which, at that time, constituted a grave threat to the Christian faith. To that end, he wrote a monumental work, in five books, known by the Latin title *Adversus haereses* (*Against Heresies*).[4] In it, he not only refutes the errors of the Gnostics but contrasts their teaching with the correct doctrine of the Church, of which he offers a clear and persuasive synthesis. Another work of his has come down to us: *Proof of the Apostolic Preaching*, while other works have been lost.

As far as Marian doctrine is concerned, Irenaeus takes up the theme of Mary considered as *new Eve* and significantly develops the ideas of the apologist Justin. Finally, it is solidly based on the Pauline doctrine of "recapitulation", which becomes the foundation for his soteriology.

Recapitulation in Christ

According to St. Paul, the Redeemer brought together or "recapitulated" in himself all the things and events that had happened since the first creation, reconciling everything with God. In this view, the salvation of man appears as a second creation, which is essentially a kind of repetition of the first creation. Through this second creation, God rehabilitates his original plan of salvation, which had been interrupted by Adam's fall; he takes it up again and reorganizes it in the person of his Son, who becomes for us the second Adam. And, if the whole human race fell into perdition because of the sin of one man (cf. Rom 5:12ff.), it was necessary that God's Son should become man. He, as the fountainhead of a new humanity, could then realize

---

[4] Unfortunately, we do not possess the original Greek text of the *Adversus haereses* in its entirety. However, we have a complete Latin version, which due to its antiquity has great value. It seems to have been known to St. Cyprian, so it can be dated around 250. Migne, in PG 7, has the Latin text and the Greek pericopes that have survived. The best critical edition is *Sources Chrétiennes* 263–64 (bk. 1), 293–94 (bk. 2), 210–11 (bk. 3), 100 (bk. 4), 152–53 (bk. 5).

God's plan of salvation by retracing, but in a contrasting manner, the same path walked by the first Adam in his rebellion against God. Irenaeus writes:

> When [the Son of God] took flesh and became man, he recapitulated in himself the long history of men, procuring for us the reward of salvation, so that in Christ Jesus we might recover what we had lost in Adam, namely, the image and likeness of God. For since it was not possible for man, once wounded and broken by disobedience, to be refashioned and to obtain the victor's palm, and since it was equally impossible for him to receive salvation, as he had fallen under the power of sin, the Son of God accomplished both of these tasks. He, God's Word, came down from the Father and became flesh; he abased himself even unto death and brought the economy of our salvation to its completion.[5]

So, faithful to the teaching of St. Paul, Irenaeus' doctrine of recapitulation clearly brings out the two great objectives achieved by Christ in his redemptive work. First, there is a negative result: the destruction of sin and death, which are the two main consequences of the disobedience of Adam. There is also a positive result: the restoration of the entire human race in the image of God, which had been destroyed by original sin.[6] The second Adam achieved these goals through his complete obedience to the Father, thus counterbalancing the disobedience of the first Adam and victoriously renewing the ancient conflict against Satan.[7] It can be said, then, that all things have been made new in the second Adam.[8]

Mary's Role in the Economy of Salvation

It is in this context of the doctrine of recapitulation of all things in Christ that Irenaeus explains the role of the Blessed Virgin in the divine plan of salvation, referring to the Eve–Mary parallel. While Justin, as we have seen, had touched on this theme casually, Irenaeus produces a more developed and profound theological reflection:

---

[5] *Adv. haer.* 3, 18; PG 7, 932.
[6] Ibid.
[7] Ibid., 5, 21; PG 7, 1171.
[8] Ibid., 4, 34; PG 7, 1083–84.

> Even though Eve had Adam for a husband, she was still a virgin. . . .
> By disobeying, she became the cause of death for herself and for the
> whole human race. In the same way, Mary, though she also had a
> husband, was still a virgin, and by obeying, she became the cause of
> salvation for herself and for the whole human race. . . . The knot of
> Eve's disobedience was untied by Mary's obedience. What Eve
> bound through her unbelief, Mary loosed by her faith.[9]

Irenaeus clearly establishes a perfect parallel between the two
women, in terms of both convergence and divergence, just as the
apostle Paul had done with Adam and Christ. Eve and Mary, though
both were married, were still virgins. But while Eve disobeyed, causing ruin and death for herself and the human race, Mary by obeying
became the cause of salvation. Eve's disobedience imposed the bonds
of spiritual slavery upon the human race; Mary's obedience broke
these bonds, returning man to his original freedom. Eve's disobedience is the consequence of her unbelief; Mary's obedience is the fruit
of her faith. In another passage, where the Eve–Mary comparison is
discussed in parallel with the Pauline comparison between Adam
and Christ, Irenaeus attributes to the Virgin the title "advocate of
Eve":

> Eve was seduced by the word of the [fallen] angel and transgressed
> God's word, so that she fled from him. In the same way, [Mary] was
> evangelized by the word of an angel and obeyed God's word, so that
> she carried him [within her]. And while the former was seduced into
> disobeying God, the latter was persuaded to obey God, so that the
> Virgin Mary became the advocate (*advocata*) of the virgin Eve.
>
> And just as the human race was bound to death because of a virgin,
> so it was set free from death by a Virgin, since the disobedience of one
> virgin was counterbalanced by a Virgin's obedience.
>
> If, then, the first-made man's sin was mended by the right conduct
> of the firstborn Son [of God], and if the serpent's cunning was bested
> by the simplicity of the dove [Mary], and if the chains that held us
> bound to death have been broken, then the heretics are fools; they are
> ignorant of God's economy, and they are unaware of his economy for
> [the salvation of] man.[10]

---

[9] Ibid., 3, 22; PG 7, 959–60.
[10] Ibid., 5, 19; PG 7, 1175–76.

These texts clearly show that Irenaeus not only attributes to Mary a role within the work of redemption; he specifies that this role is strictly connected to the Savior's actions, in the same fashion that Eve had a role, albeit negative, with regard to the first Adam. Finally, the holy Virgin is not limited to carrying out her role on her own separate plane, parallel to that of Eve. She does something more: she interferes with Eve's historical plane because, by her simplicity, she destroys the pride and cleverness of the serpent, the author of the evil that befell Eve.

But Irenaeus goes even farther. In his *Proof of the Apostolic Preaching*, he expressly states that, just as Adam was recapitulated in Christ, even so Eve has been recapitulated in Mary:

> Adam had to be recapitulated in Christ, so that death might be swallowed up in immortality, and Eve [had to be recapitulated] in Mary, so that the Virgin, having become another virgin's advocate, might destroy and abolish one virgin's disobedience by the obedience of another virgin.[11]

We have cited these three texts in chronological order, and it is easy to observe a certain progressive development. The principle of recapitulation is integrated with the principle of "recirculation", which introduces a note of salvation history into the theology of Irenaeus. While the principle of recapitulation affirms that humanity (fallen because of its first head, Adam) had to be brought back to God by another man—Christ—who would be its second head, the principle of recirculation affirms that this process of restoration accomplished by the Savior had to correspond step by step, but in an opposite way, to the story of the fall. Mary enters this process as the antitype of Eve.

With this vision, the bishop of Lyons shows a desire to consider human history as a unified phenomenon, in which the New Testament is nothing other than the continuation of the Old Testament. The single divine economy, interrupted by Adam, with whom Eve was associated, is resumed and brought to its complete perfection by Christ, with whom Mary is associated.

---

[11] *Proof of the Apostolic Preaching* 33, SC 62, pp. 83–86. This paragraph might be viewed as an expression of the core of Irenaeus' thought. He returns to this theme repeatedly.

In this perspective we can understand why Irenaeus calls Mary *causa salutis*, precisely because she is the antitype of Eve, who was *causa mortis*. Her role is not limited to her purely biological and negative status as Virgin Mother; no, her cooperation includes moral and spiritual motives. For example, her obedience to the word of God was conscious and voluntary; her consent to the plan of salvation had a soteriological character, since she knew that the Incarnation of God's Son was happening for the sake of human redemption.

In the second and third texts cited, our author refers to Mary by the title *advocata*. This is the first time in the history of ancient Christian literature that this title is used for Mary. Unfortunately, the original Greek versions of these texts have been lost, so that we do not know for certain what Greek term was translated by the Latin word *advocata*. The Armenian version seems to indicate that the original Greek word was *paráklētos* (defender, advocate, intercessor).[12] But in what sense can Mary be Eve's advocate? Irenaeus specifies: by her obedience. He does not in any way appear to mean that Mary made intercession or offered her merits on Eve's behalf. She simply did the opposite of what Eve had done; that is, she obeyed, and thus removed the deplorable consequences of Eve's disobedience. Therefore Eve is no longer condemned as being responsible for the ruin of the human race, because this ruin has been removed by Mary's obedience.[13]

The bishop of Lyons captures the reader's attention by the particularly strong terms in which he expresses his own theological convictions. He affirms beyond the shadow of a doubt the active and efficacious presence of the Blessed Virgin in the history of salvation and does so with remarkable determination. The influence of his teaching on later mariological developments is immediately apparent. Present-day doctrine about Mary's collaboration in the redemption of man and the mediation of divine grace has its distant but discernible roots in the teaching of the great bishop of Lyons.

---

[12] As a matter of fact, in another text Irenaeus apples the term *paráklētos* to the Holy Spirit, in opposition to the term *prosecutor*, meaning the devil: "So that where we have an accuser, we may also have an advocate" (*Adv. haer.* 3, 17; PG 7, 930).

[13] Cf. Eberhard Neubert, *Marie dans l'Église anténicéenne* (Paris: J. Gabalda, 1908), p. 264.

READING

THE NEW ADAM AND THE NEW EVE

The apostle Paul, in his letter to the Galatians, clearly states that "God sent his Son, born of a woman" (Gal 4:4). And in his letter to the Romans, he says, "his Son, born of David's seed according to the flesh, constituted Son of God in power, according to the Spirit of holiness that raised him from the dead, Jesus Christ our Lord" (Rom 1:3–4).

Had it been otherwise, his descent into Mary would have been superfluous. For why would he have descended within her, if he did not need to take something from her? Furthermore, if he had not taken anything from Mary, he would not have been accustomed to eating earthly food . . . nor, after fasting forty days, like Moses and Elijah, would he have felt hunger pangs (cf. Mt 4:2), and if his body had not felt the need for nourishment, neither would his disciple John have written of him: "Jesus, tired from the journey, sat down" (Jn 4:6). Nor would David have foretold of him: "They have added to the sorrow of my wounds" (Ps 69:27). Nor would [Jesus] have wept over Lazarus (cf. Jn 11:35) or sweated drops of blood (cf. Lk 22:44) or said, "My soul is exceedingly sad" (Mt 26:38), nor would blood and water have flowed from his pierced side (cf. Jn 19:34). These are all signs that he took flesh from the earth, recapitulating this flesh in himself to save his own creation.

For this reason, Luke presents a genealogy that runs from the Lord's birth back to Adam, comprising seventy-two generations (cf. Lk 3:23–38). Thus he joins the end to the beginning and shows [Jesus] is the One who recapitulated in himself all the scattered peoples since the time of Adam and all the languages and human generations, including Adam himself. Hence, Paul called this same Adam "the type of the one who was to come" (Rom 5:14), because the Word, the Craftsman of all things, had already formed, in Adam, the economy concerning the humanity in which the Son of God would clothe himself. At first, God made man animal [=physical], apparently so that he could be saved by the spiritual Man (cf. 1 Cor 15:46). Since the Savior was preexistent, [his creature] who needed salvation had to come into existence also, so that the Savior would not exist to no purpose.

In accordance with this design, the Virgin Mary was found obedient when she said, "Behold your handmaid, O Lord; let it be done to me according to your word" (Lk 1:38). But Eve disobeyed, and she did so while still a virgin.

Even though Eve had Adam for a husband, she was still a virgin. For "they were both naked" in paradise "and were unashamed" (Gen 2:25), since they had been created a short time previously and had no idea about the generation of children; indeed, they first had to become adults, and only then did they begin to multiply. By disobeying, Eve became the cause of death for herself and for the whole human race. In the same way Mary, though she also had a husband, was still a virgin, and by obeying, she became the cause of salvation for herself and for the whole human race.

For this reason, the law calls a woman engaged to a man his wife, even though she is still a virgin; this indicates the parallel (*recirculatio*) between Mary and Eve. Just as, once something has been bound, it cannot be loosed except by undoing the knot in reverse order, even so the first knots were untied by the [undoing of the] second ones, and, inversely, these last free the first. It works out that the first knot is untied by the second, and the second causes the loosing of the first.

This is the reason why the Lord declared that the first would be last and the last would be first (cf. Mt 19:30). And the prophet affirms the same thing when he says, "Sons shall be born to you in place of your fathers" (Ps 45:16). The Lord, having become "the firstborn of the dead" (cf. Col 1:18) and having received the ancient fathers in his bosom, regenerated them into the life of God, becoming himself the first of the living (cf. Col 1:18), as Adam had become the first of the dying. That is why Luke began his genealogy from the Lord and then worked back to Adam: to show that it was not the fathers who regenerated the Son, but rather the Son who regenerated them into the gospel of life. And so the knot of Eve's disobedience was untied by Mary's obedience. What Eve bound through her unbelief, Mary loosed by her faith.

—Irenaeus of Lyons, *Adversus haereses* 3:22

5

BEGINNINGS OF MARIAN DOCTRINE IN THE
LATIN CHURCH: TERTULLIAN

Christianity spread very early in the West, thanks to the unity of the Roman Empire, which created a geographical and political situation favorable to the spread of the gospel. And yet, within Christian writings in Latin, Marian doctrine appears rather late compared to the East. From Rome, the Christian message reached all the regions of the Empire, spreading the good news of the Savior God who had become man by being born of a Virgin. As already in the East, so in the West the figure of the Virgin Mother initially remains in her Son's shadow. At least up to the Council of Nicaea (325), it is not easy to understand when the believers of that time became aware of the meaning and importance of the role played by the Mother of Jesus in the economy of salvation. We are even less able to say whether, and to what extent, a Marian cult existed in those first centuries. The historical information in this regard is quite scarce.

Northern Africa, the region that produced Tertullian, the first Christian author of the Latin language, included a vast territory in the northern sector of the continent, from Libya to Morocco. It seems that Christianity spread into this part of the Roman Empire very early; but the factors that could explain the phenomenon remain obscure. A certain bond of reverence that the Church in northern Africa sought to maintain with the Church of Rome[1] leads one

---

[1] It is sufficient to recall the example of St. Cyprian who, although not recognizing any jurisdictional primacy of the bishop of Rome (cf. *De unitate Ecclesiae* 4; *Epist.* 71, 3), always exhibited a deep and sincere veneration for the Roman Church, to which he attributes a primary role in the task of ensuring the faith and unity of the universal Church (cf. *Epist.* 59, 14).

to think that the former was first evangelized by the latter, and quite early on. In fact, numerous African martyrs died as early as 180,[2] and when, in 225, the Synod of Carthage was convened, the bishops of that proconsular province and of Numidia already numbered seventy.[3]

In addition to Tertullian, we can recall other northern African authors who, in relatively early times, made their contribution to Christian literature and theology in the Latin language: Cyprian, bishop of Carthage and martyr (d. 258), and two lay theologians: Arnobius (d. ca. 327) and Lactantius (d. ca. 330). Compared to Tertullian, however, these authors wrote little about Mary.

Tertullian's Personality

We know little about the life of Quintus Septimus Florens Tertullianus. He was born at Carthage around 155 to a Roman family of pagan religion, and his father was a centurion of the proconsular cohort. After studying jurisprudence, Tertullian practiced as a lawyer in Rome, winning for himself a significant reputation. Converting to Christianity around 193, he returned to Carthage and placed his exceptional talents at the service of the Christian faith. There is no question that his talents must be recognized, even if, at a certain point in his life, he allowed himself to be taken in by the heresy of the Montanists, who professed overly rigorous principles of morality. Tertullian died sometime after 200.

His numerous writings exercised a determining influence in the formulation and development of Christian doctrine in the West, especially trinitarian theology and Christology. We recall, for

---

[2] These are the martyrs of Scillium, in Numidia, killed at Carthage on July 17, 180 (cf. "The Acts of the Scillitan Martyrs", in Herbert Musurillo, trans., *The Acts of the Christian Martyrs* [Oxford: Clarendon Press, 1972], pp. 86–89). Also near Carthage, around 203, was the martyrdom of Perpetua, Felicity, and companions (cf. "The Martyrdom of Saints Perpetua and Felicitas", in Musurillo, *Christian Martyrs*).

[3] We have the testimony of St. Cyprian (*Epist.* 70, 1; 71, 4; 73, 3) and of St. Augustine (*De unico baptismo contra Petilianum* 13, 22; *De baptismo contra Donatistas* 3, 12, 17). Cf. Hefele-Leclerq, *Histoire des Conciles*, vol. 1, pt. 1 (Paris, 1907), pp. 154–56.

example, that Tertullian was the first writer to use the word "Trinity" and to attribute the term "person" to the Father, the Son, and the Holy Spirit. In the person of Christ, he clearly sees the presence of two natures, human and divine, without confusion, so that each of the two natures completely preserves its own properties. Divinity carries out the functions proper to it, such as working miracles and every other supernatural action. Humanity is expressed in the operations and reactions proper to it; for example, Jesus suffers from hunger in the desert; he is tempted by the devil; he feels thirst next to Jacob's well when he meets the Samaritan woman; he weeps at the tomb of Lazarus; he experiences mortal agony in the Garden of Gethsemane; he dies on the Cross. Tertullian's Christology anticipates the declarations of the Council of Chalcedon (451) by two and one-half centuries.

God Incarnate

Tertullian was a strong defender of Christ's humanity, which some of the heretics of his time denied, conditioned as they were by a pessimistic conception of matter and all that had to do with matter in this world. These heretics thought that, since matter is radically evil and is the origin and cause of the evil that exists in the world, then the Son of God could not have assumed a human body. For this reason some of them, called Docetists, denied Jesus a material body equal to that of other men. They held that his body was only apparently real, like a kind of phantasm, devoid of any real existence.

Against these errors, Tertullian vigorously affirms the reality of the human nature of Jesus Christ. In a polemic against the heretic Marcion he writes:

> The Son of God was born: I am not ashamed at this, because it is shameful. The Son of God died: and this is believable, because it is absurd. He was buried and rose: this is certain, because it is impossible. But how could these statements be true in the case of Christ if he himself did not truly exist and did not truly have what he needed to be crucified, to die, to be buried, and to rise; namely, a body filled with blood, given structure with bones, woven with nerves, shot through with veins, capable of experiencing birth and death?

Undoubtedly, then, Christ had a human body, because it was born from a human being. And so this flesh is mortal in Christ, because Christ is man and the Son of man.[4]

Tertullian's insistence on the reality of the flesh of the Son of God made man reaches the point of exaggeration when he ascribes ugliness and deformity to Christ:

His body possessed no earthly beauty; even less did it possess heavenly splendor. Even if the prophets among us had not given any report of his ignoble appearance, the very sufferings and insults he endured speak of it. The sufferings attest to the reality of his human flesh; the insults prove its ugliness.[5]

These few examples suffice to make us understand how Tertullian could have been just as rich in genius as he was sometimes lacking in a sense of balance. However, the goodness of his intentions is beyond doubt. He made these gratuitous statements while caught up in the heat of debate. His main concern was to defend the true human nature of the Lord Jesus, who, by means of his human nature, brought the work of our salvation to its completion.

Tertullian's Severity toward Mary

It does not seem that our author is directly concerned about, or sympathetic toward, the Virgin as a person. To the contrary, one must acknowledge that it was characteristic of him to render one of the most severe and rash judgments of the holy Virgin known to patristic literature. He poorly interpreted the Gospel passages that mention the brothers of Jesus (cf. Mt 12:46–50; Mk 3:31–35; Lk 8:19–21). According to him, the Lord was reproving his Mother together with his brothers. It is known that the word "brother" is used in the Gospel to indicate relatives in general, but Tertullian, as we shall see, understands it to mean sons of the same parents. The text that interests us is the following:

---

[4] *De carne Christi* 5, 4–5; PL 2, 806.
[5] Ibid., 9, 2; PL 2, 817.

[Jesus] was justly indignant that persons so close to him should stand outside while strangers were in the house with him, hanging on his every word. He was indignant above all because they were seeking to take him away from his solemn task. He did not ignore them, but disavowed them. Therefore, in response to the question, "Who is my mother, and who are my brothers?" he responded, "No one except those who hear my words and put them into practice." He transferred the terms indicating blood relationship to others whom he considered closer to him because of their faith.[6]

In this text also, Tertullian not only shows himself to be confident and peremptory in his judgments but reveals his lack of a sense of proportion. In order to emphasize and exalt the person of Jesus, he does not hesitate to criticize his close relatives when necessary.

Mary Guarantees the Humanity of Christ

Although Tertullian does not show particular sympathy for the person of Jesus' Mother, he undoubtedly exhibits an extreme interest in Mary's function in the mystery of the incarnate God. He insists on the reality of Mary's maternity, in order to remove any shadow of doubt about the real and authentic humanity of her Son. Against the Gnostics, he writes:

> You say that he was born *through* a virgin, not *of* her; that he dwelled *in* her womb, but was not *of* her womb, because the angel said to Joseph in a dream: "For that which is born in her is from the Holy Spirit" (Mt 1). It does not say "*of* her". The fact is that the angel, even if he meant to say "born *of* her", had to say "born *in* her", because that which was born of her was already inside her. The two expressions, then, are equivalent.[7]

According to our author, Mary especially guarantees the truly human roots of the body of the Son of God, since through her Jesus is connected to preceding generations:

> He is the blossom of the shoot sprung from the root of Jesse. But just as the root of Jesse is the family of David, and the shoot sprung from

---

[6] *Adversus Marcionem* 4, 19, 11; PL 2, 435.

[7] *De carne Christi* 20, 1; PL 2, 830–31.

the root is Mary, a descendent of David, and the blossom of the shoot is the Son of Mary, called Jesus Christ, is he not the fruit? . . . Therefore it is now a well-known fact that the flesh of Christ is inseparable, not only from Mary, but also from David through Mary, and from Jesse through David.[8]

The word "fruit", in this passage, is an allusion to the words Elizabeth said to Mary: "Blessed is the fruit of your womb" (Lk 1:42).

Mary Conceived Christ as a Virgin

Even though the conception of Christ in the womb of Mary was a true conception, it did not happen according to the laws of nature. Tertullian emphasizes its virginal character:

> He who was already the Son of God, generated by the seed of God the Father, that is, by the Spirit, desiring also to become Son of man, decided to assume flesh from man's flesh, but without man's seed. He who had the seed of God did not need the seed of man. Just as, before his birth from the Virgin, he had God for a Father, without having a human mother, in the same way after being born from the Virgin, he had a woman for a mother without having a human father. In short: he is a man who possessed divinity, since he is human flesh possessing the Spirit of God. His flesh was produced from a human, without human seed; his spirit comes from the seed of God.[9]

The nervousness and incisiveness of Tertullian's style are striking. It seems that he wants to block his adversaries' objections before they can get the words out of their mouths, leaving them no possibility of replying. He is so convinced of the truth of the faith that he is not able to cultivate any tolerance for the uncertainties of others, let alone their deviations from the truth. His thesis is not a matter of debate: Jesus is God because he possesses the Spirit of God, and he is man because he has received a real body from Mary, in an absolutely extraordinary fashion. For Tertullian, then, one does not hesitate about the exact terms with which to affirm the mystery of the Incar-

---

[8] Ibid., 21, 5; PL 2, 833–34.
[9] Ibid., 18, 1–3; PL 2, 828.

nation. Christ assumed flesh from a human creature, who became his Mother and who conceived him virginally.

No other ancient Christian writer so strongly stressed the identity between the flesh of Christ and the flesh of Mary. But this idea became so fixed in his mind that he lost a correct view of other aspects of the mystery of the Incarnation.

Tertullian Denies Mary's Perpetual Virginity

The better to demonstrate the reality of Christ's flesh, our author goes so far as to deny that his mother could have remained a virgin in giving birth. Let us read some realistic comments about the birth of Jesus from Mary:

> Virgin because she abstained from man; non-virgin because she gave birth. . . . Virgin when she conceived, she became a wife when she gave birth. . . . Who really opened her maternal womb, if not the one who opened the womb that had been closed [in his conception]? Normally, conjugal relations open the womb. Therefore [Mary's] womb was all the more opened, since it had been more closed. Consequently it is more accurate to call her non-virgin, than virgin.[10]

The case of Tertullian teaches that the claim of clarity at any cost about the mysteries of faith, especially when accompanied by a polemical spirit, is a dangerous attitude. It is impossible to understand by reason alone how a real body, such as the body of Jesus, could have been born without destroying the mother's physical virginity. Faith must know how to bear the test of obscurity.

On the basis of an alleged necessity to give a moral example, Tertullian also denies Mary's virginity after giving birth:

> She was a virgin who gave birth to Christ, but after his birth she was married to one man, so that both ideals of holiness [namely, the virginal ideal and the married ideal] might be exemplified in the parentage of Christ, in the person of a mother who was both virgin and married to one husband only.[11]

---

[10] Ibid., 23, 1–5 passim; PL 2, 835–36.
[11] De monogamia 8, 2; PL 2, 989.

Since these are his convictions, Tertullian has no problem, as we saw earlier, in seeing the brothers of Jesus mentioned in the Gospel as normal sons whom Mary and Joseph would have had in their married life, after the virginal conception of Jesus.

It might seem strange that a Christian author should have been able to write such things about the Mother of the Lord without reactions from his contemporaries. The explanation may come from the uncertain mentality of Christians in the first centuries. Their ideas about the one and triune God, about Jesus Christ, and about his Mother still had a long way to go before achieving the clarity that would result from theological disputation, controversies with heretics, and the dogmatic reflection of later centuries.

Because of his erroneous ideas about the virginity and sanctity of the Mother of the Lord, the Marian texts of Tertullian subsequently remained unknown for the most part. Nevertheless, some of them do have real theological value, such as the passage from *De carne Christi* in which he explains the Eve–Mary parallel:

> Eve believed the serpent; Mary believed Gabriel. The fault that Eve introduced by believing, Mary, by believing, erased. But [one might object] at the devil's word, Eve did not conceive in her womb. To the contrary, she did conceive; for from that moment the word of the devil became in her a seed by which she conceived as an outcast and gave birth in sorrow. Finally she gave birth to a fratricidal devil [Cain]. Mary, on the other hand, bore him who would one day bring salvation to Israel, his brother in the flesh and his executioner. God, then, sent his Word into [Mary's] womb, so that he, the good Brother, might erase his wicked brother's record.[12]

This is an extremely valuable witness. It confirms that the Eve–Mary parallel was known in the West during the first Christian centuries, and that the mystery of the Mother of God was beginning to become an object of theological reflection in the entire Church.

---

[12] *De carne Christi* 17, 5; PL 2, 828.

READINGS

MARY THE VIRGIN EARTH

First of all, we need to show the reason why the Son of God had to be born of a Virgin. The initiator of a new birth had to be born in a new way, and Isaiah had predicted that the Lord would give a sign of this. What is that sign? "Behold, the virgin shall conceive in her womb and bear a Son" (Is 7:14). Therefore the Virgin conceived and bore Emmanuel, God-with-us.

And this is the new birth: that man is born in God when God is born in man, having assumed the flesh of the old seed, but without using this seed, in order to reform the flesh through a new seed, a spiritual seed, and to purify the flesh after having eliminated all its ancient stains. But, as it happened, this whole new manner of birth was prefigured in the ancient wise design that depended upon a virgin. When man was created by God's action, the earth was still virgin, not yet pressed down by man's toil, not having been sown. We know that, from this virgin earth, God created man as a living soul.

If, then, the first Adam was introduced in this way, all the more reason that the second Adam, as the apostle said, had to come forth from a virgin earth, that is, from a body not yet violated by generation, by God's action, so that he might become the spirit who gives life. However, lest my introduction of Adam's name appear meaningless, why did the apostle call Christ "Adam" (cf. 1 Cor 15:45), if his humanity did not have an earthly origin? But here, too, reason comes to our aid: through a contrary operation, God recovered his image and likeness, which had been stolen by the devil.

For just as the death-creating word of the devil had penetrated Eve, who was still a virgin, analogously the life-building Word of God had to enter into a Virgin, so that he who had fallen into perdition because of a woman might be led back to salvation by means of the same sex. Eve believed the serpent; Mary believed Gabriel. The fault that Eve introduced by believing, Mary, by believing, erased.

—Tertullian, *De carne Christi* 17, 1–5; PL 2, 827–28

IN WHAT SENSE MARY IS CALLED "WOMAN"

Let us now see whether the apostle also restricts the term to the same meaning it has in Genesis, which applies it to the female sex (cf. Gen 2:23), when he calls the Virgin Mary "woman" (cf. Gal 4:4), just as Genesis called Eve "woman". Writing to the Galatians, he says, "God sent his Son, born of a woman", which establishes that she is a virgin, even if Ebion opposes this interpretation.

I also acknowledge that the angel Gabriel is sent to the Virgin, and when he declares her blessed, he locates her among women and not among virgins: "Blessed are you among women" (Lk 1:42). The angel also knew that a virgin can also be called woman.

Someone thinks that he has given a clever explanation of these two passages in saying that, because Mary was married, it is for this reason that both the angel and the apostle call her "woman". For someone who is married is also, in a certain way, *nupta* [that is, wedded, no longer a virgin]. However, between being "in a certain way" *nupta* and being truly *nupta*, there is a difference that applies in this case. In other cases, married and *nupta* go together.

Instead, they [St. Paul and Gabriel] called Mary "woman", not as if she were already *nupta*, but simply because she is a female, even though still a virgin, and this is the original sense in which the word "woman" was used (cf. Gen 2:23).

—Tertullian, *De virginibus velandis* 6, 1; PL 2, 945–46

6

TWO GREAT MASTERS
OF THE SCHOOL OF ALEXANDRIA:
CLEMENT OF ALEXANDRIA AND ORIGEN

Egypt was another region of the Roman Empire in which the Christian faith was widespread in the earliest times. Already in the first century (the apostolic age), there were Christian communities in Egypt that, according to the surviving evidence and historical documentation, must have possessed a remarkable fervor and dynamism. Marian doctrine and devotion appear to have developed very early in this favorable environment, showing signs of particular vitality.[1]

It was in Egypt that the first Marian prayer known to us was composed, in the third century. The Greek text of the *Sub tuum praesidium* was discovered in a fragment of papyrus in the John Rylands Library in Manchester, England.[2] This prayer, in the course of the centuries, has become widely known: it entered into many Eastern and Western liturgies and greatly contributed to the reawakening of attention to and interest in the doctrine of Mary's divine motherhood. In the Rylands Library papyrus, the term *Theotókos* is readily discernible; further, the prayer expresses the faith of Christians in the Virgin's power of intercession, addressing her

---

[1] The history of the Marian tradition in Egypt, from its beginnings up to the present day, has been traced with magisterial competence by Gabriele Giamberardini, *Il culto mariano in Egitto*, 3 vols. (Jerusalem: Franciscan Printing Press, 1974–1978).

[2] M. C. H. Roberts and E. G. Turner, eds., *Catalogue of the Greek and Latin Papyri in the John Rylands Library, Manchester* (Manchester: Manchester Univ. Press, 1938), 3:46; F. Mercenier, "L'Antienne mariale grecque la plus ancienne", *Le Muséon* 52 (1939): 229–33; O. Stegmüller, "Sub tuum praesidium: Bemerkungen zur ältesten Ueberlieferung", *Zeitschrift für katholische Theologie* 74 (1952): 76–82.

with the term *rhýsai* (to deliver) which, in the Our Father, is addressed to God.

The birth and spread of Marian doctrine in Egypt are tied to the names of such great Christian authors as Clement, Origen, and, a little later, Athanasius and Cyril. The first two were among the first great masters of the famous school of Alexandria, the oldest center of Christian learning and sacred sciences in the history of Christianity.

Clement of Alexandria (d. ca. 215)

Clement is known for having tried to reclaim Gnostic theology on behalf of Christianity. At that time, Gnosticism was already widespread and had proliferated in various currents of thought. It taught that man's salvation came more from knowledge of divine mysteries than from the way he lived his life. Clement wanted to show that the true gnostics are Christians, because, in them, faith becomes the light of authentic knowledge of mysteries and brings about union with God himself. The true Christian carries within him Christ, the eternal Word, the perfect image of God.

As for Mary, Clement calls her Mother of the Lord, because the Word of God was truly conceived within her womb.[3] He also witnesses to the Church's faith in the mystery of Mary's perpetual virginity:

> It appears that even today many hold that Mary, after the birth of her Son, was found to be in the state of a woman who has given birth, while in fact she was not so. For some say that, after giving birth, she was examined by a midwife, who found her to be a virgin.[4] These things are attested to by the Scriptures of the Lord, which also give birth to the truth and remain virginal, in the hiddenness of the mysteries of truth. "She gave birth and did not give birth", Scripture[5] says, since she conceived by herself, not as a result of union with a man.[6]

---

[3] *Stromata* 6, 15; PG 9, 349; GCS 15, 496.

[4] A reference to the *Protoevangelium of James* 19:1–20, 1; see James Keith Elliott, *The Apocryphal New Testament* (Oxford: Clarendon Press, 1993).

[5] Actually, this comes from the apocryphal Pseudo-Ezekiel, which other ancient Christian authors also cite as canonical. Cf. Tertullian, *De carne Christi* 23; PL 2, 790.

[6] *Stromata* 7, 16; PG 9, 529–30; GCS 17, 66.

The mystery of the Virgin Mother reminds him of the mystery of the Church, which is also mother and virgin:

> The Lord Jesus, fruit of the Virgin, did not proclaim women's breasts to be blessed, nor did he choose them to give nourishment. But when the Father, full of goodness and love for men, rained down his Word upon the earth, this same Word became the spiritual nourishment for virtuous men. O mysterious marvel!
>
> There is one Father of all, there is one Word of all, and the Holy Spirit is one and the same everywhere. There is also one Virgin Mother, whom I love to call the Church. Alone, this mother had no milk, because she alone did not become a woman. She is virgin and mother simultaneously; a virgin undefiled and a mother full of love.
>
> She draws her children to herself and nurses them with holy milk, that is, the Word for infants. She had no milk because the milk was this child, beautiful and familiar: the body of Christ.[7]

The mystery of Mary, virgin and mother, quickly begins to become the archetypal model of the mystery of the Church. For the Church too, by preaching the word, gives birth to her own children like a mother, while keeping intact the virginity of her faith in the Lord.

Origen (d. 253)

A formidable thinker and author of innumerable works, many of which unfortunately have been lost, Origen is rightly considered the "Father of Eastern theology". The historian Eusebius of Caesarea has passed on to us an abundance of information about Origen's life, activity, and writings.

Born to a deeply Christian family around 185, he received a first-rate secular and religious upbringing. He was only eighteen when the bishop Demetrius called him to replace Clement as the director of the catechetical school of Alexandria, of which he became the most well-known exponent and which, thanks to his teaching and guidance, attained an unprecedented level of prestige.

The example of his Christian life also became a reference point for

---

[7] *Paedagogus* 1, 6; PG 8, 300–301; GCS 12, 115.

his numerous disciples, many of whom were still pagans and belonged to heretical sects. During his thirty years of activity at the school of Alexandria, Origen had occasion to make various trips that enabled him to come into contact with other ecclesial communities, both in the East and in the West. He spent some time in Rome, during the pontificate of Zephyrinus, around 212.

In 232, because of conflicts that arose between him and the bishop of Alexandria, Origen moved for good to Caesarea in Palestine, where the local bishop entrusted to him the task of founding another catechetical school. At Caesarea, Origen continued to teach for another twenty years, until his death in 253, following the maltreatment and tortures he endured during the persecution of Decius.

The controversies that surround Origen and his teachings, both during his life and after his death, cannot obscure his greatness; he left an indelible mark on the history of theology, biblical exegesis, and spirituality. Moreover, by the integrity of his Christian conduct, he witnessed to the gospel to the point of heroism. Tradition counts him among the greatest mystics of the Church. The only obstacle to his canonization is posed by some of his erroneous interpretations of Christian doctrine, which, however, he never held or defended in bad faith.

Origen was one of the authors who argued with great effectiveness against the Gnostic sect of the Docetists, who reduced the humanity of Christ to a mere appearance. He isolated the cause of their error in the inability to admit that Jesus, who possessed a divine nature, could have been born of a human creature. He accused them of not knowing how to read correctly the words of the Gospel, which clearly attest to the event of Jesus' birth. Later, Origen reproved Marcion for having gone so far as to expunge from the sacred text the account of Christ's birth because he was incapable of understanding it.[8] Origen defends the historical reality of the event in no uncertain terms, although his formulation was subsequently rejected by official Church teaching on the Incarnation. Our author held the preexistence of Christ's soul. Influenced by Platonic philosophy, he thought that souls existed before their union with the body and that the soul of Christ was united to the Divine Person of

---

[8] *Commentary on John* 10, 6; PG 14, 316; SC 157, 396–98.

the Word even before the Incarnation, when it was united to the body virginally conceived by the power of the Holy Spirit in the womb of the Virgin Mary.

a. Mary, Mother of God

Origen's main concern was to demonstrate that Mary's motherhood is real and normal, above all on the level of natural reality. Let us investigate some of his texts.

> Those who believe in Jesus who was crucified in Judea under Pontius Pilate, but do not believe that he was born of the Virgin Mary, believe and do not believe in the same Person.[9]

He admonishes the faithful to read the Scriptures attentively and with a spirit of faith, and not to let themselves be deceived by false teachers:

> Therefore, it is wise to accept the meaning of Scripture and not to pay attention to those who say that [Jesus] was born through Mary, not of her. The prescient apostle has said: "But when the fullness of time had come, God sent his Son, born of a woman, born under the law, to redeem those who were under to the law" (Gal 4:4). Observe that he did not say: "born *through* a woman", but rather, "born *of* a woman".[10]

Yet Origen insists that, in order to be Mother of God, Mary must above all be a real and proper Mother of that Son whom the Gospel testifies was born of her. As to the divine character of her motherhood, the Church historian Socrates furnishes us with an interesting piece of information about Origen's convictions. He writes that Origen, in his commentary on the letter to the Romans (a lost fragment), expounds the reasons why it is correct to attribute to Mary the title "Mother of God". Socrates, in tracing the history of Nestorianism, tries to demonstrate that Nestorius was wrong to reject the term *Theotókos*, because in Jesus Christ "there are not two beings, but one single being", and he continues:

---

[9] Ibid. 20, 30; PG 14, 641–44; GCS 10, 367.
[10] *Commentary on the Letter to the Galatians*, PG 14, 1298.

Reasoning in this way, the ancients did not hesitate to call Mary *Theotókos*. . . . Origen, too, in the first volume of his commentary on the apostle's letter to the Romans, gives a full explanation of why Mary is called *Theotókos*.[11]

One needs to keep in mind that the Marian title *Theotókos*, in all probability, originated in Egypt, Origen's homeland, and that he not only used it to indicate Mary's function, but that he, according to the testimony of Socrates, was particularly convinced of its correctness and so went to great lengths to explain its significance and the reasons that justified it.

b. Mary, Virgin Mother

Origen considers virginity to be the most mysterious and marvelous aspect of Mary's motherhood. He makes it quite clear that, above all, this is a question of faith:

> If someone believes that he who was crucified under Pontius Pilate was a holy person, who came to bring salvation to the world, but does not believe in his birth of the Virgin Mary and the Holy Spirit, thinking instead that he was born of Joseph and Mary, then this person lacks an indispensable condition for possessing the complete faith.[12]

To the contrary, Jesus was born exclusively from the Virgin Mary, from whom he took his own human flesh. Origen poses the question exactly in the terms in which it had to be phrased for the mentality of his time. According to the biology of that time, the conception of a baby was caused solely by the male semen, while the mother's womb was considered to be only the receptacle in which it developed. In such a perspective, the words of Origen appear clear when he notes that the birth of Christ represents a completely different case from that of all other human beings, who are born from a man by means of a woman:

> In the case of any man, it is appropriate to say that he was born "by means of a woman", because before he was born of a woman, he took

---

[11] *History of the Church* 7, 32; PG 67, 812.
[12] *Commentary on John* 32, 16; PG 14, 784; GCS 10, 452.

his origin from a man. But Christ, whose flesh did not take its origin from a man's seed, is rightly said to have been born "of a woman".[13]

Further, the virginal conception of Jesus took place without any of the passion that normally accompanies conjugal relations and therefore stains the soul of the human creature from its birth. Instead, the virginal conception happened in such a way that Christ's human nature was free from concupiscence and unbridled passions. Therefore, notes Origen, the apostle Paul says that Jesus was sent in a body similar to the sinful flesh (cf. Rom 8:3) but which, in reality, is not sinful flesh. Thus, the soul of Christ, free from concupiscence, could readily achieve a perfect union between the flesh and the divine Word, which assimilated this human flesh as fire assimilates iron.[14] In this view, Origen is convinced that the virginal conception of Jesus was not a sort of privilege for his Mother but, rather, a service she owed to the mystery of the Word made flesh.

c. Mary, Ever-Virgin

When it comes to the mystery of Mary's perpetual virginity, Origen not only has no doubts but seems directly to imply that this is a truth already recognized as an integral part of the deposit of faith. It would appear that one of his declarations ought to be interpreted in this sense:

> There is no child of Mary except Jesus, according to the opinion of those who think correctly about her.[15]

The expression "think correctly" in all probability means thinking according to the doctrine of revealed faith.

He praises the intention of those who, in order to defend Mary's perpetual virginity, accept the explanation of the apocrypha regarding the so-called brothers of the Lord. These would be sons fathered by Joseph during a previous marriage. Then he goes on:

> Those who speak thus mean to safeguard Mary's dignity in the virginity she conserved until the end, so that that body chosen to serve

---

[13] *Commentary on the Letter to the Romans* 3, 10; PG 14, 956–57.

[14] *Treatise on First Principles (Peri Archon)* 2, 6, 5–6; PG 11, 214; SC 252, 318–20.

[15] *Commentary on John* 1, 4; PG 14, 32; GCS 10, 8–9.

the Word, who said, "The Holy Spirit will come upon you and the power of the Most High will overshadow you" (Lk 1:35), did not know any relations with a man, after the point that the Holy Spirit came down upon her and the power of the Most High overshadowed her.

I consider it to be in conformity with reason that, with regard to the purity which consists in chastity, Jesus was the first among men, while Mary was the first among women. It is the act of a wicked man to attribute the first place in virginity to anyone else.[16]

In his writings, Origen frequently expresses his own esteem and admiration for the Christian practice of virginity. It allows one to conform himself to the Mother of the Lord, in whom he sees an outstanding model of the true Christian, the spiritual man, the perfect disciple of Christ. Also, through the virginal life, the faithful can share in Mary's maternal function:

Every incorrupt and virgin soul, having conceived by the Holy Spirit in order to give birth to the will of the Father, is a mother of Jesus.[17]

Thus, doing the will of the Father means, according to our author, giving birth to the divine Word, who is, in himself, the will of the Father.

In the context of the mystery of Mary's perpetual virginity, there occurs the problem of the marriage she contracted with Joseph. Origen is the first Christian author to give well-developed explanations of this fact:

I ask myself why God, after having decided that the Lord was to be born of a virgin, did not choose a young woman without a fiancé, but instead chose [Mary], who was already engaged. If I am not mistaken, the reason is this: the Lord had to be born of a virgin who was not only engaged to be married but also, as Matthew writes, already entrusted to the care of a man (who had not yet known her, however), to avoid any disgrace to the virgin, should she be seen with a swollen belly.

On this subject, I have found a fine observation in a letter of the martyr Ignatius, second bishop of Antioch after Peter,[18] who fought

---

[16] *Commentary on Matthew* 10, 17; PG 13, 876–77; GCS 40, 21–22.
[17] *Fragments on Matthew* 281; GCS 41/1, 126.
[18] *To the Ephesians* 19, 1.

with the wild beasts during a persecution in Rome. Mary's virginity was hidden from the prince of this world, hidden thanks to Joseph and her marriage to him. Her virginity was kept hidden because she was thought to be married.[19]

This double reason given by Origen will be fully exploited by later authors, some of whom will go so far as to say that God wanted to use the marriage between Mary and Joseph to deceive the devil, while Origen limits himself to saying that God simply kept hidden the mystery of Mary's virginity.

d. Mary's Holiness

To indicate the exalted holiness of the Mother of the Lord, the Eastern Church has used the term *panaghía* (all-holy), which has become common in theological and liturgical language. It is possible that this title began to be attributed to Mary in the Church of Alexandria. As far as Origen is concerned, we encounter the title more than once in his writings[20] and, while some scholars consider it an interpolation,[21] others see no plausible reason to share this suspicion.[22]

According to Origen's dynamic concept of Christian perfection, understood as a journey or continual progress toward higher forms of the spiritual life, Mary could not have been totally holy from the beginning of this journey. For this reason, he readily admits the presence of some imperfections or defects in her. For example, he asserts that the sword foretold by Simeon was none other than the doubt and scandal that arose in her during her Son's Passion:

> What ought we to think? That while the apostles were scandalized, the Mother of the Lord was immune from scandal? If she had not experienced scandal during the Lord's Passion, Jesus did not die for

---

[19] *Homilies on Luke* 6, 3–4; PG 13, 1814–15; SC 87, 144–46.

[20] Cf. Giamberardini, *Culto mariano*, 1:126, n. 192.

[21] Cf. Cipriano Vagaggini, *Maria nelle opere di Origene*, Orientalia Christiana Analecta, 131 (Rome: Pontificium Institutum Orientale, 1942), p. 158, n. 91. This is one of the best studies on Origen's mariological thought, together with that of Henri Crouzel, "La Théologie mariale d'Origène", in *Origène: Homélies sur St. Luc*, intro., SC 87.

[22] Cf. Giamberardini, *Culto mariano*, 1:126–27.

her sins. But if "all have sinned and fall short of the glory of God" and if all "are justified and saved by his grace" (Rom 3:23), then Mary, too, was scandalized in that moment. This is what Simeon is prophesying about: . . . Your soul will be pierced by the sword of unbelief and will be wounded by the sword point of doubt.[23]

From this text also emerges the intention to support such a conclusion by resorting to a dogmatic reason: the universal value of the redemption accomplished by Christ.

But usually Origen, faithful to the more ancient Alexandrian tradition, tends to emphasize the Virgin's holiness and virtues, always in the context of her condition as one still making progress. He regards her as assiduous in reading and meditating upon Scripture, open to the influence of the Holy Spirit, who pours into her the light of prophecy at the moment she pronounces her *Magnificat*; he calls her humble and poor, but rich in faith, persevering in spiritual knowledge. In times of trial, he sees her as capable of overcoming difficulties, obediently accepting the revelation of mysteries. Among the holy persons of the Old and New Testaments, he attributes a place of honor to the Mother of the Lord, unique among all women.

Origen's response to those who held that Mary had been rejected by her Son because, after his birth, she had conjugal relations with Joseph, truly makes one reflect:

If Mary is proclaimed blessed by the Holy Spirit [through the mouth of Elizabeth], then how can the Lord have rejected her?[24]

It appears that all of Origen's admiration for the Mother of the Lord is expressed in this assertion: Mary was proclaimed blessed by the Holy Spirit himself.

---

[23] *Homily on Luke* 17, 6–7; PG 13, 1845; SC 87, 256–58.
[24] Ibid. 7, 4; PG 13, 1818; SC 87, 158.

READINGS

"SUB TUUM PRAESIDIUM"

Under your mercy we take refuge, O Mother of God. Do not reject our supplications in necessity, but deliver us from danger, [O you] alone pure and alone blessed.

—from the Rylands Library papyrus,
text reconstructed by Gabriele Giamberardini

"MY SOUL MAGNIFIES THE LORD"

Two faculties, the soul and the spirit, express a twofold praise. The soul celebrates the Lord while the spirit praises God; not that praising the Lord is different from praising God, since the One who is God is also the Lord, and the One who is the Lord is also God.

We ask ourselves how the soul could magnify the Lord. For if the Lord cannot be subject either to growth or to diminution, being who he is, why does Mary now say, "My soul magnifies the Lord"?

If I consider that the Lord and Savior is "the image of the invisible God" (Col 1:15), and if I see that my soul is made "in the image of the Creator" (Gen 1:27), to be the image of the image (since my soul is not, properly speaking, the image of God but has been formed unto the likeness of the original image), then I will be able to comprehend the matter by putting it in these terms: Just as painters of images, after choosing (for example) the face of a king, apply their artistic ability to copying a unique model, in the same way each of us, by transforming our own soul into the image of Christ, reproduces an image of him, smaller or larger, sometimes hidden and dirty, but sometimes shining and luminous and corresponding to the original model.

Therefore, when I have enlarged the image of the image, that is to say my soul, and have magnified it in my deeds, thought, and words, then the image of God becomes larger, and the Lord himself, whose image is my soul, is magnified in that soul. And as the Lord grows in our image, so, if we are sinners, he diminishes and decreases.

Precisely speaking, the Lord neither diminishes nor decreases. It is we who, instead of putting on the image of the Savior, clothe ourselves in other images. In place of the image of the Word, of wisdom, of justice, and all the other virtues, we put on the likeness of the devil, so much so that we can be called "serpents, brood of vipers" (Mt 23:33). We also put on the costume of lions, dragons, and wolves when we become cruel, venomous, wily; and even assume the likeness of a goat or pig when we are too inclined to sensual pleasures.

I remember saying one day, while explaining the passage from Deuteronomy where it is written, "Do not make any image of a man or a woman, nor an image of any living thing" (Dt 4:16–17), that according to "the spiritual law" (Rom 7:14), some form themselves after the image of a man, others into a woman, others resemble birds, reptiles, and serpents; still others resemble God. If you read this explanation, you will understand how these words are to be understood.

Now, first Mary's soul magnifies the Lord, and then, her spirit rejoices in God. Unless we first believe, we will not be able to rejoice.

—Origen, *Homilies on Luke* 8, 1–4; PG 13, 1820–21

THE APOSTLE JOHN RECEIVES MARY AS HIS MOTHER

Thus we should be bold and say that while the Gospels are the firstfruits of Scripture as a whole, the firstfruits of the Gospels is the Gospel of John, whose profound meaning cannot be perceived except by him who rested his head on Jesus' breast and who received Mary to be his mother also.

He who wishes to be another John must become so in order to be pointed out by Jesus as another John, that is to say, another Jesus. While Mary has no son other than Jesus, as it appears to those who think correctly about her, nevertheless Jesus said to his Mother, "Behold your son" (Jn 19:26), and not, "Behold, this man also is your son." In other words, he said to her, "This man is Jesus, whom you bore."

Indeed, when someone is perfect, it is no longer he that lives, but Christ lives in him (cf. Gal 2:20); therefore when he speaks of him to Mary, he says, "Behold your son, that is, Jesus Christ."

—Origen, *Commentary on John* 1:6; PG 14, 32

MARY, HUMBLE AND LOWLY

I do not consider it worth the trouble to contest accusations offered without seriousness and as a joke [by Celsus]: "Was the Mother of Jesus pretty, perhaps, and was it because of her beauty that God, who by his nature cannot fall in love with an incorruptible body, embraced her? Wasn't it less than fitting that God should fall in love with a woman who was neither rich nor of royal blood, since no man had knowledge of her, not even her neighbors?" He also asserts, joking, that "when the carpenter began to hate her and discarded her, neither God's power nor her protestations of fidelity could save her. No"—he concludes—"all this has nothing to do with the kingdom of God." In what way does this differ from the villainies that some prefer to speak on the streets, whose words are unworthy of any serious attention?

—Origen, Against Celsus 1, 39; PG 11, 733

7

MARY IN THE EARLY CHURCH IN ROME

Although the Church of Rome enjoyed a position of primacy as the see of Peter's successor, it was not in the forefront of the theological debates and developments of the first centuries. This is not to say that it was ignored or undervalued by other Christian communities. History appears to testify that exactly the opposite was the case. For example, there are the eloquent and impressive declarations of the bishop Ignatius of Antioch, who died at Rome as a martyr around the end of the first century. He used words of extraordinary praise and admiration for the Roman Church, in a letter addressed to the Christians of that community:

> The church which presides in the place of the region of the Romans, worthy of God, worthy of honor, worthy of blessedness, worthy of praise, worthy to be chaste, which presides in charity, is signed with the name of Christ and with the name of the Father.[1]

We also know that, around the end of the first century, under the pontificate of Clement I, the Church of Rome intervened energetically and with authority on the occasion of certain regrettable events in the Christian community of Corinth.[2]

Its absence from the theological debates of that period is probably to be explained by the fact that the doctrinal problems that so impassioned and divided Eastern Christianity had not taken hold in the West. One should also take into consideration the different Roman-Western mentality, which inclined more toward practical questions than to theological speculation. Nonetheless, it is precisely in ancient Rome that we observe a phenomenon of extreme interest from the

---

[1] *Letter to the Romans* 1.
[2] *Letter to the Corinthians.*

point of view of the history of religion: namely, the presence of the figure of the Virgin Mother in iconography.

Mary in the Art of the Catacombs

In the ancient catacombs of Rome, an abundance of artistic evidence can be found that is important for understanding the Christian faith and life of the time. This takes the form of numerous frescoes, which may be admired even today, in more or less good condition, and which usually depict scenes and characters from the Old and New Testaments.

For the Christians of that day, these pictures constituted a form of easy catechesis, aimed especially at simple and illiterate persons, who perhaps would not benefit from an approach utilizing written documents of revelation and Church doctrine. But, certainly, they were expressions of the faith and piety of the Christian people as a whole, who saw the ideas and images that nurtured their faith depicted in these iconographic pictures.

It should be noted that the Virgin Mother is present from the beginning in these frescoes, which combine catechesis and Christian devotion. While in some examples her presence is of secondary importance, in others she appears as the central figure, depicted as a genuine protagonist. The biblical scenes in which Mary is portrayed are those of the prophetic announcement of her motherhood, the Annunciation by the angel, and the adoration of the Magi. There is a constant reference to the mystery of the Incarnation in which the relationship between Christ and his Mother is made obvious. "These paintings," says Wilpert, "better than any written document from the period of the persecutions, characterize the position of Mary in the Church of the first four centuries and show that, in terms of substance, she was the same person then that she would later become."[3]

The Virgin with Prophet is the theme of a famous fresco that is still admired today in the catacombs of Priscilla, on the via Salaria.

---

[3] J. Wilpert, *Die Malereien der Katakomben Roms*, vol. 1 (Freiburg im Breisgau: Herdersche Verlagshandlung, 1903), p. 197.

Although the lower portion is deteriorated, the pictorial group can be considered complete in that it does not lack any essential character. The Virgin, clothed in a stole and short veil, is seated in an attitude of meditation, with her head inclined slightly forward, toward her right shoulder. With both hands, she holds in her lap the naked baby Jesus, whose head is turned around, as if someone had called him. On the left side of the scene stands the erect figure of a prophet, holding the scroll of the Scriptures in his left hand and pointing toward the Virgin with his right index finger.

The figure of this prophet has been variously interpreted by experts. Some, pointing to the eight-rayed star over Mary's head, maintain that it is the prophet Balaam, who foretold, "A star shall come forth out of Jacob, and a scepter shall rise out of Israel" (Nb 24:17). Others consider it more probable that it is Isaiah, the prophet par excellence of the Messiah: "Behold, a virgin shall conceive and bear a son, and shall call his name Emmanuel" (Is 7:14). It seems more normal to think of Isaiah, when one considers the figure of the prophet pointing his finger toward Mary. As for the symbolism of the star, it is true that Isaiah does not use it when speaking of the coming of the Messiah, but he does describe, in inspired poetry, the fullness of light that will arise at the birth of the Messiah-Redeemer: "Arise, shine; for your light has come, and the glory of the LORD has risen upon you" (Is 60:1).

Undoubtedly, this is the oldest and most beautiful pictorial representation of the Virgin Mother to have survived from early second-century Roman Christianity.

A later portrayal of the Virgin in the *orans* posture and with the child in her lap was discovered in the so-called Great Cemetery (*Cimitero Maggiore*), on the via Nomentana. This fresco dates from the middle of the fourth century.

The Gospel account of the Annunciation became part of the art of the catacombs fairly early. We find it in a fresco in the catacombs of Priscilla, from the end of the second century, and in a crypt of the catacombs of Sts. Peter and Marcellinus, where the fresco appears to date from the third century.

These two frescoes have a particular meaning and importance not only for paleo-Christian art, but also for the history of theology and devotion. While in other Gospel scenes the leading character is

Christ, and Mary appears as a secondary figure, in the Annunciation there is no doubt that she is the principal protagonist.

The creators of these frescoes must have wanted to interpret the special feelings of the early Christians of Rome for the Mother of the Lord, in particular their respect and admiration for her. The angel, dressed in the same clothes that are observed in the pictures of the saints, is portrayed standing in front of the figure of the Virgin, with his right hand raised, as if about to speak. Mary, by contrast, receives the divine message while seated on a chair. Undoubtedly this detail is meant to indicate her superiority over the angel.

The fresco in the catacombs of Priscilla deserves particular consideration. It is not presented as one panel out of a series of depictions of the mysteries of the Lord's life. Had it been so, the scene would have to be interpreted as one moment within a pictorial sequence. Instead, the Annunciation is a single, completely isolated fresco, the only scene on an entire wall. This shows that, in this case, the artist was directly concerned with the figure of Mary and the mystery of the Virgin Mother.

The Adoration of the Magi is the catacomb painting in which Mary is most frequently depicted. She is always portrayed seated in a chair, with the young Jesus in her arms, while the Magi are shown in the act of approaching to adore the child and to offer their gifts. Jesus is clearly the center upon which all the elements of the fresco converge. It is toward him that the Magi address themselves, and it is he who is being presented by his Mother. Her seated position shows that she was regarded by the artist as someone who deserved special attention and respect.

In these pictorial elements, sober as they are, we see certain traces of the important place that the Blessed Virgin had begun to have, very early on, in the faith and devotion of the Christian people of the first centuries. Art is a very eloquent witness, because it does not speak to the ears but directly to the soul, through its lines and colors.

A Witness to the Apostolic Tradition: Hippolytus of Rome (d. 235)

Between the end of the second century and the first decades of the third century, there lived in Rome an author who continues to arouse notable interest on account of his valuable information on the constitution and life of the Church during the first three centuries. This was the priest and martyr Hippolytus. He was almost certainly not of Latin origin, but, having become a priest of the Roman Church, he carried out his ministry and produced his prolific writings in the imperial capital. Both austere and ambitious, he set himself against Pope Callixtus, whom he accused of laxism in the treatment of Christians who had fallen into grave sin. His followers elected him bishop of Rome, in opposition to Callixtus, and so he became the first antipope in the history of the Church. Arrested by the imperial authorities and deported to Sardinia together with Pope Pontianus, Hippolytus was reconciled with the Church before his death in 235.

His body was carried back to Rome and buried by Pope Fabian in the cemetery of the via Tiburtina, which today is called the cemetery of St. Hippolytus. He was soon venerated and invoked as a martyr. This is attested to by a graffito near the cemetery entrance: *Ippolite, in mente habeas Petrum peccatorem* (O Hippolytus, remember Peter, a sinner).

In his works there are numerous allusions and references to the Blessed Virgin, which are strictly tied to a christological context. Hippolytus is aware that the heresies that change right doctrine about Jesus Christ inevitably affect his Mother as well. She has an essential role in the mystery of the Incarnation, so that, if the nature of her relationship with the Son of God become man is not exactly defined, the purity of faith in the mystery of the incarnate Word is endangered.

Hippolytus accuses the heretics of offering a deformed image of Christ or of affirming outright the existence of more than one Christ. This happened in the extreme case of certain Gnostics who discovered no fewer than three Christs: the first being the trinitarian Word; the second, a kind of demiurge (that is, an intermediary being between God and creation); and the third being the man Christ, born of Mary to become our Savior.

To tell the truth, Hippolytus himself fell into erroneous statements about the mystery of the Son's eternal generation from the Father within the trinitarian mystery. But his reflections on the Incarnation are put in terms in perfect conformity with the teaching of the faith. He explains more than once how the Son of God had to assume our flesh from the Virgin Mary in order to save us:

> Being outside of the flesh, the Word of God took upon himself the holy flesh from the holy Virgin; like a bridegroom, he prepared for himself that garment which he would weave together with his sufferings on the Cross. . . . In this way he intended to obtain salvation for man, who was perishing.[4]

In another work, Hippolytus offers a clear and complete synthesis of the Church's faith in the mystery of the Incarnation:

> Let us believe, blessed brothers, according to the tradition of the apostles, that God the Word came down from heaven and entered into the holy Virgin Mary. Thus, receiving his flesh from her and taking a human (that is, rational) soul and becoming everything that man is, except for sin, he might save fallen man and confer immortality on all men who believe in his name.[5]

Struck by the hidden depths of this event, Hippolytus is instinctively moved to ask the Virgin herself if she can shed some light on this mystery:

> Tell me, O blessed Mary, whom did you conceive in your virginal womb? Yes, even the firstborn Word of God, who came down from heaven into you and was formed, the firstborn man, in your womb, so that the firstborn Word of God might appear united with the firstborn of man.[6]

Our author underscores the superiority of Christ over all created things, insisting on giving him the titles "firstborn of the Father" and "firstborn of the Virgin", inspired respectively by St. Paul and the evangelist Luke. We reproduce a significant text:

> The Son is the firstborn of all: firstborn of God, so that it would be clear that he is the Son of God and the second after the Father; firstborn before the angels, so that it would be clear that he is Lord of the angels; firstborn of the Virgin, so that it would be evident that he

---

[4] *Christ and Antichrist* 4; PG 10, 732; GCS 1, 2, 6–7.
[5] *Against Noetus* 17; PG 10, 826–27.
[6] *Eranistes,* Dial. 1; PG 83, 88.

re-creates in himself the first-formed Adam; firstborn from the dead, being himself the firstfruits of our resurrection.[7]

The title "firstborn of the Virgin" will be commonly attributed to Jesus in a later era, when it will be invoked as one of the biblical-patristic foundations of the doctrine of Mary's spiritual motherhood in regard to all men. For, if Jesus is Mary's firstborn, she must have other children; namely, all men saved by the sacrifice of the Redeemer. But, in Hippolytus' time, it was still too early for a reflection of this kind.

Hippolytus attributes to John, the Forerunner, the role of first herald of the good news of the Savior's conception in the womb of the Virgin by the working of the Holy Spirit. He states that this great announcement of salvation was directed toward the children reborn from the womb of the Church. This is why the good news was proclaimed by a child still hidden in his mother's womb.

We can certainly render a positive judgment of Hippolytus' Marian doctrine. He was one of the earliest Christian writers to appreciate the importance of Mary's role in the mystery of the Incarnation and of human salvation.

Novatian, a Heretic Who Defends Mary's Maternity

Novatian was also a priest of the Roman Church and a contemporary of Hippolytus. The reputation with which he has passed into history is anything but flattering, and, to tell the truth, various errors are encountered in his writings. Among other things, he denies that Christ's death has any expiating effectiveness, which would reduce it to a mere proof of his human nature. Also, he places an exaggerated emphasis on the faith and morality that a Christian is called to practice in this life, and he undervalues the efficacy of God's working through grace and the sacraments. Moreover, he clings to utopian ideals about the constitution of a totally pure and holy Church, going so far as to provoke a schism when Pope Cornelius was elected in 251.

---

[7] *Commentary on Daniel* 4, 11; GCS 1, 1, 212–14.

However, Novatian was a man of considerable intellectual stature and left us a work on trinitarian theology that, taken as a whole, constitutes a fundamental stage in the doctrinal development of the Latin Church.[8] He probably died as a martyr. If this is so, by the supreme act of martyrdom Novatian may have saved his own his life, which, from a Christian point of view, was hardly edifying.

We must however recognize that, notwithstanding the errors found in his teachings, Novatian expressed himself correctly and with respect when speaking of the Blessed Virgin. He defended her maternity against those heretics who denied it in any way. He disputed with them rather emphatically:

> We do not recognize the Christ of the heretics who [they say] was only an appearance and not real . . . nor that Christ who does not have a body like ours because, they maintain, he took nothing from Mary.[9]

To the contrary, Novatian defends the reality of Christ's body, born of the Virgin Mary. He fully recognizes that to deny this would be equivalent to denying the reality of salvation, which he understands as the response of faith to the teaching of the Son of God become Son of Man.

Unfortunately, his concept of Mary's divine motherhood remains subtly marred by the subordinationist mentality with which he treats the problem of the relation between the Father and Son within the trinitarian mystery.

Concluding this brief glance at the situation of the Roman Church in the first centuries, we can recognize that, even in Rome, there was no lack of concern over the danger that some heresy was infiltrating the faithful. On the whole, however, the doctrinal situation appears fairly tranquil. The faith and devotion of Roman Christians toward the Mother of the Lord could be characterized as untroubled and rewarding, if we may be permitted to draw conclusions from the catacomb frescoes mentioned above. The Mother who holds the Son of God within her arms must have infused cour-

---

[8] Cf. R. J. De Simone, *The Treatise of Novatian, the Roman Presbyter on the Trinity*, Studia ephemeridis Augustinianum, 4 (Rome: Institutum patristicum, 1970).

[9] *On the Trinity* 10; PL 3, 929.

age and the strength to persevere into the Christians of this Church, which in her early centuries could reckon innumerable martyrs among her faithful.

READINGS

CHRIST, VIRGINAL FLOWER

In calling him who descended from Judah and David "the lion's cub", the prophet [Jacob] indicated the Son of God become man; and by saying, "From a sprout, my son, you went up" (Gen 49:9), he foretold the fruit that flowered from the holy Virgin, not generated by David's seed, but conceived by the working of the Holy Spirit, sprung up from the earth as from a bud. For Isaiah says, "A shoot shall sprout from the stump of Jesse, and a branch shall flower forth from his roots" (Is 11:1). The one whom Isaiah calls a branch, Jacob calls a sprout; for the Word first sprouted [in the womb], then flowered in the world.

—Hippolytus, *Christ and Antichrist* 8; PG 10, 733–36

GENERATED BY THE FATHER ACCORDING TO THE SPIRIT, BY HIS MOTHER ACCORDING TO THE FLESH

For Scripture says, "Jacob loved him [Joseph] because he was the son of his old age" (Gen 37:3). Thus in a world that had become old and was entirely lost, the Son of God, who had been manifested and born of the Virgin, appeared to the eyes of the Father "the son of old age". Even before all ages, from everlasting, he is with God.

"By the blessing of the breasts and of the womb of your father and your mother" (Gen 49:25–26, Septuagint). Blessing of breasts: or rather, of the two Testaments, from which came forth the preaching that announced the future appearance of the Word in the world; breasts with which he nurses and feeds us, presenting us to God as sons. Or he designates with these words the breasts of Mary, from which he took suck, breasts that were blessed and of which a woman, crying out, said, "Blessed is the womb that bore you and the breasts that you sucked!" (Lk 11:27).

By saying in addition, "And of the blessing of the womb of your father and your mother", the prophet is foretelling a spiritual mystery. For he could have said, "And of the blessing of the womb of your mother", to indicate, with this expression, Mary, in whose womb the Word was carried for nine months. Yet he did not say this; instead he says, "and from the blessing of the womb of your father and your mother". Joining the two ideas in this way, he made them a single reality, so that it would be clearly understood that both that which exists according to the spirit and that which is according to the flesh belong to this one Person. For the Word proceeded from one heart of the Father and from the holy womb [of Mary], being born from one womb of the Father, as he says through the mouth of the prophet, "My heart speaks a good Word" (Ps 45:1).

On the other hand, in the last days, he came forth, according to the flesh, from a virginal womb after having been carried for nine months, so that, after having been born a second time from the womb of his Mother, he might manifest himself visibly. Therefore he says, also through the prophet, "Thus says the LORD who formed me from [my Mother's] womb to be his servant" (Is 49:5).

—Hippolytus, *On the Blessings of the Patriarchs* 1;
PO 27, 108–12

8

THE END OF THE ANTE-NICENE ERA

The period from the second half of the third century until the Council of Nicaea (325) was a time of considerable historical importance. Radical changes in the relationship of the Roman Empire to the Christian Church took place during this period. After having been outlawed and persecuted, the Church achieved a legitimate status. This meant that the civil society's attitude of reserve, suspicion, and hostility toward the Church could start to fade away.

Although the policies of the Roman emperors, from the edict of Constantine on, favored the progressive replacement of pagan religion by Christianity, they also led to the unhealthy phenomenon of Caesaro-papism. This was often a serious problem, not only for the pastoral governance of the Church, but also for the working of the Magisterium.

At the close of this period, theological activity remained in a period of stasis. Accordingly, we find relatively little literary evidence of any significant development in Marian doctrine. With the rise of the Arian heresy, Christianity was caught up in a grave doctrinal crisis that called into question the dogma of the Trinity and its christological implications. Consequently, Christian leaders devoted all their theological reflection and apologetic work to defending orthodoxy against the heretical deviations of Arius and his followers, whose influence had spread virtually everywhere among the population of the Roman Empire, infecting even the barbarian peoples.

The dominant theme in the theological debate at that time was the eternal consubstantiality of the Word of God with the Father. Compared with the central mystery of the Blessed Trinity, Marian doctrine remained somewhat in the shade. Few hints of it are found in works of this period.

In Roman Africa, *Cyprian*, bishop of Carthage and martyr (d. 258), was the first author to see a reciprocal connection between the text of Genesis 3:15 and Isaiah 7:14:

> It is written in the prophet Isaiah: "And the Lord spoke again to Ahaz saying, "Ask for a sign from the Lord your God. . . . Therefore the Lord himself will give you a sign: Behold, a virgin shall conceive in her womb and bear a son, and shall call his name Emmanuel. He shall eat curds and honey; before he knows or brings forth evil, he will exchange it for the good" (Is 7:10–15). God had predicted that the seed destined to crush the head of the devil would come forth from a woman. In Genesis, it is written: "I will put enmity between you and the woman, between your seed and hers. He will crush your head and you will strike at his heel" (Gen 3:15).[1]

Around 330, the Latin poet *Juvencus*, of Spanish origin, composed a poetic work entitled *Evangeliorum Libri*, a kind of paraphrase in verse of the four Gospels. In it, the author sets forth a sober, delicate, and charming image of the Blessed Virgin. When Juvencus presents the Gospel episodes that mention Mary, he portrays her as a real protagonist alongside her Son.[2]

In the East appears the famous *Gregory the Wonderworker* (d. ca. 270), who studied under Origen for five years at the school of Caesarea in Palestine. Tradition incorrectly attributes numerous pseudo-epigraphic Marian homilies to Gregory the Wonderworker. Gregory of Nyssa wrote his biography, in which we find the Wonderworker portrayed as the recipient of the first reported Marian apparition in the history of the Church.

READING

MARY APPEARS TO THE YOUNG GREGORY THE WONDERWORKER

While [Gregory] was passing a sleepless night because of these worries, someone appeared to him in human form, aged in appearance,

---

[1] *Book of Testimonies* 2, 9; PL 4, 704; CSEL 3, 1, 73.

[2] Ibid., 1, 52–79; CSEL 24, pp. 6–7; 1, 296–306, pp. 18–19; 2, 135–38, p. 47; 2, 725–32, p. 74.

clothed in garments denoting a sacred dignity, with a face characterized by a sense of grace and virtue. Gregory, looking frightened, rose
from his bed and asked him who he was and why he had come.

The other, in a subdued voice, after soothing his distress, told
Gregory that he had appeared by divine will, because of the questions
that Gregory found ambiguous and confusing, to reveal to him the
truth of pious faith. After hearing these words, Gregory regained his
serenity and began to observe the other man with a certain joy and
wonder.

The other then held up his hand, as if to point out, with his index
finger, something that had appeared opposite him. Gregory, turning
his gaze in the direction indicated by the other man's hand, saw before him another figure, which had appeared not long before. This
figure had the appearance of a woman, whose noble aspect far surpassed normal human beauty. Gregory was again disturbed. Turning
away his face, he averted his glance and was filled with perplexity;
nor did he know what to think of this apparition, which he could not
bear to look upon with his eyes. For the extraordinary character of
the vision lay in this: that though it was a dark night, a light was
shining, and so was the figure that had appeared to him, as if a burning lamp had been kindled there.

Although he could not bear to look upon the apparition, Gregory
heard the speech of those who had appeared, as they discussed the
problems that were troubling him. From their words, Gregory not
only obtained an exact understanding of the doctrine of the faith but
also was able to discover the names of the two persons who had appeared to him, for they called each other by name.

For it is said that he heard the one who had appeared in womanly
form exhorting John the Evangelist to explain to the young man the
mystery of the true [faith]. John, in his turn, declared that he was
completely willing to please the Mother of the Lord even in this matter and that this was the one thing closest to his heart. And so the
discussion coming to a close, and after they had made it quite clear
and precise for him, the two disappeared from his sight.

—Gregory of Nyssa, *Life of St. Gregory the Wonderworker*,
PG 46, 909–12

PART TWO

*From the Council of Nicaea
to the Council of Ephesus (431)*

Prologue

The fourth century coincides with the golden age of ancient Christian literature. It is the period of the great Fathers of the Church, among whom we begin to notice a more developed and specific interest in the Mother of the Lord. In this century, Marian literature is enriched by the contributions of such great names as Athanasius, Epiphanius, Cyril of Jerusalem, Ephrem the Syrian, Basil, Gregory Nazianzen, Gregory of Nyssa, and John Chrysostom in the Eastern Church. In the Western Church, we meet Hilary of Poitiers, Ambrose, Jerome, and Augustine, to mention only the greatest. These personages dominate the Christian culture, which, thanks to them, begins more and more to influence the science, art, and thought of that time.

With regard to the Mother of the Lord, we can establish that not only Marian doctrine but Marian devotion as well were beginning to gain ground and to be expressed in the Church's liturgy.

As early as the middle of the fourth century, we find significant developments in Marian devotion in the East. For example, the Church of Jerusalem was already celebrating the feast of the Presentation of Jesus in the Temple (*Hypapantē*). While this remained fundamentally a christological feast, it left ample room for a commemoration of the Blessed Virgin, especially in homilies commenting on Simeon's words to Mary about the sword that would pierce her soul (cf. Lk 2:35). According to the testimony of Egeria, this feast was celebrated forty days after Epiphany; that is, on February 14.[1]

The figure of the Virgin becomes steadily more familiar, especially in monastic environments and, in a general way, in the lives of those Christians who consecrated themselves to the Lord as virgins. The political situation also favored the spread of consecrated virginity. After the Edict of Milan (313), the official tolerance accorded by the emperor Constantine to the Christian religion effectively put an end

---

[1] *Peregrinatio Aeterae* 26; CSEL 39, 77.

to persecutions. Consequently, martyrdom was no longer an eventuality for which the Christian had to prepare himself. Previously, a Christian had to be prepared to face martyrdom with steadfast courage and with a sense of gratitude toward the Lord, should he demand the supreme witness of faith and love through the sacrifice of one's life. In the new state of affairs, there was a steady increase in the number of Christians who saw a life consecrated to God in perpetual virginity as a way to render the kind of witness previously manifested in the acceptance of martyrdom. In the context of this new mentality, it seemed obvious to present the Mother of the Lord as the most sublime model of life for consecrated virgins.

ATHANASIUS OF ALEXANDRIA
(d. 373)

One of the Fathers who made the greatest contribution to new interest in the person and mission of the Virgin Mary in the plan of salvation was Athanasius, bishop of Alexandria in Egypt. He strongly defended the true Christian doctrine of the divinity of Jesus Christ against Arius and his followers, who denied it. St. Gregory Nazianzen called him "pillar of the Church".

Athanasius was born in Alexandria around 295. He was ordained a deacon in 319 by his bishop, Alexander, who made him his secretary. It was in this role that Athanasius accompanied Alexander to the first ecumenical council, held at Nicaea in 325. On this occasion he so distinguished himself by his gifts, by his vigor, and by the effort he put into the debate against the Arians that in 328 he was called to succeed Alexander as bishop.

The Arians, who considered him their most dangerous enemy, made his life very trying and troublesome. He was opposed, calumniated, rejected by some parts of his own Church. He even had to resist the orders of the emperor Constantine, who claimed to have readmitted the heresiarch Arius to communion with the Church. Constantine, being unable to bend the bishop of Alexandria to his will, condemned him to exile at Trier, in Gaul, after which a group of bishops hostile to Athanasius deposed him from his episcopal throne.

After the death of Constantine in 337, Athanasius was able to return to his Church of Alexandria, but, because of the machinations of his enemies, he had to return to exile five times. Only in 336 was he able finally to return to his see and be restored to his office as bishop, which he carried out until his death in 373.

Athanasius' contributions to Marian doctrine derive their value from his important efforts in the christological debate of his time and from the clear and courageous positions he assumed in defending the divinity of the Son of God. But Athanasius was also capable of successfully emphasizing the ascetical and moral aspect of the example of Mary, a theme that, as we have noted, had become customary in the monastic circles of that time. In this he follows a trail already blazed by his predecessor, Alexander, who addressed himself to the Virgin in these words:

> Also, you have the conduct of Mary, who is the type and image of that life which belongs to heaven.[1]

An Important Anonymous Witness

The idea expressed by Bishop Alexander appears in a fascinating document, published together with the so-called *Proverbs of the Council of Nicaea*. Here is the text:

> Mary is like a wise virgin. Who could describe the beauty of the Mother of the Lord, who was loved by God because of his works? Therefore, his beloved Son made his dwelling in her. . . . Mary is called Mother of the Lord and this she truly is, because she brought to light him who created her. . . . Neither did she lose her virginity when she gave the Savior to the world; to the contrary, she preserved it intact, like a precious treasure. Mary had never seen the face of a stranger, and it is for this reason that she was confused when she heard the voice of the angel Gabriel.[2]

The text continues, giving some curious details about Mary's behavior. This seems to be material drawn from the apocryphal gospels. Here are some examples:

> She did not eat to give pleasure to her body but only according to the demands of nature. . . . When her mother came and got her, she could not speak a single word about her condition (as a pregnant vir-

---

[1] Quoted by Athanasius in his *De virginitate*, found in a Coptic translation and edited by T. Lefort, in *Le Muséon* 42 (Louvain, 1929): 197–275 and 240–64. For the text cited, see p. 259.

[2] Felix Artur Julius Haase, "Die koptischen Quellen zum Konzil von Nicaea, Kap. 34–35", *Studien zur Geschichte und Kultur des Altertums* 10 (1929): 50ff.

gin), because she had sworn an oath to herself that she would not speak a word about it to anyone in this world. She always sat with her face turned toward the East, because she prayed continually. Her brothers wished to see her and speak with her, but she did not want to receive them. Since the angels visited her at different times, they could observe her exemplary manner of life and admire it. She would sleep, but only according to necessity. The Lord, who knows his entire creation well, saw in it nothing like Mary. Therefore he chose her to be his Mother. If, then, a girl wants to be called virgin, she must resemble Mary.[3]

Apparently, this description of Mary's personality corresponds to an ideal of consecrated virginity as it was conceived in the fourth century. When one sets out to find personal models to imitate, there is always the risk that these will be manipulated to conform to preconceived ideals. This also happens in the case of Mary, whose authentic image, traced in sober but marveling lines by the Gospels, has at times been retouched by religious groups looking for an affirmation and sublimation of their ascetical objectives.

Athanasius Defends Mary's Motherhood

The bishop of Alexandria became a vigorous defender and assertor of the teaching of revelation on the Mother of the Lord. Against the followers of Arius, he unequivocally holds that Jesus is the Son of God, generated by the Father from eternity, and thus possessing the Father's identical divine nature. On the basis of this premise, he does not hesitate to give the name "Mother of God" to her who generated him in his mortal nature. Athanasius uses the term *Theotókos*, which in 431 would be introduced into the official documents of the Council of Ephesus:

> Christ, being God, became man for our sake and was born of Mary, Mother of God, to free us from the devil's power.[4]

He is fond of emphasizing the salvific purpose of the Incarnation, which allows him to argue for an (at least) indirect link between Mary's motherhood and human redemption:

---

[3] Ibid.
[4] *On Virginity* 3; PG 28, 256; TU 29, 2, 38.

It was for our sake that Christ became man, taking flesh from the Virgin Mary, Mother of God.[5]

The salvation of men demanded the destruction of the power of sin, and Jesus took our human flesh from Mary precisely in order to redeem from slavery those who were being held prisoner by sin:

> When, at the end of the time ordained, he was born of Mary to destroy sin (for this is why the Father decided to send his own Son, born of a woman, born under the law), then he, having taken a body, became man.[6]

But numerous heretics were teaching every kind of error about the human nature of Jesus. Some held that his body was only an appearance, a sort of phantasm, whose function was to conceal the splendor of divinity, which man could not bear. Others taught that the Son of God could not have assumed a human body because of the intrinsically wicked nature of matter, which therefore was absolutely unworthy to be united with divinity. Others, to the contrary, asserted that the flesh of Christ was not like our own but was a sort of divine or heavenly flesh, having descended directly from heaven. It merely passed through Mary's womb but did not have its origin from her. There were also some who stated that when Jesus was conceived in and born of Mary, he was a mere man, who only later was clothed with divinity.

Against all these errors, Athanasius affirmed the real birth of the Son of God from the Virgin Mary. Jesus assumed a body like ours, even though his conception had occurred in an extraordinary manner, outside of the norms of nature:

> If the Son of God had wanted merely to appear, He could certainly have assumed any kind of body, even one better than ours. Instead it was our own kind of body that He took, and not just in any way. He took it from a pure and unstained Virgin, who had not known man. This body was pure and not corrupted by union with man. For since He is indeed the All-powerful and the Craftsman of all things, He made for Himself a temple within the Virgin; that is to say, a body.[7]

---

[5] *Against the Arians* 3, 29; PG 26, 385.

[6] Ibid. 3, 31; PG 26, 388–89.

[7] *On the Incarnation of the Word* 8; PG 25, 109; ed. Thomson (Oxford: Clarendon Press, 1971), p. 152.

The Virgin's Child Is God

For Athanasius, as for many other Fathers, the miracle of the virginal conception is a clear sign of the divinity of the Baby born of the Virgin:

> When He came among us, He formed Himself a body, taking it from a Virgin to offer a proof of His divinity which could not be ignored. It had to appear clearly that He who fashioned this body is the Maker of all things. For who, seeing a body being born of the Virgin alone, without the intervention of man, could fail to understand that He who appears in that body is the Maker and ruler of other bodies also?[8]

Athanasius points out that the virginal birth of the Son of God is an absolutely unique fact. No saint, prophet, or patriarch of the Old Testament was born virginally. The birth of Jesus is a mystery that goes totally beyond our power to understand:

> No one can describe His bodily generation. No one can point to a father who begot Him in the flesh, because His body did not come from a man, but from the Virgin alone.[9]

God foretold this unfathomable mystery through the voice of the prophet Isaiah (cf. Is 7:14). The prophecies and the miracle of the virginal conception are signs that God gave to man to help him receive the inexpressible mystery of the Lord of the universe, who became man. Faith needs divine support and assistance to overcome the limits of human weakness.

Mary Ever-Virgin

Athanasius, who was a great promoter of the monastic life, insists strongly on Mary's perpetual virginity, which he presents as a paradigm of the highest holiness to virgins who have consecrated their lives to the Lord.

He emphasizes, above all, that Mary's perpetual virginity is a truth clearly taught by the Gospel. For, had Mary had other children, she

---

[8] Ibid. 18; PG 25, 128; Thomson, p. 178.
[9] Ibid. 37; PG 25, 160; Thomson, p. 224.

would have been taken into their care after the death of Jesus. Instead, Jesus entrusted his Mother to the apostle John:

> For, if she had had other children, the Savior would not have ignored them and entrusted his Mother to someone else; nor would she have become someone else's mother. She would not have [abandoned her own] to live with others, knowing well that it ill becomes [a woman] to abandon her husband or her children. But, since she was a virgin, and was his Mother, he gave her as a mother to his disciple, even though she was not really John's mother, because of his great purity of understanding and because of her untouched virginity.[10]

The bishop of Alexandria masterfully exalted the highly exemplary function of Mary's perpetual virginity:

> Mary, who gave birth to God, remained a virgin to the end [in order to be a model for] all to come after her.[11]

In this brief text, our author's thought is clear and unequivocal: Mary's perpetual virginity is, above all, demanded by her divine motherhood. It follows that her virginity becomes a paradigm of holiness that should be proposed for the imitation of the faithful. He explains it this way:

> The Holy Scriptures, which instruct us, and the life of Mary, Mother of God, suffice as an ideal of perfection and the form of the heavenly life.[12]

Athanasius is sometimes fond of going into details that make the blessed Virgin's exemplary qualities concrete. In this he appears to be inspired by the apocrypha:

> Mary was a pure virgin. . . . She loved to do good works. . . . She did not want to be seen by men but prayed God to be her judge. . . . She remained at home always, leading a hidden life. . . . She gave generously to the needy what surplus she had earned by the work of her hands. . . . She prayed to God as one person speaks to another. . . . Her speech was reflective and her voice subdued. . . . She purposed to

---

[10] *De virginitate*, in *Le Muséon* 42:243–44.
[11] Ibid, 244.
[12] Ibid., 255.

make some advances each day and did so. . . . She did not worry about dying. She was even sad and sighed every day because she had not yet reached the gates of heaven.[13]

The example offered by the life of Mary, according to the bishop of Alexandria, will one day prove itself to have been extremely fruitful:

How many virgins Mary will meet! How she will embrace them and lead them to the Lord's feet! What joy among the angels when they see an image of their own purity in the bodies of virgins! How the Lord will present them to his Father, saying: "All these were and are [virgins] like Mary, my Mother!"[14]

READINGS

MARY GREETS ELIZABETH

[Mary] greets Elizabeth: the Mother of the Master greets [the mother] of the servant; the Mother of the King greets the mother of the soldier; the Mother of God greets the mother of the man; the Virgin greets the married woman. She greets Elizabeth with an outward greeting, and when the two greet each other in a visible manner, the Holy Spirit, who dwelt in Mary's womb, incites him who is in Elizabeth's womb, as one who urges on his friend, "Hurry, get up!"

Therefore he who dwelt in Elizabeth's womb leapt. And behold: [Christ spoke to him] saying, "Go forth; make straight my paths, so that I may realize the plan [economy] that has been determined for me." When Mary and Elizabeth greeted one another, Christ also greeted John in his mother's womb, as it is [said] in the Gospel: "It happened that, when Elizabeth heard Mary's greeting, the baby stirred in her womb for joy."

Come now, raving Arius: do you not hear that he who is in Mary's womb and he who is in Elizabeth's womb are exchanging greetings,

---

[13] *Letter to Virgins*, in *Le Muséon* 42:244–45.
[14] *De virginitate*, in *Le Muséon* 42:248.

while the son of the barren woman announces to the whole world: "Behold the Son of God in the womb of the holy Virgin, Mary."

But you say, "How does this happen?" Listen, and I will tell you. The moment John heard his Master's voice, he greeted him through the mouth of his mother, and then he rejoiced and delighted to hasten forth from his mother's womb, in advance of his Master. Then, unable to contain his joy, he cried out, through his mother's mouth, addressing the Virgin: "Blessed are you among women and blessed is the fruit of your womb. But who am I that the Mother of my Lord should come to me?"

My dear friends, do not think that John was the instrument; Elizabeth is the instrument, and John speaks through her mouth. Now, just as John was not an instrument, so also the Savior greets John, by the greeting Mary addresses to Elizabeth through the mouth of his mother.

—Athanasius, *Homily of the Papyrus of Turin*,
ed. T. Lefort, in *Le Muséon* 71 (1958):214

IN PRAISE OF THE BLESSED VIRGIN

O noble Virgin, truly you are greater than any other greatness. For who is your equal in greatness, O dwelling place of God the Word? To whom among all creatures shall I compare you, O Virgin? You are greater than them all. O [Ark of the New] Covenant, clothed with purity instead of gold! You are the Ark in which is found the golden vessel containing the true manna, that is, the flesh in which divinity resides. Should I compare you to the fertile earth and its fruits? You surpass them, for it is written: "The earth is my footstool" (Is 66:1). But you carry within you the feet, the head, and the entire body of the perfect God.

If I say that heaven is exalted, yet it does not equal you, for it is written: "Heaven is my throne" (ibid.), while you are God's place of repose. If I say that the angels and archangels are great—but you are greater than them all, for the angels and archangels serve with trembling the One who dwells in your womb, and they dare not speak in his presence, while you speak to him freely.

If we say that the cherubim are great, you are greater than they, for the cherubim carry the throne of God (cf. Ps 80:1; 99:1), while you hold God in your hands. If we say that the seraphim are great, you are greater than them all, for the seraphim cover their faces with their wings (cf. Is 6:2), unable to look upon the perfect glory, while you not only gaze upon his face but caress it and offer your breasts to his holy mouth. . . .

As for Eve, she is the mother of the dead, "for as in Adam all die, even so in Christ shall all be made alive" (1 Cor 15:22). Eve took [fruit] from the tree and made her husband eat of it along with her. And so they ate of that tree of which God had told them: "The day you eat of it, you shall die" (Gen 2:17). Eve took [fruit] from it, ate some of it, and gave some to her husband [that he might eat] with her. He ate of it, and he died.

In you, instead, O wise Virgin, dwells the Son of God: he, that is, who is the tree of life. Truly he has given us his body, and we have eaten of it. That is how life came to all, and all have come to life by the mercy of God, your beloved Son. That is why your spirit is full of joy in God your Savior!

—Athanasius, *Homily of the Papyrus of Turin*,
ed. T. Lefort, in *Le Muséon* 71 (1958):216–17

2

EPHREM THE SYRIAN
(ca. 306–373)

The Marian doctrine of the Syrian Church reaches its most sublime expression in the poetry of Ephrem. He is rightly called "the harp of the Holy Spirit" and deserves the additional title of "Marian Doctor". The profound artistic inspiration that pervades his writing, especially his compositions in verse, together with its lofty doctrinal tone and intense spirituality, made a deep impression on the subsequent Syrian tradition. Other important writers in that tradition make significant references to Mary; among them are Narsai (d. 502) and James (Jacob) of Sarugh (d. 521).

Ephrem was born at Nisibis, in Syria, around 306. He was baptized as a youth and was ordained a deacon in the church of his birthplace. In 363, Nisibis fell into the hands of the Persians, and Ephrem followed the large contingent of his compatriots who migrated to Edessa. There he continued the catechetical activity that he had already carried out in Nisibis and in so doing established a new school, which came to be called "the school of the Persians". He died in 373, leaving a collection of works that is still impressive today, even though some of his works have been lost and the authenticity of others is disputed. His poetic activity seems to have been inexhaustible. The historian Sozomen informs us that Ephrem wrote no fewer than three million lines of verse.[1] He is undoubtedly to be considered the greatest poet of the patristic age, and he was the first to lay such stress on the mysteries and the grandeurs of the Mother of the Lord.

His verses not only overflow with beauty of form and lyricism but also express rich religious and theological thought. The poet reveals

---

[1] *Storia Ecclesiastica*, PG 67, 1088 B.

his feelings of deep awe and admiration when considering the holy Virgin and her virtues. He is always finding new views, new images, and new concepts to express what he feels deep inside himself. One might say that his poetic inspiration never tires of celebrating the fascinating figure of Mary.

This extraordinary richness of thought and style has an explanation. Ephrem does not merely recite; he expresses what is in his heart. One can see that he loves the Blessed Virgin passionately and tenderly, that she is an important person for him, that he feels intimately bound to her because of their common Christianity, and that he considers himself obliged to give her recognition. At the same time, his relationship with Mary is marked by an easy familiarity that, without showing disrespect, encourages confidence and faithful prayer.[2]

In Love with the Beauty of the Virgin

Mary is the most marvelous creature who exists, after Jesus. St. Ephrem feels irresistibly attracted to this creature, who becomes for him the source of the highest inspiration. In his boundless enthusiasm, he manages to pay a sort of affectionate compliment to the Son, while extolling the greatness of his Mother:

> Only you [Jesus] and your Mother
> are more beautiful than everything.
> For on you, O Lord, there is no mark;
> neither is there any stain in your Mother.[3]

In a charming comparison, he presents the Virgin as the receptacle of the divine light, that is, of that Son who came to dwell in her and who is the root cause of her perfection:

---

[2] For the Marian thought of Ephrem, cf. Edmund Beck, "Die Mariologie der echten Schriften Ephräms", *Oriens Christianus* 40 (1956):22–39; Ignacio Ortiz de Urbina, "La Vergine Maria nella teologia di S. Efrem", *Symposium Siriacum*, 1972 (Rome: Pont. Inst. Orient. Studiorum, 1974), pp. 65–104.

[3] *Carmina Nisibena* 27, 8; CSCO 219, 76.

The eye becomes pure
when it is united with the light of the sun,
and receives strength from its vigor
and clarity from its splendor;
it becomes radiant with its ardor
and adorned with its beauty. . . .
In Mary, as in an eye,
the Light has made a dwelling and purified her spirit,
refined her thoughts, sanctified her mind,
and transfigured her virginity.[4]

Ephrem's insistence on Mary's spiritual beauty and holiness, and on her freedom from any stain of sin, has led some scholars to hold that he was aware of the privilege of the Immaculate Conception and to point to him as a witness to the dogma.[5] Yet it does not appear that our author was familiar with the problem, at least not in the terms in which it was made clear by later tradition and the dogmatic definition of 1854. In one passage he even uses the term "baptized" to indicate her Son's saving intervention in her regard:

Handmaid and daughter
of blood and water [am I] whom You redeemed and baptized.[6]

God's grace-giving choice made Mary the object of a sort of biblical envy that compares Mary to the prophetic city of Bethlehem:

Blessed are you, Bethlehem, whom fortified towns
and fortified cities envied.
Mary, like you, women envied—
and virgin daughters of powerful men.
Blessed is the girl He found worthy to indwell,
and also the town He found worthy to inhabit.[7]

---

[4] *Hymns on the Church* 36, 1–2; CSCO 199, 87–88.

[5] Cf. Fr. X. Mueller, "Die unbefleckte Empfängnis Marias in der syrischen und armenischen Ueberlieferung", *Scholastik* 9 (1934): 161–220; Ignacio Ortiz de Urbina, "Vale el testimonio de san Efren en favor de la Immaculada?" *Estudios Eclesiasticos* 28 (1954): 417–22.

[6] *Hymns on the Nativity* 16, 10; CSCO 187, 76; *Ephrem the Syrian: Hymns*, trans. Kathleen E. McVey, CWS (New York: Paulist Press, 1989), p. 150.

[7] Ibid., 25, 12; CSCO 187, 119; CWS, p. 203.

Even Mary's name reflects the grace and greatness of her person, so intimately linked to that of the Son of God:

> Blessed are you also, Mary, whose name is great and exalted because of your Child. Indeed you were able to say how much and how and where the Great One, Who became small, dwelt in you.[8]

The Mystery of the Mother of God

Ephrem's religious and poetic enthusiasm for the holy Virgin has its robust and deep roots in the awareness of the ineffable reality that this privileged creature bore. This reality is that of the Son of God who became also the Son of Mary. Ephrem repeats this often, in different ways:

> He formed his individuality, the Image, in the womb,
> and he formed in all wombs all persons.[9]

Our doctor feels compelled to specify, against the heretics, that the life of Jesus consists of concrete and real facts, not fictitious apparitions. He shows how the reality of one event presupposes the reality of others, while the denial of one reality implies the denial of all the others:

> His death on the Cross attests to his birth from the woman. For anyone who dies must have been born as well. . . . Therefore, the human conception of Jesus is demonstrated by his death on the Cross. If anyone denies his birth, the Cross proves him wrong.[10]

Thus Ephrem defends the unquestionable reality of Mary's motherhood in its human aspect. But he also insists on the transcendent aspect of the person of Christ, thereby affirming the divine character of Mary's motherhood as well:

> Whoever believes that he had his beginning in Mary is set straight [and taught] that his divinity is before all ages.[11]

---

[8] Ibid., 25, 14; CSCO 187, 120; CWS, p. 203.
[9] Ibid., 4, 177; CSCO 187, 36; CWS, p. 102.
[10] *Sermon on Our Lord* 2, CSCO 271, 2.
[11] Ibid.

The holy doctor shows that he is irresistibly attracted to the arcane aspect of this mystery, in which a creature is raised to an incomprehensibly lofty role:

> By power from Him Mary's womb became able
> to bear the One who bears all.[12]

This unfathomable mystery evokes questions full of surprise and wonder:

> The womb of Sheol conceived him and burst open;
> and how did the womb of Mary sustain Him?
> With His voice He split stones upon graves;
> and how did Mary's bosom sustain Him?
> You came to humiliation to save all:
> glory to You from all who were saved by You.
> Who is able to speak about the hidden Son
> Who came down and put on a body in the womb?[13]

Our author tries to gain an insight into the Virgin's astonishment, seeing her involved in an event far above our powers of comprehension:

> Who will dare speak to her son
> as in prayer, to the hope of his mother
> as God, to her beloved [child] and her son
> as man. In fear and love
> it is right for Your mother to stand before You. . . .
> I became a haven for Your sake,
> great Sea. Behold, the psalms
> of Your father David and also the words
> of the prophets, like ships
> discharged in me Your great wealth.[14]

We stand before the mystery of the divine election. Not even Mary can understand why the Lord's choice has fallen upon her humble person. Yet, when God chooses one of his creatures to carry

---

[12] *Hymns on the Nativity* 4, 182; CSCO 187, 36; CWS, p. 102.

[13] Ibid., 4, 190–93; CSCO 187, 36–37; CWS, p. 103.

[14] Ibid., 9, 1–4; CSCO 187, 55; CWS, p. 125.

out a mission, that creature can become an extraordinary instrument in his hands. Such was the Virgin Mary. Therefore, Ephrem never tires of emphasizing the transcendent significance of Mary's motherhood:

> A wonder is Your mother: the Lord entered her
> and became a servant; He entered able to speak
> and He became silent in her; He entered her thundering
> and His voice grew silent; He entered Shepherd of all;
> a lamb He became in her; He emerged bleating.[15]

The Exceptional Virgin

It seems that Ephrem thought of virginity as a prerogative of Mary's person. The prophecies and symbols of the Old Testament prefigured her in this light. The virgin earth that gave birth to Adam, the virgin Eve, the bush, burning yet unconsumed, that Moses saw on Mount Sinai, the famous prophecy of Isaiah, and other figures as well are to be applied to Mary's virginity. Finally, in Jesus' Resurrection from the tomb, Ephrem perceives a posthumous confirmation of his virginal birth from Mary:

> The womb and Sheol shouted with joy and cried out
> about Your resurrection. The womb that was sealed,
> conceived You; Sheol that was secured,
> brought You forth. Against nature
> the womb conceived and Sheol yielded.
> Sealed was the grave which they entrusted
> with keeping the dead man. Virginal was the womb
> that no man knew. The virginal womb
> and the sealed grave like trumpets
> for a deaf people, shouted in its ear.[16]

This text is one of many that show how Ephrem celebrated, above all, Mary's bodily integrity in the conception and birth of Jesus.[17] He considers the virginal conception of Christ to be a unique and magnificent miracle, possible only because a God was being born:

---

[15] Ibid., 11, 6; CSCO 187, 62; CWS, p. 132.
[16] Ibid., 10, 7–8; CSCO 187, 59; CWS, p. 130.

> If difficult things for You are not difficult
> but easy, so that the womb conceived You
> without intercourse, and without seed
> the womb gave birth to You, it is easy for the mouth
> to be fruitful and to multiply Your great glory.[18]

This exceptional privilege conferred on Mary becomes a kind of model of how the Lord will intervene on behalf of Christian virgins. It is also a reason for the praise that they and the whole people of God raise to him:

> Praise to You [who] purify your flock
> as Your mother, and Your chaste women
> as the one who bore You, and Your handmaids
> as the one who nursed You. From them and from her
> and from all of us glory be to Your name![19]

Ephrem offers an explanation of this wonder. Mary became fertile through the word of God pronounced by the angel Gabriel, which penetrated her through her ear:

> Just as their very bodies have sinned and die, and as the earth, their mother, is cursed (cf. Gen 3:17–19), so because of this body which is the incorruptible Church, his earth is blessed from the beginning.
> This earth is Mary's body, the temple in which a seed has been deposited. Observe the angel who comes and deposits this seed in Mary's ear. It is with this very clear word that he began to sow: "Salvation is with you; you are blessed among women" (Lk 1:28). And Elizabeth confirmed this word, saying once more: "You are blessed among women" (Lk 1:42), showing that because of the first mother who was cursed, the second Mother bears the name of blessed.[20]

This image of the conception occurring through the ear was to inspire many Christian artists, who reproduced the motif in their paintings.

---

[17] Cf. Paul Krueger, "Die somatische Virginität der Gottesmutter im Schrift-ume Ephräms des Syrers", *Alma Socia Christi*, vol. 5 (Rome: Academia Mariana Internationalis, 1952), pp. 46–86.

[18] *Hymns on the Nativity* 15, 6; CSCO 187, 74; CWS, p. 146.

[19] Ibid., 12, 11, CSCO 187, 65; CWS, p. 135.

[20] *Diatessaron* 4, 15; SC 121, 102.

Figure of the Church

As already referred to in the text above, Ephrem perceived the profound analogy that exists between the Virgin Mary and the Church. He declares explicitly that Mary is a figure of the Church:

> The Virgin Mary is a symbol of the Church, when she receives the first announcement of the gospel. And, it is in the name of the Church that Mary sees the risen Jesus.[21] Blessed be God, who filled Mary and the Church with joy. We call the Church by the name of Mary, for she deserves a double name.[22]

In a passage from the *Diatessaron*, Ephrem goes so far as to identify the Church with Mary, entrusted by Jesus to John:

> He walked upon the sea (cf. Mt 14:25–31); he appeared in the cloud (cf. Mt 17:5); he liberated his Church from the circumcision; he replaced Joshua, son of Nun, with the virgin John, and to him he entrusted Mary (cf. Jn 19:25–27), his Church, as Moses consigned his flock to Joshua (cf. Dt 31:7–8).[23]

Mary and the Church resemble each other in their anxiousness to see Christ and in their promptness in recognizing him:

> Three angels were seen at the tomb:
> these three announced that he was risen on the third day.
> Mary, who saw him, is the symbol of the Church
> which will be the first to recognize the signs
> of his Second Coming.[24]

Further, the Church and Mary have in common the effort to ensure that believers have the true bread of life, the Eucharist:

> The Church gave us the living Bread,
> in place of the unleavened bread that Egypt had given.

---

[21] In his writings, Ephrem repeatedly fails to distinguish between the Mother of Jesus and Mary Magdalen, to whom the Lord appeared on the day of the Resurrection (cf. Jn 20:11–18).

[22] *Sermo ad noct. Resurr.*, ed. Lamy, 1:534.

[23] *Diatessaron* 12, 5; SC 121, 216.

[24] *Hymns on the Crucifixion* 4, 17; CSCO 249, 47.

Mary gave us the refreshing bread,
in place of the fatiguing bread that Eve had procured for us.[25]

From this point forward, Mary and the Church are presented as two realities that will become more and more intimately connected in patristic reflection.

Eve–Mary

In his writings, Ephrem fully develops the Eve–Mary comparison, which is based on the foundational concepts of light and darkness, death and life, the triumph of good over evil, the role of the woman alongside the man.

Mary and Eve are like a kind of eye for the world, yet how different one is from the other! While the one eye is closed to the light, the other radiates splendor on all men, who in this way will retrieve their lost unity:

> Behold the world! To it were given two eyes:
> Eve was the left eye, the blind eye; the right eye,
>   the luminous eye is Mary.
> Because of the eye that grew dark, the whole world became dark.
> Then men, groping in the shadows,
> will consider every stone on which they stumble
> to be a god.
> They have called lies the truth.
> But when the world once more begins to shine, by the other eye
> and the light of heaven taking up a dwelling in the cavity
>   of this eye,
> then men will rediscover unity, perceiving that what they
>   had found
> was the downfall of their lives.[26]

In his *Harmonization of the Gospels*, Ephrem returns more than once to this comparison. Parallels and contrasts are equally in evidence:

---

[25] *Hymns for the Unleavened Bread* 6, 6–7; CSCO 249, 11.
[26] *Hymns on the Church* 37, 5–7; CSCO 199, 90.

Mary gave birth without having relations with a man. As in the beginning Eve was born from Adam without a carnal relationship, so it happened for Joseph and Mary, his wife. Eve brought to the world the murdering Cain; Mary brought forth the Lifegiver. One brought into the world him who spilled the blood of his brother (cf. Gen 4:1–16); the other, him whose blood was poured out for the sake of his brothers. One brought into the world him who fled, trembling because of the curse of the earth; the other brought forth him who, having taken the curse upon himself, nailed it to the Cross (cf. Col 2:14).[27]

Applying Genesis 3:15 to Mary, Ephrem presents her as the one who conquers the serpent that made Eve his victim:

Because the serpent had struck Eve with his claw, the foot of Mary bruised him.[28]

Ephrem is the first Christian author to call Mary spouse of Christ; this seems to be a veiled reference to Eve, who was already married to Adam while he was still a virgin:

For I am [Your] sister from the House of David,
who is a second father. Again, I am mother
because of Your conception, and bride am I
because of your chastity. Handmaiden and daughter
of blood and water [am I] whom You redeemed and baptized.[29]

The great doctor of Syrian Christianity is one of the first Fathers of the Church who allows living sentiments of love and devotion toward the Mother of God to emanate from his writings. These sentiments are oriented, above all, toward the sense of admiration that is certainly one of the defining characteristics of his devotion to Mary.[30]

---

[27] *Diatessaron* 2, 2; SC 121, 66.

[28] Ibid., 10, 13; SC 121, 191.

[29] *Hymns on the Nativity* 16, 10; CSCO 187, 76; CWS, p. 150.

[30] Cf. H. M. Guindon, "Une dimension objective du culte marial chez Saint Ephrem de Syrie: l'Admiration", *De primordiis cultus Mariani*, vol. 3 (Rome, 1970), pp. 213–28.

READING

MERVELOUS MOTHER

Our Lord, no one knows
how to address Your mother. [If] one calls her "virgin,"
her child stands up, and "married"—
no one knew her [sexually]. But if Your mother is
incomprehensible, who is capable of [comprehending] You?

REFRAIN: *Praise to You for Whom, as Lord of all, everything is easy.*

For she is Your mother—she alone—
and Your sister with all. She was to You mother;
she was to You sister. Moreover, she is Your betrothed
with the chaste women. In everything,
behold, You adorned her, Beauty of Your mother.
For she was betrothed according to nature
before You came; yet she conceived
outside of nature after You came,
O Holy One, and she was a virgin
although she gave birth to You chastely.
Mary acquired by You all the attributes
of married women: conception with her
without sexual union, milk in her breasts
not in the usual way. You have suddenly made
the parched earth into a source of milk.
If she carried You, Your great mountain
lightened its burden. If she fed You
[it was] because You hungered. If she gave you a drink
[it was] because you willed to thirst. If she embraced You,
the coal of mercy preserved her bosom.
A wonder is Your mother: the Lord entered her
and became a servant; he entered able to speak
and he became silent in her; he entered her thundering
and his voice grew silent; he entered Shepherd of all;
a lamb he became in her; he emerged bleating.
The womb of Your mother overthrew the orders:

The Establisher of all entered a Rich One;
He emerged poor. He entered her a Lofty One;
He emerged humble. He entered her a Radiant One,
and he put on a despised hue and emerged.
He entered, a mighty warrior, and put on fear
inside her womb. He entered, Nourisher of all,
and he acquired hunger. He entered, the One who gives drink to all,
and he acquired thirst. Stripped and laid bare,
He emerged from [her womb], the One who clothes all.

—Ephrem the Syrian, *Hymns on the Nativity*,
trans. Kathleen E. McVey, CWS, pp. 131–32

3

EPIPHANIUS OF SALAMIS
(d. 403)

The fourth century is considered the Golden Age of patristic literature. At the same time, we must recognize that the Fathers received a
critical impetus to preaching, writing, and working from the heresies
raging about them, heresies that had reached peak intensity and had
diversified into numerous and complex forms. The attacks of the
heretics were directed principally against the Divine Person of the
incarnate Word. Indirectly, however, they implicated all the important aspects of the mystery of the Incarnation.

The Blessed Virgin was one of the leading protagonists in the mystery of the Incarnation and was one of the first to become an object of
false doctrinal manipulations on the part of heretics. Along with their
denial of the divinity or the humanity of Jesus, they denied Mary's
virginity or the divine character of her motherhood or the human
reality of her motherhood.

One of the most forceful and untiring defenders of these truths of
the faith, which were solemnly proclaimed by the Council of Nicaea
(325), was St. Epiphanius, bishop of Constantia (the ancient Salamis)
on the island of Crete. He passed on to later Christian generations a
Marian doctrine that is among the best developed of his time; it is
undoubtedly the most copious.

Epiphanius was born in a village near Gaza, in Palestine, around
325. He spent his youth in Egypt, where he received his initial education, learned languages that enabled him to have some useful
ecclesial experiences, and came to know various monastic communities. Returning to Palestine, he founded a monastery, which
would last for about thirty years, and had his first battles with the
various heretical movements of the day. The orthodoxy of his doc-

trine and his reputation for holiness caused him to be named bishop of Salamis and metropolitan of the island of Cyprus.

The duties and demands of his pastoral ministry led him to write at length in defense of the faith and the authentic teaching of the Church. Yet his writings also reveal certain character flaws: impulsiveness and partiality in making judgments and insufficient control of his own emotional reactions. In the context of his temperament, some of his hostilities are explainable; in particular, his severity and overwhelming hostility toward the great Origen, motivated also by the fact that, in his day, the most influential supporters of Arianism used Origen's teachings to support their own position.

Alongside the inevitable shadows, however, rich personal qualities and indisputable merits also emerge from Epiphanius' temperament and writings. As an author of doctrinal works, he was very successful, not only during his life, but after his death as well; he had a profound influence on later generations of Christians. St. Jerome, his contemporary, proffered this rather flattering testimonial on his behalf:

> Epiphanius, bishop of Salamis in Cyprus, wrote several books *Against Heresies* and many others, which the learned eagerly peruse because of their content and common folk love to read because of their style.[1]

The works of Epiphanius remain an eloquent document that reveals the faith professed by the Christian communities of Palestine, Egypt, and Cyprus. He died in 403, while returning to his episcopal see after a voyage to Constantinople.

The pages that speak of Mary are scattered more or less throughout the works of the bishop of Salamis but especially in his two principal works: the *Ancoratus*, or "Anchor of Faith", a sort of compendium of Christian doctrine,[2] and the *Panarion*, or "Basket", a thorough study and confutation of eighty heresies (this work is usually cited as *Adversus haereses*).[3]

---

[1] *De viris illustribus* 114; PL 23, 746.

[2] PG 43, 12–236; crit. edit. by Karl Holl, GCS 25 (Berlin: Akademie-Verlag, 1980).

[3] PG 41, 173–1200; 42, 12–773; crit. edit. by Karl Holl, GCS 25 (1915), 154–464; GCS 31 (1922); GCS 37 (1933). On the Marian thought of Epiphanius, cf. D. Fernandez, *De Mariologia Sancti Epiphanii* (Rome, 1968); E. Megyer, *Mariologia Sancti Epiphanii* (Rome, 1969); Jean Galot, "Déviation du culte marial et saine tradition:

His Polemical Mariology

Epiphanius had polemics in his blood and in his pen. Not wrongly was he considered the hammer of heresies. He himself unconsciously confesses this on the last page of his *Ancoratus*, where he offers his own version of the Nicene Creed. It is a formula substantially faithful to that of the Council, but—according to Epiphanius—"more suited to combating raging errors".[4] Naturally, the bishop of Salamis has no objections to the doctrine defined by the Fathers of Nicaea. He is referring, rather, to the necessity of expressing the doctrine in such a way that it might most effectively combat errors, so that even the newly baptized, to whom the *Credo* was entrusted, would be able to reject and oppose them.

In reading his works, one gets the clear impression that his Marian doctrine developed out of his polemic against two heresies we can call mariological in the proper sense of the word, because they directly threatened orthodox belief in the mystery of the Blessed Virgin. The two heresies came from two sects, the Antidicomarianites and the Kollyridians.

Epiphanius speaks profusely about the Antidicomarianites in chapter 78 of the *Panarion*,[5] presenting them as heretics who denied, above all, the perpetual virginity of Mary and held that she had normal marital relations with Joseph after the birth of Jesus. The sect of the Kollyridians,[6] widespread in Arabia, Thrace, and Scythia, was made up predominately of women who practiced exaggerated and aberrant forms of worship directed to the Mother of the Lord. The author informs us that these women would offer her oblations consisting of a kind of bread (*kollýra*), as if to a god. This bread would then be consumed in the manner of a true sacramental communion.[7] In rebutting these heresies, Epiphanius had a way to expound his own Marian doctrine in which, along with the themes that by then had become traditional, new intuitions and teachings appear.

Saint Epiphane et les Colliridiens", *De primordiis cultus Mariani*, vol. 3 (Rome 1970), pp. 291–301.

   [4] *Ancoratus* 120; PG 43, 233 A.

   [5] PG 42, 700–740.

   [6] *Haer.* 79; PG 42, 740–56.

The Ever-Virgin Mother of God

Against those who denied and diminished the divinity of Christ (Arians) or his humanity (Apollinarians), our author affirms the divine-human unity of the Person of the incarnate Word and, consequently, the real and divine maternity of Mary:

> [Jesus] is both man and God at once; mysterious for men, he who cannot be contained. As man, however, he is truly born of Mary, having been begotten without manly seed.[8]

In Christ, the bishop of Salamis sees the Son who was to be born of the Virgin, according to the prophecy of Isaiah (7:14), and is thus Emmanuel, God-with-us. And so he does not hesitate to give the Virgin the title *Theotókos* (God-bearer), which appears twice in his writings:

> Without manly seed, he made himself a holy body, taking it from the *Theotókos* Mary, "born of a woman" (Gal 4:4) according to the Scriptures, after he had taken our human nature. Then, as man, he could say: "My God", while, in his eternal nature as Son, he could say: "My Father".[9]

Taking on the Antidicomarianites, Epiphanius decisively confronts the problem of Mary's perpetual virginity. He firmly believes that she was always a virgin, even after the birth of Jesus, and he appears inclined to base his certainty on the universal consensus of the faithful:

> Is not the very name [virgin] sufficient witness? Is it not enough to convince you, you quarrelsome fellow? Was there ever anyone who dared pronounce the name of holy Mary without immediately adding the title "Virgin"?[10]

Accordingly, he follows the tradition that saw St. Joseph as an old widower (of eighty years), whom God wanted to stand beside the

---

[7] *Haer.* 78; 23; PG 42, 736. For more on this heretical sect, cf. Franz Joseph Dolger, "Die eigenartige Marienverehrung der Philomarianiten oder Kollyridianer in Arabien", *Antike und Christentum*, 1, 2 (1929): 107–40.

[8] *Ancoratus* 32; PG 43, 76 A–B.

[9] Ibid., 30; PG 43, 72 B.

[10] *Haer.* 78, 6; PG 42, 705 D.

young Mary as her sole guardian and guarantor of her reputation. Hence, the brothers of Jesus spoken of in the Gospels would be Joseph's children from a previous marriage. Moreover, Christ's decision to entrust his Mother to the disciple John confirms that Mary had no children by Joseph[11] and that she lived as a virgin throughout her life.

The New Eve

In the *Panarion*, our author dedicates two whole paragraphs to the Eve–Mary theme. Returning to the old teaching of Justin and Irenaeus, he adds a further development, which represents the best we can find on this teaching in the Fathers of the Greek Church.[12] Among other things, he writes that Mary, not Eve, is the true Mother of the living. Eve's physical motherhood was merely a figure of a more perfect motherhood, which was realized in Mary, who, conceiving and giving birth to Christ the Lord, brought to light the true life of men.

Going back to the explanation of Irenaeus, the bishop of Salamis sees the Blessed Virgin's obedience to the word of God as a contrast to the disobedience of Eve, the way in and through which the true—that is, eternal—life came down from heaven for all men.[13]

The Eve–Mary parallel also suggests the Mary-Church parallel. This reflection hinges upon the text of Genesis on the creation of woman:

> Notice, I pray you, how precise Scripture is. Of Adam, it is said that he was formed, while, in the case of Eve, it does not say that she was formed but rather that she was built up. "He took"—it says—"one of his ribs and built it up into a woman" (Gen 2:21), to show that the Lord formed himself a body from Mary, but that the Church was

---

[11] Ibid., 78, 10; PG 42, 713 C–716 A.

[12] Cf. T. Camelot, "Marie la nouvelle Eve, dans la patristique grecque du Concile de Nicée à Saint Jean Damascène", *La Nouvelle Eve*, vol. 1, *Etudes mariales*, 1954, p. 160.

[13] *Haer.* 78, 18; PG 42, 728 C–729 A.

built up from his side, when it was pierced and the mysteries of blood and water were poured out for our redemption.[14]

Mary's Earthly End

As far as we know, no Christian author before Epiphanius had ever raised the question of the end of the Blessed Virgin's earthly existence. He was the first who tried to bring together the data from a tradition that, along the course of the centuries, had absorbed many different ideas.

In the *Panarion*, he formulates some hypotheses that may correspond to convictions some early Christians held about the end of Mary's earthly life.

In one brief text, in which our author uses a verb in the future tense, some have seen a denial of Mary's Assumption into heaven:[15]

> How will holy Mary not possess the kingdom of heaven with her flesh, since she was not unchaste, nor dissolute, nor did she ever commit adultery, and since she never did anything wrong as far as fleshly actions are concerned, but remained stainless?[16]

According to this hypothesis, the bodily enjoyment of heavenly glory will be a future reward for Mary, just as it will be for all the redeemed.

In another and better-known text, Epiphanius seems to leave the door open for the assumptionist hypothesis, although he does not state it openly in this sense. The passage is long but worth the trouble to reproduce:

> If anyone holds that we are mistaken, let him simply follow the indications of Scripture, in which is found no mention of Mary's death, whether she died or did not die, whether she was buried or was not buried. For when John was sent on his voyage to Asia, no one says that he had the holy Virgin with him as a companion. Scripture simply is

---

[14] Ibid., 78, 19; PG 42, 729–32.

[15] Cf. J. Niessen, *Die Mariologie des hl. Hieronymus* (Münster, 1913), p. 225 n.; Berthold Altaner, "Zur Frage der Definibilität der Assumptio", *Theologische Revue* 44 (1948): 132.

[16] *Haer.* 42, 12; PG 41, 777 B.

silent, because of the greatness of the prodigy, in order not to strike the mind of man with excessive wonder.

As far as I am concerned, I dare not speak out, but I maintain a meditative silence. For you would find (in Scripture) hardly any news about this holy and blessed woman, of whom nothing is said concerning her death.

Simeon says of her: "And a sword shall pierce your soul, so that thoughts out of many hearts may be laid bare" (Lk 2:35). But elsewhere, in the Apocalypse of John, we read that the dragon hurled himself at the woman who had given birth to a male child; but the wings of an eagle were given to the woman, and she flew into the desert, where the dragon could not reach her" (Rev 12:13–14). This could have happened in Mary's case.

But I dare not affirm this with absolute certainty, nor do I say that she remained untouched by death, nor can I confirm whether she died. The Scriptures, which are above human reason, left this question uncertain, out of respect for this honored and admirable vessel, so that no one could suspect her of carnal baseness. We do not know if she died or if she was buried; however, she did not ever have carnal relations. Let this never be said! [17]

The identification of the woman of the Apocalypse with the Virgin Mary is interesting. It may be the first Marian interpretation of this scriptural text.

Later, Epiphanius appears to reorder his thought into three clearly formulated hypotheses:

If the holy Virgin is dead and has been buried, surely her dormition happened with great honor; her end was most pure and crowned by virginity.

If she was slain, according to what is written: "A sword shall pierce your soul" (Lk 2:35), then she obtained glory together with the martyrs, and her holy body, from which light shone forth for all the world, dwells among those who enjoy the repose of the blessed.

Or she continued to live. For, to God, it is not impossible to do whatever he wills; on the other hand, no one knows exactly what her end was. [18]

---

[17] Ibid., 78, 11; PG 42, 716 B–C.
[18] Ibid., 78, 23; PG 42, 737.

Devotion to the Virgin

Epiphanius greatly admired the Mother of the Lord and did not hesitate to express this admiration, inviting all the faithful to praise her:

> Mary, the holy Virgin, is truly great before God and men. For how shall we not proclaim her great, who held within her the uncontainable One, whom neither heaven nor earth can contain?[19]

We are not on shaky ground if we see St. Epiphanius as a forerunner of the numerous fifth-century homilists who tirelessly sing marvelous songs of praise to the holy Virgin. In any case, he leaves us some valuable considerations about Marian devotion and indicates some appropriate directions for it. He is quick to define the proper meaning and purpose of honor paid to Mary, whom he calls the "holy vessel" in which the Lord was carried:

> Whoever honors the Lord also honors the holy [vessel]; who instead dishonors the holy vessel also dishonors his Master. Mary herself is that holy Virgin, that is, the holy vessel.[20]

Our author has no doubts that the honor paid to the holy Virgin ultimately redounds to God himself; however, he hurls polemics against the Kollyridians; he rejects their idolatrous and pagan devotional excesses, to which we have already referred. He makes a clear distinction between the worship owed to God and the devotion that one ought to render to his Mother:

> Yes, Mary's body was holy, but it was not God. Yes, the Virgin was surely a virgin and worthy of honor; however, she was not given us for us to adore her. She herself adored him who was born of her flesh, having descended from heaven and from the bosom of the Father.[21]

Still engaged in polemic against the Kollyridians, he rejects their pretense of granting the priestly ministry to women, appealing to a Marian argument:

> If God had so arranged things that the priesthood would be entrusted to women and that they would exercise a canonical role in the

---

[19] Ibid., 30, 31; PG 41, 460 C.

[20] Ibid., 78, 21; PG 42, 733 A.

[21] Ibid., 79, 4; PG 42, 745 C–D.

Church, first of all, before any other woman in the New Testament, he would have granted the priesthood to Mary, who was so honored that she carried the universal King in her womb.[22]

The bishop of Salamis, though viewing Mary with a great sense of veneration, praise, and honor, calling her "Ever-Virgin", "*Theotókos*", and "holy", denies her the worship, or *proskýnēsis*, that is due to God alone.[23]

The Marian teachings of St. Epiphanius, though rarely profound, retain historical value within the Christian tradition because of his complete, faithful, and authoritative witness to the Marian beliefs of the Church of his time. His answers to theological questions, as we have noted, are not always definitive or completely satisfactory, but they do open up many new perspectives for the great Marian theologians and homilists of the fifth century. With regard to Marian doctrine, then, it is just to call the bishop of Salamis "top of the line" among the Fathers of the Eastern Church.[24]

READINGS

DEATH FROM EVE, LIFE FROM MARY

"Hail, full of grace, the Lord is with you" (Lk 1:28). This is she who was prefigured by Eve and who symbolically received the title of mother of the living (cf. Gen 3:20). For Eve was called mother of the living after she had heard the words, "You are dust and to dust you shall return"(Gen 3:19), in other words, after the fall. It seems odd that she should receive such a grand title after having sinned. Looking at the matter from the outside, one notices that Eve is the one from whom the entire human race took its origin on this earth. Mary, on the contrary, truly introduced life itself into the world by

---

[22] Ibid., 79, 3; PG 42, 744 A–B.

[23] "Mary should be honored, but only God should be worshiped" (ibid., 79, 9; PG 42, 753 D).

[24] Cf. G. Jouassard, "Deux chefs de file en théologie mariale dans la seconde moitié du IVe siècle: St. Epiphane et St. Ambroise", *Gregorianum* 42 (1961): 5–36.

giving birth to the Living One, so that Mary has become the Mother of the living.

Indeed the words: "Who gave woman wisdom and skill in embroidery?" (Job 38:36), refer to two women: one is the first Eve, who skillfully wove the visible garments of Adam, whom she herself had reduced to nakedness. To this toil, then, she had been destined. Just as nakedness was discovered because of her, so to her was given the task of reclothing the sensible body against visible nakedness.

To Mary, instead, God entrusted the task of giving birth, for our sakes, to him who is the lamb and the sheep; from his glory, as from a veil, by the power of his immortality, a garment is skillfully woven for us.

But we must consider another marvelous aspect of the comparison between Eve and Mary. Eve became for men the cause of death, because through her death entered the world. Mary, however, was the cause of life, because life has come to us through her. For this reason, the Son of God came into the world, and, "where sin abounded, grace superabounded" (Rom 5:20). Whence death had its origin, thence came forth life, so that life would succeed death. If death came from woman, then death was shut out by him who, by means of the woman, became our life.

And as in paradise Eve, still a virgin, fell into the sin of disobedience, once more through the Virgin came the obedience of grace, when the joyful announcement was given that eternal life in the flesh was descending from heaven. For God said to the serpent: "I will put enmity between you and the woman, between your seed and hers" (Gen 3:15). Woman's seed is found nowhere; and so it is in a figurative sense that this enmity is applied to Eve in relation to her and the serpent and to that which was represented by the serpent, namely, the devil and envy.

But all this cannot be perfectly fulfilled in her. Instead, it will be realized truly in the holy, elect, and unique seed, which comes from Mary alone and not from relations with man. This seed came to destroy the power of the dragon, that is, the tortuous and fleeting serpent, who boasted of holding possession of the whole world.

For this reason, the Only-begotten was born of a woman for the ruin of the serpent, that is to say, the ruin of false doctrine, of corruption, of deceit, error, and lawlessness. He is the one who truly opened the womb of his Mother (cf. Ex 13:12). For all the other firstborn sons who preceded him were not able—to speak with decency—to realize a condition of that sort. Only the Only-begotten opened the virginal womb. That happened to him alone and to nobody else.

—Epiphanius, *Adversus haereses* 78, 17–19;
PG 42, 728 B–729 C

MARY, VIRGINAL WORKSHOP OF THE INCARNATION

It was the same holy Savior, descending from heaven, who deigned to bring about our salvation in a virginal workshop, being generated a second time by Mary, having been conceived by the working of the Holy Spirit. Clothed in flesh—"The Word became flesh" (Jn 1:14)—without changing in his nature, although uniting a human nature to divinity, being a perfect being from the Father. For our sake, he came into the world in order to fulfill the perfect economy and to bring about our salvation.

Gifted with the perfection of the Father, he took a human body and a human soul and became man in our midst, not in mere appearance but in truth, molding himself a perfect humanity from Mary, the Mother of God, by the Holy Spirit. The Word did not dwell among us as he had before, such as when he spoke through the prophets, living and working in them by means of his power. Instead, *the Word* himself *became flesh*.

However, in becoming man, he did not change his own nature, nor did he exchange his divinity for humanity; although to the fullness of divinity, which was proper to him, and to his hypostasis as the Word of God, he united humanity. A perfect humanity, I say, meaning everything that is found in man, just as it exists in man.

—Epiphanius, *Ancoratus* 75; PG 43, 157 B–D

4

CYRIL OF JERUSALEM AND THE
JERUSALEM CATECHESES

We have a precious collection of twenty-three catechetical discourses or lectures, dating from the fourth century and traditionally attributed to St. Cyril of Jerusalem. St. Jerome himself, a contemporary of Cyril, vouches for this tradition.[1] The collection is divided into two parts. The first eighteen catecheses, prefaced by an introductory discourse, were addressed to those catechumens who were called *illuminandi*, that is, those who were receiving the requisite "illumination", or instruction, before being admitted to baptism and the other sacraments. Therefore this type of catechesis is also called baptismal catechesis. Today, scholars readily attribute these eighteen lessons to Cyril.

The second part of the collection is comprised of five catecheses called "mystagogical", consisting of a more profound and detailed exposition on the celebration of the Christian mysteries, that is, the sacraments. This was expounded to the neophytes during Easter Week, after they had received baptism during the Easter Vigil. The attribution of these five catecheses to Cyril has been contested. Following the evidence of some manuscripts, some scholars attribute them to John, Cyril's successor as bishop of Jerusalem. While they also constitute an important documentation of catechetical activity in that Christian community, they are less useful for our purpose because they contain no references to the Blessed Virgin.

We have no reliable information about the place and date of Cyril's birth. Nor do we know anything about the events of his life until his episcopal consecration in the year 348. Some historians have suggested that he tended to be friendly toward Arianism. In fact, he

---

[1] *De viris illustribus* 112; PL 23, 746.

was at different times deposed from and restored to his episcopal see of Jerusalem, either by local synods of bishops or by civil authorities. However, shortly after Cyril's episcopal consecration, the Arians accused him of being a defender of the Nicene faith, and this removes any doubt about his orthodoxy. In 381, he took part in the first Council of Constantinople. He governed the Church at Jerusalem until his death in 387.

Cyril's catecheses possess great historical and doctrinal value. They describe the journey that candidates took in preparation for baptism; they explain and illustrate the truths of the faith and the precepts of the Christian life in a simple, spontaneous, and lively manner; their convincing and effective oratory exhorts and encourages the listener to personal struggle; they reveal new hopes and indicate final goals.

Their mariological value lies in the fact that they allow us to see clearly how doctrine about the Virgin Mother of God fit into the structure of the teaching imparted to fourth-century catechumens as they prepared for baptism.[2]

Mary in Cyril's Catechetical Program

The bishop of Jerusalem begins his catechetical series by explaining to the candidates the interior dispositions they ought to cultivate when preparing to receive baptism. He exhorts them to be sorry for their sins and illustrates the nature and value of baptism, in order clearly to present the goals they hope to reach. At this point, in *Catechesis IV*, Cyril offers the catechumens a synthetic exposition of the "ten dogmas"—a kind of summary of all the teachings of the faith. Touching on the dogma of the Incarnation of the Son of God, Cyril stresses the cooperation that the Virgin Mother offered, in mysterious collaboration with the Holy Spirit, to bring about the Incarnation:

> Believe that this only begotten Son of God came down from heaven to earth for our sins, taking our own same humanity, subject to trials like our own. He was born of the holy Virgin and the Holy Spirit.[3]

---

[2] On the Marian content of the catecheses, cf. D. Fernandez, "Maria en las catequesis de san Cirilo de Jerusalén", *Ephemerides Mariologicae* 25 (1975): 143–71.

[3] *Catecheses* 4, 9; PG 33, 465 A.

In this preamble, one can already see how Cyril's Marian teaching mainly gravitates toward the mystery of the incarnate Word, who remains the one and only protagonist of this inexpressible mystery. Alongside him, however, other characters act, offering their own particular cooperation in the mystery. Among these secondary characters, the Virgin Mother plays the most visible and important role. This is what Bishop Cyril tries to make his catechumens understand about the earthly Mother of the Son of God. He presents her as playing a very real role, just as real, in fact, as the consequences of the Incarnation of God the Savior:

> He was made man, not in appearance only or as a phantasm, but in a real way. He did not pass through the Virgin, as if through a channel; rather he truly took flesh from her and by her was truly nursed, really eating and really drinking just as we do.
>
> For if the Incarnation were a mere appearance, such would be our redemption as well. In Christ there were two aspects: man, who was visible in him, and God, who remained invisible. He really ate as we do, as man (for he had the passions of the body in common with us); but as God he fed the five thousand with five loaves; he truly died as man, but as God he raised a dead man from a sleep of four days; as man he really slept in the boat, but as God he walked upon the waters.[4]

Clearly, then, the mystery of the Incarnate Word is the context in which the Jerusalem Church approaches the mystery of Mary.

Mary, Virgin Mother of the Word Incarnate

What has been said above appears even more clearly in *Catechesis XII*, where the figure of the Blessed Virgin occupies more space. This catechesis, which has as its specific theme the Incarnation of the Lord, has much to say about the Virgin Mary and her role as well. The discourse is inspired by the words of the Creed: "He became incarnate, and was made man", and by the prophet's proclamation: "Behold, the virgin shall conceive and bear a son, and shall call him Emmanuel" (Is 7:14).

---

[4] Ibid., 465 B–468 A.

Although the talk, as a whole, obviously revolves around the figure of Christ, his Mother is also included in the explanation of the mystery:

> O students of purity and disciples of chastity, let us celebrate, with lips full of purity, the God born of the Virgin.[5]

Cyril does not avoid the difficulties that can arise when one examines such a mysterious event. The catechumens, too, may have raised some of these difficulties, given the widespread presence of heretical doctrines. Therefore, he teaches them how to handle the objections of heretics and Jews, above all by confronting them with the words of Scripture. With regard to the Jews specifically, Cyril proposes this line of reasoning:

> It would be opportune to pose this question to Jews: Was the Prophet Isaiah being truthful or false when he said that the Emmanuel would be born of a virgin? If they accuse him of being a liar, they are not doing anything odd: they are accustomed not only to accuse the prophets of lying but to stone them. If, on the other hand, the prophet is truthful, accept the Emmanuel. He who is to come and he whom you await, was he or was he not born of a virgin? If not, you are accusing the prophet of falsehood. But if you are waiting for something that will happen in the future, why do you reject what has already happened?[6]

In addition to the unbelief of the Jews, the errors of the heretics afforded Cyril the opportunity to make some precise definitions:

> We accept that the Word of God truly became man, not by the will of a man and woman, as the heretics say, but in conformity with what the Gospel says: "He became man by the Virgin and the Holy Spirit", and that this happened not in appearance but in reality. He became man of the Virgin, and you must now listen to the exposition of this doctrine and accept the proofs for it, because the heretics make many errors about this topic.[7]

One of the more serious objections had to do with the very possibility of a virginal conception. Both Jews and heretics were sceptical

---

[5] Ibid., 12, 1; PG 33, 725 A.
[6] Ibid., 12, 2; PG 33, 728 B–C.
[7] Ibid., 12, 3; PG 33, 728 C–729 A.

that a virgin could have given birth without relations with a man.[8] Cyril formulates a criterion to follow in confronting this and similar objections. It is not human reasons that count but the testimony of Scripture:

> Do not accept the testimony of a man, unless you are taught by Sacred Scripture about the Virgin, about the where, the when, and the how.[9]

It was necessary to explain to the catechumens the reasons why God chose the Incarnation as the way to save men. This is why Cyril's talk on the fittingness of the Incarnation induces him to bring up the Eve–Mary parallel:

> Death came through a virgin, Eve. It was necessary that life also should come through a virgin, so that, as the serpent deceived the former, so Gabriel might bring glad tidings to the latter.[10]

Faithful to the principle set forth above, Cyril also turns to the testimony of Scripture:

> Let us again ask whence he comes and how. Isaiah tells us: "Behold, the Virgin shall conceive and bear a Son, and shall call his name Emmanuel" (Is 7:14).[11]

But the Jews disagreed on the interpretation of the text of Isaiah; according to them the baby in question was Hezekiah, son and successor of King Ahaz, to whom the prophet addressed the prophecy. Cyril invites his listeners to reflect on the meaning of the word "sign":

> Let us read, then, the Scripture: "Ask for a sign from the Lord your God, in the depths or in the heights" (Is 7:11). Now then, a sign has to be something extraordinary. For the water from the rock was a sign, and the parting of the sea, and the turning back of the sun, and things of that sort. But what I am about to say has greater argumentative force against the Jews: . . . the prophecy happened within the sixteen years [of Ahaz's reign], Hezekiah was born at least nine years earlier. What need was there to make a prophecy about someone who

---

[8] Cf. ibid., 12, 4; PG 33, 729 B.
[9] Ibid., 12, 5; PG 33, 729 B–C.
[10] Ibid., 12, 15; PG 33, 741 B.
[11] Ibid., 12, 21; PG 33, 753 A.

had already been born before his father became king? Indeed, he does not say: "she conceived", but: "the virgin shall conceive", in the style of a prediction.[12]

The Virgin's Son, the object of the messianic prophecies of the Old Testament, cannot be anyone except Christ.

Divine Character of Mary's Motherhood

Like all the pre-Ephesus Fathers, Cyril does not insist on the use of the technical term *Theotókos* when speaking of Mary's divine motherhood. In the *Catecheses* it is found only once:

> Dear friends, we possess many true witnesses about Christ. The heavenly Father bears witness through the Son; the Holy Spirit bears witness, descending bodily in the form of a dove; the archangel Gabriel bears witness, bringing the glad tidings to Mary; the Virgin *Theotókos* bears witness to him; the blessed place of his manger bears witness on his behalf.[13]

Cyril, however, never betrays any lack of certainty when discussing the divine character of Mary's motherhood, and there is no doubt that he propounded it to his catechumens as a truth of the Christian faith. He speaks of Jesus as the only begotten Son of God, of whom Mary is "Mother according to the flesh",[14] and calls him "God, born of the Virgin".[15] In a peremptory tone, he reminds his audience that they must see both true God and true man in Christ; as such, he must be adored as a single whole, without separating his divinity from his humanity:

> It is not holy to worship a mere man, but neither is it pious to state that he is only God, excluding his humanity; for, even if Christ were fully God—as he really is—but had not assumed humanity, we would be estranged from salvation. Let us worship him as God but believe also that he was made man. It is not useful to assert that he is man,

---

[12] Ibid., 12, 22; PG 33, 753 B–C.
[13] Ibid., 10, 19; PG 33, 685 A.
[14] Ibid., 7, 9; PG 33, 616 A.
[15] Ibid., 12, 1; PG 33, 725 A.

while prescinding from divinity; neither is it helpful to salvation to confess his divinity without confessing his humanity.[16]

This brief passage is a splendid synthesis of the theology of the hypostatic union. It affirms that, in the Divine Person of Christ, humanity and divinity are inseparable. This is why the Virgin, even though she gave Jesus his human nature only, is rightly proclaimed to be the Mother of God.

The Virginal Birth of Christ

According to the bishop of Jerusalem, Jesus' virginal birth from Mary is a miracle made necessary by motives of the utmost fittingness. The catechumens had to understand this well, in order to oppose the derision of the pagans who mocked the Virgin Birth:

> It was fitting that he who is all pure and the master of virginity should come forth from a virginal bridal chamber.[17]

He explains this fittingness by establishing a link between this great mystery of the faith and the custom that had already been introduced among the priests of his day; namely, abstaining (at least periodically) from the rights of marriage:

> If a man who is functioning worthily as a priest of Jesus abstains from women, how could Jesus himself have come by means of a man and a woman?[18]

Citing Psalm 22:9, "It is you who brought me forth from the womb", Cyril draws the attention of his catechumens to it:

> Heed well the expression: "You brought me forth from the womb." It means that he was conceived and brought forth from the Virgin's womb without the involvement of man. It is different when one is begotten according to the laws of marriage.[19]

---

[16] Ibid., 12, 1; PG 33, 728 A.
[17] Ibid., 12, 25; PG 33, 757 A.
[18] Ibid.
[19] Ibid.

As for the Jews' objections to the virginal birth of Christ, Cyril finds them incomprehensible. If they believe that God made fertile such sterile and aged wombs as that of Sarah, Abraham's wife, how could they hold that it was absurd for the same God to have made fertile, virginally, the young womb of Mary?[20] This is the very miracle to which the Gospel attests when it speaks of the intervention of the Holy Spirit and of the power of the Most High. In addition to the creation of Jesus' flesh, Cyril explains, this intervention brought about the sanctification of the Virgin, thus making her worthy to collaborate in such an incredible event.

Mary, Wondrous Model of the Virginal Life

The birth of the Son of God from a Virgin Mother, as well as her perpetual virginity, greatly exalted the virginal state within the Church and made a chaste life highly attractive to all the faithful, whatever their state in life. In this climate of widespread asceticism, one can understand the easy, confident tone of the final exhortation of *Catechesis XII*:

> Let us all, by God's grace, run the race of chastity, young men and maidens, old men and children, without abandoning ourselves to lust, but praising the name of Christ. Let us not disregard the glory of chastity, which is the crown of the angels and a superhuman state of life!
>
> Let us respect our bodies, which ought to shine like the sun. Let us not stain the body, which is so beautiful and so great, through brief pleasures. Sin is brief and lasts but a little while; the shame of sin lasts a long time, forever.
>
> Those who profess chastity are angels dwelling on earth. The virgins have their portion with the Virgin Mary. Let us be rid of every sought-for ornament, every dangerous glance, every wanton movement, every scent that leads to lustful pleasure. Instead, let there be in all the sweet smell of prayer, of good works, and of bodily holiness, so that the Virgin's Son may say to us also, chaste men and crowned women: "I will dwell in their midst, and I will walk with them; I will be their God, and they shall be my people" (Lev 26:11–12).[21]

---

[20] Cf. ibid., 12, 28; PG 33, 760 B–C.
[21] Ibid., 12, 34; PG 33, 768 A–769 A.

Mary and the Role of Women

From one of Cyril's statements, we might cull a starting point for a theology of woman:

> At first, the feminine sex was obligated to give thanks to men, because Eve, born of Adam but not conceived by a mother, was in a certain sense born of man. Mary, instead, paid off the debt of gratitude: she did not give birth by means of a man, but by herself, virginally, through the working of the Holy Spirit and the power of God.[22]

Cyril seems to want to say that the Blessed Virgin restored woman's dignity, reestablishing her position of equality with regard to man and ennobling her role as mother. Mary's response to God, who spoke to her through the mouth of an angel, reminds women that they, too, are partners, not only of men, but of God himself.

The prestigious catechist of the Jerusalem Church, through his simple, spontaneous, and lively style, tries to make his disciples understand that the figure of Mary is essential to understanding the mystery of Christ. God, incarnate and made man, appears in all his mysterious divine-human reality and in his glory as the Savior of men only if he is presented alongside his Mother, from whom he received the body that made him Emmanuel, God-with-us.

READING

MARY, JOSEPH'S VIRGINAL SPOUSE

Let us reject those who say that the Savior's birth was the accomplishment of a man and a woman; those who dare to say that he was born of Joseph and Mary, solely because it is written: "And he took [her as] his wife" (Mt 1:24). Let us remember Jacob, who before taking Rachel, said to Laban: "Give me my wife" (Gen 29:21). Just as she was called Jacob's wife before the marriage celebration solely because promises had been exchanged, so also Mary was called Joseph's wife, because she was betrothed.

---

[22] Ibid., 12, 29; PG 33, 761 B–C.

Note how precise the Gospel is when it says: "In the sixth month the angel Gabriel was sent by God, to a town of Galilee named Nazareth, to a virgin betrothed to a man named Joseph" (Lk 1:26–27), and so forth. Again, when the census was taken and Joseph had to enroll himself, what does Scripture say? "Then Joseph went up from Galilee also, to register together with Mary, his betrothed spouse, who was with child" (Lk 2:4–5). And even though Mary was with child, it does not say, "his wife", but "his betrothed spouse". Indeed, God—says Paul—sent his Son, not born of a man and a woman, but of a woman (cf. Gal 4:4) only, that is, of a virgin. We have shown that a virgin is called a woman. For from a Virgin was born the One who makes souls virgins.

You marvel at what has happened. Did she not also marvel who gave him birth, seeing that she said to Gabriel: "How will this happen since I do not know man?" (Lk 1:34). But he answered: "The Holy Spirit will come upon you, and the power of the Most High will cover you with its shadow; hence, the holy Child to be born will be called Son of God" (Lk 1:35).

Pure and spotless is this birth. For where the Holy Spirit breathes, all pollution is taken away, so that the human birth of the Only-begotten from the Virgin is undefiled.

If, then, the heretics speak against the truth, the Holy Spirit himself will convict them; against them will rise the anger of the overshadowing power of the Most High and, in the Day of Judgment, Gabriel will rise up against them with severity; the manger that held the Lord will reprove them. The shepherds who received the glad tidings, the host of angels who sang praises and hymns saying: "Glory to God in the highest and peace on earth to men of good will" (Lk 2:13–14), the temple into which he was brought after forty days, the pair of turtle doves offered for him, Simeon who took him in his arms and the prophetess Anna who was present there: they will all bear witness against the heretics.

—Cyril of Jerusalem, *Catecheses* 12, 31–32; PG 33, 764–65

5

THE CAPPADOCIAN FATHERS:
BASIL OF CAESAREA (d. 379)

Cappadocia was one of the most important geographical areas of the Eastern Church. Even today it is a favorite destination of travelers making pilgrimages to the sites of ancient Eastern Christianity. It became a Roman province during the reign of Tiberius, around A.D. 17, and was divided into two provinces when Diocletian reorganized the territories of the Roman Empire at the end of the third century. Presently, it is part of the republic of Turkey.

Christianity came to Cappadocia quite early. We know that there were Jews from Cappadocia among those who heard the preaching of Peter at Jerusalem on the day of Pentecost (cf. Acts 2:9). The Prince of the Apostles himself included the Christians of Cappadocia among the addressees of his first letter (cf. 1 Pet 1:1), and perhaps he himself evangelized the region for the first time. Others think that the first evangelizer of Cappadocia was the apostle Paul, during his voyage to the region of Galatia.

The Christian religion must have spread very rapidly, since the names of several Cappadocian bishops from the second and third century are known to us. It also happens that, in addition to the bishops, there were chorbishops, or rural bishops, and that there were ten bishops of the Cappadocian Church present at the Council of Nicaea.

It appears that Cappadocian Christianity experienced periods of exceptional fervor. This is demonstrated by its numerous martyrs[1]

---

[1] We know from St. Basil that he was accustomed to celebrate public worship with his faithful in honor of the martyrs of Caesarea and that he invited Christians of other regions to visit the places where their memory was kept (cf. *Letter* 176; PG 32, 653 B; *Letter* 252; PG 32, 940 B; *Letter* 282; PG 32, 1017 C).

and its role in the conversion to the gospel of other neighboring regions, such as Armenia.

In the fourth century, Cappadocia gave birth to three exceptional men who became bishops and are numbered among the greatest Fathers of the Eastern Church. These were Basil of Caesarea, his friend Gregory Nazianzen, and his brother Gregory of Nyssa. Thanks to their genius, to their profound theological and biblical learning, and to the fruitfulness of their pastoral activity, these men brought glory to all of Eastern Christianity. To them, we could add Amphilochius, a cousin to Basil and Gregory of Nyssa, who was bishop of Iconium from 373 to 394.

The interest of the Cappadocian Fathers in the Mother of the Lord could find a likely explanation in the close relations between them and Alexandrine Christianity, which boasted of an ancient and consistent Marian tradition. The Marian texts found in the writings of the Cappadocians are few in number; however, they have significant theological value, above all because they are inspired by the unbreakable and fundamental relationship between the Blessed Virgin and her Son.[2]

We begin with Basil, a pastor of awe-inspiring greatness and of singular relevance for today. His works continue to have a strong influence on many different areas of the Christian world, such as culture, patristics, liturgy, and monastic spirituality.

He was born at Caesarea in Cappadocia around 330, of a family with a solid Christian tradition. His grandmother Makrina was a faithful disciple of St. Gregory the Wonderworker; his mother, Emmelia, was the daughter of a martyr; two of his brothers became bishops and are also venerated as saints: St. Gregory of Nyssa and St. Peter of Sebaste. His older sister, Makrina, is known to tradition as an exemplary model of the ascetic life.

Basil first attended the schools of Caesarea and Constantinople, then went to Athens (in 351) to perfect his knowledge of rhetoric. He returned to Caesarea around 356 and, after having practiced as a rhetorician for a short time, entered the monastic life. He received

---

[2] For the Marian thought of the Cappadocian Fathers, cf. Georg Söll, "Die Mariologie der Kappadozier im Lichte der Dogmengeschichte", *Theologische Quartalschrift* 131 (1951): 163–88, 288–319, 426–57.

baptism and undertook a long journey through Egypt, Palestine, Syria, and Mesopotamia, with the intention of meeting the ascetics who abounded in those regions. Once back in his native land, he founded many monasteries, for whom he composed his two famous *Monastic Rules*.

He was ordained priest in 364 and was consecrated bishop of Caesarea and metropolitan of Cappadocia in 370. During the nine years of his episcopate, Basil revealed his exceptional abilities as pastor, leader, and organizer. He founded hospitals, shelters for indigents, and hospices for foreigners; he organized relief operations in times of famine and epidemic. His wide-ranging activity did not prevent him studying and deepening his understanding of Christian theology and spirituality, for he knew how to maintain a harmonious balance between thought and action. He died in 379. Those of his texts that hold the greatest interest for Marian doctrine are the *Homily on the Generation of Christ* and *Letter 260*.[3]

Mary, Workshop of the Incarnation

In the Blessed Virgin, our author sees the Mother of Emmanuel, foretold by the prophet:

> Thus was fulfilled the mystery ordained before all ages and announced of old by the prophets: "Behold, the virgin shall conceive in her womb and bear a son and shall call his name Emmanuel, which translated means: God-with-us" (Is 7:14).
>
> This ancient name also contains the revelation of the whole mystery, namely, that God will be with men. For it says: Emmanuel, which means God-with-us.
>
> No one, then, ought to let himself be led astray by the calumnies of the Jews, who assert that the prophet was speaking of a young woman and not of a virgin. Then the text would say: "Behold the young

---

[3] Basil's Marian thought has been exhaustively studied. Some bibliographical pointers are: Söll, "Mariologie"; Georges Gharib, "Basilio 'devoto' di Maria?" *Mater Ecclesiae* 15 (1979): 32–36; Luigi Gambero, "La Madonna negli scritti di San Basilio", *Mater Ecclesiae* 15 (1979): 37–45; idem, "Cristo e sua Madre nel pensiero di Basilio di Cesarea", *Marianum* 44 (1982): 9–47; idem, *L'omelia sulla generazione di Cristo di Basilio di Cesarea: Il posto della Vergine Maria*, Marian Library Studies, new series, vols. 13–14 (Dayton, Ohio: Univ. of Dayton, 1981–1982).

woman shall conceive in her womb." In any case, it is the most absurd thing imaginable to think that what was given to us by the Lord as a sign should be something so common and familiar to nature.

What does the prophet really say? "And the Lord went on to speak with Ahaz thus: 'Ask for yourself a sign from the Lord, in the depths or in the heights.' And Ahaz said: 'I will not ask and I will not tempt the Lord' " (Is 7:10–12). And a little later it continues: "Therefore the Lord himself will give you a sign. Behold the virgin shall conceive in her womb" (Is 7:14).

Then, since Ahaz does not ask for a sign, neither in the depths nor from the heights, so that you might understand that he who descended into the lowest regions of the earth is the same who rose above all the heavens (Eph 4:9–10), the Lord himself gave a sign: a sign truly extraordinary and portentous, far superior to the common law of nature: the same woman is both virgin and mother; and though remaining in the holy condition of virginity, she also obtains the blessing of childbearing.[4]

Thus, Emmanuel did not limit himself to coming among us but assumed our mortal flesh as well. This unheard-of mystery took place in Mary's womb. That is why Basil insists:

> The author sees the incarnate God; he sees Emmanuel, born of the holy Virgin. The meaning of Emmanuel is: God-with-us. For this reason he prophetically cries out: The Lord of hosts is with us. This shows us that it was he himself who appeared to the holy prophets and patriarchs.[5]

The mysterious and transcendent origin of the Virgin's Son, surpassing his own Mother who gave him birth, shows that he is a Divine Person:

> His origin was not from Mary, nor does he belong to her time. What, then? "In the beginning was the Word, and the Word was with God, and the Word was God" (Jn 1:1). Eternal substance, impassible generation, majesty of nature, which he possesses in union with the Father.[6]

---

[4] *On the Holy Generation of Christ* 4; PG 31, 1465 B–1468 A.

[5] *Commentary on Psalm 45*, 6; PG 29, 425 C.

[6] *Against Eunomius* 2, 15; PG 29, 601 B–C.

In this text we once again see the Basil of the anti-Arian struggle, who, even when he illustrates the mystery of Jesus' human birth, always begins with the even more unfathomable mystery of his eternal birth from the Father. Basil is convinced that, if he fails to take this first generation into account, it will be impossible to evaluate adequately the nature and significance of the Incarnation. To bring about this wondrous event, God had to collaborate with a woman, since, according to the plan of salvation, the incarnate Word had to descend from human ancestors. Otherwise, the involvement of a woman would have been superfluous. In the following terms, Basil attacks the heretics who wanted to revive the error of Valentinus:

> All this (what the Redeemer accomplished on our behalf) is destroyed by those who say that the Lord came in a heavenly body. If the God-bearing flesh (*theophóros sárx*) did not have to be taken from the dough of Adam, what need was there for the holy Virgin?[7]

Mary is called to collaborate with God's almighty power by offering her own body. Basil, with a sense of profound realism, calls Mary's womb a "workshop":

> But what is the workshop (*ergastērion*) of this economy? The body of a holy Virgin. And what are the [active] principles of this birth? The Holy Spirit and the overshadowing power of the Most High.[8]

In Mary's womb, then, the Lord worked the miracle of the Incarnation. The Holy Spirit and the power of the Most High are called the agents of this indescribable phenomenon. In virtue of this intervention from on high, the eternal Son of God became true man.

Mary's motherhood does not raise any problematic questions for the bishop of Caesarea. He does not hesitate to call her Mother of God (*Theotókos*)[9] and calmly accepts the effects of this on her role as a mother. Through Mary, God came down upon earth; he made his dwelling among men; he became our equal, that is, one of our race; he made us his friends and intimate companions.[10]

---

[7] *Letter* 261; PG 32, 969 B–C.
[8] *On the Holy Generation of Christ* 3; PG 31, 1464 A.
[9] Ibid., 5; PG 31, 1468 B.
[10] Cf. ibid., 6; PG 31, 1473 B.

Mary's Virginity and the Faith of Christians

Our doctor presents the mystery of Mary's virginity in two distinct phases: virginity up until the moment of Christ's birth and her perpetual virginity. The Lord determined that Mary should remain a virgin until the moment of the divine Son's birth, as a condition of her collaboration in the mystery of the Incarnation of the Word:

> Since the humanity of that time had nothing to equal Mary's purity, as to be able to accommodate the working of the Holy Spirit, but was totally constrained by marriage, the Blessed Virgin was chosen, since her virginity was totally uncontaminated by marriage.[11]

With this argument, Basil seems to imply that Mary had formed the intention of remaining a virgin even during her marriage. Indeed, he states that her virginity was not lessened even when, after her marriage, she was able to have regular conjugal relations. Inasmuch as she abstained from these relations, she appears instead as a perfect model of total openness to the action of the Holy Spirit.

As for the matter of Mary's perpetual virginity, Basil admits that, in theory, once the mystery of the Incarnation had taken place, Mary could have renounced virginity without compromising God's plan of salvation in any way. In practice, however, he defends the perpetual virginity of the Lord's Mother without hesitation, adducing as proof the religious sensibility and convictions of believers:

> For "he did not know her"—it says—"until she gave birth to a Son, her firstborn" (Mt 1:25). But this could make one suppose that Mary, after having offered in all purity her own service in giving birth to the Lord, by virtue of the intervention of the Holy Spirit, did not subsequently refrain from normal conjugal relations.
>
> That would not have affected the teaching of our religion at all, because Mary's virginity was necessary until the service of the Incarnation, and what happened afterward need not be investigated in order to affect the doctrine of the mystery.
>
> But since the lovers of Christ [that is, the faithful] do not allow themselves to hear that the Mother of God (*Theotókos*) ceased at a given moment to be a virgin, we consider their testimony to be sufficient.[12]

---

[11] Ibid., 3; PG 31, 1464 B–C.
[12] Ibid., 5; PG 31, 1468 B.

The bishop of Caesarea considers that the consensus of the faithful is a more than sufficient argument to establish that the perpetual virginity of the Mother of God is an indispensable requirement of ecclesial faith.

Marriage to Joseph

In the homily on the generation of Christ, our author shows that he is very interested in the Virgin's marriage to St. Joseph. He justifies it by referring to well-known arguments, drawn from the writings of Origen. Among others, he offers the witness of St. Ignatius of Antioch:[13]

> An ancient author offered another reason. The marriage with Joseph was planned so that Mary's virginity might remain hidden from the prince of this world. For the external forms of marriage were adopted by the Virgin, almost as if to distract the Evil One, who has always preyed on virgins, ever since he heard the prophet announcing: "Behold the virgin shall conceive and bear a son" (Is 7:14). With this marriage, then, the tempter of virginity was deceived. For he knew that the coming of the Lord in the flesh would entail the destruction of his dominion.[14]

But the motivations that Basil stresses are primarily those of a moral character. He wishes, above all, to affirm the religious character of Christian marriage:

> A virgin, who was then given in marriage to a man, was found worthy for the service of [the Incarnation], so that virginity might be honored and marriage not be despised. For virginity was chosen as being apt to sanctification, but with the betrothal, the precepts of marriage were also included.[15]

The marriage also had the purpose of creating a context that protected and safeguarded the virginity of Jesus' Mother:

> In Joseph, Mary had a spouse and guardian of her life, so that there would be a witness who was familiar with her purity and so that

---

[13] *Letter to the Ephesians* 19, 1; PG 5, 660 A.

[14] *On the Holy Generation of Christ* 3; PG 31, 1464 C.

[15] Ibid., PG 31, 1464 A–B.

calumniators would not be given the pretext to accuse her of having violated her virginity.[16]

Mary as a Moral Figure

Basil does not make any explicit statements about the Virgin Mother's holiness. He limits himself to calling her holy, to recalling her purity and perseverance in holy virginity. In a homily, he stresses her poverty:

[Christ] lived in the house of a builder and a poor mother.[17]

However, he considers himself justified in affirming that the Virgin's holiness was not totally without shadow. He refers to the doubt that she suffered at the moment of her Son's Passion, which Simeon had foretold, using the metaphor of the sword:

Simeon calls a sword (cf. Lk 2:35) the word that has the power to test and discern thoughts, that penetrates unto the division of soul and spirit, of joints and marrow (cf. Heb 4:12).

Indeed every soul, at the moment of the Passion, underwent a kind of doubt, just as the Lord said: "You will all be scandalized because of me" (Mt 26:31). Therefore Simeon prophesies that Mary herself, while standing by the Cross observing what was happening and hearing what was being said, after the witness of Gabriel, after the secret revelation of the divine conception, after the great showing of miracles, would have known some wavering in her soul. Indeed it was necessary that the Lord should taste death for all and that, having become a sacrificial victim for the world, he should justify all by his blood.

Even you [O Mary], who learned about the Lord from above, will be affected by doubt. This is the sword.

"That thoughts out of many hearts may be revealed" (Lk 2:35). This means that, after the scandal caused by the Cross of Christ, the Lord wished a ready remedy to follow, both for the disciples and for Mary, confirming their hearts in faith in him.[18]

---

[16] Ibid., PG 31, 1464 B.

[17] On Humility 6; PG 31, 536 C.

[18] Letter 260; PG 32, 965 C–968 A.

Like the disciples, Mary also experienced doubt at the foot of the Cross. But Jesus strengthened the faith of his disciples and his Mother, so that she subsequently became a shining example of faith.

In conclusion, we can perceive how the bishop of Caesarea preferred to bring out Mary's role within the context of the mystery of the Incarnation, instead of praising her attributes or her personal merits. In this perspective, we can see how his Marian thought was essentially shaped by Christology, from which it draws its confidence and vigor.

READINGS

CHRIST'S TRUE BIRTH FROM MARY

Joseph, speaking with the other prisoners of their own dreams (cf. Gen 40:8), clearly uses the expression: "by means of (*diá*) God", instead of the expression: "of (*ek*) God". Paul, to the contrary, uses the preposition *ek* in the place of *diá*, when he says, for example: "Born of (*ek*) woman" (Gal 4:4), instead of: "Born by means of (*diá*) a woman".

Indeed, he clearly explained to us elsewhere how it is proper for a woman to be born of man and for a man to be born by means of woman, in the place where he states: "As woman is born of man, so man is born by means of woman" (1 Cor 11:12).

Here, however, the apostle makes clear the difference in the usage of these two expressions and simultaneously corrects, in passing, the false doctrine of those who held that the Lord's body was spiritual.

He wants to show that the flesh that became the bearer of God (*theophóros sárx*) was molded out of human material; and for this reason he prefers to use the more meaningful term. For the expression: "by means of a woman" could give rise to the suspicion that it refers to Christ being born by passing through a woman. Instead, speaking of generation "of a woman" indicates with sufficient clarity the communion of nature between the Son and his Mother.

There is no contradiction, then. The apostle simply demonstrates with what facility the terms can be substituted for one another.

—Basil, *On the Holy Spirit* 5, 12; PG 32, 85 B–C

JOSEPH'S CONDUCT TOWARD MARY

"Before they came to live together, she was found with child by the working of the Holy Spirit" (Mt 1:18). Joseph found both things: both the conception and its cause, namely, the intervention of the Holy Spirit. Therefore, fearing to be called the husband of such a woman, he "wanted to send her away quietly" (Mt 1:19), not daring to make public what had happened to her.

But being just, it was his lot to have mysteries revealed to him. For "while he was thinking of these things, the angel of the Lord appeared to him in a dream, saying: 'Do not fear to take Mary as your wife' " (Mt 1:20). You should not have thought it necessary to conceal a fault from wicked and suspicious people. For you have been called just: it would not be the action of a just man to pass over sins in silence. "Do not fear to take Mary as your wife." Joseph showed that he had not disdained her, nor had he showed disgust at her, but that he feared because she was full of the Holy Spirit. "That which is born in her is the work of the Holy Spirit" (ibid.).

—Basil, *On the Holy Generation of Christ* 4;
PG 31, 1464 C–1465 A

6

GREGORY OF NYSSA
(d. ca. 394)

Basil exhibits extraordinary gifts as a pastor and man of action; the other two great Cappadocians are equally impressive in other ways. Gregory Nazianzen possessed the fluid eloquence of a formidable orator; Gregory of Nyssa had impressive talents as a thinker and mystic. These three eminent Fathers ably continued the difficult struggle, begun by Athanasius, against the Arian heresy, which denied the divinity of Christ. Ultimately, this struggle led to the definitive triumph of the Nicene faith, which proclaimed the Son's full divinity, eternity, and consubstantiality with the Father. Their direct adversary was another Cappadocian, Eunomius of Cyzicus, a dangerous heretic who had resurrected the Arian heresy under a veneer of subtle and insidious rationalism.

Another important polemical objective pursued by the two Gregories was the struggle against Apollinarianism, which refused to recognize a complete and normal human nature in the incarnate Word.

With these two premises, it is easy to foresee how the Marian thought of the two Gregories would develop within the context of these two pressing christological exigencies.

The foremost mystical and speculative theologian of the Cappadocians was Gregory of Nyssa, younger brother of St. Basil. At first he had a career as a rhetorician and even contracted marriage, but very soon he entered a monastery founded by his brother in Pontus to dedicate himself to the ascetic life. In 371, he was consecrated bishop of Nyssa, where he had to face many serious problems of an administrative and pastoral character, because of the opposition of the Arians. In 376 Gregory was deposed by a synod of Arian bishops, with the connivance of the imperial court, but in 378, after the death of the Emperor Valens, he was able to return to his own see. Together with Gregory Nazianzen, he played an active and authoritative role during the Council of Constantinople in 381. We find him again in 394 at the Synod of Constantinople. This is the last piece of biographical information we have of Gregory of Nyssa. The most probable hypothesis is that he died that same year.

Many of his works have survived, varied in content: dogmatic tracts, exegetical works, ascetical and liturgical writings, and part of his correspondence. In many cases, valuable content is combined with undeniable literary and stylistic excellence.

St. Gregory speaks of the Virgin especially in his homily on the birth of Christ, as well as in his treatise on virginity, his commentary on the Song of Songs, his life of St. Gregory the Wonderworker,[1] and his polemical works against Eunomius and Apollinaris. Brief references to Mary are found in other writings as well. With regard to the problem of the authenticity of the homily on the birth of Christ,[2] which has some important Marian content, I hold that it should be considered resolved in favor of authenticity.[3] There is a homily on the Annunciation[4] by Pseudo-Chrysostom attributed to Gregory of Nyssa, noteworthy from the point of view of mariological doctrine and for its formal beauty; I do not think, however, that Gregory's authorship of it can be upheld.[5] Nevertheless, we will take it into consideration later on.

---

[1] We have already given the passage from the *Life of St. Gregory the Wonderworker* where Gregory of Nyssa speaks of an apparition of the Mother of God to this saint (cf. pt. 1, chap. 8, reading).

[2] PG 46, 1128–49.

[3] Cf. Jean Daniélou, "Chronologie des sermons de Saint Grégoire de Nysse", *Revue des sciences religieuses* 29 (1955): 346–72.

[4] PG 62, 763–70.

[5] The arguments of Caro in favor of the Cappadocian origin of this composition can be shared, as can his dating of it around the end of the fourth century; but the problem of its authorship remains unresolved for the moment. Cf. R. Caro, *La homilética mariana griega en el siglo V*, Marian Library Studies, new series, vol. 4, no. 2 (Dayton, Ohio: Univ. of Dayton, 1972), pp. 538–45; Luigi Gambero, "Un'omelia pseudo-crisostomica sul Vangelo dell'Annunciazione", *Marianum* 47 (1985): 517–35.

Mary's Role in the Incarnation

The Marian thought of Gregory of Nyssa becomes clear in his polemic against Apollinaris of Laodicea, a prominent figure in the Eastern Church during the second half of the fourth century. Wishing to safeguard the hypostatic union of the human nature and the divine nature in the incarnate Word, Apollinaris taught that these were joined to a body that lacked a rational soul, the place of which was filled by the divine Word himself.

To defend Christ's complete and perfect humanity, Gregory insists on the reality of Mary's motherhood. He writes:

> Along with all those who profess the orthodox faith, I too declare my belief that the same [Jesus] is God and man, but not in the manner in which Apollinaris thinks. For the divinity does not become earthly, nor does the humanity become something heavenly, as he maintains; rather, the power of the Most High, through the Holy Spirit, overshadowed the human nature and was formed therein; that is to say, the portion of flesh was formed in the immaculate Virgin. For this reason, the Child born of her is called Son of the Most High. In truth, the divine power makes possible a certain affinity of human nature with God, while the flesh makes it possible for God to have a certain relation with man.[6]

Precisely because the Son of God became incarnate in Mary's womb, she is rightly called Mother of God. Gregory therefore, wishing to defend himself against the insinuations of certain innovators, proposes the title *Theotókos* as a criterion of orthodoxy:

> If then we preach in a loud voice and testify that Christ is the power and wisdom of God (cf. 1 Cor 1:24), always immutable, always incorruptible, and that, although dwelling in a mutable and corruptible body, he himself is not thereby polluted but even purifies what was polluted, what is our crime, and why are we hated? What is the meaning of these new altars erected against us?
>
> Is it because we preach a different Jesus? Do we point to another? Is it because we proclaim a different Scripture? Has one of us, perhaps, dared to call the Virgin Godbearer (*Theotókos*) a Manbearer, as we hear some of them irreverently doing?[7]

---

[6] *Against Apollinaris* 6; PG 45, 1136 C–D.

[7] *Letter* 3; PG 46, 1024 A. The tone of this letter reveals Gregory's disappointment with the controversies he found when he visited the Christian community

Christ's human nature, then, was not a preexistent reality but was assumed in the womb of Mary and possessed all the requisites of a human being, bound to a body and a soul. Mary's Son is the new and perfect man:

> When the Holy Spirit came upon the Virgin and the power of the Most High overshadowed her, the new man was formed in her. He is called new because he was fashioned by God, not in the usual human way, but differently, so that he would become a dwelling of God, not made by human hands. For the Most High does not dwell in places made by hands; not, that is, in dwellings built by human effort.
>
> Then, Wisdom built herself a house (cf. Prov 9:1), and the overshadowing power formed within it an image as a kind of sign. Then, the divine power mixed itself with both the elements of which human nature consists; I mean to say the soul and the body, mixing itself equally with the one and the other.
>
> Both of these elements are subjected to death because of disobedience: for the soul, death consists in separation from true life; for the body it is corruption and dissolution. Of necessity, I say, death had to be driven out through the reuniting of these two elements with life. For just as divinity was united to both of the elements of man, so striking signs of a superior nature will be manifest in both elements.[8]

The Wonder of Mary's Virginity

In his Christmas homily, Gregory speaks at length about the mystery of Mary's virginity. The messianic prophecies of the Old Testament had foretold that Jesus had to be born of a virgin. Obviously the prophecy of Isaiah is not forgotten:

> Hear Isaiah crying out: "A child is born for us; a Son is given to us" (Is 9:6). Learn from the same prophet how the baby is born, how a son is given. Was it according to the law of nature? The prophet denies it. The Master of nature does not obey the laws of nature. But how is the child born? Tell me. The prophet answers: "Behold, the

---

of Jerusalem. After returning to Nyssa, he felt obliged to recall the faithful of Jerusalem to the faith of the fathers, especially with regard to the Incarnation.

[8] *On the Resurrection*, homily 1, PG 46, 616 B–C.

virgin shall conceive in her womb and bear a son, and they shall call his name Emmanuel" (Is 7:14), which, translated, means: God-with-us.

O marvelous event! The Virgin becomes a mother and remains a virgin! Observe this new ordering of nature. All other women, in order to remain virgins, do not become mothers; when a woman becomes a mother, she no longer has her virginity. Here, instead, the two terms are applied to the same person. For it is the same woman who is presented as mother and as virgin, for just as her virginity posed no obstacle to her giving birth, neither did her childbearing destroy her virginity. Indeed, it was fitting that [the Redeemer], having entered human life to make us all incorruptible, should Himself originate from an incorruptible birth. In fact, according to our usual way of speaking, a woman who has not had relations with a man is called "incorrupt".[9]

But our author recalls that the same event was prefigured in an even earlier Old Testament theophany, namely, in the image of the burning bush that Moses saw on Mount Horeb:

> It seems to me that, already, the great Moses knew about this mystery by means of the light in which God appeared to him, when he saw the bush burning without being consumed (cf. Ex 3:1ff.). For Moses said: "I wish to go up closer and observe this great vision." I believe that the term "go up closer" does not indicate motion in space but a drawing near in time. What was prefigured at that time in the flame of the bush was openly manifested in the mystery of the Virgin, once an intermediate space of time had passed.
>
> As on the mountain the bush burned but was not consumed, so the Virgin gave birth to the light and was not corrupted. Nor should you consider the comparison to the bush to be embarrassing, for it prefigures the God-bearing body of the Virgin.[10]

The bishop of Nyssa attributes great value to the sign, which arouses wonder and awe when one observes it attentively—these dispositions being essential for anyone who encounters the super-natural. For the sign, through its sensible content, draws us into the

---

[9] *On the Birth of Christ*, PG 46, 1133 D–1136 B.

[10] Ibid. On this theme, cf. M. Gordillo, "La virginidad transcendente de María Madre de Dios en San Gregorio de Nisa y en la antigua tradición de la Iglesia", *Estudios Marianos* 21 (1960): 117–55.

vision of faith in the divine mystery and helps us acquire a certain mystical understanding of it.

Gregory gives a moral explanation to the mystery of the Lord's virginal birth. He who came to free men from the corruption of evil was born, appropriately, through an incorruptible generation. Consequently, Mary's virginity, which connotes physical integrity, was for the Fathers a sign of moral integrity and, therefore, a sign of holiness.

Zechariah, Martyr for the Sake of Mary's Virginity

Gregory of Nyssa helped spread a curious tradition, according to which the priest Zechariah, father of John the Baptist, was slain in the Temple. This happened when Zechariah, having learned that Jesus' Mother was still a virgin, allowed her to remain in the Temple, in the place reserved for virgins. In Gregory's words:

> Everything Zechariah said was a foretelling of the future. Led by the prophetic spirit to the knowledge of hidden mysteries, and aware of the mystery of virginity that surrounds the incorrupt birth, he does not remove the Virgin Mother from the place in the Temple that the law reserves to virgins. He explains to the Jews how the Creator and King of all creation holds human nature subject to himself, together with all other things, so that he governs it according to his pleasure and is not controlled by it.
>
> Thus it is within his power to create a new kind of generation, which does not prevent a mother from remaining a virgin. This is the reason why Zechariah does not remove Mary from the place in the Temple reserved to virgins. The place in question was an area located between the temple [court] and the altar.[11] The Jews, having heard that the King of creation, according to his divine pleasure, had come through a new kind of birth, and fearing to be subject to a king, slew Zechariah while he, in his capacity as priest, was offering the sacrifice in front of the altar, because he had witnessed to the events relating to [Christ's] birth.[12]

---

[11] According to this tradition, the father of John the Baptist is to be identified with Zechariah, son of Barachiah, of whom Jesus speaks (cf. Mt 23:35).

[12] *On the Birth of Christ*, PG 46, 1137 A–B.

This seems to have been a fairly widespread tradition in Gregory's time. Other authors speak of it as well; it suffices to recall Origen[13] and Basil.[14]

Did Mary Make a Vow of Virginity?

In interpreting Mary's response to the angel Gabriel (cf. Lk 1:34), Gregory goes so far as to think that she expressed an intention or vow of virginity, to which she purposed to remain faithful even after having heard the angelic message. Let us examine the text:

> What is Mary's response? Listen to the voice of the pure Virgin. The angel brings the glad tidings of childbearing, but she is concerned with virginity and holds that her integrity should come before the angelic message. She does not refuse to believe the angel; neither does she move away from her convictions. She says: I have given up any contact with man. "How will this happen to me, since I do not know man?" (Lk 1:34).
>
> Mary's own words confirm certain apocryphal traditions. For if Joseph had taken her to be his wife, for the purpose of having children, why would she have wondered at the announcement of maternity, since she herself would have accepted becoming a mother according to the law of nature?
>
> But just as it was necessary to guard the body consecrated to God as an untouched and holy offering, for this same reason, she states, even if you are an angel come down from heaven and even if this phenomenon is beyond man's abilities, yet it is impossible for me to know man. How shall I become a mother without [knowing] man? For though I consider Joseph to be my husband, still I do not know man.[15]

Earlier, Gregory had spoken of Mary being offered to God by her own mother, even before she was born. Is this a kind of consecration that was made on Mary's behalf or something that she did personally? Although he does not say so explicitly, he appears to lean toward the second hypothesis. In this case, Gregory would be the first author to propose that Mary took a vow of virginity.

---

[13] Cf. *In Matthaeum comment.*, series 25, GCS 38, 42–43; PG 13, 1631 A–B.

[14] *On the Holy Generation of Christ* 5; PG 31, 1468 C–1469 A.

[15] Ibid., PG 46, 1140 C–1141 A.

READING

CHRIST, CHOSEN FRUIT OF VIRGINITY

Among the myriads of men born of Adam, succeeding him as long as his nature will continue through successive births, only [Jesus] came to light through a new way of being born. Nature did not collaborate at all in bringing that birth about; it was solely at the service of that birth. For this reason [the Song of Songs] says that he who is bright and ruddy (cf. Song 5:10) from having dwelled in this life in flesh and blood is the only one, among all the myriads of men, to have been chosen as the fruit of virginal purity.

His conception did not result from the union of two humans; his birth was not polluted in any way; there were no labor pangs; his bridal chamber was that of the power of the Most High, which covered virginity like a cloud; the bridal torch was the splendor of the Holy Spirit; his bed was a personal condition devoid of vices; his nuptials were incorrupt.

He who is born in such conditions is justly considered to have been chosen from among all the myriads of men; this means that he did not exist because of the marriage bed. In fact, his birth alone occurred without labor pains, and he alone began to exist without sexual relations. Indeed, for her who remained incorrupt and who had no knowledge of such relations, the word "birth" does not seem appropriate, because virginity and birth do not go together.

As the Son has been given to us without a father, so the Child has been born without a birth. As the Virgin herself did not know how the body that received divinity was formed in her own body, so neither did she notice the birth. Even the prophet Isaiah affirms that her giving birth was without pain, when he says: "Before the pangs of birth arrived, a male child came forth and was born" (Is 66:7).

Therefore, he was chosen to introduce a twofold innovation into the order of nature, since he did not begin to exist because of sin, nor was he born in pain. This happened for an understandable reason; there is nothing absurd about it. Just as she who introduced death into nature by her sin was condemned to bear children in suffering and travail, it was necessary that the Mother of life, after having conceived in joy, should give birth in joy as well. No wonder that the angel said to her, "Rejoice, O full of grace!" (Lk 1:28). With these words he took from her the burden of that sorrow which, from the beginning of creation, had been imposed on birth because of sin.

—Gregory of Nyssa, *On the Song of Songs* 13;
PG 44, 1052 D–1053 B

7

GREGORY NAZIANZEN
(d. 390)

He has passed into history as "Gregory the Theologian". A contemporary of St. Basil, he was born around 330 at Arianzus, a village near Nazianzus, where his father was bishop. He attended the famous catechetical schools of Caesarea in Palestine and Alexandria in Egypt. Later he joined Basil at Athens, planning to complete his studies of rhetoric. There, the two young men established a friendship that remained firm for the rest of their lives. Returning to his native land around 357, Gregory received baptism and, some time later, was ordained to the priesthood by his father. In 371, Basil, who had been bishop of Caesarea for one year, consecrated his friend Gregory bishop of Sasima. In 379, Gregory was called to govern the Nicene community of Constantinople, made up of a small minority of Christians faithful to the dogma proclaimed at the Council of Nicaea and isolated amid an overwhelming Arian majority. Gregory consecrated the little church of the Resurrection for the use of this community, and there he preached and offered the sacraments.

With regard to this church and to the special relationship between it and the Mother of the Lord in Gregory's time, we have an interesting witness from the fifth-century Church historian Sozomen:

> Shortly after promulgating this law, Theodosius went to Constantinople. At that time the Arians, led by Demophilus, still controlled the churches; Gregory of Nazianzus, however, led those who professed their faith in the consubstantial (*homooúsion*) Trinity.
>
> There was a little house that had been transformed into a church by men who followed this creed. It had been entrusted to Gregory and to those who had the same faith he did. There he would call together the assembly of the faithful.

Later, this little church became one of the most famous churches of the imperial city, and it is still famous today, not only because of the beauty and completeness of its structure, but also for the frequent favors that were received there through manifestations of divine power. For a divine power (*theía dýnamis*) was manifested there to persons both watchful and asleep, which brought relief to many oppressed by illness and other woes.

It is believed that this power came from the Virgin Mary, Mother of God. For in such wise is she wont to appear.

This church was called *Anastasia* [= Resurrection], because, it seems to me, the Nicene doctrine, which had been oppressed or, so to speak, slain by the power of the heretics, there rose from the dead and returned to life through Gregory's preaching.[1]

Gregory remained at the Church of the Resurrection until 380, when the newly elected emperor Theodosius solemnly enthroned him in the cathedral of Constantinople, the Church of the Apostles.

In 381, the Council of Constantinople ratified his election as patriarch of the imperial capital, but the procedure was contested by the bishops of Macedonia and Egypt. Gregory, discouraged and disgusted, renounced his patriarchal see and retired to Cappadocia, where he dedicated himself primarily to the monastic life and applied himself intensively to writing. He died there in 390.

Among his works, forty-five sermons stand out, which won him his reputation as one of the greatest theologians and orators of antiquity. In his writings, few passages are dedicated to the Blessed Virgin; however, some of these references have significance for the history of Marian doctrine and devotion. Among other things, it appears that Gregory was the first author to propose the title *Theotókos* as a criterion of orthodoxy. In addition, he has left us a valuable witness to the faith of the Christian people in the value of Mary's intercession.

A Criterion of the True Faith

For Gregory, accepting the Marian title *Theotókos* represents an indispensable condition for possessing orthodox faith. Anticipating the

---

[1] *Storia ecclesiastica* 7, 5; PG 67, 1424–25.

doctrine that would be defined in 431 at the Council of Ephesus, he holds that this title guarantees the divine-human unity of the person of the incarnate Word, as well as guaranteeing the truth of the mystery of the Incarnation:

> If anyone does not admit that holy Mary is Mother of God (*Theotókos*), he is cut off from the Godhead. If anyone claims that Christ merely passed through Mary, as if passing through a channel, but denies that he was formed within her in a divine way (because there was no intervention of a man), and in a human way (that is, according to the laws of conception), he is equally godless.
>
> If anyone says that a man was formed first, who only afterward was clothed with divinity, let him be condemned. For that would not be a generation of God but a denial of divine generation. If anyone introduces the notion of two sons, one born of God the Father and the other born of the Mother, instead of a single and identical Son, let him be deprived of the adoption of sons, promised to those who believe aright.[2]

This long passage from a famous letter of Gregory to the priest Cledonius shows how our author rightly holds, against Apollinaris of Laodicea, that the dogma of Mary's divine motherhood is the linchpin of the Church's doctrine about the incarnate Word and the mystery of human salvation. The text mentions nearly all of the most dangerous errors about the Incarnation; Mary appears as a point of reference that helps us eliminate heretical threats to the truth.

The Divine–Human Exchange

In the mystery of the Incarnation, the bishop of Nazianzus discerns a wondrous exchange between God and Mary. She offered him the gift of her undiminished virginity, while the Lord, for his part, intervened in an extraordinary manner to bring about her purification, in advance. He empowered her human abilities, to make her worthy of the unique event of the Incarnation:

> He was conceived by the Virgin, who had first been purified by the Spirit in soul and body; for, as it was fitting that childbearing should

---

[2] *Letter* 101; PG 37, 177 C–180 A.

receive its share of honor, so it was necessary that virginity should receive even greater honor.[3]

From this doctrine of Mary's purification before the conception of Christ emerges an intuition of that truth which, in 1854, the Church would define as the dogma of the Immaculate Conception.

His birth from a woman in no way diminishes the greatness and dignity of the Son of God because, Gregory explains, the fact of becoming man does not in any way imply the renunciation of his original divine condition. For the Word of God, incarnation means assuming that which he was not, while remaining what he is:

> He is born, but he has already been generated; he is born of a woman, but also from a Virgin. The former is human, the latter divine. In his human nature, he has no father; in his divine nature, he has no mother. Both of these [conditions] belong solely to divinity.
>
> He was dwelling in her womb, but he was recognized by the Prophet[4] who, while himself still dwelling in the womb, began to rejoice at the nearness of the Word for whose sake he was born.[5]

Virginal Temple of the Incarnate Word

In the Incarnation, the Blessed Virgin becomes the temple of the Lord's body, while he, in turn, is the temple of divinity:

> They are not few in number who say that the God-man was born from the Virgin's womb, which the Spirit of the great God formed, constructing a pure temple to house the Temple. For the Mother is the temple of Christ, while Christ is the Temple of the Word.[6] For, just as the venomous serpent held our nature under the yoke of wicked transgression, it was then so arranged that, through the nature of a more divine Man, the evil might be mended and the horrible power of the lying dragon beaten down.

---

[3] *Sermon* 38, 13; PG 36, 325 B.

[4] A reference to St. John the Baptist, forerunner of Jesus (cf. Lk 1:41).

[5] *Sermon* 29, 19; PG 36, 100 A–B.

[6] The symbolism of the temple, applied either to the Lord's body or to the womb of the Virgin Mother, recurs frequently in the writings of the Church Fathers.

For this reason, he entered the womb; he honored one half of our lineage, but left the other half, because he was born of an intact Virgin. She, after having conceived in her inmost parts, illuminated by divinity, brought him to light when her time came. Then, the sovereign Word put on our heavy flesh and filled the temple with pure divinity. For me, in both natures, he remained one single God.[7]

While the earlier Fathers had reserved the symbolism of the temple for the human nature of Christ, later on, Mary's womb was also called the temple of the incarnate Word. In these texts of Gregory Nazianzen, the two symbolisms are combined.

Further, based on our author's testimony, this symbolism must have been fairly widespread in the theological language of his time.

The two temples are, we might say, *acheropiti*, or not made by hands, because they were erected by the Holy Spirit himself. In this passage, Gregory amplifies the content of the Gospel account of the Annunciation, where it is said only that the flesh of the Word is the work of the Holy Spirit. Gregory adds that Mary's womb, too, was fashioned by a special intervention of the Spirit, by which a virginal body was made capable of conceiving a human being. Mary's virginity then, in the mystery of the Incarnation, is a divine miracle: Mary's inmost parts were illuminated by divinity.

This entire event, involving the incarnate Word, the Holy Spirit, and the Virgin Mother, was willed by God to bring about the salvation of the human race from evil and from the devil's oppression.

God, however, who does not exclude any part of human nature from salvation, appears to have excluded the male sex from the honor he accorded to the female sex, when he became incarnate in Mary's womb even though she did not know man. Gregory does not consider, in this text, that the male sex has already been sublimely honored by the very existence of Mary's Son.

Prayer to Mary

The bishop of Nazianzus is one of the earliest Fathers from whom we have any mention of prayer addressed to Mary for obtaining her protection and assistance.

---

[7] *Poems about Others* 7, 180–94; PG 37, 1565 D–1566 A.

We have recalled at the beginning of this chapter, citing Sozomen, the miraculous manifestations of the Lord's Mother in Gregory's Church of the Resurrection, in response to the invocations of the oppressed. In one of his sermons, Gregory himself, recounting the story of a virgin named Justina, tells us that the faithful were accustomed to address Mary directly, requesting her help in particular necessities. At the end of this chapter we reproduce his lengthy account of this incident. The account appears to have considerable historical importance because, in it, a prestigious and authoritative figure (Gregory) speaks of prayer addressed to Mary as something common and accepted in the Church of that time.

Mary, Model of the Virginal Life

Our author does not limit himself to teaching Mary's virginity on the doctrinal level but also presents its exemplary and ascetical value. Also, he asserts that the Christian practice of virginity was inaugurated by Mary herself:

> As a painter, when drawing inanimate images on wooden panels, first traces the forms with light brush strokes, then with bolder ones, and finally completes the entire image with colors of every kind, so virginity, an inheritance of Christ the everlasting, was first manifested in a few persons and remained obscured during the time that the law was in force. For, under the law, the colors showed themselves weakly and the hidden splendor [of virginity] sparkled in only a few persons.
>
> But after Christ was born of a chaste and virgin Mother, not bound by carnal chains and like unto God (for it was necessary that Christ should come into the world without marital relations and without a father), virginity began to sanctify women and drive away the bitter Eve. It took away the laws of the flesh, and, through the preaching of the gospel, the letter gave way to the spirit, and grace entered in.
>
> Then virginity shone out clearly before mortals; it appeared in the world freely, as the liberator of a helpless world. It is as superior to matrimony and to the conditions of life as the soul is superior to the body and as the wide heavens are superior to earth, as the lasting life of the blessed is superior to the fleeting life of earth, as God is superior to man.[8]

---

[8] *Moral Poems* 1, 189–208; PG 37, 537 A–538 A.

READING

THE VIRGIN JUSTINA CALLS UPON MARY

There once lived a virgin of noble ancestry, endowed with the most perfect manners. Hear ye and exult, O virgins, and all who honor modesty and love purity. For this story is an elegy to both categories.

The virgin, Justina, was extraordinarily beautiful to behold. Of her divine David sings together with us, saying: "The daughter of the king is clothed in beauty" (Ps 45:14). True spouse of Christ, hidden beauty, living image of God, inviolate sanctuary erected to the Godhead, inaccessible sacred ground, enclosed garden, sealed fountain (thus Solomon also adds something),[9] reserved for Christ alone.

I do not know why or how the great Cyprian was seized with passion for this absolutely uncompromising and virtuous virgin. And yet his greedy eyes, which of all the organs of the body are the most lively and eager, reached out to grasp even the most untouchable things. But Cyprian was not only possessed with love for her; he also tempted her. What singular stupidity, if he was hoping to seduce her, or rather what gross shamelessness in trying anything of the kind, and persisting in his attempts!

The devil also, from the beginning, insinuated himself into paradise to tempt the first man and stood amidst the angels when he sought to tempt Job; he did not even hesitate in the presence of the Lord himself, who was to defeat and condemn him definitively by his death; he tried to tempt him who cannot be affected by any temptation when, in the outward appearance of God, the devil saw the second Adam and, as it were, claimed to make him capitulate as had the first. He was totally unaware that, by attacking the humanity of Christ, he had struck a blow against the Godhead. Why then is it strange that, by means of Cyprian's passion, he makes an attempt against the holy soul and virtuous body of Justina?

Nevertheless, he tempted her, using as an intermediary, not one of those women who are old hands at the trade, but an absolute devil who relished bodies and pleasures. For the rebellious and envious

---

[9] Cf. Song 4:12.

powers readily accept a task of this kind, because they are trying to add many others to their own ruin. And the payment for this mediation was in sacrificial victims and libations and that affinity which is contracted through the blood and odor of the victims. For such a reward has to be paid to those who do these favors.

But pure and divine souls are quick to discover in this the sport of the devil, even though he is very subtle in deceiving and various in his attacks. Thus the maid, as soon as she noticed the presence of evil and sensed the threat, what did she do and what method did she oppose to the artifice of the evil one? Despairing of all other remedies, she took refuge in God and against this detestable passion took as her defender her husband, that is, the same who had freed Susanna from the wicked elders and saved Thekla from a tyrannical courtier and from an even more tyrannical mother.

But who is this husband? He is Christ, who strengthens our spirits and raises up those who are drowning; he hurls the legion of wicked spirits into the abyss; he snatches away the just man from the pit in which he had been placed as food for lions and, stretching out his hands, binds the proud; he frees from the whale the fleeing prophet who, even while inside the whale, had kept the faith. And, in Assyria, he frees the children from the flames; they are kept cool by an angel, and to the three children a fourth is added.

Recalling these and other circumstances and imploring the Virgin Mary to bring her assistance, since she, too, was a virgin and had been in danger, she entrusted herself to the remedy of fasting and sleeping on the ground.

—Gregory Nazianzen, *Sermon* 24, 9–11;
PG 35, 1177 C–1181 A

8

AMPHILOCHIUS OF ICONIUM
(d. after 394)

Amphilochius was born between 340 and 345 in Diocaesarea of Cappadocia. He was probably a cousin of Gregory Nazianzen and became an intimate friend of the three great Cappadocians. After studies in Antioch and Constantinople, he returned to his native city, intending to embrace the life of a hermit, but, in 374, Basil convinced him to accept episcopal consecration as bishop of Iconium and metropolitan of the ecclesiastical province of Lycaonia. He governed his church with zeal and wisdom and participated effectively in the dogmatic controversies of his time, refuting heretics.

In 381, at the Council of Constantinople, he was one of the Fathers who distinguished themselves by their orthodoxy and hard work, thus gaining the esteem and praise of the emperor, Theodosius. The last information we have about his life dates from 394, when he took part in the Synod of Constantinople. We have no word on the exact year of his death. He has always been recognized as a patristic authority, and the ecumenical councils, ever since Ephesus (431), present him as such.

Among the small number of his written works that have survived, we find two homilies, one for Christmas and one for the Hypapante, that help us to know his Marian thought.[1]

Like Basil, Amphilochius thinks that the Blessed Virgin suffered anguished doubts during the drama of her Son's Passion and death:

> As you see, Simeon called a "sword" the many thoughts that wounded her breast and reached unto the joints and marrow. The Virgin Mary fell into these thoughts, because she did not yet know about the power

---

[1] Cf. Ignacio Ortiz de Urbina, "Mariologia Amphilochii Iconiensis", *Orientalia Christiana Periodica* 23 (1957): 186–91.

of the Resurrection and did not know that it was near. And so, after the Resurrection, the sword was no longer ambiguous, but a cause for joy and exultation. Simeon, therefore, called the Cross a sign of contradiction, and so it was at the time when the sword of these thoughts was piercing the Virgin.[2]

On a personal level, the bishop of Iconium appears to harbor feelings of sincere and profound admiration for the Mother of the Lord. Contemplating her presence and her mission in the work of salvation, he can do nothing less than cry out:

O Mary, O Mary! The Maker of all things was your firstborn Son![3]

He also puts words of high praise into Simeon's mouth:

It is enough, O Virgin, to be called the Mother. It suffices to be the nurse of him who nurtures the world. It is a great thing to have held within your flesh the One who upholds all things.[4]

READING

THE NEW EVE GIVES BIRTH TO THE SALVATION OF THE WORLD

In what does this new and wondrous doctrine consist? What is this benevolence of divine Providence, which in becoming mortal reveals its omnipotence? What a grand and most wise strategy against the devil! The world, which had once fallen under the power of sin because of a virgin, is now restored to freedom because of a Virgin. Through the virginal birth, a great multitude of invisible demons has been cast down into Tartarus.

The Lord took the same form as his servants, so that the servants might become conformed to God again. O Bethlehem, city sanctified and made the common inheritance of men! O crib, O crib, you share in the glory of the cherubim and share the same honor as the seraphim! For he who from all eternity is divinely raised above those thrones now reposes bodily in you.

---

[2] *On the Hypapante* 8; PG 39, 57 C.
[3] *On the Birth of Christ* 4; PG 39, 41 A.
[4] *On the Hypapante* 8; PG 39, 56 C.

O Mary, O Mary, the Maker of all things was your firstborn Son! O humanity, who became the bodily substance of the Word and for that reason became more honorable than the spiritual virtues of heaven!

For Christ did not want to clothe himself in the form of archangels or in the form of the immaterial figures of the principalities, virtues, and powers; rather, through you, he clothed himself in your form, which had fallen and become like that of the brute animals.

The healthy do not need a physician. But that nature, which was weighed down by many diseases, obtained such a great physician that, once healed of its disease, it recovered a state of health even better than when it had been well before.

But where now is that hostile and bewildered dragon? Where is that cursed and execrable dragon, who had claimed that his throne would be raised to the heights of heaven?

—Amphilochius of Iconium, *On Christmas* 4;
PG 39, 40 D–41 B

9

JOHN CHRYSOSTOM
(d. 407)

In fourth-century Syria, the Syriac-language Christian communities had a great singer of the Blessed Virgin's praises in the person of St. Ephrem. By contrast, the Greek-speaking Christians appear to have exhibited a certain reserve in her regard. The greatest representative of the Greek-speaking Syrian Christians was St. John Chrysostom, one of the greatest theologians and orators of the Eastern Church. The theological formation he received in the school of Antioch clearly shaped his Marian doctrine; it also steered him toward some questionable exegetical interpretations, which are sometimes disconcerting.

John was born in Antioch in Syria between 344 and 354. As a youth, he began to serve his native Christian community in various ways: first as a lector, then as a deacon, and, finally, as a priest. As a young man he had also lived for some years as a hermit.

After his priestly ordination, in 386, he dedicated himself seriously and with great success to preaching, acquiring extraordinary fame in the exercise of this sacred ministry, to which he owes the name *Chrysostomos*, which means "golden mouth".

In 397, he was elected archbishop and patriarch of Constantinople, an office he held for ten years, amid unbelievable trials and persecutions. The courage, constancy, and patience with which he fought for truth, justice, and the affirmation of moral values marked his life until the end of his earthly days.

In 407, while on his way to exile at the Black Sea, he died before reaching his destination, worn out by fatigue and the hardships of the journey. In 438, his mortal remains were brought back to Constantinople in triumphant procession. The emperor, Theodosius II, fell to his knees before the bier, begging pardon for the actions of his mother, the empress Eudoxia, who had persecuted Chrysostom bitterly.

The Greek Church continues to honor him as one of the three "great ecumenical Doctors", together with St. Basil and St. Gregory Nazianzen. Western Christians also consider him one of the greatest Fathers and Doctors of the Church.

John Chrysostom and the Blessed Virgin

At first glance, our doctor does not appear particularly interested in Marian doctrine, and some of his comments about the Mother of Jesus are bound to leave the reader baffled. We may better understand these facts if we remind ourselves that Chrysostom received his education in the school of Antioch, where the accent was placed more on the human nature of Christ than on his divinity. Further, the Marian title "Mother of God" (*Theotókos*), already used by different Eastern Fathers at that time, was almost unknown among the Antiochene theologians.

Nor should we forget that Chrysostom was primarily a moralist first and a speculative theologian second. His primary concern was focused on the practical problems of Christian conduct. Given this emphasis, he does not hesitate to attribute defects and imperfections to Mary, drawing his audience's attention to them as a way of giving them examples of attitudes and conduct to be avoided or corrected in their religious and moral life. In particular, he interprets certain Gospel passages in such a way as to attribute defects to the Virgin such as unbelief or vanity. Commenting on the episode of the Mother and brothers of Jesus (cf. Mt 12:46–50), John explains that the Master meant to reprove his relatives for their unbelief, seeking to correct them:

> Jesus cared about his Mother so greatly that, on the Cross, he entrusted her to the disciple whom he loved more than all the others, showing his great solicitude for her. However, in this case he acts differently, in order to care for his Mother and his brothers. For, since they thought that he was a mere man, giving in to vainglory, he drives this disease out of them, not reproving them, but correcting them. . . .

Jesus did not want to cause his Mother to doubt; he acted to free her from that tyrannical disease, to induce her, little by little, to form a fitting idea of who he was, persuading her that he was not only her Son but also her Lord.[1]

At the wedding at Cana, Chrysostom sees Jesus' words to his Mother as another reproof:

"They have no wine" (Jn 2:3). By asking for this favor, Mary was trying to win the guests over but also to render herself more conspicuous. And perhaps Mary gave in to a purely human feeling, just as his brothers did when they said: "Manifest yourself to the world" (Jn 7:14), desiring to gain glory for themselves through his miracles. For this reason Jesus answers her rather brusquely, saying: "Woman, what have you to do with me? My hour has not yet come" (Jn 4:4).[2]

In his commentary on the Gospel of the Annunciation, our author makes a rather serious inference about the possible reaction of the Virgin when she discovered her pregnancy. Considering the problem of why God had the mystery of Christ's conception announced to Mary before it happened, Chrysostom gives this answer:

He did it to spare her serious unease and great distress. There was cause for fear, lest she, not knowing the true reason for her pregnancy, imagine that there was something wrong with her and proceed to drown or stab herself rather than endure disgrace.[3]

Apparently, Chrysostom pictures Mary as an ordinary woman, with ordinary qualities and weaknesses; presumably, the Christian communities of Antioch and Constantinople were not startled by statements like this. In other settings, such as Alexandria, the reaction would probably have been quite different.

However, when John begins to consider the role Mary played in the economy of salvation, his attitude toward her becomes full of admiration, respect, and praise. It is expressed in terms of firm fidelity to Christian tradition about Mary's greatness. He dedicates

---

[1] *Homily on Matthew* 44, 1; PG 57, 465.

[2] *Homily on John* 21, 2; PG 59, 130.

[3] *Homily on Matthew* 4, 5; PG 57, 45.

considerable attention to the mystery of Mary's virginal motherhood, which he considers a wondrous paradox that only faith can
grasp.[4]

The Mystery of the God Incarnate

John Chrysostom perceives that the utterly mysterious conception
of Jesus resists every attempt at rationalization:

> Neither the angel Gabriel nor the evangelist Matthew can say any-
> thing except that the birth of Christ was the work of the Holy Spirit,
> but neither of the two explains how the Spirit did this, since such a
> mystery is totally beyond words. Do not believe that you have under-
> stood the mystery, just because you hear the words "of the Holy
> Spirit". For even after we have learned this, there remain many things
> we do not know about. For example: How could the Infinite be con-
> tained in a womb? How could the Virgin give birth and continue to
> be a virgin? Tell me, how did the Spirit fashion that temple? How did
> he take from his Mother, not all of her body, but only a part that he
> augmented and formed?
>
> The evangelist clearly states that Christ came forth from the
> Virgin's body in these words: "That which is conceived in you" (Mt
> 1:20), and Paul does the same: "Born of a woman" (Gal 4:4), in order
> to stop the mouths of those who say that Christ passed through his
> Mother's womb as if through a channel.[5]

This text underscores both the absolute transcendence of the mystery of the Incarnation of God's Son in Mary's womb and the incapacity of the human mind to penetrate its essence. Chrysostom
affirms the certainty of our faith, which rests on an explicit divine
revelation; at the same time, he rejects the absurdity of an old Gnostic heresy that was reemerging in his day, leading to disastrous interpretations of God's economy of salvation. The text continues as
follows:

---

[4] On the Marian teaching of Chrysostom, cf. P. Dieu, "La Mariologie de saint
Jean Chrysostôme", *Mémoires et rapports du Congrès Marial de Bruxelles*, vol. 1
(Brussels, 1922), pp. 71–83; G. M. Ellero, *Maternità e virtù di Maria in S. Giovanni
Crisostomo* (Rome, 1964).

[5] *Homily on Matthew* 4, 3; PG 57, 43.

Had it been so, what need would there have been for the Virgin's womb? And what would he have had in common with us, because his flesh would have been different from ours, since it would not have been derived from the same human substance as ours? In what way would he have been descended from the root of Jesse? How could he be called shoot and flower of this root? How could he have been called Son of man? On what pretext could Mary have been called his Mother? How would he have come forth from David's line? How did he take the form of a slave (1 Phil 2:7)? How could one hold that "the Word became flesh" (Jn 1:14)? And how could Paul have told the Romans that "from them [= the Jews] came Christ according to the flesh, he who is God over all" (Rom 9:5)?[6]

He concludes this argument with a clear definition of the proper attitude of faith:

Based on all these proofs and on many others besides, we establish that Jesus came forth from us and from our human substance and that he was born of the Virgin's womb, but how this happened we do not see. So do not pry into the mystery, but humbly accept what God has revealed, and do not be curious about what God keeps hidden.[7]

The language is very concrete and practical; we do not lose sight of the fact that Chrysostom is addressing the Christian people and giving them precise norms of conduct.

The Miracle of the Virgin Mother

Our doctor has no doubts that Jesus was born of Mary virginally. He considers the virginal conception a miracle that forms part of God's hidden design; it was already foretold in the Old Testament by such prophetic events as the miraculous conceptions of barren women such as Sarah, Anna, and Elizabeth:

When a Jew asks you: "How did the Virgin give birth?" say to him, "How did the old and barren woman give birth?"

For, in this case, there were actually two obstacles: the woman's great age and the weakness of nature. In the Virgin, instead, there was

---

[6] Ibid.
[7] Ibid.

only one obstacle: her abstention from marital relations. In this way, the barren woman prepares the way for the Virgin. But so that you might understand why there were sterile women previously, so that the virginal birth might be believed in, hear the words Gabriel spoke to the Virgin. He appeared to her and said, "You shall conceive in your womb and bear a son and call him Jesus" (Lk 1:31).

She remains troubled and amazed; then she says, "How will this happen to me, since I do not know man?" (Lk 1:34). How does the angel reply? "The Holy Spirit will come upon you and the power of the Most High will overshadow you" (Lk 1:35).

Do not look for conformity with the natural order of things, since what has happened transcends the natural order.[8]

In the sign foretold by the prophet Isaiah (Is 7:14), the event promised by God is the virginal birth of Christ. So comments Chrysostom:

If she had not been a virgin, there would have been no sign, since a sign has to be something out of the ordinary and beyond the laws of nature, something new and unexpected, something that makes an impression on those who see it and hear of it.

That is why it is called a sign, because it stands out. This would not be the case if it could be confused with other common events; so that, if the discourse refers to a woman who gives birth according to the law of nature, why would this be called a sign, since it is something that happens every day?

Therefore, in beginning his speech, he did not say simply: Behold, a virgin, but: Behold, *the* Virgin. By adding the article, he indicates a unique virgin, distinct from all the others.[9]

Elsewhere, Chrysostom makes the acute observation that Mary's husband, Joseph, was not greatly troubled by the Virgin Birth, despite its extraordinary nature, because he was familiar with the Scriptures:

Joseph would not have remained so undisturbed, hearing from the angel the word "virgin", had he not already heard the same word from Isaiah. For a man who had meditated at length on the words of

---

[8] *Homily on Genesis* 49, 2; PG 54, 446.
[9] *Commentary on Isaiah* 7, 5; PG 56, 84.

the prophet, the miracle of a Virgin Mother ceased to seem novel and became something familiar.[10]

Implicit in this analysis is a rule that holds true for the Christian life in general. The believer who nurtures his faith by assiduously meditating on Scripture acquires such a familiarity with God's action in history and in human existence that he is no longer amazed when certain supernatural events appear to contradict the normal course of natural events.

Mary's Perpetual Virginity

John quite explicitly affirms this truth also. In his day, there were still some who continued to propose the old objection that Mary did not remain a virgin after having given birth to Jesus because the Gospel states that Joseph did not know her until she gave birth to her Son (cf. Mt 1:25). According to these persons, Mary lived a normal conjugal life with Joseph after giving birth to Jesus. But Chrysostom opposes this interpretation of the Gospel:

> The expression "until" need not lead you to believe that Joseph knew her subsequently; rather, it is used to inform you that the Virgin was untouched by man until the birth of Jesus. Scripture is accustomed to using the expression "until" without intending thereby to establish a limited period of time. . . . The evangelist uses this expression to establish what happened before the birth of Jesus, leaving it up to you to infer what happened afterward.[11]

According to our doctor, Mary's perpetual virginity, although not explicitly affirmed by Scripture, is a truth deducible from Scripture itself, based on a reflection he sets forth in the following terms:

> He himself has said what you needed to learn about him: that the Virgin was untouched by man until the birth. He leaves it to you to draw the obvious and necessary conclusion, namely, that this righteous man (Joseph), even after Christ's birth, refrained from

---

[10] *Homily on Matthew* 5, 2; PG 57, 56.

[11] Ibid., 5, 3; PG 57, 58.

approaching her who had become a mother in such a manner and had been found worthy of a new kind of childbearing.[12]

In this text, we find a genuine syllogism, in which one is supposed to draw a necessary and obvious conclusion (*akólouthon kaì hōmologēménon*) from Joseph's personal holiness.

Another classic objection to Mary's perpetual virginity was based on the mention of the so-called "brothers of Jesus" (cf. Mt 12:46–50; Mk 3:31–35; Lk 8:19–21). Chrysostom responds by referring to the scene of Mary at the foot of the Cross:

> If [after Jesus' birth] Joseph had known Mary and lived with her as his wife, why would our Lord, on the Cross, have entrusted her to his disciple, commanding him to take her into his own home, as if she had no one else to take care of her?
>
> Why then, you ask, are James and others called the "brothers" of Jesus Christ? They are called brothers of Jesus in the same way that Joseph is called Mary's husband. God wanted to cover this great mystery with many veils, so that the divine birth might remain hidden for a time.[13]

Virginity Prefigured in the Old Testament

Our author finds a prophetic image of Mary's virginity in the virgin soil from which the earthly paradise sprang up, even though it had not been sown:

> Therefore he called it "Eden" or "virgin soil", because this virgin [the soil of paradise] was a type of that other Virgin. As the first soil produced for us the garden of paradise without any seed, so the Virgin gave birth to Christ for us without receiving any manly seed.
>
> In case a Jew should ask you how the Virgin could give birth, answer him thus: How could a virgin soil make wondrous plants spring up? For, in the Hebrew language, "Eden" means "virgin soil".[14]

He also resorts to the Eve–Mary parallel in reference to the earthly paradise, which in this context becomes a type of heaven:

---

[12] Ibid.
[13] Ibid.
[13] *The Changing of Names* 2, 3; PG 51, 129.

A virgin drove us out of paradise; through a Virgin we have found eternal life.[15]

Since Irenaeus and Justin Martyr, the Eve–Mary parallel had become more and more prominent in Christian thought. In this parallel, virginity was one of the important terms of comparison. Following this ancient tradition, John presents Mary as the antithesis of Eve and thus as an important protagonist in the work of salvation.

Despite the lacunae evident in Chrysostom's writings and homilies on the Blessed Virgin, some of his Marian writing reveals the greatness of his genius, especially when he touches on the themes of motherhood and virginity. His teaching on Mary's virginity would become a classic defense of this truth.

The witness of this outstanding Father of the Eastern Church still retains undiminished value for Marian doctrine; it has left an indelible mark on Christian tradition.

READING

CHRIST, WHO HAD NO FATHER AND NO MOTHER

The Son of God has no father and no mother. But how? Yes, he is without a father according to his earthly generation; he is without a mother according to his heavenly generation. For he had neither a father on earth nor a mother in heaven.

Without genealogy. Those who foolishly pry into his nature should pay attention, since some think that the expression "without genealogy" refers to his divine generation. But the heretics do not want even to retain this; they also make this generation the object of their rash speculation. The more moderate among them allow that this word refers to Christ's heavenly generation, but they also hold that the expression "without genealogy" cannot in any way apply to his earthly generation. Let us demonstrate to them that Paul spoke of two generations, one of earth and the other of heaven (cf. Heb 7:3). Moreover, if the earthly generation fills us with amazement, the

---

[14] *Commentary on Psalm* 44, 7; PG 55, 193.

divine generation presents us with an even more profound mystery. For this reason Isaiah also says, "Who will recount his generation?" (Is 58:8).

Isaiah, it is said, was speaking of his divine generation. What, then, shall we say to Paul, who speaks of two generations and then adds "without genealogy"? He added the phrase "without genealogy" so that you would believe that he is without genealogy, not only according to his divine generation, in which Christ is without a mother, but also in relation to his earthly generation, in which he is without a father.

For this reason, after having discussed both generations, he adds: "without genealogy". For the earthly generation is incomprehensible, so that we do not even dare to turn our glance to the heavenly generation. Now, if the outer courts of the temple are so fearsome and inaccessible, who will dare penetrate into the reserved inner courts? I know well that Christ was generated from the Father, but I do not know how. I know well that he was born of a Virgin, but neither in this case can I comprehend how it happened. We profess the fact of the two generations, but we remain silent about the how of both; we are not capable of expressing it.

Now, when speaking of the Virgin, even though I do not know how he was born of her, nevertheless I affirm that he was generated; so I do not discard the fact simply because I do not know how it happened. You should do the same, then, when speaking of the Father. Even if you do not know how the Son was generated, nevertheless you profess that he was generated. Should a heretic ask you how the Son was generated by the Father, brush aside the essence of his question and say to him: "Come down from heaven, show me how he was born of the Virgin, and then ask me your question!" Hold firm on this point; press him; do not allow him the comfort of withdrawing and taking refuge in the labyrinth of his arguments.

—John Chrysostom, *The Obscurity of Prophecies* 1, 2;
PG 56, 166–67

10

LATIN CHRISTIANITY: HILARY OF POITIERS
(d. 367)

As was the case with the Eastern Fathers, it is during the fourth century that the Western Fathers begin to show a notable interest (compared to the past) in the figure of Mary and in Marian doctrine. Usually they study and contemplate her in light of the mystery of the Incarnation. In the Old Testament, they perceive the long preparation for the coming of the incarnate Word; in the Church, they see the mystery's fruitful continuation and eschatological fulfillment.

One of the first Latin Fathers of the fourth century is St. Hilary of Poitiers, the most influential Western theologian of his day. He was also quite attentive and sensitive to the mystery of Mary.

He was born to a noble pagan family in Poitiers, in Aquitaine, during the first decades of the fourth century. He received a sound literary and philosophical education. His impassioned search for the truth impelled him to widen the field of his studies, and it was thus that he came to know the sacred Scriptures. Through them, he was led to conversion and baptism.

In 350, he was consecrated bishop of his native city and began that long period of pastoral labors which lasted until his death. His ministry revealed his exemplary pastoral qualities; he was totally dedicated to caring not only for his local Christian community but for the Church universal as well. In fact, his episcopate was served during a rather stormy period of ecclesiastical history. Arianism, which denied the divinity of the Son of God, had achieved its greatest extent and the summit of its strength. In the West, Hilary was the most tenacious and formidable adversary of this lamentable heresy. Among other things, he openly defended St. Athanasius of Alexandria, the greatest champion of Eastern anti-Arianism.

For these reasons, Hilary himself was deposed from his episcopal see in 356 and exiled to Asia Minor. But, after three years, the emperor Constantius II sent Hilary back home, at the suggestion of the Arians themselves, since he was creating serious difficulties for the heretics even in his place of exile. Once back in Gaul, he continued to be a leader of Western Christianity, especially through his untiring opposition to heresy. For this reason, he was called the "Athanasius of the West".

In fact, in character as well as action, Hilary greatly resembled the intrepid bishop of Alexandria. Like Athanasius, Hilary combined goodness and strength, patience and invincibility, and showed the same pastoral and leadership ability. Hilary's temperament was honest and humane. He was an openminded man, capable of understanding the views of others, even those of his adversaries. Even in the fog of anti-heretical polemics, his conduct was always governed by a profound respect for man, in whom he discerned the image of God. Hilary died in 367.

Hilary's Marian Thought

The Mother of the Lord has a place of considerable importance in the writing of St. Hilary. He considers her an exceptional religious personality who stands out among all the other figures of the primitive Church because of her glorious virginity. Further, Mary plays a unique role in the economy of salvation, though this role is obviously subordinate to her Son's absolutely necessary and essential role. Still, Mary's function in God's plan of salvation is so significant that she is associated with Christ as an object of the messianic prophecies of the Old Testament.

Hilary holds that the virginal conception of Jesus must have been such an overwhelming and sublime experience for his Mother that she could not imagine any choice other than a life lived in perpetual virginity. It became unthinkable for her to contemplate a conjugal life in the normal sense of the term.

Mary's divine-human motherhood does not pose any problem or difficulty for Hilary. He appreciates the Virgin's contribution to the work of redemption, since he holds that the mystery of the Incarnation itself had a direct effect on human salvation. We recall Hilary's insistence on the fact that the Blessed Virgin, in accepting the gift of salvation from God, did so in faith and without reserve; thus, she became the symbol and model of redeemed humanity. But let us now take a closer look at some of the most prominent and characteristic points of the Marian teaching of the bishop of Poitiers.

Christ's Genealogy according to Matthew

Commenting on Matthew's Gospel, Hilary offers us an unusual explanation concerning an alleged error committed by the evangelist in recounting Jesus' genealogy. The evangelist writes:

> So all the generations from Abraham to David were fourteen generations, and from David to the Babylonian captivity fourteen generations, and from the Babylonian captivity to Christ fourteen generations (Mt 1:17).

To the contrary, while the first two series number fourteen generations each, the third, from the Babylonian captivity to Christ, contains only thirteen generations. Hilary has his own explanation for this anomaly:

> There are fourteen generations indicated until Mary, but we only count thirteen generations. In reality, this will not appear as an error to those who know that our Lord Jesus Christ did not take his origin from Mary alone. In fact, the idea of his eternal generation is also included in his bodily generation.[1]

Thus, according to Hilary, the evangelist was not mistaken or forgetful, because the one birth of Christ ought to be reckoned as containing two generations: his birth from Mary, as man, and his divine eternal birth, from the Father. Although the author avoids any polemical tone in this text, doubtless there is an implicit reference to the Arians, who denied that the Word of God was generated by the Father from all eternity.

Matthew, then, added together the generation from the Father and the generation from Mary, as if he wished to declare that the eternal Son of God and the Son of Mary are one and the same Person.

---

[1] *In Matthaeum* 1, 2; PL 9, 920–21.

With this interpretation, Hilary offers us an example of his thoughts on how one ought to read the Bible. The true believer must go beyond a purely superficial interpretation of the sacred text, because the word of God, in addition to its literal sense, conceals a deeper, spiritual or allegorical meaning. This deeper meaning has to be understood before one can achieve a full and perfect comprehension of the text.

The Gospel Speaks on Mary's Behalf

This capacity to penetrate to the deeper meaning of the Scriptures appears indispensable when one encounters the mystery of Mary's virginity. Referring to the baptismal profession of faith, the bishop of Poitiers emphasizes that the case of Christ's conception is unique: Mary gave birth by herself. Mary alone generated the body of the Lord, without the intervention of man. He admits that other opinions were found in his day, opinions not in conformity with the witness of Scripture or the authentic tradition of the Fathers.

Some considered Mary an adulteress; others taught that she conceived Christ through normal relations with Joseph; still others claimed that she had relations with Joseph, at least after the conception of Christ. By harboring thoughts of this kind, all these persons were condemning their own incapacity to penetrate the deep meaning of God's word in a spiritual way. Hilary explains:

> So that no ambiguity should arise about his birth, Joseph himself was chosen as a witness to the fact that Christ was conceived by the working of the Holy Spirit. Since Mary was his espoused wife, he receives her as his wife. Thus the expression "He knew her after the birth" means that Mary receives the title of wife. The text, then, asserts that he knew her, not that he was joined to her.[2]

In this text, Hilary openly sets out to defend Mary's perpetual virginity. Probably under the influence of the Roman legal mentality, he introduces a distinction between marriage (*sponsalia*) and matrimony (*coniugium*). Mary gave birth while still a *sponsa*, or fiancée; afterward, Joseph recognized her as his *coniux*, or wife, but without

---

[2] Ibid., 1, 3; PL 9, 921.

joining himself to her physically (*cognoscitur enim, non admiscetur*). It is like saying that she became his wife legally, but without any consequences on the physical level.[3]

The Gospel appears to offer another pseudo-argument against Mary's virginity when it speaks of the brothers of Jesus. Hilary replies with two counter-arguments:

> Now, if these were Mary's sons, instead of children that Joseph had fathered during a previous marriage, then, at the moment of the Passion, Mary never would have been given to the apostle John as his mother, when the Lord, addressing the two of them, said, "Woman, behold your son", and to John, "Behold your mother" (Jn 19:26–27). For the Lord, to help her face her solitude, left her, in his disciple, the love of a son.[4]

Following the *Protoevangelium of James*, Hilary explains that the brothers of Jesus were sons of Joseph from his first marriage. He also observes that, if Mary had had other children, it would have been more logical for the Lord to entrust her to them instead of to John.

The Gospel also recounts Jesus' much-discussed response to the unnamed person who had announced the arrival of his Mother and his brothers:

> Who is my mother, and who are my brothers? . . . Whoever does the will of my Father in heaven is brother, and sister, and mother to me (Mt 12:48–50).

Various authors have interpreted these words to mean that Jesus was repudiating his Mother. To the contrary, Hilary reads it in a key favorable to Mary:

> In this way he presents himself as the model for all, both for how to act and how to think. Thus, he claimed for himself the right and title to any relatives, to be understood not in reference to condition of birth, but in terms of remaining in communion with the Church.
>
> In any case, since Jesus gave his Mother a great proof of his affection for her at the moment of his Passion, we cannot think that he had feelings of disgust toward her.[5]

---

[3] Cf. M. Peinador, "Et non cognoscebat eam donec peperit filium suum primogenitum", *Estudios Marianos* 8 (1948): 359.

[4] *In Matthaeum* 1, 4; PL 9, 922.

[5] Ibid., 12, 24; PL 9, 993.

The Moral Figure of Mary

Following the tradition of the Eastern Fathers, with whom he had prolonged contact during his years of exile, Hilary always considered it normal for Mary to have had some small imperfections. Once again it is the Gospel that offers a reason for expressing this opinion. Commenting on the Psalm: "My soul is consumed with desire for your judgments" (Ps 119:20), he recalls Simeon's words to Mary and adds his own curious statement:

> A sword will pierce the soul of blessed Mary, so that the thoughts of many hearts might be laid bare (cf. Lk 2:35). If this Virgin, made capable of conceiving God (*capax illa Dei Virgo*), will encounter the severity of his judgment, who will dare to desire this judgment? [6]

Our author does not mention any specific defect or imperfection in Mary's conduct but seems to hold that some such flaw exists, if even Mary must face the judgment of God. However, this is an isolated observation, to which Hilary does not return. Perhaps he was also influenced by the Western mentality, which was already tending to see the Virgin as absolutely holy, untouched by any guilt or defect.

---

[6] *Tractatus super Psalmum* 118, 12; PL 9, 523.

READINGS

MARY IN THE ECONOMY OF SALVATION

Other witnesses explicitly affirm that the economy of salvation proceeds from the Father's will. The Virgin, the birth and body [of Christ], and, in turn, the Cross, death, and descent among the dead constitute our salvation. For the Son of God was born of the Virgin and the Holy Spirit for the sake of the human race.

In so doing, he places himself at his own service and, overshadowing the Virgin with his power (that is, with the power of God), he planted the initial seed of his body and set up the beginning of his life in the flesh. In this way, having become man in his birth from the Virgin, he took upon himself the nature of human flesh so that, through this commingling, the body of the whole human race was sanctified in him. And as all men have found in him their foundation, through his willingness to assume a bodily nature, so he was restored, in turn, to all men through his invisible existence. Thus the invisible image of God did not refuse the shame of being born in a human manner, passing through conception, birth, crying, cradle, and all the humiliations proper to our nature.

And we, with what worthy gift shall we respond to a love so full of benevolence? Behold the one, only begotten God, whose origin from God is absolutely inexpressible, planted like a seed in the womb of the holy Virgin, developing little by little, taking on the form of a tiny body.

He who contains all things, in whom and through whom everything receives existence, behold he comes to light according to the human law of birth. He at whose voice archangels and angels tremble, at whose voice heaven, earth, and all the elements of this world are unraveled, hark, the sound of his newborn wailing! The Invisible and Ungraspable, before whom sight, senses, and touch proclaim their helplessness, wrapped up, in a cradle.

—Hilary of Poitiers, *De Trinitate* 2, 24–25; PL 10, 66

PREGNANT VIRGIN

O Christ, for us the twice-born God!
Born once, from God unborn;
Born twice, when the childbearing Virgin
Brought you into the world,
Embodied and still God!

—Hilary of Poitiers, *Hymns* 1, 5–8; CSEL 65, 209

FAITH IN THE INCARNATION

Gabriel pronounces; Christ is received into the Virgin's body.
The womb swells because of the holy Offspring.
We are exhorted to believe in something new,
        and never seen before:
A childbearing Virgin.

—Hilary of Poitiers, *Hymn on Christ* 11–13, CSEL 65, 218

AMBROSE OF MILAN
(d. 397)

In the writings of St. Ambrose, we find the first important Marian doctrine within Western Christianity, in terms not only of quantity but also of quality, as we encounter rare heights of illuminating reflection. This might be surprising, considering that he did not have the makings of a great theologian. Nevertheless, he had the understanding and ability necessary to search through the storehouse of tradition (with both hands!), especially the tradition of the Eastern Church. This search was prompted by his sudden and unexpected election as bishop, which impressed upon him the urgent need to provide himself with a sound doctrinal formation. He knew that this was something he lacked, something he absolutely needed in order to dedicate himself to his new pastoral mission.

The future bishop of Milan was born to an aristocratic Christian family of Trier, in Gaul, around 339. When his father, prefect of the local praetorium, died prematurely, his mother decided to return to Rome with her sons, Satyrus and Ambrose, to be reunited with her daughter, Marcellina. In Rome, Ambrose studied rhetoric and law. In 370 he was sent to Milan as *vir consularis* for Emilia and Liguria.

At Milan, Ambrose intervened, by virtue of his office, to bring about peace between the Arians and the Catholics. Upon the death of Auxentius, the Arian bishop of Milan, Ambrose was called to succeed to the episcopacy by both parties, in the year 373 or 374. It appears that he was only a catechumen at the time; nevertheless, he was quickly admitted to baptism and, one week later, was consecrated bishop of Milan.

Under the guidance of the priest Simplicianus, he immediately devoted himself to the study of Scripture and the teaching of the Fathers and quickly became one of the best-prepared pastors in the

Church of his time. As bishop, he carried out an effective and astute program of pastoral action, especially in the struggle against the Arian heresy and against an attempt to restore paganism. He died in 397.

From his writings, we can collect a truly abundant and substantive amount of Marian material. This makes it easy to understand his decisive influence on the development of Marian doctrine in the West. In particular, Ambrose made a definitive contribution to a portrayal of the Mother of the Lord as devoid of any defect or imperfection, radiant with exceptional greatness and holiness.[1]

Mary and the Ideal of Virginity

Reading the writings of St. Ambrose, one gets the clear impression that his extraordinary interest in the Mother of the Lord stemmed from his unbounded admiration for the virginal life consecrated to God.[2] Indeed, when he speaks of Mary, this very often leads to a

---

[1] The Marian doctrine of St. Ambrose has been the object of numerous studies. Here we mention only the most exhaustive and up-to-date: J. M. Bover, "La mediación universal de María según san Ambrosio", *Gregorianum* 5 (1924): 24–45; A. Pagnamenta, *La mariologia di S. Ambrogio* (Milan, 1932); E. Vismara, "Il testamento del Signore nel pensiero di S. Ambrogio e la maternità di Maria SS. verso gli uomini", *Salesianum* 7 (1945): 7–38, 97–143; J. Huhn, "Das Mariengeheimnis beim Kirchenvater Ambrosius", *Münchener Theologische Zeitschrift* 2 (1951): 130–46; idem, *Das Geheimnis der Jungfrau-Mutter Maria nach dem Kirchenvater Ambrosius* (Würzburg, 1954); G. Jouassard, "Deux chefs de file en théologie mariale dans la seconde moitié du IVe siècle: St. Epiphane et St. Ambroise", *Gregorianum* 42 (1961): 5–36; G. Rigamonti, *Maria ideale di vita cristiana nella dottrina di S. Ambrogio* (Milan, 1960); Charles William Neumann, *The Virgin Mary in the Works of St. Ambrose* (Fribourg: University Press, 1962) (foundational study); M. Bertagna, "Elementa cultus mariani apud sanctum Ambrosium mediolanensem", *De primordiis cultus Mariani*, vol. 3 (Rome, 1970), pp. 1–15; M. S. Ducci, "Senso della tipologia mariana in S. Ambrogio e suo rapporto con lo sviluppo storico e dottrinale", *Ecclesiastica Xaveriana* 21 (1971): 137–92; idem, "Sviluppo storico e dottrinale del tema Maria-Chiesa e suo rapporto con il pensiero teologico mariano di S. Ambrogio", *Ephemerides Mariologicae* 23 (1973): 363–404; S. Folgado Flores, "María modelo de la Iglesia en San Ambrosio", *Estudios Marianos* 39 (1974): 57–77; idem, "Contorno teológico de la virginidad de María en S. Ambrosio", *Marianum* 44 (1982): 286–315; S.-L. Bastero de Aleizalde, "Paralelismo Eva-María en S. Ambrosio de Milan", *Estudios Marianos* 50 (1985): 71–88.

[2] Cf. G. Jouassard, "Un Portrait de la Ste Vierge par St. Ambroise", *Vie spirituelle* 90, (1954): 477–89.

discussion of virginity, a topic that Ambrose is obviously inclined to emphasize. Writing to his sister, Marcellina, who had consecrated herself to the Lord as a virgin, he expresses himself thus:

> The first impulse to learn is inspired by the nobility of the teacher. Now, who could be nobler than the Mother of God? Who more splendid than she, whom Splendor chose? Who more chaste than she, who gave birth to a body without bodily contact? What should I say, then, about all her other virtues? She was a virgin, not only in body but in her mind as well, and never mixed the sincerity of her affections with duplicity.[3]

After this text there follows a long and precise list of the qualities and virtues that our author attributed to the Mother of the Lord, from humility to prudence, from diligence in labor to charity, from temperance to hiddenness, from modesty to reserve, and still others. Ambrose not only enumerates these qualities but describes them in some detail, as if he had been able to establish this extraordinary Virgin's conduct with his own eyes. The peremptory quality of his closing evaluation is striking:

> This woman is the model of virginity. For such was Mary, that the life of this one woman may be an example for all.[4]

In addition to being the truest and most sublime model of the virginal life, Mary establishes an emotional bond with virgin souls; this enables her to present them before the Lord and to speak to him in their name and on their behalf:

> Oh, how many virgins will she meet! How many will she embrace and bring to the Lord, saying, "By her chastity, she has kept unstained the bridal chamber of my Son!"[5]

In this way, the imitation of Mary is presented as a fitting task for all those who have embraced the ideal of virginity. But the bishop of Milan does not limit himself to this; he adds that the life of the Blessed Virgin offers a paradigm of Christian conduct for all believers, as is said in the text cited above, which is also cited by Vatican II.[6]

---

[3] *De virginibus* 2, 7; PL 16, 220.
[4] Ibid., 2, 15; PL 16, 222.
[5] Ibid., 2, 16; PL 16, 222.
[8] Cf. *Perfectae caritatis*, no. 25.

Mary Is a Virgin Because She Is Mother of God

Love for virginity, then, prompted Ambrose to dwell upon and exalt Mary's extraordinary virginity. However, he does not lose sight of the fact that this condition is a consequence of her vocation to divine motherhood. Citing Isaiah 7:14, he considers the virginal birth of Christ a sign of his divinity:

> Such an incredible and unheard-of birth needed to be announced to her before it could be believed. A virgin giving birth is the sign of a divine mystery, not a human one. And so he says, "Let this be a sign for you: Behold, the virgin shall conceive in her womb and bear a son" (Is 7:14). Mary had read this passage; therefore, she believed that the prophecy would come true, but she could not have read about how it would happen.[7]

The event foretold by Isaiah, in its mysterious and miraculous aspects, acquires the value of a sign indicating both a special presence of God and the transcendent fruit of this presence; namely, the child:

> [Jesus] is born of the Virgin, so that you might believe that he comes from God.[8]

The bishop of Milan stresses how fitting it was that the Son of God should become incarnate by means of a virginal birth:

> What birth according to the flesh could be more fitting for God than this one, in which the immaculate Son of God, even in assuming a body, should maintain the purity of an immaculate birth? Surely the sign of the divine event consists in his being born of a virgin, not from a woman.[9]

For Ambrose, the Eve–Mary parallel is another opportunity to bring out the link between divine motherhood and virginity:

> Come then, O Eve, who now are called Mary; you not only received an incentive to virginity but also gave us God.[10]

---

[7] *Expositio in Lucam* 2, 15; PL 15, 1639.
[8] *De fide* 5, 54; PL 16, 687.
[9] *Expositio in Lucam* 2, 78; PL 15, 1663.
[10] *De institutione virginis* 33; PL 16, 328.

The texts cited above show how the Marian doctrine of the bishop of Milan is placed firmly within a christological context. The eternal generation of the Word is, as it were, "balanced" by his birth within time. The truth of his temporal birth is an integral part of faith in the person of God incarnate:

> If we admit his generation from the Father, then let us also admit his birth from Mary, so that our faith might be complete.[11]

The faithful are confronted by two inseparable mysteries of the Christian faith, regarding one and the same Person: the incarnate Word, subject both to an eternal, trinitarian generation and to a virginal birth from a woman:

> Though he remains the eternal God, he undergoes the mysteries of the Incarnation while remaining one and undivided; for the One is both and is present in both, that is, in his divinity and in his body. For there is no difference between the One who proceeds from the Father and the One who is born of the Virgin; no, he is the same who comes from the Father in one way and comes from the Virgin in another way.[12]

Mother of God the Savior

From the preceding texts we can clearly see Ambrose's polemical intention against the Arians, who were making a strong comeback during the first years of his episcopate.[13] Ambrose entered the struggle against the Arian heresy with energy and conviction. During the years between 378 and 382, he wrote several works of solid dogmatic content and vigorous apologetic tone, including his *De Fide*, *De Spiritu Sancto*, and *De Incarnationis dominicae sacramento*. Although the Arians did not refuse to call Mary *Theotókos*, they understood the term in an improper sense, because they considered the Word to be, not a true God, but rather a creature of the Father.

---

[11] *De benedictionibus patriarcharum* 51; PL 14, 723.

[12] *De Incarnationis dominicae sacramento* 35; PL 16, 862.

[13] After the crisis they experienced following their condemnation at the Synod of Sirmium (375 or 378), the Arians were able to renew their efforts thanks to the support of the Goths, who, after the battle of Hadrianopolis (377–378), moved into the territories of the Roman Empire.

Ambrose underscores the unity of Christ in the duality of his natures, and, using his own version of the principle of the communication of idioms,[14] he repeats against the heretics that Mary is the true Mother of Christ, the Mother of the Lord,[15] the Mother of God.[16]

In Ambrose's day, Mary's motherhood was also contested by the Manichees, who professed a form of Docetism according to which Christ's body was not real but only a phantasm. Presenting the notion that Jesus was truly born of a human mother as an incontestable fact, Ambrose concludes that he is man in the full sense of the term. he repeats this in several ways:

> He is Son of man because the Virgin is a human creature. That which is born of flesh is flesh; that which is born of a human being is called man.[17]

> Christ assumed, not some thing resembling flesh, but the reality of our flesh: a true body.[18]

Our doctor is aware that this error leads to dangerous consequences for the Christian life and for salvation:

> If one does not believe that he has come, neither will he believe that he has taken flesh; thus, he would have appeared as a phantasm and as such would have been crucified. No, he was truly crucified for our sake; he is truly our Redeemer.
> Whoever denies this truth is a Manichee, a denier of Christ's flesh; for this reason he will not receive the remission of sins.[19]

To refute the reality of the flesh of Christ, then, is to deny the reality of salvation. In line with the patristic tradition, Ambrose attacks this error by calling attention to the reality of Mary's motherhood. For example, against those who held the heavenly origin of the flesh of Christ, he writes:

---

[14] *De Incarnationis dominicae sacramento* 36; PL 16, 862–63.

[15] Ambrose prefers this title (cf. *Expositio in Psalmum* 118, 7, 24; *Expositio in Lucam* 1, 33; 2, 1, 2, 35; *De officiis* 1, 69; *De virginibus* 2, 21; *Exhortatio virginitatis* 35, 93).

[16] He uses the title *Mater Dei* twice (cf. *Hexaemeron* 5, 65; *De virginibus* 2, 7) and is the first Latin author to do so.

[17] *Enarratio in Psalmum* 39, 18; PL 14, 1115.

[18] *De sacramentis* 1, 17; PL 16, 440.

[19] *Epistola* 42, 12–13; PL 16, 1176.

The flesh of Christ did not come down from heaven, because he assumed it from the Virgin on earth.[20]

The error that attributed a heavenly origin to the body of Christ stems from the ancient Valentinian Gnosis, but Ambrose was probably thinking more specifically of Apollinaris of Laodicea, to whom this error was wrongly attributed. In his polemic against this heresy, the bishop of Milan appears to follow closely the teaching of Athanasius in his *Letter to Epictetus*.[21] He is quite categorical on this point, because he understands well that to deny the true humanity of Christ and, consequently, the true motherhood of Mary is to deny the reality of redemption. This is the viewpoint of Athanasius, which Ambrose espouses completely. His text is explicit:

We understand what was written about the Incarnation of the Lord: "The Lord created me" (Prov 8:22) to mean that the Lord Jesus was created from the Virgin to redeem the Father's works. And truly, one cannot doubt that this was said in reference to the mystery of the Incarnation, when the Lord assumed flesh to free his works from slavery to corruption and to destroy, by the suffering of his body, the one who held the power of death.[22]

In this perspective the meaning and value of Mary's motherhood within the mystery of salvation are clear. Her contribution to human redemption is found in her giving a human nature to the Son of God, so that he could save us by means of our own nature. Here, Ambrose simply repeats a text that is common in earlier patristic tradition:

What was the reason for the Incarnation? It has to be this: the flesh that had sinned had to be redeemed by the same flesh.[23]

He is called "made" because of his birth from the Virgin. . . . He bore our flesh in his own flesh, bore in his body our weakness and curses, in order to nail them to the Cross.[24]

---

[20] *De sacramentis* 6, 4; PL 16, 474–75.

[21] *Epist. ad Epictetum* 2; PG 26, 1053. Cf. E. Weigl, *Untersuchungen zur Christologie des hl. Athanasius,* Forschungen zur christlichen Literatur- und Dogmengeschichte, vol. 12, no. 4 (Magonza-Paderborn, 1914), pp. 55f.

[22] *De fide* 3, 46; PL 16, 623–24.

[23] *De Incarnationis dominicae sacramento* 56; PL 16, 868.

[24] *Sermo contra Auxentium* 25, passim; PL 16, 1015.

Mary gave Christ a nature capable of suffering and dying, so that the Son of God was able to take upon himself the sufferings of men and so redeem humanity through his own suffering and death. This is why Mary, in the exercise of her motherhood, is seen to be strictly connected to the work of our redemption. This is the main perspective in which Ambrose views the motherhood of the holy Virgin. She is the true Mother of Christ, the Mother of the Redeemer. On this point also, the similarities to Athanasius are obvious.[25]

Mary, a Remarkable Woman

The bishop of Milan totally ignores the defects that some of the Fathers attributed to Mary on the basis of certain New Testament passages. To the contrary, Ambrose draws an attractive portrait of the Virgin, full of holiness and spiritual beauty.

In his commentary on the Gospel of Luke, we find a key for understanding everything Ambrose thought about Mary's extraordinary religious character. Referring to her words to the angel, "How will this happen, since I do not know man?" (Lk 1:34), he offers the following commentary:

> She does not appear to have doubted the event but asked how it would take place. Clearly, if she asked how it would happen, she must have believed in its fulfillment. Thus she merited to hear the words, "Blessed are you, because you have believed" (Lk 1:45).
>
> Yes, truly blessed for having surpassed the priest [Zechariah]. While the priest denied, the Virgin rectified the error. No wonder that the Lord, wishing to rescue the world, began his work with Mary. Thus she, through whom salvation was being prepared for all people, would be the first to receive the promised fruit of salvation.[26]

For Ambrose, the Annunciation constitutes the central mystery of Mary's life and mission. In this direct encounter with the saving God, her existence assumed a fundamental direction. Thenceforth, her life would be characterized by profound faith and by total and absolute obedience to God.

---

[25] Cf. *Epist. ad Epictetum* 5; PG 26, 1057.
[26] *Expositio in Lucam* 2, 17; PL 15, 1640.

The comparison between Zechariah and the Virgin also expresses a profound thought that seems to be inspired by the ancient Eve–Mary parallel. Mary, by her conduct, repaired the error of the priest, just as the idea of reparation was present from the beginning in the classic Eve–Mary parallel.

Mary is presented as the first to receive the fruit of salvation, the first creature redeemed by Christ, because she received the mission to collaborate in a unique way in human salvation. For Mary, the mystery of the Incarnation was the fulfillment of her personal salvation; her salvation was christological, as it is for all other men. The Redeemer began his saving work with his own Mother.

Ambrose has no doubts that Mary's faith was illuminated and goes so far as to demonstrate that it would be impossible to perceive any unbelief in the words of Mary at the Annunciation; that would be like admitting that the Holy Spirit came down upon Mary to reward her unbelief.[27]

Our doctor explicitly attributes other virtues to the Blessed Virgin, as can be seen in another text:

> If she asked what this greeting meant, it was out of modesty, for she was troubled. She asked out of prudence, for she was surprised by this new formula of blessing, which is not found elsewhere and which had never been encountered until this moment.
>
> This greeting had been reserved for Mary alone. Indeed she alone is called "full of grace", since only she obtained that grace which no one else had merited: to be filled with the Author of grace.
>
> Thus Mary blushed; Elizabeth did the same. Let us learn the difference between the woman's shyness and the Virgin's shyness. In the case of the woman, it indicates the extent of her own chastity; in the Virgin, the grace of chastity increases.[28]

Elsewhere our author praises the Virgin's modesty, which moved her to learn from such poor and humble people as the shepherds, whose words, deeds, and reactions she kept in her heart. This modesty imparts an eloquent lesson to the faithful, who ought not to refuse to learn from the priests.[29]

---

[27] Ibid., 2, 14; PL 15, 1638–39.

[28] Ibid., 2, 8–9; PL 15, 1636.

[29] Ibid., 2, 54; PL 15, 1654.

Ambrose also exalts the exceptional courage shown by Mary at the foot of the Cross, when all of Jesus' friends abandoned him:

> His mother stood before the Cross, and, while the men fled, she re-mained undaunted. . . . She did not fear the torturers. . . . His Mother offered herself to his persecutors.[30]

He calls the Mother of the Lord *sancta Maria* and *sancta Virgo* with notable frequency; it appears indisputable that he excluded from Mary any stain of sin whatsoever.

Mary and the Church

Ambrose is the first Christian author to call Mary the type and image of the Church; here, the study of his thought is particularly impor-tant for understanding later Christian tradition. In a text also cited by Vatican II [31] he observes:

> Well [does the Gospel say]: married but a virgin; because she is the type of the Church, which is also married but remains immaculate. The Virgin [Church] conceived us by the Holy Spirit and, as a virgin, gave birth to us without pain. And perhaps this is why holy Mary, married to one man [Joseph], is made fruitful by another [the Holy Spirit], to show that the individual churches are filled with the Spirit and with grace, even as they are united to the person of a temporal priest.[32]

The Mary–Church parallel is based on the virginal motherhood of both, a motherhood that has the same supernatural fructifying prin-ciple: the Holy Spirit. However, there is not only a relationship of resemblance between the Virgin and the Church; there is also an operative relationship, made possible by the unity between Christ and his Mystical Body. For, in conceiving Christ, Mary also con-ceived us in the Church:

> From Mary's womb there came into the world that heap of grain, surrounded by lilies (cf. Song of Songs 7:1), when Christ was born of her.[33]

---

[30] *De institutione virginis* 49; PL 16, 333.

[31] *Lumen gentium*, no. 63.

[32] *Expositio in Lucam* 2, 7; PL 15, 1635–36.

[33] *De institutione virginis* 94; PL 16, 342.

From the context, it is understood that Ambrose interprets this verse from the Song of Songs in such a way that the lily stands for Christ, while the heap of grain stands for the faithful. The holy Virgin, in giving birth to Christ for the salvation of the world, contracted a maternal relationship with all men on a spiritual level. She contributes to the building up of the Church into the body of Christ. The context allows us to interpret in this sense another text, which describes the profound communion between Jesus and the faithful:

> The inheritance of the Lord are the sons (cf. Ps 127:3), the reward of the fruit that has come forth from Mary's womb. He is the fruit of the womb. . . . Mary is the branch; the flower of Mary is Christ, who, like the fruit of a good tree, according to our progress in virtue, now flowers, bears fruit in us, and is reborn through the Resurrection that returns life to his body.[34]

READINGS

MARY, HIGHEST MODEL OF THE VIRGINAL LIFE

Virginity is thus proposed to us, as if in a picture, in Mary's life. From her life, the beauty of her chastity and her exemplary virtue shine out as from a mirror. Here you may well receive instruction on how to lead a life in which virtue, instructed by example, shows you what you must do, correct, or avoid.

The first impulse to learn is inspired by the nobility of the teacher. Now, who could be nobler than the Mother of God? Who more splendid than she, whom Splendor chose? Who more chaste than she, who gave birth to a body without bodily contact? What should I say, then, about all her other virtues? She was a virgin, not only in body, but in her mind as well, and never mixed the sincerity of her affections with duplicity:

Lowly of heart, serious in her speech, prudent in spirit, sparing in words, devoted to reading, she did not place her hope in changeable

---

[34] *Expositio in Lucam* 2, 24; PL 15, 1641–42.

riches but in the prayer of the poor. Industrious in her work, modest in her speech, she let God, not man, judge her thoughts. She offended no one; she had goodwill toward all; she respected her elders; she did not envy her peers. She fled ostentation, followed reason, and loved virtue. When did she ever offend her parents with so much as a glance? When did she ever disagree with her neighbors or despise the lowly? When did she ever make fun of the weak or avoid the needy? There was no leering in her glance, no arrogance in her words, nothing immodest in her movements. Never an agitated movement, never a hurried step, never a raised voice. The very appearance of her person reflected the holiness of her mind and expressed her goodness. A beautiful house has to appear beautiful even before you reach the front door, and as soon as you enter you have to know that there is nothing dark inside it. In the same way our mind, if not caught in the shadows of bodily obstacles, will disclose its interior light to the outside world.

What, then, shall I say about her temperance in food and of her industriousness? She did not eat more than nature required, while her industriousness surpassed natural powers. When working, she allowed herself no respite; when eating, she multiplied her fasts. And when she felt the need for food, she chose ordinary foods, just enough to keep her from dying, rather than delicacies. She slept out of necessity rather than desire, and, even when her body was resting, her spirit kept vigil, either reviewing things she had read, or continuing interrupted thoughts, or considering what she had to do the next day, or planning future tasks.

She never went out of the house except to go to the synagogue, and even then she was accompanied by her parents or relatives. Committed to staying hidden inside her house, she never showed herself in public without being guarded by a trustworthy companion. Her best guardian, however, was always herself. Her conduct and her words commanded respect; she never raised her foot off the ground without taking a step on the path of virtue.

The virgin has a guardian, yes, but she herself should be the guardian of her honesty. There will be many from whom she can learn (if she has the capacity); if she has virtue as her teacher, then her every act will be a lesson. Thus Mary observed everyone, as if she had something to learn from everyone, and every one of her actions was informed by virtue, so that she was more like a teacher than a disciple.

This is how the evangelist describes her; this is how the angel found her and how she was when the Holy Spirit chose her. But why should I prolong this discussion of details by saying that she was loved by her family and praised by strangers, if she was worthy to become the Mother of the Son of God? The angel found her alone in the most secluded room of the house, where she would not be distracted or disturbed. She did not desire the company of other women when she was being kept company by holy thoughts. She felt even less alone when she was by herself. Indeed, how could she have been alone when she enjoyed the company of so many books, so many archangels, so many prophets?

When Gabriel found her in the place where he was accustomed to visit her, she was troubled by the sight of an angel in human guise, but when she heard his name, she recognized him as someone known to her. She, who felt like a stranger when in the presence of a man, did not feel strange to be in the presence of an angel. He showed her how piously he listened and how modestly he looked at her. Finally, when greeted, she is silent; but, when questioned, she responds. And while at first she was troubled, afterward she promises obedience.

The divine Scripture tells us how loving she was with her family. When she knew that God had chosen her, her humility became even greater, and she hurried into the hills, to see her cousin Elizabeth; not, however, to assure herself of the facts, since she had already believed the announcement: "Blessed are you"—Elizabeth would greet her—"because you believed" (Lk 1:45). And she remained with her for three months. During this long period of time, she did not look to be confirmed in her faith but to show her charity. And this after the baby in Elizabeth's womb, who enjoyed grace even before he had nature, had already greeted Mary as Mother of the Lord by leaping up.

Mary, who had been troubled by the sight of the angel, now remains calm before the succession of such miracles as the pregnancy of the barren woman, motherhood in a virgin, speech from a mute, the adoration of the Magi, the expectation of Simeon, and the witness of the stars. And, the Gospel says, "She kept all these things in her heart" (Lk 2:19). Even though she was Mother of the Lord, she wanted to learn his precepts. She, who had given birth to God, desired to know God still better.

What to say about the fact that, when she goes up to Jerusalem for the yearly solemnity of Passover, she is always accompanied by Joseph? In the virgin, every virtue must always be accompanied by modesty. Modesty and virginity must be inseparable, because without modesty there is no virginity. Therefore, even when going to the Temple, Mary does not go out without a guardian of her chastity.

This is the model of virginity; in truth, such was Mary, whose life alone is sufficient to instruct everyone. So, if we find the author pleasing, let us approve the author's work, so that whoever desires her same prize may imitate her example. How many different virtues shine out in a single Virgin! Modest hiddenness, banner of faith, devout obedience. She was a virgin in her home, a companion in service, a mother in the Temple.

Oh, how many virgins will she meet! How many will she embrace and bring to the Lord, saying, "By her chastity, she has kept unstained the bridal chamber of my Son!"

—Ambrose, *De virginibus* 2, 6–16; PL 16, 220–22

MARY AT THE FOOT OF THE CROSS

His mother stood before the Cross, and, while the men fled, she remained undaunted. Consider whether the Mother of Jesus, who did not lose her courage, could ever lose her virginal purity. With eyes full of pity, she looked upon her Son's wounds, by which, as she knew, would come the redemption of the world. She, who did not fear her Son's killers, assisted at his generous martyrdom.

Her Son hung upon the Cross; his Mother offered herself to his persecutors. If she had been there for no other reason than to be slain before her Son's Cross, then she would deserve praise for her maternal affection, because of which she did not want to outlive her Son. But if she wanted to die along with her Son, it was because she looked forward to rising with him. Well did she know the mystery, that she had given birth to One who was to rise; moreover, she knew that her Son's death would happen for the good of all. Thus, by her death, she hoped to add something to the common good.

Her Son's Passion, however, had no need of help, just as the Lord had foretold long ago: "I looked, but there was no one to help; I was appalled, but there was no one to uphold; so my own arm brought me victory" (Is 63:5).

—Ambrose, *De institutione virginis* 49; PL 16, 333

For her part, Mary did not fail to live up to her station as the Mother of Christ. When the apostles fled, she stood before the Cross and gazed tenderly on the wounds of her Son, because she was waiting, not for her Son's death, but for the salvation of the world. Did she, the hall of the King, who knew that the world would be redeemed by her Son's death, think that her own death could add anything to the grace given to all? But Jesus, for the redemption of all, had no need of assistance, not he who had said, "I am like a man without help, alone among the dead" (Ps 88:6). He accepted his mother's affection, but he did not seek human assistance.

—Ambrose, *Expositio in Lucam* 10, 132; SC 52, 200

JEROME
(d. 419)

A contemporary of St. Ambrose and St. Augustine, Jerome also made a considerable contribution to the development of Marian tradition within Western Christianity, especially with his commentaries on Sacred Scripture and his polemical tracts against those who appealed to Scripture itself to deny the virginity of the Mother of God.[1]

Tradition tends to consider Jerome the most cultured man of his time. The foundation of his education was a vast and profound knowledge of classical learning, which made him an exceptional writer of the Latin language. He also knew Greek and Hebrew. More than a theologian, he stands out as a supreme exegete; the Council of Trent speaks of him as the greatest doctor of scriptural exegesis.

Jerome was born in the town of Strido, in Dalmatia, around 342. At the age of eleven he was sent to study in Rome, where he was baptized at age nineteen. As a young man, he dedicated himself to a wide variety of activities, frequently alternating experiences of the monastic life with long voyages, on which he had the chance to get to know the various Fathers of the Church who were his contemporaries.

Returning to Rome around 382, he was hired by Pope Damasus as his secretary and founded several monastic communities. After Damasus' death, Jerome returned to the East, where he spent many years making pilgrimages to the holy places and leading a solitary life of prayer, study, and writing. His activity as writer and exegete was

---

[1] Cf. J. Niessen, "Die Mariologie des hl. Hieronymus: Ihre Quellen und ihre Kritik" (dissertation, Westfälische Wilhelms-Universität, Münster, 1913).

truly impressive. He died in 419 (or 420), and his remains were interred in the grotto of Bethlehem. Later they were transferred to the crypt of St. Mary Major in Rome.

Controversy over Mary's Virginity

Because of the war Jerome was obliged to wage against the heretics Helvidius and Jovinian, the virginity of the Mother of the Lord became the dominant theme of his Marian thought. His work *On the Perpetual Virginity of Mary against Helvidius* might have become a genuine treatise on Marian exegesis had it not been dominated by an excessive preoccupation to demonstrate the superiority of virginity over matrimony. Jerome emphasized this theme in order to crush the thesis of his adversary, who held the equal value of both states of life from a Christian point of view.

Helvidius, a Roman layman and friend of Auxentius (the Arian bishop of Milan before St. Ambrose), proposed Mary as a model of both states of life, whether as a perfect virgin before the birth of Jesus or as exemplary wife and mother afterward. Tertullian had already held this same position.[2] According to Helvidius, the "brothers of Jesus" mentioned in the synoptic Gospels (cf. Mt 12:46–50; Mk 3:31–35; Lk 8:19–21) were in fact sons born to Mary and Joseph, as Tertullian also thought.

To this argument, which Helvidius claimed to draw from Scripture, Jerome responds point by point, with an irony and sarcasm that undoubtedly hit the bull's-eye. Here is a telling example:

> Regarding the words of the Gospel: "Before they came together, she was found to be with child by the power of the Holy Spirit" (Mt 1:18), [Helvidius] observes: "No one, when speaking about someone who is not going to eat lunch, says, 'Before he ate lunch.'"
>
> I don't know whether to laugh or cry. Should I accuse him of lack of experience or just carelessness? Suppose someone should say, "Before eating lunch at the harbor, I set sail for Africa." Would this mean that his statement could not be valid unless he had to eat lunch at the harbor some day? Or if we wished to say, "The apostle Paul, before departing

---

[2] *De monogamia* 8, 2; PL 2, 989.

for Spain, was put in chains in Rome." Or to say—which is quite likely—"Helvidius, before repenting, was struck down by death."

Now does Paul have to go to Spain immediately upon his release? Must Helvidius repent after his death, even though Scripture says, "In the underworld who will give you praise?" (Ps 6:5)? Although the preposition "before" often indicates a consequence, sometimes it merely shows what was being planned beforehand.[3]

And see what conclusion Jerome draws from this argument about Mary's perpetual virginity:

> Therefore, it is not necessary that the things one was planning to do should really happen, should something else intervene to prevent them from happening. Thus, when the evangelist says, "Before they came together", he means that the time of the wedding is near and that things have reached the point that she who had been considered engaged was about to become a wife.[4]

Later, he sets about, with growing virulence, to demolish Helvidius' exegesis of Matthew 1:25, "And he did not know her until she gave birth to a Son":

> On this point especially, my adversary works up a sweat, laboring to no purpose, striving to make the term "to know" (*cognoscere*) refer to sexual relations rather than to knowledge, as if anyone had ever denied this fact and as if any intelligent person could ever have imagined any assertions as stupid as those he refutes.
>
> Then he means to prove that the adverb "until" (*donec* or *usque*) designates a limited period of time and that, when said time is concluded, there occurs an event that, up until that point in time, had not yet taken place, as in the following passage: "And he did not know her until she gave birth to a Son." It is obvious, he says, that he knew her after she gave birth and that the birth of the child simply delayed sexual relations.
>
> To prove this point, he gathers together many examples from the Scriptures and brandishes his sword in the dark, like the blindfolded gladiators,[5] making his tongue vibrate with his own noise, wounding no one but the members of his own body.[6]

---

[3] *De perpetua virginitate Mariae adversus Helvidium* 4; PL 23, 195.

[4] *Ibid.*, 4; PL 23, 195–96.

[5] Cf. Cicero, *Epistulae ad familiares* 7, 10, 2.

[6] *De virginitate perpetua* 5; PL 23, 198.

Then follows Jerome's refutation, which shows how effective he was, not only because of his formidable *vis polemica*, but especially because of his capacity to give a lesson in method to his opponent by descending to his level and attacking him with his own arguments. We give a brief summary:

He concedes to Helvidius the validity of giving a sexual interpretation of the verb *cognoscere*, which is also supported by the Bible. But if Helvidius assumes the semantic ambivalence of the term, he should also accept the ambivalence of the terms *donec* and *usque*, which also have a double meaning in the Scriptures.

Having cleared the field of these presumed difficulties, Jerome affirms Mary's perpetual virginity with a declaration that forms an argument of convenience. This same argument will be found later, in various other Fathers and early Christian authors:

> Would he [Joseph], who knew such great wonders, have dared touch the temple of God, the dwelling place of the Holy Spirit, the Mother of his Lord?[7]

In another work, Jerome addresses the threat posed to Mary's perpetual virginity by the term "firstborn":

> "He did not know her until she gave birth to her firstborn Son.". . . Based on this passage, some perversely suppose that Mary had other children, maintaining that a son is not called "firstborn" unless he has siblings. To the contrary, the divine Scriptures are accustomed to call someone "firstborn", not because other siblings come after him, but because he is born first.[8]

This response was already becoming a stereotypical formula in the authors who discussed this question. This shows that a crystallization of common arguments was beginning to occur within Church teaching.

Later, in his treatise against Helvidius, Jerome articulates a hermeneutical principle of great importance that will be taken up by subsequent exegetical tradition:

> While on the one hand we do not deny what is written [in the Bible], on the other hand we do reject what is not written. We believe that

---

[7] Ibid., 7; PL 23, 200.
[8] *In Evangelium Matthaei* 1, 1, 25; PL 26, 26.

God was born of a Virgin, because we read it. We do not believe that Mary consummated her marriage after giving birth, because we do not read it.[9]

For Jerome, as for Ambrose, defending Mary's perpetual virginity meant underscoring the superiority of the virginal life consecrated to God over married life. We also know that, in Jerome's day, there was a strict connection between the phenomenon of the extraordinary increase in the monastic life and communities of virgins, and the growth of faith in Mary's perpetual virginity. In this circumstance, we can discern a further example of the mysterious ways in which the Holy Spirit guides the Christian people toward an ever clearer understanding of the revealed deposit of faith.

Jerome, however, does exhibit some scepticism regarding the theme of *virginitas in partu*, possibly because this truth, which is not explicitly affirmed in Scripture, was handed down by the apocrypha. His description of Jesus' birth is almost too realistic:

> If every day the hands of God form babies in their mothers' wombs, why blush to think that Mary, after the birth of Jesus, became a real wife? If they find this disgraceful, then they should not believe that God was born by passing through the genital organs of a Virgin. According to their view, this would be more shameful than believing that a virgin was joined to her husband after the birth of her child.
>
> Now add, if you will, the other humiliations of nature: the womb growing larger for nine months, the nausea, the birth, the blood, the swaddling-clothes. Picture to yourself the baby wrapped in the usual protective membranes. Do not omit the uncomfortable manger, the crying of the Child, the circumcision on the eighth day, the time of purification for declaring pure that which had been impure. We do not blush; we are not silent about these matters. The greater the humiliations he suffered for me, the greater my debt to him.[10]

And so, when the Synod of Milan (390) condemned the heretic Jovinian, who denied Mary's virginity in giving birth, Jerome appeared indirectly implicated in the condemnation. Entreated by his friend Pammacchius to clarify his position and to justify himself, Jerome wrote his treatise against Jovinian, in which he not only

---

[9] *De virginitate perpetua* 19; PL 23, 203.
[10] Ibid., 23, 202.

avoided committing himself to a clearly stated position but caused quite a scandal because of his intemperate style and the exaggeration of some of his statements. Jerome remained somewhat hesitant in confronting the theme of virginity *in partu*. The attitude of Ambrose, Augustine, and many other Fathers before and contemporary with him, who had taken a stand in favor of virginity during birth, did not render Jerome more favorable to this aspect of Marian doctrine.

Mary Ever-Virgin

Notwithstanding his problematic opinion about the Virgin Birth, Jerome speaks of Mary as a perpetual virgin; a virgin before and after the birth of Jesus, who never had marital relations with her own husband. That shows his understanding of virginity as abstaining from sexual relations, rather than as physical integrity, which he would not consider an indispensable condition of virginity.

However, faced with the concerns of those who wanted explanations of how the Blessed Virgin gave birth to her Son, Jerome offers an answer that is clouded by his own personal incertitude, as well as by his awareness that he is in the presence of a great mystery:

> Holy Mary, blessed Mary, Mother and Virgin, virgin before giving birth and virgin after giving birth! I marvel that a virgin is born of a virgin and that after the virgin's birth, his Mother remained a virgin.[11]

Our doctor seeks an explanation of this incomprehensible prodigy in the appearance of the risen Christ to his disciples in the upper room:

> Do you want to know how he was born of a Virgin and how, after his birth, his Mother remained a virgin? The doors were locked, yet Jesus entered. There is no doubt that the doors were locked. He who entered through the locked doors was not a phantasm or a ghost but a true body. For what did he say? "Look at me and see that a ghost does not have flesh and bones as I do" (Lk 24:39).[12]

[11] *Homilia in Joannem* 1, 1–14; CCL 78, 521.
[12] Ibid.

Both the appearance of the risen Lord and the Virgin Birth, in their mysterious and miraculous aspect, are manifestations of God's omnipotence, and it is not possible to know their inner workings:

> Simply attribute to the power of God the fact that he was born of the Virgin, and that this Virgin remained a virgin even after giving birth.[13]

Notwithstanding, then, his slightly uncertain ideas about the specific fact of *virginitas in partu*, our doctor has no doubts that Mary remained a virgin, not only prior to the mystery of the Incarnation of the Son of God and until his birth, but for the rest of her life. Her bonds to Joseph continued on an entirely spiritual and affective level, excluding any physical relationship; hence, according to Jerome, her husband lived a virginal life as well. Here is what he writes in his polemic against Helvidius:

> You say that Mary did not remain a virgin. I, instead, claim to affirm something even more: namely, that Joseph also remained a virgin for Mary's sake, so that a virgin Son might be born from a virginal marriage. For if there was no place for fornication in a holy man like Joseph, and if it is not written that he had another wife, and if for Mary, who was considered his wife, he was a guardian rather than a husband, we conclude that, along with Mary, he who merited to be called father of the Lord remained a virgin.[14]

Also, Jerome rejects the apocryphal reports that Joseph, when he married Mary, was an old widower, with children from a previous marriage. The so-called "brothers of Jesus" were simply cousins, according to the meaning of the Hebrew word.

Mary in the Prophecies of the Old Testament

It is easy for Jerome, as a great biblical scholar, to trace the Virgin's pre-history in the prophecies and characters of the Old Testament.

Applying to Mary the text of Isaiah 7:14, Jerome inquires as to the exact meaning of the term *'almāh*:

---

[13] Ibid.

[14] *De virginitate perpetua* 19; PL 23, 213.

It means: hidden virgin; that is, not only a virgin, but more intensely so, because not all virgins are hidden and withdrawn from the fortuitous glance of men.[15]

Mary is the one to whom Jeremiah's prophecy applies:

"Can a bride forget her jewels, or a virgin her girdle" (Jer 2:32). Always in this very prophecy it is said that a great miracle occurred involving this woman: The woman will surround the man and the virgin's womb will contain the Parent of all.[16]

The heretics erred about the birth of Jesus, because they failed to understand the prophecy of Ezekiel 44:1–2:

Only Christ opened the closed doors of the virginal womb, which continued to remain closed, however. This is the closed eastern gate, through which only the high priest may enter and exit and which nevertheless is always closed.[17]

In the "fruits of the earth" of Psalm 67:6, and in the flower and lily of Song of Songs 2:1, Jerome sees the Virgin's Son:

Do you want to know what this fruit is? It is the virgin from the Virgin, the Lord from the handmaid, God from a human creature, the Son from a mother, the fruit from the earth.[18]

In the cloud of Psalm 78:14 and Isaiah 19:1, Jerome discerns a prefiguration both of Christ and of his Mother:

As for the light cloud, we must either interpret it rightly as the body of the Savior, because it was light and not weighted down with any sin, or surely we ought to see in the light cloud holy Mary, who was not weighed down by any manly seed.[19]

Mary is also the land that was promised to David (cf. Ps 97; = Ps 96 Vulgate, title) and restored to him:

The land of David is holy Mary, Mother of the Lord, "who was born of David's seed according to the flesh" (Rom 1:3). What was

---

[15] *Adversus Iovinianum* 1, 32; PL 23, 266.

[16] Ibid., PL 23, 267.

[17] *Contra Pelagianos* 2, 4; PL 23, 563.

[18] *Tractatus de Psalmo* 66; CCL 78, 38.

[19] *Tractatus de Psalmo* 77, 14; CCL 78, 72.

promised to David was fulfilled in Mary's virginity and birth, where a virgin is born from a Virgin.[20]

But he thinks especially of Eve, whose downfall was repaired by Mary, who leads man back to the paradise from which he had been driven out:

> Observe the cleverness of the ancient foe. He ferociously preyed upon the substance of the just man [Job]. . . . He left him nothing but his tongue and his wife, so that one tempted him while the other blasphemed. The devil remembered the old trick by which he had once ensnared Adam through the woman . . . thinking that he could always trap men by using woman. But he did not consider that, if a man was ruined by a woman once, now the whole world has been saved through a woman. You are thinking of Eve, but consider Mary: the former drove us out of paradise; the latter leads us back to heaven.[21]

Mary's Holiness

Jerome is certain that Mary's excellence makes her unique. He directly compares her to the holy day of Easter:

> As the Virgin Mary, Mother of the Lord, holds the first place among all women, so, among all other days, today [Easter] is the mother of all days.[22]

Often in his writings he refers to Mary as "holy" and describes her as full of the grace of the Spirit.[23] Her holiness is greater than that of Elizabeth and Zechariah:

> Indeed how inferior they are, in terms of holiness, to blessed Mary, Mother of the Lord! She, aware of God dwelling in her, freely proclaims: "For behold, henceforth all generations will call me blessed!" (Lk 1:48).[24]

---

[20] *Tractatus de Psalmo 96*, 1; CCL 78, 440.

[21] Ibid.; CCL 78, 444–45.

[22] *In die dominica Paschae*, CCL 78, 545.

[23] Cf. *Epist.* 22, 38; PL 22, 422.

[24] *Contra Pelagianos* 1, 16; PL 23, 533.

Among Mary's personal virtues, as emphasized by Jerome, some appear as an ornament of her virginity:

> "A shoot shall sprout from the stump of Jesse, and from his roots a bud shall blossom" (Is 11:1). The shoot is the Mother of the Lord, simple, pure, and sincere, who was not joined to any seed coming from without.[25]

Mary's poverty is manifest especially in the story of Bethlehem, where she is forced to give birth in a stall. From this testimony, the poor can draw comfort:

> Whoever is poor should be consoled by this: Joseph and Mary, the Mother of the Lord, had neither servant nor handmaid. They came to Bethlehem by themselves from Nazareth. They did not have a pack horse. They are masters and servants at the same time. This is new! They go into an inn, not into the city, for, in their timid poverty, they dare not approach the rich. Admire the greatness of their poverty: they go to an inn. The Gospel does not say that it was on the road, but in an alley, off the main road.[26]

Another aspect of Mary's moral character brought out by Jerome is the practice of meditation:

> What is the meaning of the words "she meditated"? It has to mean: she kept it in her heart, she made herself consider it. Someone explains it this way: she meditated in her own heart because she was holy and had read the Sacred Scriptures.[27]

Jerome had such a lofty concept of Mary's purity and holiness that he attributed to her a title that she merited based on the gift of the divine motherhood:

> Take as your example blessed Mary, whose purity was so great that she merited to be the Mother of the Lord.[28]

Thus Jerome proposes Mary as a model whom all Christians ought to imitate, especially those who lead a virginal life. Christians who

---

[25] *Epist.* 22, 19; PL 22, 406.
[26] *Homilia de nativitate Domini*, PLS II, 189.
[27] *Ibid.*, 191.
[28] *Epist.* 22, 38; PL 22, 422.

strive to imitate the example of the holy Virgin also become mothers of the Lord.

READING

WHY MARY CONCEIVED WHEN SHE WAS ALREADY ENGAGED

If anyone is confused by the fact that the Virgin conceived when she was an engaged woman, and not as a maiden who had no fiancé and was not married, as the Scripture says, let him know that there are three reasons for this. First, through the genealogy of Joseph, to whom Mary was related [by marriage], her ancestry is also revealed. The second reason was so that she would not be stoned by the people as an adulteress, according to the law of Moses. The third reason is so that, during the flight to Egypt, she would have the comfort of a guardian rather than a husband.

In that circumstance, indeed, who would ever have believed the Virgin if she had said that she conceived by the power of the Spirit and that the angel Gabriel had come to communicate God's will to her? Instead, everyone would have condemned her as an adulteress, as they did with Susanna, just as today, when the whole world believes, the Jews still claim that in the prophecy of Isaiah, "Behold, a virgin shall conceive and bear a son" (Is 7:14), the Hebrew text has the word "young woman" instead of "virgin", that is, 'almāh instead of bethûlāh. But against them we will speak more effectively elsewhere.

Finally, with the exception of Joseph, Elizabeth, Mary herself, and a few others who heard from them how things stood, everyone thought that Jesus was the son of Joseph, so that even the evangelists, wishing to express the opinion of the people (which is the purpose of true history), called Joseph the Savior's father, as in the following passages: "Inspired by the Spirit, [Simeon] came to the temple, and when his parents brought the child Jesus to fulfill the law" (Lk 2:27). And elsewhere: "His father and his mother were amazed at what was being said about him" (Lk 2:33). And again: "His parents went every year to Jerusalem for the Passover festival" (Lk 2:41). Again: "When the days of the festival were over, they began their journey home, while the boy Jesus remained in Jerusalem without his parents noticing" (Lk 2:43). Listen to what Mary herself says about Joseph, she who had answered Gabriel by saying "How will this happen to me since I do not know man?" (Lk 1:34): "Son, why have you done this to us? Behold, your father and I have been looking for you anxiously" (Lk 2:48).

These pronouncements are not made in the style of the Jews; not, that is, of a people who are joking, as many would argue. The evangelists call Joseph his father; Mary also calls him father. Not because, as I have said above, Joseph was the true father of the Savior, but because everyone believed him to be his father, in order to safeguard Mary's good reputation.

—Jerome, *De virginitate perpetua beatae Mariae*
adversus Helvidium 4;
PL 23, 187–88

13

AUGUSTINE OF HIPPO
(d. 430)

St. Augustine, Bishop of Hippo, was not only a true giant of Western theology; he was undoubtedly one of the greatest geniuses of all time. He had a remarkable understanding of the human condition and perceived man's irrepressible yearning for the Infinite. His efforts in the christological controversies, his keen understanding of the Church, his untiring zeal for the care of souls, and, not least, his singular conversion experience are among the factors that markedly influenced his Marian doctrine. His teaching appears very open to the problems of his time, which he experienced and pondered with all the understanding and passion of his rich and complex personality.

Aurelius Augustine was born in Tagaste, in northern Africa, on November 13, 354. Even though he was given a Christian upbringing by his mother, St. Monica, his youth and young adulthood were characterized by moral disorder and a total lack of interest in questions of religion, according to his own account in his *Confessions*. But reading Cicero's *Hortensius* provoked a salutary crisis of conscience, which led to a complete reexamination of his existence, its meaning, content, and purpose.

The fruit of this laborious internal process was a radical conversion of his life to Christ. It was the year 386; he was then living in Milan. After being baptized by St. Ambrose, he decided to give up both the teaching profession and marriage, in order to consecrate himself entirely to the Lord's service.

While he and his mother, Monica, were at Ostia, preparing to set sail for Tagaste, she suddenly took ill and died before they could begin their voyage. Augustine returned alone to Africa, where, with some friends, he began to lead an ascetical life, following the monastic model. He continued to lead this life even after being ordained a priest. Around 396, he was consecrated coadjutor bishop of Hippo, and the following year he assumed the pastoral leadership of the diocese. He dedicated himself zealously and without rest to the spiritual care of the faithful; his pastoral efforts embraced a wide range of activities. As a result, not only his own Christian community but the universal Church as well benefited from his prodigious activity as a preacher of God's word, as a writer, thinker, and theologian. And not only that: he was also a pastor, concerned with all the portions of the Lord's flock entrusted to him. As a result, he became a legislator and organizer of the monastic life and defended the purity of the faith against the attacks of the heretics. He died in Hippo on August 28, 430, while the city was caught in the grip of the Vandals' siege.

A Mariology for the Future

The extraordinary genius of the bishop of Hippo is also evident in his reflections on the mystery of the Lord's Mother. He continued the tradition of Marian theology, which had already reached considerable heights in other Fathers before and contemporary with him, while also leaving the impress of his own understanding, influenced by the originality of his great conversion experience. His intuitions and perspectives on Marian doctrine are singularly profound and anticipate the statements of the Second Vatican Council.[1] Suffice it to say that Augustine is the Father of the Church most often cited by the Council and that citations of or references to his works and teaching are to be found in almost all of the conciliar documents.

In his Marian doctrine, which anticipates the perspectives of Vatican II by centuries, Augustine examines the Blessed Virgin in relation to the mystery of her Son and to the Church; this allows him to give the proper place to her person and mission within salvation history.[2]

---

[1] Cf. A. Eramo, *Mariologia del Vaticano II vista in S. Agostino* (Rome, 1973).

[2] The Marian texts of Augustine have been collected more or less in their entirety. Among them: Michele Pellegrino, *S. Agostino: La Vergine Maria*, 2d ed. (Milan: Alba, 1987); D. Casagrande, *Enchiridion Marianum Biblicum Patristicum* (Rome, 1974), pp. 562–635; Sergio Alvarez Campos, *Corpus Marianum Patristicum,* vol. 3 (Burgos, 1974), pp. 266–437; Georges Gharib, Ermanno Toniolo, Luigi

Mary and the Predestination of Christ

A first objective that may be pursued when examining the Marian doctrine of the bishop of Hippo is the attempt to understand whether his statements about the Virgin can be connected to some of his central ideas, in order to discover their intrinsic coherence and common motivation. It seems to me that this central theme might be Augustine's doctrine of predestination. Although it has given rise to controversy throughout the history of theology, this theme remains indispensable for understanding his thought.

Augustine considers himself bound to develop a deeper under-standing of the question, in order to defend the dogma of the abso-lute gratuity of divine grace, in opposition to the Pelagian heresy. He concludes that this gratuity is such an essential reality that the incar-nate Word himself, as man, is subject to divine predestination:

> I repeat: there is no more outstanding example of predestination than the Mediator himself. The faithful Christian who wishes to under-stand this well should pay attention to this example, for in it he will find himself.[3]

Immediately after the example of Christ comes the example of his Mother. For the Lord, in his absolute and inscrutable will, chose a Mother from whom to be born as man. She is the second in a series of events that he arranged for the realization of his plan of salvation:

> Then [at the foot of the Cross] he recognized her; yet, he had always known her. Even before he was born of her, he knew his Mother in

---

Gambero, G. Di Nola, *Testi mariani del primo millennio*, vol. 3 (Rome, 1990), pp. 306–77. Considering the interminable bibliography, we limit ourselves to citing some works that seem most useful for our attempt at synthesis: P. Friedrich, *Die Mariologie des hl. Augustinus* (Cologne, 1907) (the first systematic investigation); F. Dominguez, *Ideología mariana de San Agustín* (Bogota, 1946); Victorino Capanaga, *La Virgen María según San Agustín* (Rome, 1956); J. Moran, "La mariología de San Augustín a través de la bibliografía", *Revista Española de Teología* 3 (1963): 333–66; C. Sorsoli, "Vergine e Madre: La Madonna nel pensiero di S. Agostino", in *Maria mistero di grazia*, ed. E. Ancilli (Rome, 1974), pp. 67–87; Luigi Gambero, "La Vergine Maria nella dottrina di Sant'Agostino", *Marianum* 48 (1986): 557–99.

[3] *De dono perseverantiae* 24, 67; PL 45, 1033.

her predestination. Before he, as God, created her from whom he would be created as man, he knew his Mother.[4]

The Virgin's future destiny depends on this supreme divine act, in which God knows and chooses her. He writes elsewhere:

> And so he created a Virgin, whom he had chosen to be his Mother: a woman who did not conceive according to the law of sinful flesh; that is, not by the instinct of fleshly concupiscence. Rather she, with pious faith, merited to receive the holy seed within her. He chose her, to be created from her.[5]

The choice of Mary was not determined by any factor on a human level. The Lord created and chose her according to his unsearchable designs:

> Therefore, God sent his Son in the likeness of sinful flesh. Thence he came, but he did not come thus. For the Virgin conceived him, not by desire, but by faith. He came into the Virgin, who existed before the Virgin. He chose the Mother he had created; he created the Mother he had chosen.[6]

Augustine thinks that God's initial choice of the Virgin was not determined by any foreseen merit of hers. Mary, then, is a pure grace of the Lord, given to the incarnate Word and to all humanity.

Virgin Mother of the Incarnate God

It was to carry out this function that Mary was chosen by God. Her two prerogatives (to be both mother and virgin) define her personal relationship with the incarnate Word and with the Church, by expressing the nature of her mission within salvation history.

Augustine holds that Mary's role as Mother in the event of the Incarnation must be considered an indispensable condition for safeguarding the true faith. To the heretics who denied Mary's motherhood, supporting their claim with the fact that Jesus called her "woman" (cf. Jn 2:4), he opposes the words of the same evangelist,

---

[4] *In Joannem*, tr. 8, 9; PL 35, 1455; *Nuova Biblioteca Agostiniana* (NBA) 24, 202.
[5] *De peccatorum meritis et remissione* 2, 24, 38; PL 44, 175; NBA 17/1, 176.
[6] *Sermo* 69, 3, 4; PL 38, 442; NBA 30/1, 386.

who called Mary the Mother of Jesus, not once, but twice in the very same passage (cf. Jn 2:1, 3):

> Nevertheless, if we ask them, "How do you know that Christ said, 'Woman, what have you to do with me?'" they respond that they believe the Gospel. Why do they not believe the Gospel when it says, "The Mother of Jesus was there" and "He said to his Mother"?
>
> If the Gospel is lying about this, why believe it when it states that Jesus said, "Woman, what have you to do with me?" Why do these wretches not sincerely believe that the Lord responded in this way, not to a stranger, but to his Mother, and why do they not piously try to find out why he answered in this way?[7]

It is necessary, then, to put one's faith in the word of God; otherwise, it is impossible to be Christians or to obtain salvation. Hence Augustine writes:

> We believe that Christ was born of the Virgin Mary because it is written thus in the Gospel; we believe that he was crucified and died, because it is written thus in the Gospel; and we believe that he was truly born and truly died because the Gospel is the truth. Just why he willed to subject himself to all the weaknesses of the flesh he assumed in the womb of a woman is a hidden design, known to him alone.[8]

The bishop of Hippo has no doubts about the divine character of Mary's motherhood; he sees in the virginity of the Lord's Mother a miraculous sign of the divinity of the Child she bore. In one of his Christmas homilies he says:

> It was not the visible sun that made this day holy for us, but the sun's invisible Creator, when the Virgin Mother brought to light, out of her fruitful womb and virginal body, the Creator made visible for us, the same invisible God who had also created the Virgin. Virgin in conceiving, virgin in giving birth, virgin with child, virgin mother, virgin forever. Why do you marvel at this, O man? God had to be born in this way, when he deigned to become man. Thus did he make her, who was made by her.[9]

---

[7] *In Joannem*, tr. 8, 7; PL 35, 1454; NBA 24, 1554.

[8] *Contra Faustum* 26, 7; PL 42, 483; CSEL 25, 736.

[9] *Sermo* 186, 1; PL 38, 999; NBA 32/1, 12.

According to Augustine, the divine plan, which required Mary to collaborate as a virgin, did not exclude a free choice on her part:

> Thus Christ, in being born of a Virgin who, before knowing to whom she was to give birth, had made up her mind to remain a virgin, preferred to show his approval of holy virginity rather than to impose it on her. Even so, in the woman within whom he took the form of a slave, he wanted her virginity to be freely chosen.[10]

According to this text, Mary had intentionally offered her virginity to God in a kind of vow even before the Annunciation; this vow arose spontaneously from her own will, without any imposition or coercion. This act, then, would have been prompted by her feelings toward the Lord, before he made known his plans to her. By insisting on the free character of virginity consecrated to God, Augustine accentuates its spiritual component, which gives value to the physical aspect as well.

In the West, Augustine appears to be the first Father of the Church to have expressed the conviction that Mary made a vow of virginity. We know that, in the East, Gregory of Nyssa thought the same way.[11]

According to Augustine, the proof of this vow may be deduced from Mary's own words in response to Gabriel. Indeed he is convinced that, if Mary had intended to lead a normal conjugal life, she would not have been amazed by the angel's words:

> Because she had made a vow of virginity and her husband did not have to be the thief of her modesty instead of its guardian (and yet her husband was not its guardian, since it was God who guarded it; her husband was only the witness of her virginal chastity, so that her pregnancy would not be considered the result of adultery), when the angel brought her the news, she said: "How can this be, since I do not know man?" (Lk 1:34). Had she intended to know man, she would not have been amazed. Her amazement is a sign of the vow.[12]

---

[10] *De sancta virginitate* 2, 4; PL 40, 398; CSEL 41, 238.

[11] *Oratio in diem natalem Christi*, PG 46, 1140. The authenticity of this homily, however, remains open to question, even if there is a strong presumption in its favor.

[12] *Sermo* 225, 2; PL 38, 1096–97; NBA 32/1, 378. Cf. *Sermo* 291, 5; PL 38, 1318.

Mary and the Church[13]

Even though our doctor recognizes the holy Virgin's sublime dignity and her unique, privileged mission in the divine economy, he does not hesitate to consider her a part or member of the Church. He states categorically that Mary's place is within the Church, with which she is profoundly and indissolubly linked. In a certain sense, the Church is absolutely greater than Mary:

> Mary is holy, Mary is blessed, but the Church is better than the Virgin Mary. Why? Because Mary is part of the Church, a holy member, an outstanding member, a supereminent[14] member, but a member of the whole body nonetheless. If she is a member of the whole body, the body is undoubtedly greater than one of its members.[15]

Taking St. Paul's theology of the Mystical Body as his point of departure, Augustine is convinced that no Christian can be outside of the body of Christ,[16] the Church of which Christ is the Head. Mary cannot be an exception to this rule. She is the Mother of the Head on the level of the flesh, but in the order of salvation she belongs to the whole Christ, as a member, because she, too, has been saved by Christ. Moreover, he attributes to the Lord's Mother a

---

[13] On this specific theme there is an abundant bibliography, of which we give a selection of titles: T. Janez Barrio, "María y la Iglesia según el pensamiento agustiniano", *Revista Agustiniana de Espiritualidad* 4 (1962): 22–46; I. M. Dietz, "Maria und die Kirche nach dem hl. Augustinus", in *Maria et Ecclesia*, vol. 3 (Rome, 1959), pp. 201–39; S. Folgado Flores, "María virgen y madre de Cristo, tipo de la Iglesia según San Agustín", in *Scripta Mariana* 3 (1980): 87–121; idem, "El binomio María–Iglesia en la tradición patrística del siglo IV–V (S. Ambrosio–S. Agustín)", in *Maria e la Chiesa oggi*, Atti del 5° Simposio Mariologico Internazionale (Rome 1985), pp. 91–142; J. Huhn, "Maria est typus Ecclesiae secundum Patres, imprimis secundum S. Ambrosium et S. Augustinum", in *Maria et Ecclesia*, vol. 3 (Rome 1959), pp. 163–99; E. Lamirande, "Marie, l'Église et la maternité dans un nouveau sermon de saint Augustin", *Ephemerides Mariologicae* 28 (1978): 253–63.

[14] The expression *supereminens membrum* was introduced, without reference to Augustine, in *Lumen gentium*, no. 53.

[15] *Sermo Denis* 25, 7; *Miscellanea Agostiniana*, 163.

[16] Cf. S. J. Grabowski, *The Church: An Introduction to the Theology of St. Augustine* (St. Louis, Mo., 1957).

certain maternal relationship with regard to all the other members of the Mystical Body:

> Therefore this woman alone, not only in spirit, but also in body, is both Mother and Virgin. She is Mother in the Spirit, but not of our Head, the Savior himself, for it is she who was spiritually born from him, since all who believe in him, among whom she too is to be counted, are rightly called children of the Bridegroom. Rather, she is clearly the Mother of his members; that is, of ourselves, because she cooperated by her charity, so that faithful Christians, members of the Head, might be born in the Church. As for the body, she is the Mother of its Head.[17]

This text also confirms how Augustine preferred to conceive of Mary's spiritual motherhood as applying to the faithful as individual members of the Church, rather than toward the unity of the Mystical Body. This spiritual relationship is based on Mary's physical motherhood of Christ, the Head of the Church.

Mary's motherhood and the motherhood of the Church toward the faithful are two realities that, in Augustine's thought, are often mixed together or identified outright, as in the following text:

> How is it that you do not belong to the Virgin's birth, if you are members of Christ? Mary gave birth to our Head; the Church gave birth to you. Indeed, the Church also is both virgin and mother, mother because of her womb of charity, virgin because of the integrity of her faith and piety.[18]

Taking up Ambrose's line of thought, Augustine sees Mary as the type or model of the Church. Actually, he applies the term *typus* to the Church only once:

> Nevertheless it is true, the Church is the mother of Christ. Mary preceded the Church as its type.[19]

But the concept recurs frequently in his writings, and, in general, we can assert that it assumes important dimensions in his reflection

---

[17] *De sancta virginitate* 6; PL 40, 399; CSEL 41, 240.
[18] *Sermo* 192, 2; PL 38, 1012–13; NBA 32/1, 52.
[19] *Sermo Denis* 25, 8; *Miscellanea Agostiniana*, 164.

and brings the already happy intuitions of St. Ambrose to a significant level of development.

Usually, the terms of the comparison between Mary and the Church are virginity and motherhood:

> How much do the members of the Church deserve honor, they who guard even in their flesh the prerogative that she collectively guards in faith, by imitating the Mother of her Spouse and Lord! For the Church also is at once virgin and mother. Whose virginity do we look to if the Church is not a virgin? Whose children do we speak to if she is not a mother?
>
> Mary gave birth bodily to the Head of this body; the Church gives birth spiritually to the members of the Head. In both, virginity is no impediment to fruitfulness; in both, fruitfulness does not take away virginity.[20]

As for motherhood, the analogy remains but on a different level, because Mary is the physical Mother of the Redeemer, while the Church is the spiritual Mother of the redeemed. The situation is different with regard to virginity. Both, in addition to being obviously virgins in spirit, are also virgins in the flesh, because the Church possesses members who are virgins in body, although not all her members are virgins. As in Mary, so virginity is fruitful in the Church as well:

> Perhaps you will say to me: If she is a virgin, how can she bear children? Or, if she does not bear children, why have we given her our names, in order to be reborn from her womb?[21]
>
> I answer: She is a virgin, *and* she bears children. Imitate Mary, who gave birth to the Lord. Did not holy Virgin Mary both give birth as a virgin and remain a virgin? So also the Church: she gives birth, *and* she is a virgin. And, if you think about it, she gives birth to Christ, because those who are baptized are his members. The apostle says: "You are the body of Christ and his members" (1 Cor 12:27). If the Church, then, gives birth to the members of Christ, then the Church greatly resembles Mary.[22]

---

[20] *De sancta virginitate* 2; PL 40, 397; CSEL 41, 236.

[21] A reference to those enrolling as catechumens.

[22] *Sermo Guelferbytanus* 1, 8; *Miscellanea Agostiniana*, 447–448.

Augustine praises the free and informed *fiat* by which Mary became Mother of the incarnate Word and offered her moral cooperation in the work of salvation; he explains that all the faithful can share the spiritual motherhood of the Church by giving themselves over to the will of God. In this sense, even consecrated virgins can exercise a very fruitful motherhood:

> Holy virgins ought not to be disappointed that, keeping their virginity, they cannot become mothers in the physical sense. The only case in which it was fitting for a virgin to give birth was the case of him who, in his birth, can have no equal. Further, the birth from that one holy Virgin is a glory shared by all holy virgins; together with Mary, they are mothers of Christ, as long as they do the will of his Father. . . .
>
> Moreover, every faithful soul is a mother of Christ, and by doing the will of his Father through charity, which is a most fruitful virtue, every faithful soul transmits life to all those imprinted with the image of Christ. As for Mary, she fulfilled the Father's will; in this way, while physically she was only the Mother of Christ, spiritually she was both sister and Mother to him.[23]

Mary, Holiest of Creatures

Augustine placed the question of the holiness of the Mother of the Lord within the context of the mystery of salvation. We have already had a glimpse of this in considering the mystery of her predestination, from which it arises that God created her according to his hidden design in such a way as to make her worthy to be the Virgin Mother of his only begotten Son. In other words, he granted her certain extraordinary gifts that made her altogether exceptional.

There is, first of all, a negative aspect to Mary's personal holiness, which could be summarized thus: given her exalted vocation to be the Mother of the divine Messiah, Mary was preserved by God from every stain of sin.

Augustine holds this position in opposition to the Pelagians. They taught the same thing but gave a different explanation. Man is

---

[23] *De sancta virginitate* 5; PL 40, 399; CSEL 41, 239.

capable of living without committing sin, by the power of his will alone, and, according to them, Mary is an eloquent example of this principle.

To the contrary, Augustine, following in the footsteps of Ambrose, affirms that the holy Virgin was certainly without sin or imperfection, not, however, as a consequence of her personal effort alone, but thanks to a special grace from God. In support of this, we have a famous text from his *De natura et gratia*:

> With the exception of the holy Virgin Mary, in whose case, out of respect for the Lord, I do not wish there to be any further question as far as sin is concerned, since how can we know what great abundance of grace was conferred on her to conquer sin in every way, seeing that she merited to conceive and bear him who certainly had no sin at all?[24]

There seems no doubt that Augustine considered Mary's exemption from sin to be a great grace. But what sins does he mean? Undoubtedly he excludes any personal sin from Mary. Is it possible to hypothesize that Augustine also intended to exclude original sin? Some scholars think so and make him a forerunner of the doctrine of the Immaculate Conception. A full treatment of the question would call for a lengthy discussion. To us it seems safer to adopt the contrary position, which is held by many experts and appears more in accord with numerous Augustinian texts.[25]

---

[24] *De natura et gratia* 36, 42; PL 44, 267; CSEL 60, 263.

[25] There is an abundant bibliography on this problem. Studies include: F. S. Mueller, "Augustinus amicus an adversarius Immaculatae Conceptionis?" in *Miscellanea Agostiniana*, vol. 2 (Rome, 1931), pp. 885–914; F. Hofmann, "Die Stellung des hl. Augustinus zur Lehre von der unbefleckten Empfängnis Mariens", *Theologische Quartalschrift* 113 (1932): 299–319; J. Goetz, "Augustin und die Immaculata Conceptio", *Theologie und Glaube* 25 (1933): 739–44; B. Capelle, "La Pensée de saint Augustin sur l'Immaculée Conception", *Recherches de théologie ancienne et médiévale* 4 (1932): 361–70; I. M. Dietz, "Ist die hl. Jungfrau nach Augustinus Immaculata ab initio?" *Virgo Immaculata*, vol. 4 (Rome 1955), pp. 61–112; D. Fernandez, "El pensamiento de San Augustín sobre la Immaculada", *Analecta Baetica* (1954), pp. 13–63; C. Boyer, "La Controverse sur l'opinion de Saint Augustin touchant la conception de la Vierge", *Virgo Immaculata*, vol. 4 (Rome 1955), pp. 48–60; P. Frua, *L'Immacolata Concezione e S. Agostino* (Saluzzo, 1960); I. Falgueras Salinas, "La Contribución de San Augustín al dogma de la Immaculada Concepción de María", *Scripta theologica* 4 (1972): 355–433.

The bishop of Hippo does not limit himself to defining holiness in a negative sense. Following in the footsteps of his master, Ambrose, he attributes an extraordinary positive holiness to the Virgin, in virtue of which she can be proposed to the Christian people as an incomparable model of interior dispositions and practical life.

The holy Virgin is presented as a woman of great faith, who manifested all the power of this virtue at the moment of the Annunciation. To show Mary's faith in greater relief, Augustine contrasts it with the unbelief of Zechariah:

> Because Mary says: "How will this happen, since I do not know man?" (Lk 1:34), calumniators might accuse her of having little faith. But she is inquiring about the "how" and does not doubt the power of God. . . .
>
> Zechariah, on the other hand, who spoke more or less in the same way, is reproved as an unbeliever and punished by the loss of his voice. Why? Was it not because God does not judge according to the words we speak but according to what is in our hearts?[26]

Authentic faith necessarily includes obedience to God; these two virtues form the basic attitude of the true disciple of Christ. Referring to Matthew 12:46–50, our author considers that it was more important for Mary to be a disciple of Christ than to be his Mother. The blessedness of faith is superior to the blessedness of motherhood.[27]

Mary's faith has its origin in charity, which acts as a force that annuls concupiscence and replaces it with action in the mystery of the generation of the incarnate Word.[28] The Virgin shows her charity in our regard as well by her collaboration in our spiritual rebirth in the Church.[29]

Another personal virtue of Mary's emphasized by Augustine is her humility or holy modesty, which he sees manifested in the finding of Jesus in the Temple.[30]

---

[26] *Quaestiones in Heptateuchum* 4, 19; PL 34, 726; CSEL 28, 2, 329–30.

[27] *De sancta virginitate* 3; PL 40, 398; NBA 7/1, 76.

[28] *Sermo* 214, 6; PL 38, 1069; NBA 32/1, 226.

[29] *De sancta virginitate* 5; PL 40, 398; NBA 7/1, 80; cf. ibid., 6, 399; 80; *Sermo* 192, 2; PL 38, 1012–13; NBA 32/1, 52.

[30] *Sermo* 51, 18; PL 38, 343; NBA 30/1, 28.

All these virtues are expressed, above all, in the devotion and faithfulness with which the Virgin hears the word of God and puts it into practice.[31]

Because of the great holiness of the Mother of the Lord, Augustine urges consecrated virgins to look to her as their model par excellence. Without her, the virginal life would never have existed in the Church.[32] But the holy Virgin is also proposed by Augustine as a model of life for married women, because she was a most upright and loving wife to St. Joseph.[33]

READINGS

THE VIRGINAL BIRTH OF CHRIST IS A TRUTH OF THE FAITH

It is on the basis of this notion that we structure our thought, that we believe that God became man for us, to give us an example of humility and a proof of God's love for us. Yes, it is good for us to believe and hold with a firm and unshakeable heart that the humility with which God was born of a woman, and let himself be led off to die, amidst so many outrages, at the hands of mortal men, is the supreme medicine for healing our swollen pride and the sublime sacrament for loosing the bonds of sin.

Likewise, we should speak of the power of his miracles, especially his Resurrection. Knowing what omnipotence is, we believe in an omnipotent God and, based on knowledge either innate or acquired through our experience of appearances and forms, we make a judgment about facts of this sort, lest our faith be a fabrication.

In fact, we do not know what the face of the Virgin Mary looked like, she who was unstained and untouched, even in giving birth, by any contact with man, she from whom he was born in a wonderful way. Nor do we know the appearance of Lazarus' body, nor that of

---

[31] *De sancta virginitate* 5; PL 40, 399; NBA 7/1, 78–80; *In Joannem*, tr. 10, 3; PL 35, 1468; NBA 24, 236.

[32] *Sermo* 51, 26; PL 38, 348; NBA 30/1, 42.

[33] *Contra Faustum* 23, 8; PL 42, 470; CSEL 25, 713.

Bethany, nor the tomb, nor the stone that the Lord commanded them to roll away when he raised Lazarus, nor the new tomb, hewn out of rock, whence he rose, nor the Mount of Olives whence he ascended into heaven. We, who have never seen these things, do not know at all whether they really are as we imagine them; yet we consider it more probable that they are not as we imagine them.

For if the appearance of a face or a place or a man or any body whatever be presented to our eyes just as it appeared in our mind when we imagined it before having seen it, we are more than a little surprised, so rarely, if ever, does this happen. Nevertheless, we believe these things firmly, because we present them to ourselves according to a specific or general idea that seems sure to us.

We believe that the Lord Jesus Christ was born of a Virgin named Mary. But what is a virgin, what does it mean to be born, and what is a proper name—these things we do not believe; rather, we know them. Whether Mary's face was just as we imagine it when we speak of these things or recall them, we neither know nor believe. Therefore it is licit to say, without endangering the faith, "Perhaps she had a face like this, perhaps it was different." But no one could say, "Perhaps Christ was born of a virgin" without endangering the Christian faith.

—Augustine, *De Trinitate* 8, 5, 7; PL 42, 952;
CCL 50, 276–77

THE DIGNITY OF BOTH SEXES IS EMPHASIZED BY THE INCARNATION

To fulfill this plan, our Lord Jesus Christ became the Son of man, precisely by being born of a woman. If, instead, he had not been born of the Virgin Mary, what would have been lost? "He wanted to be man", someone will say. I agree, but he could have been a man without being born of a woman, since when he created the first man he did not need a woman.

Observe how to answer this objection. You ask, "Why did he choose a woman from whom to be born?" The answer comes, "To the contrary, why did he have to avoid a woman? Suppose I could not show you why he decided to be born of a woman; show me what he would have to avoid in a woman." But it has already been stated that, if he had shunned the womb of a woman, it would have indicated the possibility of being contaminated by her somehow. On the other hand, the more he was invulnerable by his nature to any contamination, the less he should have feared a womb of flesh, as if he could have been stained by it.

Instead, by being born of a woman, he had to show us a great mystery. In truth, brothers, we too admit that, if the Lord had wanted to become man without being born of a woman, it surely would have been easy for his majesty. For just as he was able to be born of a woman without the cooperation of a man, even so he could have been born without the cooperation of a woman. Instead, he wanted to show us something: namely, that the human creature, no matter whether male or female, did not have to lose the hope of being saved.

Now, human gender is either male or female. And if, in becoming a man, he had not been born of a woman, exactly as it had to happen, women would have lost the hope of being saved, recalling their first sin, when the first man was ensnared by the woman, and they would have believed themselves to be absolutely without hope in Christ. Christ, then, came into the world as a man, choosing the male sex on purpose, but, being born of a woman, he came to console the feminine sex, as if, addressing himself to them, he had said: "So that you may know that none of God's creatures is wicked, but rather have been perverted by a guilty pleasure, when, in the beginning, he made man, he made them male and female: I do not condemn the creatures I myself have fashioned. Behold, I am born a man; I am born of a woman. Thus I do not condemn the creatures I have made but their sins, which I did not make."

Both the sexes should recognize their own dignity, and both should confess their sins and hope to be saved. Through woman, poison was poured upon man, in order to deceive him, but salvation was poured out upon man from a woman, that he might be reborn in grace. The woman, having become Mother of Christ, will repair the sin she committed in deceiving the man.

—Augustine, *Sermo* 51, 3; PL 38, 334–35;
NBA 30/1, 7–9

PART THREE

*From the Council of Ephesus
to the Fifth Century*

Prologue

The death of Augustine occurred on the eve of an ecclesial event of immense importance for the subsequent development of Marian doctrine and devotion. This was the third ecumenical council, which was held at Ephesus in 431. Augustine had been invited to take part, undoubtedly out of respect for his prestigious reputation and for his doctrine, which had a great influence throughout the Christian West and was probably starting to win agreement in the East as well. But death took him first.

The Council of Ephesus was a typically oriental phenomenon; it met in a time of christological controversy that impassioned and divided the various Churches of Eastern Christianity. Behind the men who steered the unfolding of the Council, we once more discover opposing schools of thought, namely, the Alexandrian versus the Antiochene school. These opposing schools were engaged in a struggle rendered even more difficult by mutual misunderstandings and the ambiguous theological vocabulary of the time.

Both parties were pursuing legitimate objectives. The school of Alexandria stressed the unity of the subject Christ; the Antiochenes emphasized the differences between divinity and humanity. It was not clear how these two positions could be reconciled.

As for the West, that sector of Christianity remained on the fringe of the controversy, partly because it was stunned by the historical disaster of the barbarian invasions, but also because the Westerners were concerned with different theological problems.[1]

The Council was convened in the ancient city of Ephesus, in Asia Minor. Even before it became the site of such an important event as an ecumenical council, Ephesus was already quite famous in the

---

[1] Twenty years after Ephesus, Pope Leo the Great would recognize its universal importance in a letter to the Council of Chalcedon: "What the First Council of Ephesus established against Nestorius should still remain in force (Bishop Cyril, of happy memory, presided over that council)" (*Epist.* 93; PL 54, 939; ACO 2, 4, 52).

Greco-Roman world. Since the fourth century B.C., there had been a temple at Ephesus dedicated to a female deity who was originally known as "Great Mother"; later she was identified with the Greek goddess Artemis, the Roman Diana. This temple was considered one of the seven wonders of the world, and the statue venerated there was believed to have come down from heaven.

During the Christian era, the apostle Paul met a group of disciples of John the Baptist (cf. Acts 18:19–21) and a community of Jewish Christians (cf. 1 Cor 1:12) at Ephesus. When he came to Ephesus during his third missionary voyage, however, he was involved in a riot caused by the Ephesians' devotion to the statue of their goddess (cf. Acts 19).

According to an ancient tradition, attested to by St. Irenaeus of Lyons, it was in Ephesus that the apostle John wrote his Gospel and faced martyrdom, around the end of the first century or the beginning of the second.[2] There is another tradition that adds to the preceding one; it reports that the Mother of the Lord lived at Ephesus together with John. This tradition, which is not confirmed historically, appears to be connected with the fact that the basilica in Ephesus where the Council met was dedicated to Mary. Although the Council met in this historic city, the problems that led to it began elsewhere.

The Homily of Proclus of Constantinople

At Constantinople, the capital of the Roman Empire, a specific episode took place between 428 and 429 that led to unforeseeable consequences. During a liturgical celebration in the cathedral, in the presence of the patriarch, Nestorius, a famous orator named Proclus (who, in 434, would be called to succeed Nestorius as patriarch) preached a homily in honor of the Blessed Virgin in which he called her *Theotókos*, a Greek word meaning "Mother of God". Proclus began his exposition in praise of the Virgin with a panegyric, all interwoven with biblical images, in which the word *Theotókos* suddenly

---

[2] *Haer.* 3, 3, 4; PG 7, 855. Cf. Eusebius of Caesarea, *Storia Ecclesiastica* 3, 23, 4; PG 20, 255.

appeared. We give here the text, which, among other things, gives us a taste of fifth-century Marian homiletics:

> The reason we have gathered here today is the holy *Theotókos* Virgin Mary, immaculate treasure of virginity, spiritual paradise of the second Adam, workshop of the union of [Christ's two] natures, marketplace of the saving exchange, bridal chamber in which the Word was wedded to the flesh, living bush that was not burned by the fire of the divine birth, the true light cloud that bore the One who, in his body, stands above the cherubim, fleece moistened by celestial dew, with which the Shepherd clothes his sheep.[3]

Proclus ended the homily with an inspired profession of faith in the mystery of the incarnate Word and, after citing the prophet Ezekiel (44:1–2), declared, "Behold, holy Mary is openly proclaimed as *Theotókos*."[4]

No one had to wait for the patriarch Nestorius to react. He had been brought up in the school of Antioch, which put such an emphasis on the human nature of Jesus that it almost became a reality separated from divinity, as if a human person existed alongside a divine Person. In this christological context, Mary's relationship with her Son was also lowered in status. Since, obviously, she had given birth only to the human nature of the incarnate Word, she could not be called *Theotókos*. Nestorius held that Mary's proper title was *Christotókos*, Christ-bearer.

In this debate, the Person most directly affected was the Word incarnate. Nestorius did not admit the validity of the principle of the *communicatio idiomatum*. On the basis of this principle, because of the union of the two natures in the single Person of Christ, whatever one predicates of one nature can also be said about the other. Thus Mary, even though she gave birth only to the human nature of the incarnate Word, can be called *Theotókos*, inasmuch as the relationships of motherhood and sonship are understood to apply to persons, not to natures.

And so Nestorius firmly rejected the term *Theotókos*, which had been used by other Fathers before Proclus; he considered it

---

[3] *Oratio* 1, 1; PG 65, 681 A–B.
[4] Ibid., 10; PG 65, 692 B.

erroneous and contrary to the faith because it endangered the purity of the doctrine of the Incarnation.

Nestorius' attitude awoke a chorus of protest, not only within his diocese, but in other parts of the Christian world as well. The foremost interpreter of these protests was Cyril, patriarch of Alexandria. In writings addressed to the faithful of his Church, as well as in correspondence with Nestorius, he undertook a lively refutation of Nestorius' position. In doing so, he inaugurated a debate in which the patriarch of Constantinople gave no sign of retreat, and the patriarch of Alexandria did not intend to mitigate his accusations. Indeed, Cyril's attacks grew more and more violent, fueled not only by his desire to safeguard right doctrine but also by motives of rivalry between the two authoritative patriarchal sees.

Finally, convinced that he was unable to resolve the controversy with Nestorius directly, Cyril appealed to the authority of the pope, Celestine I. In fact, Nestorius also appealed to Rome, but the pope's reaction to him had been unfavorable from the beginning. In any case, the synod held at Rome in 430 to study the question enjoined Nestorius to retract his teaching. Nestorius then appealed to Emperor Theodosius II, who decided to call an ecumenical council to be held at Ephesus, beginning on Pentecost 431. The pope designated three legates, specifically instructing them to uphold the position of Cyril and to obtain the Council's condemnation of Nestorius.

The Council of Ephesus

Without waiting for all the bishops to arrive, or even for the papal legates, Cyril convened about one hundred fifty bishops in the church of St. Mary and declared the Council open, assuming the presidency himself. It is not clear on what basis Cyril claimed the authority to do this. As a sign of protest, Nestorius and his supporters withdrew from the assembly, so that it was relatively easy for Cyril to bring things to a rapid conclusion.

The Council Fathers received Cyril's first letter to Nestorius with approving applause. In this document, Cyril rejects the errors of the patriarch of Constantinople; he explains the mystery of the Lord's Incarnation and death in conformity with the doctrine of Nicaea and the tradition of the holy Fathers. The document speaks about Mary as follows:

> The holy Fathers do not hesitate to call the holy Virgin *Theotókos*, not in the sense that the divine nature of the Word took its origin from the holy Virgin, but in the sense that he took his holy body, gifted with a rational soul, from her. Yet, because the Word is hypostatically united to this body, one can say that he was truly born according to the flesh.[5]

When, however, Nestorius' letter in response to Cyril was read out in the assembly, there was a unanimous reaction of condemnation. The patriarch of Constantinople was excommunicated and deposed from his see. During the evening of June 22, a great throng of the Ephesian faithful unleashed their enthusiasm, accompanying the bishops to their lodgings with shouts of "Praised be the *Theotókos!*" and "Long live Cyril!"

From a procedural point of view, the condemnation of June 22 tends to arouse suspicion and perplexity, even though no dogmatic formulations were defined; the assembly merely approved Cyril's letter to Nestorius and condemned Nestorius' response. However, notwithstanding the procedural irregularities, the Church never repudiated the Council's conclusions. The Council continued, but it can be said that its important decisions, the validity and authority of which would later be recognized, were made on June 22.

On June 26, John, patriarch of Antioch, arrived in Ephesus, along with the bishops of Syria. Upon being apprised of the situation, they decided to meet in a separate council, in which Nestorius took part along with Candidianus, the imperial legate. The first act of this "anticouncil" was to excommunicate Cyril and the bishops who supported him. This created a paradoxical situation, in which both Nestorius and Cyril were excommunicate. Three days later, an imperial message arrived, in which Theodosius expressed his disappointment at Cyril's hasty and arbitrary procedure and ordered the bishops to leave things as they were and not to make any further decisions before the arrival of his representative.

On July 10, the papal legates arrived and authorized the opening of a second session of the Council, during which a letter from Pope

---

[5] Cyril, *Epist.* 4; PG 77, 48 B.

Celestine was read. In the days following, the decisions made during the first session were confirmed, in particular the excommunication of Nestorius. As a result, John of Antioch and the Syrian bishops refused to take part in the Council and were themselves excommunicated. Finally, in the month of August, the emperor's representative arrived; he announced the deposition of both Nestorius and Cyril and had them arrested. The emperor did not release the Council from his authority until September, when Nestorius withdrew to a monastery and Cyril was free to go back to his own diocese.

From a procedural point of view, one might get the impression that the Council of Ephesus came to a disappointing end. Yet, if we consider it from the perspective of the Church's faith, we need to recognize that clear and precise decisions were made from the beginning. Mary was solemnly declared *Theotókos*, as a consequence of the fact that the two natures of Christ are inseparably united in a single Divine Person. Thus the Council, which had been called to resolve an essentially christological problem, had an important mariological outcome.

Two years later, in April 433, an Edict of Union, also known as the Symbol of Ephesus, returned the Church to a state of peace and harmony. John of Antioch, in the name of the Eastern bishops, accepted the use of the title *Theotókos* for the Blessed Virgin, because the Son of God became incarnate within her. Cyril enthusiastically embraced this profession of faith. Pope Sixtus III, Celestine's successor, was warmly congratulated, along with the two patriarchs, on the happy conclusion of such a complex and distressing controversy.[6]

READING

MARY'S ROLE IN THE MYSTERY OF THE INCARNATION

We do not say that the nature of the Word was transformed into flesh, nor that it was transformed into a man composed of soul and

---

[6] The critical edition of the acts of the Council of Ephesus is by E. Schwartz, *Acta conciliorum oecumenicorum*, vol. 1, bks. 1–5 (Berlin-Leipzig, 1922–1929).

body; we do assert that the Word, being hypostatically united to a body informed by a rational soul, in an ineffable and incomprehensible way, became man and was called "Son of Man", not by his mere will and pleasure, nor by the assumption of a person; and we say that the natures are distinct, though they are joined in a true unity; yet both constitute a single Christ, a single Son; not in the sense that the diversity of the natures was taken away by the union, but in the sense that divinity and humanity, through their indescribable and hidden concourse, constitute a single Lord and Son, Jesus Christ.

Thus it can be affirmed that, even though he subsisted before all ages and was generated by the Father, he was also generated by a woman according to the flesh. But that does not mean that his divine nature took its origin from the holy Virgin or that this nature needed a second birth after his birth from the Father (indeed, it would clearly be unreasonable and foolish to say that he who existed before all ages and who is coeternal with the Father had need of a second generation in order to exist). Rather, it means that, for our sake and for our salvation, he assumed his human nature into the unity of his Person and was born of a woman; this is why it is said that he was born according to the flesh. Therefore, we must not think that the holy Virgin gave birth to some unspecified man, into whom the Word descended later; no, we must believe that there was one single reality from the first moment in his Mother's womb and that he was born according to the flesh, accepting the birth of his own body. . . .

Now then, to say that the Word became flesh is the same thing as saying that he, like us, became a sharer in flesh and blood (cf. Heb 2:14). He took our body for his own and as man was born of a woman, without losing his divinity or his birth from the Father, but remaining what he was, even when he assumed flesh.

This is what the orthodox faith affirms everywhere; this is what we find in the works of the holy Fathers. That is why they do not hesitate to call the holy Virgin *Theotókos*, not in the sense that the divine nature of the Word took its origin from the holy Virgin, but in the sense that he took his holy body, gifted with a rational soul, from her. Yet, because the Word is hypostatically united to this body, one can say that he was truly born according to the flesh.

I am writing these things even now, impelled by the love of Christ, exhorting you as a brother, entreating you in the sight of God and of his chosen angels, to believe and teach these truths together with us, in order to keep peace among the Churches, and so that the bond of concord and love among the priests of God may remain unbreakable.

—Cyril of Alexandria, *Letter II to Nestorius*;
PG 77, 44–49; ACO 1, 1, 1, 25–28

CYRIL OF ALEXANDRIA
(d. 444)

The figure of the patriarch of Alexandria has become so bound up with the history of the Council of Ephesus that it is sometimes difficult to separate the man from the Council. Consequently it is also difficult to disregard certain incidents that seem to present him in an unfavorable light (to say the least), so that he appears factious, scheming, intolerant, and Machiavellian. We may add that other events in his life seem to confirm these impressions, according to what information has survived. For the most part, however, these reports lack historical evidence and derive from currents of opinion traditionally hostile to Cyril.

It can also be admitted that, during the Council of Ephesus, Cyril exhibited some attitudes and conduct that could be criticized. But if his contemporary, Pope St. Celestine I, called him a good defender of the Catholic faith, a man of outstanding apostolic stature, and a most complete pastor, this means that Cyril's personality and behavior were, on the whole, considered positively by the Church. Nor ought we to think that Pope Celestine's observation was inspired solely by the fact that, at Ephesus, Cyril worked and fought along the lines favored by the Church of Rome. In addition, we have already cited Pope Leo the Great's positive confirmation of Celestine's opinion.

Beyond what Cyril accomplished during his thirty-two years of episcopal ministry, we know almost nothing about his life. The date of his birth at Alexandria is likewise unknown. We are told that he accompanied his uncle Theophilus, the patriarch of Alexandria, to the Synod of the Oak. Held near Chalcedon in 403, this synod deposed St. John Chrysostom from the patriarchal see of

Constantinople. Upon the death of Theophilus in 412, Cyril was elected to succeed his uncle as patriarch of Alexandria.

The first fifteen years of his episcopate remain covered, as it were, by a historical veil. When the Nestorian controversy exploded in the years 428–429, Cyril suddenly emerged as a leading player in the Church of the time. His name will forever be associated with the Council of Ephesus and the defense of the true faith against Nestorius and his followers. Cyril died in 444.

We do not need to retrace the events of Ephesus, where, as we have seen, Cyril was the protagonist (for want of a better word). Here we simply want to penetrate a little more deeply into the soul of the patriarch of Alexandria, to understand better his thoughts and feelings about the Mother of God, the *Theotókos*, whom he defended so decidedly and tenaciously against the maneuvering of Nestorius and his supporters.

Passionately Devoted to the Blessed Virgin [1]

One can safely state that Cyril of Alexandria inaugurated the much-beloved Byzantine homiletic technique in which the preacher would teach Marian truths by means of praises addressed to the Blessed Virgin. In some of his homilies, we are struck by extended sequences of praises, in which we can clearly see his unbridled admiration for the *Theotókos*, his devotion and love for her. The famous homily that he preached during the Council of Ephesus is inspired by these feelings (a longer extract from this homily is given

---

[1] The Marian doctrine of St. Cyril has been studied in its entirety by A. Eberle, *Die Mariologie des hl. Kyrillos von Alexandrien* (Freiburg im Breisgau, 1921). On specific topics, other studies may be consulted: Nilus a S. Brocardo, *De maternitate divina beatae Mariae semper Virginis Nestorii Constantinopolitani et Cyrilli Alexandrini sententia* (Rome, 1944); G. Jouassard, "Marie à travers la patristique", in *Maria,* ed. H. du Manoir, vol. 1 (Paris, 1949), pp. 122–36; idem, "L'Interprétation par saint Cyrille d'Alexandrie de la scène de Marie au pied de la croix", in *Virgo immaculata*, vol. 4 (Rome, 1955), pp. 28–47; H. du Manoir, "La scène de Cana commentée par saint Cyrille d'Alexandrie", in *De primordis cultus mariani*, vol. 3 (Rome, 1970), pp. 135–162; G. Vassalli, "Accenni e motivi per il culto mariano in San Cirillo d'Alessandria", *De primordis*, pp. 163–204.

later in this chapter). In order to exalt Mary, Cyril uses expressions that refer directly to the doctrine and life of the Church. Here is a beautiful example:

> Hail, Mary *Theotókos*, Virgin-Mother, lightbearer, uncorrupt vessel. Hail, O Virgin Mary, mother and handmaid; virgin, for the sake of him who was born virginally from you; mother, for the sake of him whom you carried in your arms and nursed with your milk; handmaid, for the sake of him who took the form of a servant. For the king entered into your city; or rather, into your womb, and he came forth from it as he wished, and your gate remained shut. For you conceived without seed and gave birth divinely. . . .
>
> Hail, Mary, you are the most precious creature in the whole world; hail, Mary, uncorrupt dove; hail, Mary, inextinguishable lamp; for from you was born the Sun of justice.[2]

Cyril's preaching and his attitude, redolent with affection and admiration, greatly contributed to the growth of Marian devotion.

In addition, thanks to the intransigence with which he defended the title "Mother of God", both before and during the Council of Ephesus, Cyril helped awaken an explicit interest in Marian dogma in the Church as well as a concern to safeguard a precious tradition of the Alexandrian Church, which was already accustomed to invoking Mary under the title *Theotókos*. It appears that this title had been customary in Alexandria for centuries.[3] At any rate, Cyril never intended to give up this term, not only for reasons of sentimental attachment to the tradition of his Church, but above all because he considered it a guarantee of faith in the mystery of the Incarnation. The Word of God was truly Son of Mary because he had assumed our human flesh within her womb; he made his own body of a human body, born of Mary. Through all this, the Word did not give up his divine nature; that would have been unthinkable and absurd. Calling his Mother *Theotókos* means admitting that there exists but a single Christ and that he is Son of God according to his eternal generation from the Father and Son of Mary according to his human and bodily generation.

---

[2] *Homily* 11; PG 77, 1032 C–D.

[3] Cf. G. Giamberardini, *Il culto mariano in Egitto,* vol. 1 (Jerusalem, 1975), pp. 111–22.

This profound mystery arouses further wonder in Cyril when he considers how it really happened, through conception and a virginal birth:

> In this case, we say that the divine body was formed by the Holy Spirit and fashioned in the holy Virgin in a way beyond words, above and beyond the laws of nature. The firstborn of the holy, the beginning of those who obtained rebirth from God by means of the Spirit, had no need whatsoever of man's seed. Of these it has been plainly said: "They who are born, not by blood, nor by carnal desire, nor by man's willing it, but from God" (Jn 1:13).[4]

Mary's Role as Mediatrix

Cyril considers that it was through the *Theotókos* that God accomplished everything concerning human salvation. His point of departure is the essential relationship between Mary and the Church, which was perfectly known to him; he builds his argument upon the lapidary statements of the earliest Fathers. In his famous *Homily* 11 (cited above), he pays tribute to the Virgin, greeting her as the instrument of a long list of God's saving actions:

> I salute you, O Mary, *Theotókos*: through you the prophets speak out and the shepherds sing God's praises . . . , the angels dance and the archangels sing tremendous hymns . . . , the Magi prostrate themselves in adoration . . . , the dignity of the twelve apostles has been exalted . . . , John exulted while still in his mother's womb, and the lamp adored the everlasting light . . . , grace ineffable came forth . . . , the true light came into the world, our Lord Jesus Christ . . . , light shone on those sitting in darkness and in the shadow of death . . . .
>
> Because of you the Gospels proclaim, "Blessed is he who comes in the name of the Lord" (Lk 19:38); through you, the churches of those who possess the orthodox faith have been founded in the cities, in the villages, in the isles . . . , the Conqueror of death and Destroyer of hell has come forth. . . . He has come, the Maker of the first creation, and he has repaired the first man's falsehood, he, who governs the heavenly kingdom. . . .
>
> Through you, the beauty of the Resurrection flowered, and its brilliance shone out . . . , the tremendous baptism of holiness in the

---

[4] *Commentary on Luke* 2, 22; PG 72, 500.

Jordan has shone out . . . , John and the river Jordan are made holy, and the devil is cast out. . . .

Through you, every faithful soul achieves salvation.[5]

Mary at the Wedding in Cana

In his commentary on John's Gospel, Cyril dwells on the marriage feast at Cana and analyzes the verbal "exchange of blows" between Jesus and his Mother. In it, he discerns a proof of Jesus' great respect for his Mother and concludes that the Lord meant to teach children that they owe their own parents the greatest possible respect:

> Further, Christ shows that the greatest possible honor is owed to parents by the fact that, out of respect for his Mother, he decided to work a miracle that he had not wanted to perform.[6]

In analyzing the miracle of water changed into wine, the bishop of Alexandria also brings out certain values to which we are very sensitive today, such as the holiness of Christian marriage and the reevaluation of the meaning of womanhood:

> Many notable things were accomplished in this one sign, his first sign. Honorable marriage is sanctified, and the curse pronounced against woman is overcome. Women will no longer bear children in sorrow, since Christ has blessed the very beginning of our lives.[7]

Mary at the Foot of the Cross

Also in his commentary on St. John's Gospel, one encounters a passage where Cyril does not hesitate to attribute a psychological dimension of womanly weakness to Mary, as he depicts her succumbing in the face of the harsh trial of Calvary:

> [The evangelist] intended to teach that the Lord's unexpected Passion scandalized even his Mother, either because of the cruel nature of his death or because of the ridicule of the Jews or because of the soldiers at the foot of the Cross, who derided the One hanging

---

[5] *Homily* 11; PG 77, 1030.

[6] *Commentary on John* 2, 1; PG 73, 225.

[7] Ibid., PG 73, 228.

upon it and dared to divide his garments right before his Mother's eyes.[8]

This commentary dates from 429; it is somewhat surprising that Cyril, who only two years later would weave such a stupendous fabric of praises to the *Theotókos* (in his homilies at Ephesus), here takes a step backward. He leans in the direction of Origen's severe interpretation of the sword of Simeon,[9] explaining that even Mary fell into the temptation of scandal and despair:

> The sword was nothing other than the trial of the Passion, a trial so violent that it drove the woman's soul to absurd thoughts.[10]

Perhaps an explanation is to be found in Cyril's incapacity to separate the figure of the Lord's Mother from his concept of woman's psychological make-up. In accord with the mentality of his time, he tended to attribute a certain weakness and lack of fortitude to women. He was not able to perceive the interior strength that made Mary unshakable in her faith, even in the midst of the trial of her Son's suffering and death.

Nevertheless, according to Cyril, Jesus showed affectionate concern for his Mother, precisely because she was in a difficult state, and entrusted her to the care of the apostle John, giving a lesson to us all:

> He was so worried about his Mother that he almost did not notice his own sufferings, which had reached their peak. Indeed, he was impassible during his sufferings. He entrusted her to his favorite disciple, that is, to John, the author of this book; he ordered him to take her into his home and treat her as his own mother. In turn, he ordered his Mother to treat the Beloved Disciple as a true son, thus fulfilling his own duty as a natural son with charity and love. . . .
>
> What useful notion does Christ present us with here? We would say, above all, that he wanted to confirm the teaching of the law. For what does the law of Moses say? "Honor your father and your mother, that it may go well with you" (Ex 20:12).[11]

---

[8] Ibid., 12, 19; PG 74, 662.

[9] Origen, *Homilies on Luke* 17, 6–7; PG 13, 1845; SC 87, 256–58.

[10] *Commentary on John* 12, 19; PG 74, 664.

[11] Ibid., PG 74, 664.

Cyril's Complex Personality

Cyril is undoubtedly one of the greatest personalities of fifth-century Christian literature, not only for the massive body of writings he has left us, but also for the positions he took regarding the most crucial theological problems of his day. His firm affirmation of the hypostatic union in Christ, even though it leaves untouched some of the important implications of this truth, greatly encouraged the theological debate that led to the dogmatic definitions of Chalcedon. His defense of the title *Theotókos* had the value of connecting the mariological debate to Christology, which gave it greater and undeniable theological significance.

There will always be the events of Ephesus to raise doubts and debate about Cyril's conduct and character. But history has shed some light on the matter and given a certain justification to his behavior. In the teaching of Cyril of Alexandria, as confirmed by the Council of Ephesus, the Church herself has recognized an authentic and exact expression of her faith in the mystery of the Incarnation and her belief about the Virgin Mother of God. Therefore, in 1882, Leo XIII solemnly declared St. Cyril of Alexandria to be Doctor of the Universal Church.

READING

THE "THEOTÓKOS", CAUSE OF JOY FOR THE WHOLE WORLD

I see the assembly of the saints, all zealously gathered together, invited by the holy Mother of God, Mary, ever-virgin. I was feeling very sad, but then the presence of the holy Fathers changed this sorrow into merriment. Now the sweet words of the hymnographer David have been fulfilled in our presence: "Behold how fair, and how pleasant it is, when brothers dwell together as one!" (Ps 133:1). Hail, we say, O holy and mystic Trinity, who have called us together in this church dedicated to Mary, Mother of God. We hail you, O Mary Mother of God, venerable treasure of the entire world, inextinguishable lamp, crown of virginity, scepter of orthodoxy, imperishable temple, container of him who cannot be contained, Mother and Virgin, through whom it is said in the holy Gospels: "Blessed is he who comes in the name of the Lord" (Mt 21:9).

Hail, you who held the Uncontainable One in your holy and virginal womb! Through you, the Holy Trinity is glorified; the precious Cross is celebrated and adored throughout the world; heaven exults, the angels and archangels rejoice, the demons are put to flight, the devil, the tempter, falls from heaven, the fallen creation is brought back to paradise, all creatures trapped in idolatry come to know of the truth.

Through you, holy baptism and the oil of gladness are administered to believers; through you, churches are established throughout the world; the peoples are led to conversion. What more shall I say? Through you, the only begotten Son of God shone forth as a light upon those who sat in darkness and in the shadow of death. Through you, the prophets made their predictions, and the apostles preached salvation to the nations; through you the dead rise, sovereigns reign, and through you the Holy Trinity reigns.

But who among men is capable of celebrating Mary most glorious? The virginal womb: such a great wonder! This miracle has me enraptured. When has it ever been heard that a builder was prevented from dwelling in a temple that he built himself? Could he, who calls his own handmaid to be his Mother, be considered deserving of shame? Behold, now: the whole universe is rejoicing. The sea obeyed, recognizing [in the fathers] its fellow servants. For while the water surged in stormy billows, the passage of the saints made it smooth and calm. The creature water remembered the voice of the Savior: "Silence! Be still" (Mk 4:39). The passage of the fathers also subdued the earth, which previously had been infested with brigands. "How beautiful the feet of those who preach the good news of peace" (Rom 10:15). But what peace is this? Jesus, our Lord, who was born from Mary, as he himself willed.

—Cyril of Alexandria, *Homily IV Preached at Ephesus against Nestorius*; PG 77, 992–96

2

PROCLUS OF CONSTANTINOPLE
(d. 446)

As far as Marian doctrine and devotion are concerned, the Council of Ephesus set in motion an important process of evolution in the Church. In point of fact, the Council fathers did not intend to define any new dogmas but to recall Christians to the orthodox faith by condemning heretical deviations. In the last analysis, even the Marian title *Theotókos*, canonized by the Council, was intended simply to express fidelity to what Nicaea had proclaimed in 325.

On the level of the practical life of the Church, however, the figure of the Mother of God began to penetrate more deeply into the thought, attention, admiration, and devotion of the people of God. The cult of Mary could be found almost everywhere, beginning in the East; more and more the faithful were tending to consider it an indispensable part of the Christian life. The liturgy was beginning to reserve an important place for the Virgin in its celebrations. Marian homiletics, which seems to have taken its first steps at the end of the fourth century, was starting to appear as a new literary genre. In addition to the feasts of the Lord that included a commemoration of his Mother, the first Marian feasts appeared.[1]

One of those who made an important contribution to this flowering of interest in the person of the Mother of God was Proclus of Constantinople, who is also a helpful and authoritative witness to it.

A Staunch Devotee of Mary

We have previously explained how Proclus was the unwilling catalyst who caused the explosion of the Nestorian controversy and how

---

[1] D. Montagna, "La liturgia mariana primitiva: Introduzione ad uno studio sull'omiletica mariana greca", *Marianum* 24 (1962): 84–128.

this controversy was concluded by the declaration of the Council of Ephesus on Mary's divine motherhood. Subsequently, he became an eloquent example of the greatly expanded Marian piety that followed the Council.

We know little of his life before the year 426, when he was consecrated bishop of Cyzicus, on the Hellespont. Proclus was never able to take possession of this episcopal see, because his faithful opposed him to the point of rejecting him. Consequently, he continued to live in Constantinople, where he won renown as a powerful preacher. In 428 or 429, he preached the famous Marian homily in which he praised the Virgin as *Theotókos*. As we have seen, this term provoked the hostile reaction of the patriarch Nestorius, who was opposed to its use for doctrinal reasons we have already explained. The homily in question was later inserted into the *Acts* of the Council of Ephesus. In 434, Proclus himself was elected patriarch of Constantinople and governed that Church until his death in 446.

Even today, scholars are divided in their judgment on the authenticity of some of the works attributed to him by the manuscript tradition. However, even if we limit ourselves to the undoubtedly genuine works, we can get a sufficiently clear and accurate idea of this brilliant preacher's Marian thought and devotion. His style was fluid and elegant, his imagination fertile, his exposition confident; he was adept at applying biblical figures and symbols to the Blessed Virgin. In his homilies, he preferred to address her in the most beautiful elegies, rather uncommon in the preceding patristic tradition. These elegies appear not so much as the fruit of a personal taste for rhetoric but as an expression of a sincere and profound admiration for the greatness of the Mother of the Lord and as an act of love and devotion to her person.

Enthusiastic Defender of the Theotókos [2]

When Proclus preached his sermon in which he called Mary *Theotókos* in the very presence of Nestorius, who rejected the title, he

---

[2] The Marian doctrine of Proclus has been studied by R. Caro, "Proclo de Costantinopla, orador mariano del siglo V", *Marianum* 29 (1967): 377–492; idem, *La Homiletica Mariana Griega en el Siglo V*, Marian Library Studies 3, vol. 1 (Dayton, 1971), pp. 76–128.

was undoubtedly motivated by reasons of a christological nature. He wanted to defend the unity of the two natures, human and divine, in the single Person of Christ. Because of this personal unity, called the "hypostatic union", it is possible to call Mary *Theotókos*.

But when he found himself caught up in the Nestorian controversy and the conclusions of the Council of Ephesus, which practically legitimated his theological position, this undoubtedly impressed upon him a special inclination toward and love for the Mother of God. In his homilies, he exalts Mary's divine motherhood as a role and dignity greater than any religious situation that a creature of this world could experience. What happened in the Virgin Mary's womb has no human parallel:

> O man, run through all creation with your thought, and see if there exists anything comparable to or greater than the holy Virgin, Mother of God. Circle the whole world, explore all the oceans, survey the air, question the skies, consider all the unseen powers, and see if there exists any other similar wonder in the whole creation. . . .
>
> Count, then, the portents, and wonder at the superiority of the Virgin: she alone, in a way beyond words, received into her bridal chamber him before whom all creation kneels with fear and trembling.[3]

In a homily on the Nativity, Proclus presents the mystery of the incarnate Word in relation to the mystery of the eternal generation of the Son by the Father. The approach leaves no doubts about his faith in the divine nature of Mary's Son. Hence, Mary is rightly called *Theotókos*:

> He who was divinely generated by the Father before all ages, the Same is generated by a Virgin today, for our salvation's sake. There above, he is the only Son, generated according to divinity, by the only Father; here below he is God, but not just a man according to humanity. There above, he is with the Father in an inexpressible way; here below, he is born from his Mother in an unspeakable way. There above, he has no mother; here below, he has no earthly father. Above, the Firstborn, before all ages; below, the firstborn of a Virgin, according to the mystery of the Incarnation.[4]

---

[3] *Homily* 5, 2; PG 65, 717 C–720 A.
[4] *Homily* 24, 15; *Le Muséon* 54 (1941): 42.

The divine character of Mary's motherhood is based, then, precisely on the fact that the Son born of her is the Only-begotten of the Father. This is also shown by the Virgin Birth:

> Precisely for this reason, the Virgin is Mother of God. Thus, even after giving birth, she remained a virgin. The birth is inexplicable because of the inaccessible mystery, but the Word became visible through the event of his Incarnation. Consider that he remained what he was and became what he was not, passible and impassible together, according to what was seen, remaining consubstantial with the Father according to his divinity and consubstantial with us according to his humanity, except in the matter of sin.[5]

Therefore, to sceptics who objected, "How can a woman give birth to God?" Proclus responded:

> I am not telling you that a woman could give birth to God, but that the incarnate God could have been borne by a woman. For to God all things are possible.[6]

Mary, Virginal Workshop

Proclus repeatedly emphasizes Mary's virginity in conceiving and bearing Jesus as a proof for the existence of two natures in Christ; these two natures are different in themselves but indissolubly united in the one Person of the Son of God, who became incarnate in Mary to save humanity by becoming man. Our author cannot conceal his wonderment before this unheard-of miracle:

> O Virgin, unmarried maid, mother without the corruption of birth, where did you get the wool from which you prepared the garment that today clothed the Master of the world? Where did you find the uterine loom on which you wove the seamless garment?[7]

The patriarch of Constantinople exalts the mystery with contagious enthusiasm that is conveyed both to his contemporary listeners and to his future readers:

---

[5] *Homily* 24, 17; in *Le Muséon* 54 (1941): 42–43.
[6] *Homily* 2, 5; PG 65, 697 D.
[7] *Homily* 4, 2; PG 65, 712 C.

Splendid and wonderful is the object of today's celebration! Splendid, because it brought men the long-awaited salvation; wonderful, because the birth transcends the laws of nature. Certainly, a mother giving birth is not unknown to nature. But grace made the one who gave birth and kept her a virgin; it made her a mother without destroying her integrity.

O earth never planted with seed, which made a heavenly fruit spring forth! O Virgin, who opened paradise to Adam! What is more, you yourself are more glorious than paradise! For paradise was the cultivation of God, but you cultivated God himself, according to the flesh.

Now let us all dance, not to celebrate the marriage of the Mother of the Lord, because she is a virgin uninitiated in marriage and without experience of it, but to honor the birth of him who is the Unstained. Though unmarried, she became a mother, without having any experience of a man. But the baby did not remain an orphan.

Then let us admire the Virgin's womb, a womb wider than creation. For she, without difficulty, enclosed within her him who cannot be contained in anyone. He who holds his Mother, along with everything else, in his hand, was held by her in her womb.[8]

The idea that Mary's virginity was an unquestionable guarantee of her Son's divinity was commonly held by the Fathers of the Church, who often observed that no man is able to leave his mother's virginity intact in being born. Our author explains it well:

If the Mother had not remained a virgin, her child would have been a mere man, and his birth not wonderful. If, to the contrary, she remained a virgin after his birth, how will the Son not be God, and the mystery indescribable? Without corruption he was born, who entered the upper room through closed doors without being hindered by them. Thomas, recognizing in him the two natures united, cried out, saying, "My Lord and my God!" (Jn 20:28).[9]

We do not recall having met, anywhere in the other Fathers, this singular interpretation of the act of faith pronounced by the apostle Thomas at the sight of the risen Christ; nor do we recall that it was ever invoked as a proof of the duality of natures in the one Person of the incarnate Word.

---

[8] *Homily* 4, 1; PG 65, 708 C–709 B.
[9] *Homily* 1, 2; PG 65, 684 A.

Salvific Character of Mary's Motherhood

In his graceful and thoughtful style, our author invites his flock to meditate on the wonderful effects of Mary's motherhood upon God's plan for human salvation. It seems that God loves to resort to incomprehensible and disconcerting means. These demand faith and acceptance from men, as well as trust in the positive effects that can be produced:

> O man, do not be ashamed of this birth. It was the cause of our salva-
> tion. For, if he had not been born of a woman, neither would he have
> died. And if he had not died, he would not have brought to nothing,
> by his death, "him who has the power of death; that is, the devil"
> (Heb 2:14).[10]

A little later, Proclus gives free rein to his enthusiasm and wonder-ment at how much the Lord accomplished in Mary when realizing his plan for human salvation:

> O womb, in which the decree of our liberation was composed! O
> belly, in which were forged weapons to oppose the devil! O field, in
> which the cultivator of human nature, without seed, made grain
> spring up! O temple, in which God became a priest, not changing
> our nature, but reclothing it, in his mercy, with that which he is, ac-
> cording to the order of Melchizedek![11]

Our homilist explains the reason why the Incarnation of the Son of God was necessary for the salvation of the human race. Since the human race was totally enslaved by sin, there was not a single human being who could assume the role of a redeemer. Only the Son of God could do it, but he had to assume human nature, based on the patristic principle that became current from Gregory Nazianzen on: only what was assumed by the Redeemer could be saved.[12] Let us cite the text of Proclus:

> When he appeared in the Virgin's womb, he clothed himself in con-
> demnation. There occurred the tremendous exchange: he gave the

---

[10] *Homily* 1, 3; PG 65, 684 A.

[11] Ibid., 684 B.

[12] Gregory's phrase is famous: "What is not assumed is not restored, but what is united to God is saved as well" (*Epist.* 101, 7; PG 37, 181–84).

Spirit; he received flesh; he was both with the Virgin and from the Virgin; with the Virgin in overshadowing her; from the Virgin in taking his flesh from her.[13]

Proclus also underscores Mary's collaboration in the work of salvation, using the traditional Eve–Mary parallel, which he expands by including the birth of Cain from Eve and within which he alludes, in a veiled manner, to the conception of Christ through hearing, through the ear:

In being born, Christ made the former entranceway of sin into a portal of salvation. For, in the place where the serpent had injected its venom through disobedience, the Word, entering by his obedience, built a living temple. Whence had emerged Cain, the firstborn of sin, thence without seed sprang Christ, the Redeemer of the human race.[14]

In another homily he adds that the effects of Mary's collaboration in the economy of salvation extend to all the dimensions of the world:

You alone cured Eve's sorrow; you alone wiped away the tears of travail; you alone bore the world's ransom.[15]

This text is particularly significant as a witness to the evolution of the traditional Eve–Mary parallel. If, for Irenaeus, Mary's intervention was for the sake of Eve, now it is considered to be beneficial for the whole human race. In other words, the affirmation of Mary's maternal power was growing more and more decisive and sure.

Mary, Boast of the Female Sex

If the figure of Mary represents a shining ideal for every believer, she is in a special way an ideal for woman, who sees the values of virginity and motherhood realized in Mary:

---

[13] *Homily* 1, 8; PG 65, 688 D–689 A.
[14] *Homily* 1, 2; PG 65, 681 C.
[15] *Homily* 5, 3; PG 65, 720 C.

What is being commemorated is the boast of the female sex, the glory of women, in her who is both mother and virgin at the same time. What a lovable and wonderful union this is! [16]

And, further on, he exhorts:

Let nature exult and human nature be glad: women are honored! Let humanity dance: virgins are exalted! [17]

Thanks to Mary, women have been liberated from the shame that was perpetuated in them because of Eve's falsehood:

Let the women hasten to come here, because here is a woman who does not point to the tree of death but gives birth to the fruit of life. Let the virgins hasten as well, because a Virgin has given birth without harming her virginity. For the Baby has come forth, leaving the curtains of the womb intact behind him, leaving the workshop of nature as he found it and adding grace as well.

Let mothers hasten, because a Virgin Mother has replaced the tree of disobedience with the tree of life. Let daughters hasten, because the obedience of a daughter cancels the shame of a mother's disobedience. [18]

Through Mary, a special blessing descended upon all women, and Proclus sets out to demonstrate this by using biblical characters as examples:

Thanks to her, all women are blessed. It is not possible that woman should remain under her curse; to the contrary, she now has a reason to surpass even the glory of the angels. Eve has been healed; the Egyptian woman [Hagar] has been silenced; Delilah has been buried; Jezebel has fallen into oblivion; even Herodias has been forgotten.

Today, a list of women is admired: Sarah is acclaimed as the fertile field of peoples; Rebekah is honored as the able conciliator of blessings; Leah, too, is admired as mother of the ancestor [Judah] according to the flesh; Deborah is praised for having struggled beyond the powers of her womanly nature; Elizabeth is called blessed for having carried the Forerunner, who leapt for joy in her womb, and for having giving witness to grace; Mary is venerated, because she became the Mother, the cloud, the bridal chamber, and the ark of the Lord. [19]

---

[16] *Homily* 1, 1; PG 65, 680 C.
[17] Ibid., PG 65, 681 A.
[18] *Homily* 4, 2; PG 65, 709 C–712 A.
[19] *Homily* 5, 3; PG 65, 720 B.

The patriarch of Constantinople considers Mary a sublime claim of glory for all women who live in accord with God's will. For the Virgin is portrayed as the antithesis of those women whose conduct had negative results for the salvific economy and as the incomparable model of conduct whom virtuous women must imitate.

The Value of Proclus

One could produce many other texts to demonstrate the important role Proclus played in the development of Marian doctrine. But his greatest and most original achievement was proposing the image of Mary within a framework of great dignity; he accentuated her maternal power to such a degree that he opened the way for the considerable growth of Marian devotion that occurred in the post-Ephesus Church. Christians understood, more and more clearly, that a creature so sublime and so near to God had to be honored with a proper cult and that she had to be gifted with a special power of intercession, so that her invocation was a justified and recommended religious act.

READINGS

MARY IN THE MYSTERY OF THE INCARNATION

What, then, is the mystery celebrated in yesterday's solemnity? The unexplainable mystery of the divinity and the humanity, a birth that leaves the Mother uncorrupt, an Incarnation that gives a form to the incorporeal Divinity, while it undergoes no passion, an extraordinary birth, a beginning for a generated One who has no beginning. For origin belongs to his human nature, while his divinity has no origin . . . ; the union of two natures and the birth of a single Son, the unconfused union of the Word with the flesh. He who yesterday was born according to the flesh is God because of what he received from the Father, but he is man because of what he took from me.

O tremendous and marvelous mystery! Who ever saw a king wearing the garments of a condemned man? What eye ever contained all of the sun's light? When was a body ever united substantially and without change to a God, other than yesterday?

When the holy Virgin offered her womb, the Word rushed in through her sense of hearing; the Holy Spirit built a living temple; the Most High emptied himself, taking the form of a slave, and, finally, the Virgin's womb carried the mystery of the divine economy.

O womb wider than the heavens! O birth pregnant with salvation! O womb, who were the bridal chamber of the clay and the potter! O mystery, which I do not know how to explain!

O birth, who gave and announced to the people, not the beginning of divine existence, not a change of nature, not a lessening of power, not a separation from the eternal Parent, but the substantial union of God and the flesh, the blessing of birth and the coming of God, the wonder hidden in God from all ages, the unfathomable mystery of the two natures, the end of the curse, the destruction of the condemnation, the eternal existence of a single and unique Son and his generation from the Virgin according to the flesh, the adoration of all creation.

—Proclus of Constantinople, *Homily 3 on the Incarnation*;
PG 65, 703–8

MARY IN THE CHOIR OF ALL CREATURES WHO OFFER GIFTS TO THE LORD

But I also want to question the Virgin against the unbelieving Jews. Tell me, O Virgin, who made you a mother before marriage? How did you become a mother, yet remain a virgin? Persuade the Jews that a Virgin gave birth; close the mouths of the unbelievers.

She, with authority, answers me thus: Why do the Jews marvel that a Virgin gave birth, seeing that they do not marvel when a dry branch produces a shoot, against nature? They see the branch, without roots, flowering indoors, and do not ask how or why it happened; instead, they are always asking questions about me! "Behold, the Virgin shall conceive in her womb and bear a son" (Is 7:14).

The Jews see the Child, and plot against the Mother; they look for the father of the Child whose Mother they do not recognize as a virgin. Why, O Jew, are you looking for the father of him who is born today? Hear him crying, "The Lord said to me: You are my son; today I have begotten you" (Ps 2:7). Am I not your parent before all ages? Another is the Father of you who are born today. Either you say that the Child born today (for he is truly on the earth) has no father, or you call him my Son. For a single son cannot be born of two fathers. "Today I have begotten you."

Today, then, the Sun of justice sprang from the virginal cloud: "The people that sat in darkness have seen a great light" (Is 9:2). Today the unsown Seed grew up out of the uncultivated plain, and the hungry world rejoices for it. Today, without conjugal relations, a birth sprang from an uncorrupt womb, and all creation brings gifts to the Child who has no father. The earth offers a crib; the rocks offer jars of water; the winds, obedience; the sea, submission; the waves, calm; the depths of the ocean, fish; the rivers, the Jordan; the wells, the Samaritan woman; the desert, John; the beasts, a foal; the birds, a dove; the mountains, a cave; the cities, Bethlehem; the Magi, their gifts; the women, Martha; the widows, Anna; the barren, Elizabeth; the virgins, Mary Mother of God; the shepherds, a hymn of praise; the priests, Simeon; the children, palms; the persecutors, Paul; the sinners, the publican; pagans, the Canaanite woman; the woman with a hemorrhage, her faith; the sinful woman, ointment; the trees, Zacchaeus; wood, the Cross; the Cross, the thief; the east, a star; the air, a cloud; Gabriel, his greeting, namely: "Rejoice, full of grace, the Lord is with you" (Lk 1:28), and the Lord is from you and the Lord is before you.

He came into you according to his good pleasure; he came from you as he willed; he came before you, before every thought of the mind, having been generated by God the Father ineffably, immutably, wondrously, impassibly, without corruption, without witnesses, without mediators, without supervisors, unspeakably and divinely. In heaven without a mother, on earth without a father.

—Proclus of Constantinople, *Homily IV on the Nativity of the Lord*; PG 65, 713–16

3

THEODOTUS OF ANCYRA
(d. before 446)

Scholars have not spent much time studying this talented and interesting author, perhaps because of still-unresolved questions about
the authenticity of some of his writings. Few of his dates are known.
He was bishop of Ancyra (modern Ankara) and for some time main-
tained a bond of friendship with Nestorius; however, at the Council
of Ephesus he disassociated himself from Nestorius' doctrinal position and became one of his most tenacious and fierce opponents. He
functioned as the Council's quasi-official theologian and delivered at
least two sermons on the Nativity of the Lord and one discourse
against Nestorius during the Council. His death is to be located between 438 and 446.

Theodotus is a profound thinker who sometimes becomes ecstatic
in contemplating the mystery of God and the Incarnation of his
Word. His writings do not reflect the interior attitude of a curious or
indiscreet man; rather, they reveal the attitude of a humble believer
who prefers to stand in adoration before truths superior to the human mind. His Marian doctrine is clearly inspired by the theology of
the incarnate Word.[1]

The Mother of God's Only Begotten Son

The majority of Theodotus' writings come from the Council of
Ephesus. This context leads him to take clear and precise positions in

---

[1] A study of the Marian thought of the homilies of Theodotus of Ancyra was
done by R. Caro, *La Homilética Mariana Griega en el Siglo V*, Marian Library Studies 3, vol. 1 (Dayton, 1971), pp. 156–97.

the debate about Mary's divine maternity. These characteristics of Theodotus' style are also evident where his sense of devotion and aesthetic wonder call for inspired language; for example, when our author, seeking to imitate the respect and veneration of the angel in the mystery of the Annunciation, addresses the Virgin in the following terms:

> The fruit of your womb is not autumnal; rather, it is a shoot of immortality. It is not a harvest that came as a gift of nature but a flower sprung from divine seed. For you gave birth to the Beginning who has no beginning, a child who is before all ages, the Virgin's Son, the Eternal who is nurtured in your womb, to him who is older than his Mother yet is nursed by her, to him who nourishes all creatures and who clothes himself in human form, to the Splendor of God who presents himself as a pauper, to the King who will have no successor. Therefore I salute you, O Virgin full of grace, Mother among virgins and Virgin among mothers, archetype of both mothers and virgins, but superior to both.[2]

Our author is familiar with the inconsistency of the objections that were formulated against the transcendent divine origin of the Virgin's Son; he does not neglect to recall to the faith those who have allowed themselves to be disturbed or led off the right path by such difficulties:

> Do not say: If the only begotten Son was begotten of the Father, how could he be born a second time of the Virgin? He is born from the Father according to his divine nature; he is born from the Virgin according to the economy of salvation. First as God, then as man.[3]

The only begotten Son does not cease to be the eternal Son of God when he is born here on earth as man, because his taking on of our humanity does not cause him to lose his divinity. For this reason, his Mother is truly the Mother of God, *Theotókos*:

---

[2] *Homily* 6, 12; PO 19, 331. R. Caro doubts the authenticity of this homily (*Homilética*, 192). To the contrary, Jugie, who published the original text preserved in the manuscript *Parisinus gr. 1171*, readily attributes it to Theodotus (cf. PO 19, 289–91, 318–35; *L'Immaculée Conception dans l'Écriture Sainte et dans la tradition orientale* [Rome, 1952], p. 83).

[3] *Homily* 2, 7; PG 77, 1377 B–C.

Consider that the Virgin, by means of her body, brings to light the Word, not of course conferring by this birth the principle of divinity (God forbid!), but so that he might make himself known to men, as God-made-man. . . . Therefore God, the Word, made a birth proper to himself; he chose the Virgin as his Mother and came forth from a womb adorned with virginity.[4]

One can understand how this event was possible if one reflects that the Creator does not abhor any part of his creation and that all his creatures are worthy of his wisdom and his perfection. It is not strange, then, that the Lord chose to become incarnate and to dwell in one of his creatures.

Virgin Mother

In Mary, motherhood and virginity are strictly connected and inter-related; for Theodotus, Mary's virginity is a proof and consequence of the divine character of her motherhood. If Mary's Son is God, then his birth could not be other than virginal or, rather, miraculous:

Have you seen how marvelous was the mystery, transcending the law of nature? Have you seen this supernatural occurrence, wrought by the power of God alone? Have you seen the Word beyond words being born? The fact that he did not destroy her virginity plainly shows that the One born is the Word of God. A woman who gives birth to mere flesh ceases to be a virgin; but the Word of God, born in the flesh, maintains her virginity, thus showing that he is the Word. And when you hear me say "Word", understand that I mean the substantial and subsistent Word, not the word one speaks forth with one's mouth.[5]

In another homily, the bishop of Ancyra repeats himself even more explicitly, appealing to the good sense of his audience:

No mother of a man has ever remained a virgin. Have you seen how this birth offers us a twofold consideration regarding the One who is born? If he had been born like us, he would have been a man, but if

---

[4] *Homily* 2, 8; PG 77, 1377 D–1380 A.
[5] *Homily* 1, 1; PG 77, 1349 B–C.

he kept his Mother a virgin, it is clear, for those who know how to think, that the One who is born is God.[6]

Before this inexpressible mystery of a Virgin Mother, Theodotus emphasizes that the Christian must be aware of what can be investigated about the mystery of God and what he must simply adhere to with faith:

> One can attempt to investigate, with the mind, those things [God] does that are consistent with our nature; as for the things he does miraculously, beyond our thought and our nature, we must hold them by faith and not scrutinize them with our reason.[7]

However, even though the Lord's birth is a matter of great importance, God brought it about in simplicity and obscurity, taking into account the weakness of man, who is unable to bear the experience of the divine power and glory. Even Mary shares in this solicitous concern of God for men:

> He comes, the Lord of all, in the form of a servant, clothed with poverty, so as not to startle his prey. He was conceived in an obscure village; he chose an obscure country place for his birth; he is born of a poor Virgin, and takes upon himself everything that poverty involves.[8]

Mary's Preparation for the Incarnation

The mission to which God called the Virgin was so important that some Fathers thought it demanded an adequate preparation. Today, we know that this preparation happened in the mystery of the Immaculate Conception, in which Mary was not only preserved from original sin and its moral consequences but filled with extraordinary graces as well. The Fathers do not appear to have known about this unique privilege; they thought that a special divine intervention took place in Mary immediately before the Incarnation, to render her

---

[6] *Homily* 2, 3; PG 77, 1372 D–1373 A.
[7] *On the Nicene Creed* 4; PG 77, 1320 A–B.
[8] *Homily* 1, 8; PG 77, 1360 C.

worthy to become the Mother of the Word incarnate.[9] Theodotus also expresses himself in this vein, resorting to the example, so common in patristic literature, of iron heated in a fire:

> If iron, once joined to fire, immediately expels the impurities extraneous to its nature and swiftly acquires a likeness to the powerful flame that heats it, so that it becomes untouchable and capable of setting any material on fire, how much more, in a superior way, did the Virgin burn when the divine fire (the Holy Spirit) rushed in? She was purified from earthly impurities, and from whatever might be against her nature, and was restored to her original beauty, so as to become inaccessible, untouchable, and irreconcilable to carnal things.[10]

Continuing with another comparison, the author clearly expresses the idea of this preparatory intervention for the work of the Holy Spirit:

> A person who has had water poured upon his head is made wet in every part of his body, from head to toe; just so, we believe that the divine Virgin Mother was also entirely anointed with the holiness of the Holy Spirit, who descended upon her. And so, in this way, she received the living God, the Word, into her virginal and fragrant bridal chamber.[11]

The Old Testament tradition held that man was not able to encounter God directly; Theodotus explains how God, when he wanted to manifest himself to man, resorted to human figures and to natural phenomena that we could perceive with our senses. For Mary, however, the Incarnation represented such a direct and strong experience of the divine that she needed an adequate personal preparation for it.

---

[9] This is the idea of pre-purification, or *procatharsis*, articulated by Gregory Nazianzen (cf. *Oratio* 38, 13; PG 36, 325; *Oratio* 45, 9; PG 36, 633; *Poemi dogmatici* 9, 68; PG 37, 461). On this theme, see M. Candall, "La Virgen Santísima prepurificado en su Anunciación", *Orientalia Christiana periodica* 31 (1965): 241–76.

[10] *Homily* 4, 6; PG 77, 1397 B–C.

[11] Ibid.

Virginal Birth and Resurrection

From the fifth century on, the comparison between Jesus' birth from Mary's virginal womb and his coming forth from the tomb in the mystery of the Resurrection recurs fairly frequently in the Fathers. Usually, they reason that he who wrought the miracle of the Resurrection was able to act with the same power in a virginal birth. But the bishop of Ancyra goes beyond this: he analyzes the different way God proceeded in working the two miracles. For while Christ, in rising from the dead, opens the tomb, he was born without opening the maternal womb:

> The Savior, after three days, came forth from the tomb, not limiting himself to opening his own tomb, but opening the tombs of many saints as well. . . . When he rose from the tomb, he opened tombs; when he was born from a womb, he did not open the womb. . . . When he is born, he leaves the Virgin's womb closed.[12]

In touching on this matter, our preacher is conscious that he has aroused the curiosity of his audience. So he goes on:

> Why, I ask? But I see that you want to know too. Let us tell, then, the reason why the tombs were opened, while the virginal womb was not opened. The reason is that his Resurrection became the causal principle of all resurrections, while the extraordinary manner of his birth was reserved to him alone.[13]

The Role of Joseph

From the beginning, the presence of Joseph in God's plan for the Incarnation has raised questions for readers of the Gospel. If the Lord had to be born of a virgin, why did he use the collaboration of a married woman? As we have already had occasion to note, the problem is not at all new; indeed, it belongs to an earlier period of patristic exegesis, from Origen onward. Theodotus, too, offers an answer of his own:

---

[12] *Homily* 5, 1; PG 77, 1413 A–B; OCP (*Orientalia Christiana Periodica*) 26 (1960): 225.

[13] Ibid.

> But how is it that Jesus, who had to be born of a virgin, was born, not of an unmarried virgin, but of a married virgin? We have to find out. Indeed, those who request an answer are many, desirous of grasping the reason why matters were so arranged.
>
> Why was he not born of an unmarried virgin? Why was it that her virginity, which was to serve the Lord's birth, did not remain totally above suspicion? Actually, the opposite might have happened. For the Virgin could have been suspected had not Joseph been married to her as her guardian. Instead, Joseph the just man takes her as his wife, to be the guardian of her virginity and the witness to the birth.[14]

This explanation allows us to understand the reason why Joseph, according to the Gospel, decided to put Mary aside secretly when he discovered her pregnancy (cf. Mt 1:19). He would have suspected her and been afraid that he had not properly carried out his task as guardian. At that moment, God himself guaranteed Mary's innocence, sending an angel to calm her husband.

We have noted how Theodotus, in his response, admits the importance of the question; it must have been very much in vogue in his day if many people were asking him about it.

The Sword of Simeon

As a protagonist in so many extraordinary events, the Virgin Mother observed, meditated, and asked herself questions (cf. Lk 2:33). The bishop of Ancyra notes that Simeon's prophecy is really the divine answer to some of the silent questions that Mary asked herself:

> To you Simeon spoke a prophecy, saying: O white, innocent dove! O holy tabernacle of our hope, in whom all holiness and magnificence reside! "This Child", whom you have borne in a way beyond words, "this Child is set for the downfall and rising of many in Israel, a sign that is spoken against. And a sword shall pierce through your own soul as well, that thoughts out of many hearts may be revealed" (cf. Lk 2:34-35).
>
> But why, O old man, do you mix sad predictions with glad tidings? Up until now, you have proclaimed "light" and "glory", and now you

---

[14] *Homily* 5, 3; PG 77, 1414 B; OCP 26 (1960): 226-27.

announce "downfall" and speak of a "sword" for the Mother. "Yes," you say, "everything will happen at the appropriate time. There will be downfall for unbelievers, rising for believers, and a sign that is spoken against. . . ."

For Mary's soul, as well, there will come a day of trial, when opposing thoughts will run through her mind.[15]

Theodotus' thought is not totally clear. He indicates that a whole series of contradictory events will put Mary's soul to the test but does not say what exactly this test will be: Unbelief? Doubt? Suffering?

Praise for the Holy Virgin

The immense gifts bestowed by the Lord in the mystery of the Incarnation awake in man a sense of recognition and the desire to repay him. Unable to do this in any other way, man expresses himself in prayer and praise, addressed either directly to God or else to those whom God has chosen for realizing his plans of mercy and love. In this spirit, Theodotus addresses Mary in touching accents of love. Here is a beautiful example:

> Hail, our desirable gladness;
> Hail, O rejoicing of the churches;
> Hail, O name that breathes out sweetness;
> Hail, face that radiates divinity and grace;
> Hail, most venerable memory;
> Hail, O spiritual and saving fleece;
> Hail, O Mother of unsetting splendor, filled with light;
> Hail, unstained Mother of holiness;
> Hail, most limpid font of the lifegiving wave;
> Hail, new Mother, workshop of the birth.
>
> Hail, ineffable Mother of a mystery beyond understanding;
> Hail, new book of a new scripture,
> of which, as Isaiah tells,
> angels and men are faithful witnesses.

---

[15] *Homily* 4, 13; PG 77, 1409 A–B.

> Hail, alabaster jar of sanctifying ointment;
> Hail, best trader of the coin of virginity;
> Hail, creature embracing your Creator;
> Hail, little container containing the Uncontainable.[16]

This kind of apostrophe addressed to the Virgin occurs frequently in Greek homilies of the fifth century onward; it constitutes a literary form called *chairetismoí*, from the Greek word *chaîre*, which translates as "hail" or "rejoice" (cf. Lk 1:28).

Besides the marvelous divine gifts stressed in the pericope above, which one can only admire and praise, in Mary there are also qualities that are more pertinent to practical living; this can give rise to the desire and will to imitate them. We have an example of this in another homily:

> Innocent virgin, spotless, without defect, untouched, unstained, holy in body and in soul, like a lily-flower sprung among thorns, unschooled in the wickedness of Eve, unclouded by womanly vanity. . . . Even before the Nativity, she was consecrated to the Creator. . . .
>   Holy apprentice, guest in the Temple, disciple of the law, anointed by the Holy Spirit, clothed with divine grace as with a cloak, divinely wise in your mind; united to God in your heart. . . . Praiseworthy in your speech, even more praiseworthy in your action. . . . Good in the eyes of men, better in the sight of God.[17]

Because of her unique vocation and her marvelous qualities as Mother of the Lord, she is saluted by the bishop of Ancyra as a model of the Christian life, especially for women, in a passage cited above (see page 261, footnote 2).

In the decades to follow, praises addressed to the Mother of God will become a widespread practice among the sacred orators of Byzantine Christianity. Very quickly, it will become part of Marian hymnody.

---

[16] *Homily* 4, 3; PG 77, 1393 B–C.
[17] *Homily* 6, 11; PO 19, 329.

READINGS

THE INCARNATION, MYSTERY OF VIRGINITY

Splendid and wonderful is the object of today's solemnity! Splendid, because it offers common salvation to men; wonderful, because it surpasses the laws of nature. For nature does not know any woman who both gave birth and remained a virgin; it is grace that made her bear and conserved her virginity. Grace made the Mother and did not damage her virginity. In truth, it was grace that guarded her chastity.

O unsown field, from which sprouted a saving fruit! O Virgin, surpassing the Garden of Eden itself! For young plants of every kind were born in Eden, springing up from the virgin soil; yet this Virgin is better than that soil. She does not make fruit trees grow but the root of Jesse, which gives the saving fruit to men. The first soil was virgin; so is this new soil. In Eden, God decreed that plants should be born; in this Virgin, the Creator himself became a sapling, according to the flesh. The first garden yielded no produce before the plants came; nor was Mary's virginity diminished by [Christ's] birth.

The Virgin became more glorious than paradise. Indeed, this was God's cultivating; according to the flesh, God cultivated her, desiring to unite himself with human nature.

Have you seen how marvelous was the mystery, transcending the law of nature? Have you seen this supernatural occurrence, wrought by the power of God alone? Have you seen the Word beyond words being born? The fact that he did not destroy her virginity plainly shows that the One born is the Word of God. A woman who gives birth to mere flesh ceases to be a virgin; but the Word of God, born in the flesh, maintains her virginity, thus showing that he is the Word. And when you hear me say "Word", understand that I mean the substantial and subsistent Word, not the word one speaks forth with one's mouth.

And so the only begotten Son of God is born, who is also called the Word. He does not begin to exist as the Word from the moment of this birth; rather, he makes this birth the principle of his becoming man. Indeed, God the Word existed before all ages, coeternal with the Father. But when he wished to become man out of love for men, he chose birth as the principle of his becoming man, not through a change in his divine nature, but through a miracle according to the will of God. Therefore, he was born as man; he kept intact her virginity as Word. For, just as our words are born without corrupting our minds, so the substantial and subsistent Word of God, in experiencing birth, does not corrupt [his Mother's] virginity.

This birth, then, surpasses the laws of nature. So do not lower yourself to the level of the ways of nature. I am presenting you with a miracle; do not put forth a line of reasoning. I tell you that it involves a birthed God who has chosen to be born; yet this birth was not the beginning of his existence in his divinity. Being God, he took a birth to himself, but it was not the birth that made him God. Wanting to become what he was not, nevertheless he remained what he had been. He chose the birth as the principle of the Incarnation. He became man without altering his nature, without eliminating the elements of the divine substance.

—Theodotus of Ancyra, *Homily I on the Nativity*
of the Lord 1–2; PG 77, 1349–52

A MORAL PORTRAIT OF THE VIRGIN

Divine Providence has given her to us, a creature worthy of the Lord, bearer of blessings. She does not incite us to disobedience but leads us to submit to God. She does not offer a deadly fruit but offers the life-giving bread. She is not timid in her reasoning but is strong in her affections. Not light in her mind, but solid in her soul. She converses with the archangel in a magnificent dialogue and shames the author of evil. Seeing the angel of the Annunciation, she was struck by wonder because he did not look like a son of Adam; nevertheless, she remained prudently attentive to what he told her, to assure herself that what was visiting her in the Temple was not the kind of deceitful benevolence that had once visited paradise. In other words, to make sure that it was not the audacity of the violator introducing himself into the house of God, as he had done in Eden. She wanted to make sure that the glad tidings were not a trick.

What did the divine messenger do then? Perceiving the Virgin's interior dispositions and perspicacity in her outward appearance and admiring her just prudence, he began to weave her a kind of floral crown with two peaks: one of joy and one of blessing; then he addressed her in a thrilling speech of praise, lifting up his hand and crying out: "Hail, O full of grace, the Lord is with you, you are blessed" (Lk 1:28), O most beautiful and most noble among women. The Lord is with you, O all-holy one, glorious and good. The Lord is with you, O worthy of praise, O incomparable, O more than glorious, all splendor, worthy of God, worthy of all blessedness.

I admire your humility, most eminent woman. "Do not fear, Mary" (Lk 1:30), spouse of God, divinely nourished treasure. To you I announce neither a conception in wickedness nor a birth in sin; instead, I bring the joy that puts an end to Eve's sorrow. To you I proclaim neither a trying pregnancy nor a painful delivery; rather, I foretell a birth of consolation and gladness. Do not judge divine things in a human way. For I am not telling you about a tearful labor or about giving birth in sadness; no, I am proclaiming the dawn of the light of the world.

Through you, Eve's odious condition is ended; through you, abjection has been destroyed; through you, error is dissolved; through you, sorrow is abolished; through you, condemnation has been erased. Through you, Eve has been redeemed.

He who is born of the holy [Virgin] is holy, holy and Lord of all the saints, holy and Giver of holiness. Wondrous is he who generated the Woman of wonder; Ineffable is he who precedes the Woman beyond words; Son of the Most High is he who springs from this highest creature, he who appears, not by man's willing it, but by the power of the Holy Spirit; he who is born is not a mere man, but God, the incarnate Word.

—Theodotus of Ancyra, *On the Mother of God and
on the Nativity*; PO 19, 330–31

4

A HOMILY ON THE ANNUNCIATION
(Fourth Century)

A sermon given by Proclus was the immediate cause of the Council of Ephesus. The Council, in its turn, strongly influenced preaching about Mary. Toward the end of the fourth century, homilies appeared that, on the strength of their content, could be called Marian; after Ephesus, however, there was a virtual explosion of Marian homilies, which multiplied steadily in subsequent centuries. In addition to homilies composed by unknown authors and those whose authorship is certain, there exist many *pseudoepigraphic* homilies, so called because they bear a false indication of authorship in their titles or "epigraphs". For this reason, in patristic collections, they are usually printed as appendices to the genuine writings of the author whose name they bear. In most cases, this would be one of the great Fathers of the fourth century.

At first, these Marian homilies appeared as commentaries on the Gospel pericopes that speak of the Virgin; these are the same passages that were read during the liturgical celebration of such feasts as Christmas and the Presentation of Jesus in the Temple (*Hypapantē*). Later, these homilies were preached during the celebration of Marian feasts.

Although the value of this abundant material is inconsistent as far as form and content are concerned, it remains a valuable documentation of the development of Marian doctrine and piety. From this copious pseudoepigraphical material, we have chosen one homily that is very valuable because of its content and formal elegance.

The Problem of Authorship

In the edition of Migne, the homily bears the title "On the Annunciation and against the Impious Arius."[1] The manuscript tradition

---

[1] PG 62, 763–70.

almost unanimously attributes it to Chrysostom, but scholars have tended to discount this attribution, and with good reason. Some codices give Gregory of Nyssa or Amphilochius of Iconium as the author. Meanwhile, the codex *Parisinus gr. 1191*, from the fifteenth century, gives the name of an unknown figure, a certain John, disciple of St. Basil. Also, in the codex *Vaticanus gr. 1098 B*, belonging more or less to the same period, a second hand, about a century after the first, has corrected the name of Chrysostom to that of John the monk, disciple of Basil the Great. Nevertheless, in the present state of the question, one cannot go beyond mere hypotheses.[2] The only conclusion that can be accepted as very likely is that the text was composed in a Cappadocian environment between 370 and 378.[3]

The homilist begins with a grandiloquent elegy for St. Basil, who had given a homily in the same church of Caesarea of Cappadocia on the previous Sunday. This initial encomium is not found in all the codices.

The homily then moves on to a commentary on the Gospel of the Annunciation, which had just been read in the course of the liturgy. We should recognize that this is a truly singular commentary, containing more than a hint of drama and poetry.

Content of the Homily

The theme of the Annunciation is explicitly enunciated by the author when he states his desire to present the mystery of the Incarnation of the Word of God; that is, the assumption of a human nature by the Word. This theme is suggested to him by the reading of the Annunciation Gospel; therefore, the main body of the homily is presented as a commentary on this text.

It tells of a personal intervention of the Son of God, who, before sending the angel Gabriel to Nazareth, explained to him the meaning of the mission he was to carry out on behalf of the Virgin and the

---

[2] Cf. Luigi Gambero, "Un'omelia pseudo-crisostomica sul Vangelo dell' Annunciazione", *Marianum* 47 (1985): 517–35.

[3] R. Caro, *La Homilética Mariano Griega en el Siglo V*, Marian Library Studies 4, vol 2 (Dayton, 1972), pp. 511–22.

meaning of the message he was to pass on to her. There follows a brief parenthesis devoted to contemplation, where the homilist expresses his sense of awe and wonder before the mystery and the divine dispositions revealed in it. Then begins a description of and commentary on the scene of the Annunciation. The angel's greeting gives the author an excuse to devise a long series of *praises* of the Virgin (*chairetismoí*), packed with lyricism and theological significance. Mary's distress, underlined in the Gospel account, is exhaustively analyzed in the homily; above all, the angel's response is extensively paraphrased and interpreted, with a marked insistence on certain points:

— The announcement is a cause for rejoicing, not a reason for distress;

— the Incarnation of the Son of God is posed not as a hypothetical situation, but as something that has already really happened within the Virgin's womb;

— this hidden event represents the fulfillment of God's promises to humanity.

At this point, Mary questions the angel about how the birth will come about since, to her, it appears completely outside of the normal laws of nature. The homilist also attributes to her a knowledge of future events that seem beyond her capacity to know at that moment.

The angel's response is once again amplified into an exhortation to Mary, telling her to accept the revelation of the mystery without useless curiosity but with faith and joy. Then the angel explains that the Son himself will teach her what she will need to know about the mystery. Finally, he proposes to her Elizabeth's extraordinary motherhood, as a pale shadow of God's even more extraordinary intervention in her case; he invites her to visit her aged cousin to show solicitude and to establish personally the truth of the words she has heard.

In reporting Mary's final statement, the homilist underlines (not without a certain rhetorical flourish) her disposition of humility and total docility to God's will. Having finished the commentary on the Gospel, the author brings his homily to a close by severely admonishing Arius. He reproves Arius for claiming to investigate a mystery that neither the Virgin nor the angel Gabriel could understand. For his part, the homilist restates his own belief in a trinitarian and christological profession of faith. The concluding doxology is also trinitarian.

READING

FROM THE HOMILY ON THE ANNUNCIATION
BY PSEUDO-CHRYSOSTOM

And he came to her and said, "Rejoice, full of grace, the Lord is with you; blessed are you among women" (Lk 1:26–28). It is now the sixth month since Zechariah was punished for his unbelief by being deprived of his speech and Elizabeth conceived her unexpected offspring. For six months, John the Baptist has been dwelling in the prison of the womb; the Forerunner has appeared in the recesses of sterility; the lamp is shining in the dark places of the womb.

At this time, then, the angel Gabriel was sent by the Sun of justice. Go — he told him — to the city of Nazareth, in Galilee, to the Virgin Mary, espoused to Joseph the builder, for I, the Builder of all creation, will espouse myself to this Virgin, for the salvation of men. Make known to her my serene coming into her, lest the Virgin, out of ignorance, be troubled in receiving me. Inform her of my love for men, for whose sake I wish to be born of her as man and to come into the world. First make known to her the plan of salvation, so that, when she sees her womb suddenly grow large, she will not be distressed.

Bring your journey to a swift conclusion. You will find me in the place to which I am now sending you. Even though I remain here, I precede you there. I will betake myself to her before you and after you; you bring her the announcement of my coming, while I, invisibly present, will confirm your words with deeds. For by her virginal womb, I plan to renew the human race; by my condescension, I want to reestablish the image I molded; I want to restore the ancient image, reshaping it. I formed the first man from a virgin earth, but the devil, making himself master, plundered him as an enemy and threw him to the earth, thus mocking my fallen image. Now I want to remold a new Adam for myself from the virgin earth, so that nature might prepare a beautiful defense and receive the just crown against him who conquered her. Then will the enemy be properly shamed.

O incomparable ocean of condescension! O infinite summit of divine love for man! The King did not send many angels or more than one foreteller; the Creator did not set into motion the hosts of the incorporeal powers; no, he sent but a single angel to be the herald of his coming, so that, through the announcement given by him alone, the Mother, who was about to receive the King, might be reassured beforehand.

And so the angel arrived at the Virgin Mary's home and, having entered, said to her: *Rejoice, full of grace!* He greeted her, his fellow servant, as if she were a great lady, as if she had already become the Lord's Mother. *Rejoice, full of grace!* Your foremother Eve, having broken the law, was condemned to bear children in pain; to you, instead, is addressed the invitation to rejoice. Eve bore Cain, thus giving birth to envy and murder; you, instead, will conceive a Son who will give life and immortality to all.

Rejoice, therefore, and dance for joy; rejoice, and tread upon the serpent's head. *Rejoice, full of grace.* For the curse has come to an end; corruption is taken away; sadness has passed; happiness is flowering; the blessed event foretold by the prophets of old has come to pass. You are the one to whom the Holy Spirit referred, speaking through the mouth of Isaiah: "Behold the Virgin shall conceive in her womb and bear a son" (Is 7:14). You are that virgin. Rejoice therefore, O full of grace. You are pleasing to the Demiurge; you are pleasing to the Maker; you are pleasing to the Creator; you are pleasing to him who delights in the beauty of souls. You have found a Spouse who will protect your virginity instead of corrupting it; you have found a Spouse who wants to become your Son because of his great love for men.

The Lord is with you! He who is everywhere is in you; he is with you, and he comes from you, the Lord in heaven, the Most High in the abyss, the Creator of all, Creator above the cherubim, Charioteer above the seraphim, Son in the womb of the Father, Only-begotten in your womb, the Lord—he knows how—entirely everywhere and entirely in you.

Blessed are you among women! For among all virgins, you have been chosen in advance; you have been made worthy to provide a dwelling for such a Lord; the Uncontainable willed that you should contain him; you house him who fills all things; you have become the most pure workshop of the divine economy; you have appeared as the worthy chariot for our King's entrance into life; you have been proclaimed the treasure, the spiritual pearl. *Blessed are you among women!*

The all-holy Virgin, hearing these words and contemplating the angel's form and voice, asked herself what manner of greeting this might be. Where might this discourse lead? What do these words mean for me? It was the angel who greeted me first. Who am I? What dignity have I achieved? I, full of grace? But how and why? The Lord is with me? But is the Lord not with anyone who fears his name? I am blessed among women? On what basis and why and how? What gift does this foretell for me? What miracle do these words speak of?

The angel, seeing her so troubled, said to her: *Do not fear, Mary.* I did not greet you in order to make you afraid. I speak to you sweetly, to make you exult. So do not harbor distress in your soul, because you carry the peace of the universe within you. *Do not fear, Mary, for you have found favor with God.* You have been made the most beautiful part of creation, more luminous than the heavens, more resplendent than the sun, higher than the angels. You were not lifted up into heaven, and yet, remaining on earth, you have drawn down into yourself the heavenly Lord and King of all.

And behold, you will conceive in your womb. The realization of this preceded my word; the mysterious conception was faster than my voice. You already carry within you, in your womb, the Lord, the Creator of all things who, from your holy and uncontaminated flesh, is building the temple of his holy flesh without any difficulty. You are carrying inside you the painter of nature, who, by his grace, is restoring his own timeworn image.

Behold you will conceive in your womb and bear a son and give him the name Jesus. He will be great. For great he is, by reason of his divinity, and great will he be in his humanity as well. *He will be called Son of the Most High. And the Lord God will give him the throne of David his father.*

For the Lord swore the truth to David and will not violate his oath. But what truth did he swear? *I will place on your throne,* he said, *the fruit of your loins.* That oath is fulfilled in this moment. *And he will reign over the house of Jacob forever, and his kingdom will have no end.* No one will be higher than this King, and no other woman will be more blessed than you who will bear him.

And Mary said to the angel: But how will this happen, since I do not know man? Joseph is espoused to me, not yet my husband; for these are the nuptial agreements, valid until the marriage bonds. How, then, will I be able to conceive without a husband? How will I be able to bear a fruit without a cultivator? Am I, perhaps, the first woman in whom the course of nature will be altered? Will the law of conception, perhaps, change for the first time in me? Will a new method of procreation take place in me alone? Will the ancient law of birth be rewritten in my case alone? O angel, clarify your enigmatic speech for me; explain to me the meaning of your words; interpret for me the force of your beautiful announcement; guide me to this unusual birth, so that I may gradually come to know the mystery to which I am going to give birth; so that I may apprehend how impossible things will become possible, and impracticable things be done, how inadmissible things may be admitted; so that I may hear how grace will improve nature, or how nature will be at the service of grace.

And answering, the angel said to her: The Holy Spirit will come upon you. You have understood who is the Artisan, do not be curious as to how; you have understood who is the Sculptor, do not ask questions about the work. You have heard that the Holy Spirit is involved; leave the fulfillment of the work to the Spirit. *The Holy Spirit will come upon you and the power of the Most High will overshadow you.* I have been ordered to say to you only this: You will conceive a Son. As to how you will conceive, he who is to be born from you will explain it clearly. I have brought you the announcement as a servant; the Lord himself will accomplish the work, and he knows how it will happen. I am the minister of the royal dispositions, not an interpreter of the divine will. I dare not teach you what I have not learned, nor dare I interpret what I have not been told, nor dare I make public the reality of the mystery. I am not capable of explaining the glad tidings.

I proclaim the prodigy but am incapable of saying how it will happen; I do not investigate what is beyond all investigation; I do not teach unreachable goals; I do not involve myself in matters that are beyond me; I do not call to account grace, which is above all discussion; I do not discuss the unexplainable birth. Truly, this spiritual conception is above all understanding; the extraordinary gestation surpasses all discourse; the saving birth transcends every inquiry.

The Holy Spirit will come upon you. The Holy Spirit knows well what he is doing; the Son knows well how to prepare a spiritual dwelling for himself. For the Maker of nature does not submit himself to the laws of nature; he alone conceives the design; he alone, according to his intention, clothes himself in the form of a servant.

The Father is aware of the Incarnation of his only begotten Son because, where the Holy Spirit is, there also is the Son, and where the Son is, there the Father also is. The Trinity is inseparable and indivisible. For, as in the beginning the Father, when he formed man, induced the Son and the Holy Spirit to act as well, saying: *Let us make man in our image and likeness* (Gen 1:26), so now, at the moment of the new creation, the Holy Trinity is present once again, in an ineffable way. The first creation was common to the Trinity; the second creation is again common to it.

Therefore, the Holy Child to be born will be called Son of God. For he is truly a holy offspring, a shoot not grown from a seed, a most holy birth. He is the Son of God according to his divinity and your Son according to his humanity. He is consubstantial with the Father according to what is understood by faith and consubstantial with you according to his visible nature. He is heavenly and earthly, invisible and visible, impassible in his divinity and passible in his humanity. And, as he is a perfect God, Jesus is also perfect man. But just as he, having become man, remained the immutable God, so you, remaining a virgin, will become the incorrupt Mother. For virginity will not be opposed to birth, nor will birth oppose itself to virginity.

Do you want to know? Apprehend the truth of the prodigy that has happened in you from a visible sign. Do you want to contemplate a figure of the mystery surrounding your conception? Look upon Elizabeth, your neighbor and relative. *For behold*—he says—*Elizabeth your cousin has conceived a son in her old age; this is the sixth month for her who was called barren; for no word is impossible for God* (Lk 1:36–37).

Elizabeth was freed from her hopeless sterility, so that her release from suffering was a proof of your untouched virginity. She, old and barren, conceived the forerunner of the King who will be born from you, so that you may believe that you carry the Savior in your womb. Go, observe Elizabeth, and, if you do not find her as I have said, then do not believe in my message.

What response, then, does holy Mary make to these words, the Virgin in body and spirit, pious, God-fearing, obedient, the honor of human nature, the gate of our life, the procurer of our salvation?

Receiving the angel's words with a good disposition, she answers him: *Behold the handmaid of the Lord; let it be done to me according to your word* (Lk 1:38). As a handmaid, I submit to the Lord's orders; as clay, I entrust myself to the hands of the Potter; let the Craftsman realize his design in me, according to his authoritative will; let him miraculously bring about the extraordinary pregnancy in me, in conformity with his love for men. Let it happen to me according to your word; let your words be fulfilled in me, and let what happens be made completely manifest and true.

And the angel left her, he who had descended from heaven, had instructed and prepared the Virgin. He had trained her, insofar as he was able. He also heard from her what was important for him to apprehend, and once more he went up whence he had come down, leaving there below him who had sent him. And the angel found him once more, there above in the heavens, adored by all the angelic band.

Now, Arius, what do you have to say about all this? Tell me, wretch, how was the Uncontainable contained within the Virgin's womb? How did she conceive as a virgin and remain a virgin, while at the same time becoming enriched by the birth of the Savior and by grace?

But you cannot answer. For if even the Mother of the mystery did not understand the mystery she bore, how could you comprehend it? If the archangel Gabriel, when questioned by the Mother of the Lord: *How will this happen to me, since I do not know man?* could not say more, but took refuge in the Holy Spirit, being unable to proffer anything more substantial, how will you be able to say what Gabriel was unable to interpret?

If no one can adequately explain the generation of Christ according to the flesh, which occurred in the last days, how dare you pry into that generation of Christ, which is heavenly, eternal, incorporeal, invisible, impassible, totally unspeakable and incomprehensible?

—Pseudo-Chrysostom, *On the Annunciation to the Mother of God and against the Impious Arius*; PG 62, 765–68

5

CAELIUS SEDULIUS
(d. ca. 440–450)

Although the influence of the Council of Ephesus was manifested more clearly in the life of the Eastern Church, we also need to recognize its strong influence in the Western Church, where it encouraged a more explicit Marian piety. Attention to and veneration of Mary had already found frequent expression in Western literature, particularly in such great authors as St. Ambrose, St. Jerome, and St. Augustine; now it was expressed in bolder and more conspicuous displays of devotion.

It was probably in the years between Ephesus and Chalcedon that a Mass of the Annunciation was introduced into the Ambrosian rite; even more important was the insertion of a commemoration of the Blessed Virgin into the Roman Canon. Latin authors who bear important witness to the positive developments of this period include St. Peter Chrysologus, especially with regard to homiletics, and the liturgical poet Sedulius, who continues the Latin tradition of writings in praise of Mary.

We know very little about the life of Caelius Sedulius, a poet much appreciated in the Middle Ages and in modern times; nevertheless, his name is well known to Christian tradition, because (among other reasons) some of his compositions have become part of the liturgical patrimony of the Latin Church. The place of his birth and the dates of his life are uncertain. Even his first name, Caelius, is attested to only in later manuscripts. We do not know when or where he was born, but it appears to have been somewhere in Italy. It appears that he spent part of his life in Greece. From the information handed down to us by other writers, it is deduced that he was a priest and that he served as a cantor in liturgical ceremonies. His death is dated somewhere between 440 and 450.

Sedulius' most famous work is the *Carmen Paschale* ("Easter Hymn"), a sort of free elaboration of the four Gospels. Often he inserts strictly personal reflections and expressions of his own feelings. In various passages in the *Carmen*, the Blessed Virgin is presented in tones of lofty inspiration, not without a certain formal beauty; the work sometimes recalls the style of the great poets of classical antiquity, both pagan and Christian.

On a historical level, the expressions of praise with which he addresses the Mother of the Lord confirm the phenomenon of increasing Marian devotion we have mentioned above. In his poetry, Sedulius sings of everything that the Marian doctrine of that time was teaching; after the Council of Ephesus, of course, this doctrine was even more richly developed. Usually, however, the poet does not dwell at length on dogmatic themes. His poetry is made up of brief, penetrating, evocative intuitions of meaning. Often, the figure of Mary will suddenly appear and just as suddenly vanish, leaving behind a lingering trace of beauty that arouses a kind of dreamy longing in the reader. The greatness of Sedulius lies precisely in his ability to make his readers intuit and sense even what he does not say.[1]

Mother of the Lamb

The biblical metaphor of the Lamb, referring to Christ, led various Fathers and Christian writers to depict his Mother as a ewe lamb. Instead, Sedulius, more realistically, refers to Mary using the metaphor of a sheep:

> Open to me the narrow way that leads the few
>   to the city of salvation,
> And grant that the lamp of the Word should shine
>   before my feet
> So that the path of my life may guide me to the confines
>   of that country
> Where the good Shepherd guards his flock, where first enters in,

---

[1] For the Marian content of Sedulius' poetry, see C. Weymann, "Der Preis der Gottesmutter bei Sedulius", *Münchener Museum* 3 (1923): 186–89; A. Bastiansen, "L'Antienne 'Genuit puerpera regem', adaptation liturgique d'un passage du Paschale Carmen de Sedulius", *Revue Bénédictine* 83 (1973): 388–97.

Clothed in white fleece, the Lamb born of the virgin sheep,
And then the whole white-clad flock.[2]

Obviously, these verses recall Revelation 14:4, where it is said that the virgins follow the Lamb wherever he goes. The reference to Mary is purely incidental; however, it is not devoid of a certain attraction linked to the realistic, tangible metaphor of the sheep. Seeing that the Book of Revelation presents Jesus as the Lamb, it spontaneously occurred to the poet that his Mother could be called "sheep", with the addition of the adjective "virgin", to specify her extraordinary personal condition. It does not appear that Sedulius was the first to use this metaphor for the Virgin Mother. We know that the nearest metaphor is that of the ewe lamb, found in an ancient Easter homily of Melito of Sardis[3] and in a homily of Proclus.[4]

The New Eve

In his *Carmen*, Sedulius introduces the classic Eve–Mary parallel, using the metaphor of a rose to give the poem's doctrinal content a tinge of lyricism:

As the tender rose springs up among prickly thorns
But does not offend in any way, since its beauty obscures
    its thorny branches,
So holy Mary, the new virgin descending
    from the branch of Eve,
Makes pure the old virgin's offense.
Just so the old nature languished, corrupted
Under the sentence of death. Once Christ was born,
Man could be born anew and cast off his old nature's stain.[5]

The image of the rose meaningfully illustrates both the person and role of Mary. As the rose blooms in the midst of thorns without

---

[2] *Carmen Paschale* 1, 79–84; PL 19, 561; CSEL 10, 21–22.
[3] *Easter Homily,* SC 123, 98, v. 514 (see pt. 1, chap. 3, reading).
[4] *Homily* 4, 2; PG 65, 712 A.
[5] *Carmen* 2, 28–34; PL 19, 595–96; CSEL 10, 46.

losing its beauty and its pleasantness, so Mary, though born from the
sinful stock of Eve, does not lose her beauty by falling into evil;
instead, she compensates for the old Eve's offense. Thus the poet,
reprising the idea of Irenaeus, assigns Mary an active role in the
economy of salvation.

In another of his compositions, an elegy of fifty-five distichs,
Sedulius again returns to this same parallel, laying down its biblical
foundation: St. Paul's comparison between Adam and Christ.

> Because of one man, all his descendants perished;
> And all are saved because of one man.
> Because of one woman, the deadly door opened;
> And life returned, because of one woman.[6]

In the same context, the poet brings out Mary's contribution to
the work of salvation, contrasting it to the disastrous conduct of
Eve:

> We are the blind offspring of the children of pitiful Eve,
> Bringing with us the shadows born of an age-old error.
> But when God deigned to assume the mortal form
> Of a human nature, then came forth from the Virgin
> A world of salvation. . . .[7]

In this passage also, the poet underscores Mary's involvement in
the saving action of Christ the Redeemer; the contrast with Eve enables him to make his thought clear: From his ancient foremother,
man received only darkness, while from the Virgin, Mother of the
God incarnate, all men were offered a world in which they might
find salvation. Here metaphors are interwoven, one with another:
this virgin earth, from which the Redeemer was born, was, in the
view of the Fathers, already prophetically anticipated in Eden, the
virgin earth that had produced the fruit of life without prior cultivation. Here, too, Sedulius is probably recalling Irenaeus, who had already called Mary "cause of salvation".[8]

---

[6] *Elegia* 5–8; PL 19, 753.

[7] *Carmen* 4, 265–69; PL 19, 697; CSEL 10, 109.

[8] *Haer.* 3, 22, 4; PG 7, 959. The Greek original of this text has not survived, but
the oldest Latin translation has the expression *causa salutis*.

The Incarnation

According to Sedulius, the words that the angel spoke to Mary in the Annunciation do not represent the first announcement of salvation. The prophets of old had already predicted it, but Gabriel came to bring the glad tidings of its realization, which happened following the Blessed Virgin's word of faith:

> After the ancient prophets told what was to come about,
> The angel revealed to untouched Mary that it was very near.
> Faith received the message, and suddenly a heavenly burden
> Filled the maiden's womb: the world's Maker
> Made himself obey the laws of birth. The unmarried Virgin
>   looks with wonder
> At her swollen belly and rejoices: she is to bear
>   her own Creator.[9]

In these few verses, Sedulius touches on all the traditional exegetical themes connected with the Gospel of the Annunciation: The angel conveys the word of the Lord; Mary responds with the adherence of her own faith; the Son of God is made man in her womb by a virginal conception (cf. Jn 1:14); he, the Creator and Lord of the world, abases himself to the point of submitting to the limits of the human condition (cf. Phil 2:6–8).

In the mystery of Christmas as well, Sedulius puts the emphasis on Mary's miraculous virginity. The birth of the Child took place yet left his Mother's womb intact:

> Nine months having passed, on the threshold of the tenth,
> That holy day shone forth on which the pregnant Virgin
> Brought the promised work to its fulfillment:
>   the Word became flesh,
> Wishing to dwell among us (cf. Jn 1:14). Then the
>   most-high Infant,
> Conserving intact the womb [*viscera*] of his temple,[10]

---

[9] *Carmen* 2, 35–40; PL 19, 596; CSEL 10, 46.

[10] The metaphor of the temple, in connection with the Incarnation, has two possible usages in the writings of the Fathers. It can indicate Christ's human nature, chosen by the incarnate Word as the temple of his divinity; alternatively it indicates Mary's womb, as in this case.

Left undamaged the pathways of his birth. He who was born
    bears witness
For the Virgin: He left her closed in coming in,
    and closed in coming forth.[11]

In these verses one can clearly notice a description of events in
rapid succession; this is typical of Sedulius' style, together with his
ability to blend the realism of the story with the fluid and musical
quality of his highly inspired verse. We may observe, for example,
the detail of Mary's reaction, as she looks at her womb after the Incarnation of the Word. Here is a young girl experiencing her first and
last pregnancy, and that glance, so spontaneous and human, reveals a
curiosity full of wonder and candor.

On the doctrinal level, Sedulius discloses very well-defined opinions in his verses. He is aware that not only God but also the Virgin
played an active role in the mystery of the Incarnation; she completed what God had promised to bring about. Further, Mary's virginity is clearly proclaimed in two aspects, directly linked to the
mystery of the Incarnation: virginity before giving birth (*virgine feta*)
and virginity in giving birth (*intemerata sui conservans viscera templi, /
inlaesum vacuavit iter*). As for Mary's virginity after giving birth:
Sedulius appears to affirm this in the reference to the classic text of
the prophet Ezekiel about the eastern gate of the Temple, through
which only the Lord passed and which remained shut nevertheless
(cf. Ezek 44:1–3). This passage recurs repeatedly in the writings of
the Fathers, who understood it as a foreshadowing of Mary's virginity. For Sedulius too, Mary's womb remained closed, even though
the Son of God entered it and came forth from it (*clausa ingrediens et
clausa relinquens*). No one but the Lord passed through the Virgin's
womb, the Lord alone.

In the following verses, the poet indulges in a series of exclamations, marveling at the wondrous effects of Jesus' birth:

What new light shines out in the world; what grace
    throughout the heavens!
What a glory it was, when Christ from Mary's womb
Came forth in new splendor! He was like a bridegroom

---

[11] *Carmen* 2, 41–47; PL 19, 597; CSEL 10, 47.

> Coming forth exultant from his gorgeous chamber,
> his pleasing form
> Beautiful beyond other men, his figure radiant,
> grace poured out upon his lips.[12]

The poet does not comment upon the external miracles recorded in the Gospel: the appearance of the angels to the shepherds; the star, the Magi. His attention and contemplation are concentrated on the miracle par excellence: the divine Infant, born of a Virgin Mother. With obvious allusions to biblical passages, he reveals his fascination with other signs that accompanied the event: light, joy, sweetness, beauty, grace. In the course of Christian tradition, all of these characteristics have been connected with the Christian celebration of Christmas.

The Angel's Prophetic Greeting

A little later on, Sedulius addresses to the Virgin an exclamation of wonder and greeting that appears to echo certain passages from the prophet Isaiah. This is found in seven verses that are the best known of the poet's work, beginning with the words: *Salve sancta parens, enixa puerpera regem.* They were introduced into the liturgy as the entrance antiphon of the Mass for the Saturday Memorial of the Blessed Virgin Mary. There is another curious detail: in medieval manuscripts, these words are usually written in red ink. Here is the text:

> Hail, O holy mother; you gave birth to the King
> Who governs heaven and earth forever, whose
> Divinity and dominion embrace everything
> in one eternal realm
> And endure without end. In your blessed womb
> You hold a mother's joy, yet you enjoy the honor of virginity.
> No woman like you was seen before, nor did one appear after;
> You alone, without comparison, were the woman
> who pleased Christ.[13]

---

[12] Ibid., 2, 48–53; PL 19, 597–98; CSEL 10, 48.
[13] Ibid., 2, 63–69; PL 19, 599–60; CSEL 10, 48–49.

This impassioned passage is a virtual synthesis of all Mariology. It brings out Mary's divine motherhood, her virginity, the exceptional holiness of the Mother of the Lord, the grace of the divine election. Similarly, the Gregorian melody to which the first verses of this text were set seems to express, by the calmness and slowness of its rhythm, the desire to dwell in contemplative admiration of the awesome wonder of the Lord's Virgin Mother for as long as possible.

Mary and the Paschal Mystery

Among the Latin poets, Sedulius is the first to refer to Mary's participation in the mysteries of Jesus' death and Resurrection, basing his work on apocryphal narratives that speak of the Risen Christ appearing to his Mother. In one passage, he places Mary among the women who hasten to the tomb on the morning of the Resurrection:

> At dawn that day
> The Virgin Mother, carrying like the other mothers
>   an offering
> Of aromatic ointment, went weeping to the
>   well-known tomb
> And found the place already empty of a body
> But full of power.[14]

As we can see, the poet does not give much detailed information about this particular situation. He gives more detail when he speaks of the risen Lord appearing to his Mother and offers some brief but interesting theological considerations:

> The synagogue withdrew, eclipsed by his face.
> Christ unites himself to the Church in fairest love.
> This illuminates the conspicuous greatness of Mary,
> Who, while always conserving the glorious name of Mother,
> Remains a Virgin ever.
> The Lord showed himself to her eyes first,
> When he revealed himself openly in the light, so that
>   the good Mother,

---

[14] Ibid., 5, 322–26; PL 19, 738; CSEL 10, 138.

Who was once the way of his arrival,
By spreading the news of the great miracles,
Became the sign of his return as well.[15]

In his reflection, the poet follows certain traditions that were widespread in the Eastern Church. He asserts that the Savior, who had come from the synagogue, now has taken himself a new bride; namely, the Church, which is illuminated by the greatness of Mary, the Virgin Mother, because the Church herself is both virgin and mother. Here we are very close to the thought of Augustine, who held that for Mary to be virgin and mother was almost an ecclesial necessity, inasmuch as she had to prefigure the Church.

Mentioning Jesus' appearance to his Mother after the Resurrection, Sedulius also gives some reasons for it. Mary received the mission of witnessing to the events and miracles wrought by her Son and to be a sign and guarantee of his Second Coming by her presence. Mary was especially qualified for this mission because she had been the way through which Jesus came to us for the first time. Thus, for the infant Church, the presence of the Virgin Mother was a kind of *memoria* of the Lord, whose glorious return all Christians must await.

Sedulius is also the author of a very beautiful hymn that the liturgy has assigned to the office of the Christmas season. Composed in iambic tetrameter, it begins with the words: *A solis ortus cardine*. It contains twenty-three strophes in all and is structured as an acrostic; that is, every strophe begins with a different letter of the alphabet, in order. This hymn verifies the freshness and creativity of Sedulius' poetic style (at the end of this chapter we reprint the six strophes that have Marian content).

This enchanting singer of the Christian mysteries, whose life and activity have remained so mysterious, has left us a precious legacy of poetry, of witness to the faith, and of Marian piety.

---

[15] Ibid., 5, 357–64; PL 19, 742–43; CSEL 10, 140–41.

READING

IN PRAISE OF THE DIVINE MOTHERHOOD

> Now, from the rising of the sun
> Unto the very ends of earth,
> Let us sing praise to Christ our Head,
> Born of the Virgin Mary.
>
> The blessed Maker of the world
> Put on the body of a slave
> Lest, setting free the flesh by flesh,
> He let be lost what he had made.
>
> The grace of heaven enters in
> The closed-up Mother's inmost parts.
> The maiden's womb bears
> A mystery unknown to her.
>
> The dwelling of a modest heart
> Suddenly becomes God's temple;
> Untouched, not knowing man,
> She spoke a word and made a Son.
>
> In childbirth she gave birth to him
> Whom Gabriel had foretold,
> Whom John had recognized,
> While still his Mother's womb enclosed him.
>
> He endured lying in the manger,
> He did not spurn the crib.
> He fed upon a little milk;
> Through him not even birds lack food.

—Caelius Sedulius, *Hymn* 2, 1–24; PL 19, 763–64;
CSEL 10, 163–64

6

PETER CHRYSOLOGUS
(ca. 380–ca. 450)

The famous preacher Peter Chrysologus has left us a collection of homilies that witness to his vast culture as well as his superb rhetorical training. Even today, these homilies pass on the human warmth with which he preached to the faithful of Ravenna. They clearly reveal their author's deep faith, doctrinal convictions, and the apostolic zeal that marked his pastoral mission in the Church. Equally precious is the information they contain about fifth-century Christian life and the development of the liturgical year in the Latin Church, especially in the Christian community at Ravenna. Chrysologus' homilies also show him to be a strong defender of the primacy of the bishop of Rome.

The historical sources for his life are rather wanting. The *Liber Pontificalis* mentions him, and we have a ninth-century biography by Agnellus of Ravenna, who coined the title *Chrysologus* (of the golden word). It appears that he was born at Imola around the year 380. It is certain that before 431 he became metropolitan archbishop of Ravenna, which was then the capital of the western part of the Roman Empire.

When the Monophysite controversy exploded, he wrote a letter to the archimandrite Eutyches, exhorting him to submit to the decision of Pope St. Leo the Great, as expounded in the pope's letter to Flavian, patriarch of Constantinople. The year of Peter's death is also uncertain; in all probability, he died in the year 450.

The historical period in which Peter governed the Church at Ravenna was crucial for working out and developing the doctrine of the Incarnation and, consequently, for understanding the Virgin Mary's role in this mystery. These are the years between the Councils of Ephesus and Chalcedon. Accordingly, for the sake of his people in Ravenna, Peter tried to be a simple and easily understood teacher of Christian faith and doctrine. He became an exemplary exponent of the teaching of the Council of Ephesus and took a very clear stand in confronting the Nestorian heresy. Alluding to the deposed patriarch of Constantinople and his supporters, he wrote:

> As for those who seek to cloud the issue with Greek confusion, blaspheming by calling Mary *anthropotókos* [mother of a man] or *christotókos* [Mother of Christ] so as to deny her the title *Theotókos*, just let them come and hear the clarity of the Latin language: "That which is born in her is of the Holy Spirit" (Mt 1:20). And that which is born of the Holy Spirit is spirit, because God is spirit.[1]

The bishop of Ravenna speaks of the Blessed Virgin especially in his discourses on the Annunciation, on the Incarnation, and on Christmas; he mentions her in passing in various other homilies as well.[2]

Mother of God and Our Lady

We have already seen how Peter defended the title *Theotókos*. However, he avoided the corresponding Latin expressions *Mater Dei* or *Dei Genetrix*, since the Latin language contained similar expressions with pagan overtones. He preferred to call the Mother of the Lord by the appellation "Virgin" or simply by her name, Mary, which he translated as *Domina*:

> Even before the angel announced God's plan, the Virgin's dignity was announced by her name; for the Hebrew word Mary is rendered in Latin as *Domina* ["Lady"]. Hence the angel calls her Lady, so that the fear proper to servitude might leave her, the Mother of the Master.

---

[1] *Sermo* 145, 6; PL 52, 590.

[2] Some bibliographical references for understanding the Marian teaching of Chrysologus: R. H. McGlynn, *The Incarnation in the Sermons of Saint Peter Chrysologus* (Chicago: Mundelein Seminary, 1956); J. P. Barrios, "La naturaleza del vínculo matrimonial entre María y José según san Pedro Crisólogo", *Ephemerides Mariologicae* 16 (1966): 321–55; F. Sottocornola, "Il contenuto mariano dei sermoni di Pietro Crisologo", *Ravennatensia* 8 (Cesena, 1983), 13–42.

For her Son's authority decreed and brought it about that she should be born and named Lady.[3]

When Peter is trying to explain the doctrine of Ephesus to his listeners, he does not attempt to interest them in doctrinal concepts. Instead, he uses clear and concrete language to stir up their personal feelings of affection toward the Virgin:

"Blessed are you among women" (Lk 1:42). The Virgin is truly blessed, for she possessed the splendor of virginity and achieved the dignity of motherhood. She is truly blessed, for she merited the grace of a heavenly conception and wore the crown of integrity. She is truly blessed, for she received the glory of the divine Son and is queen of all chastity.[4]

The preacher presents Mary's motherhood as a unique case, because it was the consequence of a miraculous and heavenly conception and because its fruit was a divine Son. Her Son cannot be contained, is above all things, and gives existence and continued being to all things. In essence, Peter's discourse is based on the concept of the totality of the person of the incarnate Word and is totally opposed to the Nestorian formulation, which emphasizes the division of the components of Christ's personhood.

The Miracle of Mary's Virginity

We have already seen how Peter continually interweaves the theme of Mary's virginity with the theme of her motherhood. Echoing the great Latin Fathers who came before him, Chrysologus defines the three phases of Mary's virginity; namely, before, during, and after childbirth:

She conceives as a virgin, she gives birth as a virgin, and she remains a virgin. Therefore, her flesh knows the power of the miracle but does not know pain. In giving birth, it gains in integrity and knows nothing of physical suffering.[5]

---

[3] *Sermo* 142, 2; PL 52, 570.
[4] *Sermo* 143, 7; PL 52, 584.
[5] *Sermo* 117, 3; PL 52, 521.

The extraordinary circumstances of Mary's virginity endow it with an important character, which Peter Chrysologus does not fail to emphasize:

> When someone conceives as a virgin, gives birth as a virgin, and remains a virgin, this is not normal; it is a sign. It is not the work of logic but of divine power. Nature's maker did it, not nature. It is not common but unique. It is divine, not human. Therefore let hapless philosophy cease trying to explain it.[6]

The phenomenon of a woman who conceives and gives birth as a virgin invalidates every empty claim of the human mind to transcend the limits of understanding. Before the workings of God's almighty power, there is no room for our pride or ambitions. The bishop of Ravenna invites his readers to learn the role Mary played in the economy of salvation.

He observes, further, that the miracle of the Virgin Mother cast Mary's own husband into wonder and perplexity. This was the person who knew her best and who was preparing to share the rest of his life with her:

> His holy soul was inflamed, struck by the newness of the affair. His bride was pregnant but a virgin; she was full of promise but not empty of chastity; she was troubled by the conception that had taken place, yet she felt sure of her own integrity. She was clothed in her maternal role but not despoiled of the honor of virginity.
>
> What should her husband do in such a situation? Accuse her of a crime? But he himself was the witness of her innocence. Reveal her sin? But he himself was the guardian of her good reputation. Charge her with adultery? But he himself was the assertor of her virginity.[7]

Joseph's crisis of conscience, as reported in the Gospel (cf. Mt 1:19–20), was the point of departure for much embellishment, both in the apocryphal literature and in the writings of the Fathers. But while the apocrypha concentrated mainly on fanciful and sensational developments of the situation, the Fathers are more concerned with finding explanations that would leave no shadow of uncertainty or doubt regarding the coherence and wisdom of God's extraordinary

---

[6] *Sermo* 148, 1; PL 52, 596.
[7] *Sermo* 145, 1; PL 52, 588–89.

acts. Therefore Chrysologus views Joseph as a man who, placed into a situation that, humanly speaking, appeared to have no possibility of a positive outcome, nevertheless managed to discern the presence of an inscrutable mystery, a divine intervention he considered himself absolutely incapable of understanding. From this, Peter draws an admonition that he addresses to his faithful, lest they fall into useless chatter:

> Therefore, O man, beware of such discussions about the birth of our Mother. Let it suffice that the angel answered: "Do not be afraid to take Mary as your wife, for what is born in her is of the Holy Spirit" (Mt 1:20).[8]

In another sermon, he repeats this admonition in even more peremptory terms, referring to the theme of faith:

> Since all things are possible for God, while for you it is impossible to duplicate even the least of his works, do not discuss the Virgin's conception, but believe it. Be piously convinced that God wanted to be born, because if you set yourself to inquiring into it, you will do yourself harm. Approach the great mystery of the Lord's birth with faith since, without faith, you will not be able to approach the least of God's works.[9]

Faith, then, is the main road on which the Christian approaches the mysteries of God. And because the virginal birth of Christ from Mary is one of these ineffable mysteries, faith remains the only possible response to the word of God and to his interventions in human history. In this perspective Mary, whom the Fathers never ceased to exalt because of her faith, becomes herself an object of faith for the Christian people.

Mary, God's Spouse

Peter Chrysologus appears to have been the first Latin Father to call the Blessed Virgin "God's spouse". Commenting upon the mystery

---

[8] *Sermo* 175, 1; PL 52, 658.
[9] *Sermo* 141, 3; PL 52, 578.

of the Annunciation, in which the Gospel presents Mary as a Virgin involved in a marriage contract (*desponsata*) with Joseph (cf. Lk 1:27), he discerns a parallel spousal relationship between Mary and God himself:

> The messenger flies swiftly to the spouse, in order to remove every attachment to a human marriage from God's spouse. He does not take the Virgin away from Joseph but simply restores her to Christ, to whom she had been promised when she was being formed in her mother's womb. Christ, then, takes his own bride; he does not steal someone else's. Nor does he cause any separation when he unites his own creature to himself, in a single body.[10]

Mary's divine marriage with her Son is compared to the human marriage she was going to contract with Joseph. The text excludes any incompatibility between the two types of marriage, because they take place on two different levels; however, Peter does not hesitate to affirm the clear superiority of the divine marriage over the human marriage. The divine marriage belongs to the eternal plan of divine election, according to which the creature is bound to its Creator before anything else; the marriage with Joseph, upon which our author does not place much emphasis, is part of the order of human possibilities. The only condition imposed by the realization of the divine plan is the attitude of total interior detachment from the human situation that would result.

Chrysologus' fluid and systematic reasoning may have been difficult for an assembly of the simple faithful to understand, given its dialectical nuances. But certainly, they could not have missed some of the more concrete phrases, based on such physical metaphors as marriage, spouses, and physical union, which Peter used in order to bring out the privileged relationship between Mary and her Son, who in another sermon is called "Bridegroom and guardian of his mother's purity".[11] Peter Chrysologus refers to Mary in the words of the Song of Songs 4:12: "My bride is an enclosed garden, a sealed fountain", which the Bridegroom built when he descended into her to realize the plan of the Incarnation.[12]

---

[10] *Sermo* 140, 2; PL 52, 576.
[11] *Sermo* 140 ter, 2; CCL 24 B, 854.
[12] *Sermo* 145, 4; PL 52, 589.

The Eve–Mary Parallel

Our preacher developed the ancient comparison between Eve and
Mary in a quite original way. Commenting upon the Gospel parable
of the leaven that a woman takes and mixes with three measures of
flour (cf. Mt 13:33), he explains:

> The woman, who had received the leaven of perfidy from the devil,
> received the leaven of faith from God. He hid it in three measures of
> flour, that is to say, in three periods of human history; namely, from
> Adam to Noah, from Noah to Moses, and from Moses to Christ.
>   Thus the woman, who in Adam ruined the entire mass of the
> human race with the leaven of death, restored the entire mass of our
> flesh in Christ with the leaven of the Resurrection. Then the
> woman, who had baked the bread of suffering and sweat, baked the
> bread of life and salvation.[13]

It is the first time that we encounter the parallel between Eve and
the woman in this Gospel parable; the woman in the story is also a
figure of the Virgin Mary, as Peter asserts in developing his thought
further:

> Through Christ, she became the true Mother of all the living, who in
> Adam had become the mother of all the dead. Christ willed to be
> born in this way, so that, as death came to all through Eve, so life
> might return to all through Mary.
>   For Mary corresponds to the typology of the leaven, she bears its
> likeness, she authenticates the figure, since she receives the leaven of
> the Word from above and receives his human flesh into her virginal
> womb, and, in her virginal womb, she transfuses the heavenly man
> into the entire mass [of dough].[14]

The author draws out the parallelism to woman in general, who,
in virtue of the actions of Christ, has again been restored to her role
as mother of the living. Yet this salvific plan manifests its firstfruits in
the person of Mary and in the role she plays. Therefore, Mary anticipates, on a practical level, the meaning of the woman in the Gospel
parable and the fruits that the Church herself is called to produce in

---

[13] *Sermo* 99, 5; PL 52, 478–79.
[14] Ibid.

the course of her mission. In other words: in contrast to Eve, Mary accomplished that soteriological task which the Church is also called to fulfill during the time of her earthly existence. The woman in the parable is a symbol already realized in Mary and a symbol that needs to be realized in the Church.

The meaning of the presence of the women at the tomb of Jesus (cf. Mt 28:1–8) is also interpreted in the light of the Eve–Mary parallel. In the earthly paradise, the woman was witness to the downfall and death of the human race; at the tomb of Christ, women witness the return of human beings to life. In the person of Mary, woman is released from the negative role that she played at the beginning of creation:

> "Mary and the other Mary came to see the tomb" (Mt 28:1). She who had taken perfidy away from paradise hurries to take faith from the tomb; she, who had snatched death from the hands of life, hastens to snatch life from the hands of death. "Mary came." The name is that of the Mother of Christ; that is, the Mother came, the woman came, so that she who had become the mother of the dying might become now the Mother of the living, and so that what had been written might be fulfilled: "She was the Mother of all the living" (Gen 3:20).[15]

Peter identifies the Mother of the Lord as "the other Mary" who went to the tomb together with Mary Magdalen. He recognizes in the two women a faith that can withstand any trial. For the women went to see the tomb, not the Lord, whom they believed already risen:

> Mary and Mary came to see the tomb; do you understand that they came, not to see the Lord, but to see the tomb? For they really believed that the Lord was already risen; therefore, they were not seeking him among the dead, since he already lived.[16]

In the person of the two Marys, Peter also recognizes the presence of the Church herself at the tomb, since the Church is made up of two ethnic groups: Jews and Gentiles.

---

[15] *Sermo* 74, 3; PL 52, 409.
[16] *Sermo* 75, 3; PL 52, 413.

Devotion to Mary

Chrysologus does not fail repeatedly to express his unbounded admiration for the mystery wrought in the Mother of the Lord and the greatness of her vocation. He sees her greatness as tied in a certain way to God's own greatness, to the point of thinking that it is impossible to comprehend God correctly without reflecting on the mystery of Mary:

> He who is not awestruck by this Virgin's spirit and who does not admire her soul is ignorant of how great God is. Heaven trembles, angels quake, creation cannot bear it, nature is helpless—yet a girl carries God in her womb; she receives him into herself and offers him a dwelling place.[17]

In his sermons on the Annunciation, he loves to repeat the angel's greeting, amplifying it with comments in which he manifests all his love and veneration for Mary. Commenting on Elizabeth's greeting, he exclaims:

> Truly blessed is she who was greater than the heavens, stronger than the earth, vaster than the globe. For she alone contained within herself that God whom the world cannot contain; she bore him who bears the world; she gave birth to her Father; she nursed him who nurtures every living thing.[18]

READING

"WHEN HIS MOTHER MARY WAS BETROTHED . . ." (MT 1:18)

It would have been enough to say: "When Mary was betrothed." What is the meaning of a betrothed woman who is a mother? If she is a mother, then she is not betrothed; if she is betrothed, then she is not yet a mother. "When Mary his Mother was betrothed." Betrothed, because of her virginity; Mother, because of her fertility; a mother who knows not man, though she does know birth. And how could she not have been a mother before his conception, seeing that she was a Virgin Mother after giving birth? When was she not a

---

[17] *Sermo* 140, 6; PL 52, 577.
[18] *Sermo* 143, 7; PL 52, 584.

birthgiver, she who gave birth to the Creator of the world? Virgin nature brought about the origin of things, while corrupt nature put an end to things. In the same way, a virgin is mother of things, and a stepmother is always the corruption of things. It is a virginal task for a virgin, by God's power, to regenerate what another virgin generated by God's power. God and virginal integrity form a heavenly couple; virginity united to Christ forms a perfect union of virtue.

What the Virgin conceives is the honor of the Spirit and not a burden of the flesh. What the Virgin bears is a mystery of God, not a conjugal secret. The birth of Christ is a work of divine majesty, not of human weakness; that the flesh suffered no injury pertains solely to the glory of divinity.

"When his Mother Mary was betrothed to Joseph, before they lived together, she was found with child by the Holy Spirit" (Mt 1:18). Why is the mystery of heavenly innocence entrusted to a betrothed woman and not to an unattached woman? Why cause anxiety for the groom and for the bride? Why should such great virtue be considered a crime and the entire work of salvation a threat? Why should the modesty of innocent persons have to undergo such a trial? Why should modesty surrender, chastity grow weary, faith be wounded, accusations arise, the facts cry out for attention, so that every possibility of an excuse is taken away? How could a betrothed woman excuse herself if they accused her of having conceived? How could she take advantage of an exterior defender when there is an internal witness to the facts? What shall we think, brothers? Consider that, in the Gospel, signs, letters, syllables, words, names, and persons always have a divine significance.

A betrothed woman was chosen, so that Christ's Church might already be symbolically indicated as bride, according to the words of the prophet Hosea: "I will make you my bride in justice and right; I will make you my bride in mercy and benevolence, and I will espouse you in fidelity" (Hos 2:19–20). Thus John says: "He who has a bride is the bridegroom" (Jn 3:29). And blessed Paul: "I have promised you to one Bridegroom, to present you to Christ as a chaste virgin" (2 Cor 11:2). She is truly a bride, who regenerates the new infancy of Christ by a virginal birth.

—Peter Chrysologus, *Sermo* 146, 3–5; PL 52, 592

LEO THE GREAT
(d. 461)

In the history of the development of christological dogma, the name of St. Leo is tied to the Council of Chalcedon (451). There, in his capacity as bishop of Rome, he intervened authoritatively and effectively in one of the most important theological controversies of the Eastern Church. While the East has always considered the conclusions of the Council a decisive moment in the evolution of the christological debate, the Western tradition has received the formula of Chalcedon as the resolution of a doctrinal crisis.

On the eve of this Council, which was to proclaim the doctrine about the mystery of the incarnate Word, Pope Leo sent an important letter, known as the *Tomus ad Flavianum*, to Flavian, patriarch of Constantinople. In it he lays out the basic lines of the Christology that would supply the foundation of the solemn definition proclaimed by the Council. It also touched indirectly on the problem of the relations between the Virgin Mary and her divine Son. However, Chalcedon was not the only event of unusual historical importance to mark the long pontificate of Leo I.

We can only hypothesize about his origins and early years. Leo was born in Rome to an Etruscan family around the end of the fourth century. During his studies, he acquired an excellent formation in theology, united with exceptional expertise in the use of the Latin language and in rhetoric. His works are written in an elegant and harmonious style. Ordained deacon, he was incardinated into the Roman clergy and soon had the chance to reveal his rich personal gifts.

In 440, he was in Gaul at the behest of the Emperor Valentinian III, charged with the mission of attempting to effect a reconciliation between two rival officers, Albinus and Aetius. While in Gaul, he was elected to succeed Pope Sixtus III to the Chair of Peter. Thus, upon his return from Gaul, he was consecrated bishop of Rome and supreme pontiff. One of his greatest concerns was to preserve intact the purity of the Catholic faith. To that end, he took strong positions in facing the heresies of his time.

There is also the story of the historical encounter of Pope Leo with Attila, the terrible king of the Huns, who, after sowing terror and death in northern Italy, had turned south with his barbarian forces and was heading for Rome. Leo convinced him to abandon his plans and to withdraw beyond the Alps.

Also decisive was Leo's intervention in the sack of Rome by Genseric and his Vandals in 455. The pontiff was able to ensure that Rome was spared the massacre and torture of the unarmed population.

His death occurred in 461, after a pontificate of more than twenty years. Among his different writings, he left a precious collection of letters and sermons that are important not only for reconstructing the events of his pontificate but also for the history of the Church and for theology. Tradition rightly awards him the title *Magnus*—the Great. He had a clear and profound awareness of the mission and primacy of the Church of Rome and of her bishop, who, as successor of Peter, guaranteed the continuity of the Redeemer's work on earth and the unity of all Christians.

His Marian teaching[1] rests on a firm christological basis. Teaching about the Son afforded him frequent and fitting occasions to speak about his Mother as well.

The Tomus ad Flavianum

After the Council of Ephesus had condemned the heresy of Nestorius, which endangered the unity of the Person of the incarnate

---

[1] Studies on the Marian teaching of St. Leo the Great: A. Spindeler, "S. Leo Magnus de parte B. Virginis Mariae in redemptione", *Maria et Ecclesia*, vol. 4 (Rome, 1959), pp. 141–52; F. Spedalieri, "La Madre del Salvatore nella Soteriologia di S. Leone Magno", *Marianum* 25 (1963): 23–38; B. Studer, "Consubstantialis Patri. Consubstantialis matri: Une antithèse christologique chez Léon le Grand", *Revue des études Augustiniennes* 18 (1972): 87–115; G. M. Polo, *Maria nel mistero della salvezza secondo il papa Leone Magno* (Vicenza 1975).

Word, an equally pernicious error began to spread throughout the East, defended and taught by Eutyches, an influential monk of Constantinople. His ideas provoked the Monophysite schism. We can obtain an exhaustive amount of information about Eutyches from the *Eranistes* of Theodoret of Cyr and in the acts of his trial before the patriarch Flavian. It seems that Eutyches obstinately appealed to some formulas of Cyril of Alexandria, invoking the authority of the deceased patriarch as well as that of the popes Julius and Felix, of Athanasius, Gregory the Wonderworker, and other Fathers.

Intending to combat Nestorian diphysitism, Eutyches fell into the opposite error of a rigid monophysitism that did away with the distinction of the natures in the incarnate Word as a consequence of the hypostatic union. The fundamental teaching of Eutyches can be summed up in the following formula: "I believe that our Lord was in two natures (*ek dúo phýseon*) before the union, but, after the union, I confess only one nature (*mía phýsis*)."[2]

Eutyches' error lay in conceiving of the unity of the Person of Christ in such a manner as to render incongruous the distinction of the two natures, so that, at the moment of the Incarnation, his human nature was in a certain way absorbed by his divinity. Therefore the Church, which already in the first centuries of her history had been obliged energetically to defend the true humanity of the Redeemer against the Docetists and the Manichees, once more found herself forced to react against a new threat to orthodoxy.

Eutyches claimed to have a good reason for denying that the incarnate Christ had an authentic human nature: he was trying to spare him the contagion of original sin, which is transmitted, inevitably, from flesh to flesh. In reality, his doctrine makes the saving action of the Redeemer useless; for, if the Son of God had not truly been made man, he would not have been able to accomplish the work of our salvation. In this problematic context, Pope Leo offers a very clear reflection:

> For we would have been unable to overcome the author of sin and death had Christ not assumed our nature and made it his own. Sin cannot defile him, nor can death hold him. For he was conceived by the Holy Spirit within the womb of a Virgin Mother, who gave birth

---

[2] ACO 2, 1, 1, 143.

to him without losing her virginity, just as she had remained a virgin in conceiving him.[3]

Leo shows how pointless was Eutyches' fear that Christ, in assuming our humanity, could have contracted original sin. What preserved Jesus from original sin was not his alleged lack of a true human nature but rather his extraordinary birth from a virgin. This was, by the way, the common belief at that time. Further on, Leo states:

> He was engendered through a new kind of birth, since the inviolate virginity did not know concupiscence when it supplied the fleshly material [of his body]. From his Mother, the Lord took [human] nature, not the [original] fault.[4]

On the other hand, Leo defines, his miraculous birth could not pose any threat to the reality of his human nature:

> In the Lord Jesus Christ, the human nature does not differ from our own, even though he was born in a miraculous manner from the virginal womb.[5]

The pontiff forcefully affirms that Mary's motherhood is an absolutely real motherhood, although there was no intervention of a man, and that Mary's motherhood guarantees the authenticity of Jesus' human nature, which remains distinct from his divinity even after the hypostatic union.

The Council of Chalcedon was opened on October 8, 451, in the church of St. Euphemia, with more than five hundred bishops present. One might say that Pope Leo had established a rather precise direction for the Council, both through the interventions of his legate, Paschasinus of Lilibeus, and, especially, by his *Tomus ad Flavianum*. When this letter was read in the session of October 10, it was well received by the fathers, who did not hesitate to accept his high spiritual authority and to recognize that "Peter has spoken through the mouth of Leo."[6]

---

[3] *Epist.* 28, 2; PL 54, 759; ACO 2, 2, 1, 25.
[4] Ibid., 4; PL 54, 767; ACO 2, 2, 1, 28.
[5] Ibid.
[6] J. D. Mansi, ed. *Sacrorum conciliorum nova et amplissima collectio*, vol 4, p. 535 (1759, reprint and continuation: Paris and Leipzig, 1901–1927).

In the three truths in which Leo saw a summary of the whole Christian faith, there is also a mention of the Virgin Mary:

> The entirety of the faithful professes its belief in God the Father almighty, and in Jesus Christ his only Son, born of the Holy Spirit and the Virgin Mary. By three beliefs, the machinations of all the heretics are destroyed.[7]

The pontiff also took it upon himself to explain how this brief summary formula of the faith, which guarantees the integrity of the two natures of Christ in the hypostatic union that took place in the womb of Mary, likewise ensures the reality of human salvation accomplished by Christ in his Incarnation:

> This birth within the confines of time took nothing away from his eternal and divine generation and added nothing to it. He offered it totally for the restoration of man, who had been deceived, in order to conquer death and, by his power, to destroy the devil, who ruled over death.
>
> For we would have been unable to overcome the author of sin and death had Christ not assumed our nature and made it his own. Sin cannot defile him, nor can death hold him. For he was conceived by the Holy Spirit within the womb of a Virgin Mother, who gave birth to him without losing her virginity, just as she had remained a virgin in conceiving him.[8]

Mary in the Prophecies of the Old Testament

St. Leo speaks of the Virgin Mother in some of his letters and in various homilies, especially those composed for the feast of Christmas. Following the tradition of the Fathers, he applies some texts of the Old Testament to her. Despite their brevity, his observations are of great importance.

He holds that the woman portrayed in the book of Genesis as the adversary of the tempting serpent and destroyer of his dominion is none other than the Mother of the Lord:

---

[7] *Epist.* 28, 2; PL 54, 757; ACO 2, 2, 1, 24.
[8] *Epist.* 28, 2; PL 54, 759; ACO 2, 2, 1, 25.

He foretold to the serpent that the woman's seed would come and crush his haughty and wicked head with his power (cf. Gen 3:15). The woman's seed is Christ, who was to come in the flesh as God and as man, born of the Virgin, to condemn the despoiler of the human race by his immaculate birth.[9]

Among the prophets who foretold the birth of Christ from the Blessed Virgin, Leo clearly gives pride of place to Isaiah, commenting on various passages:

> Again the Lord speaks through Isaiah: "Behold, the Virgin shall conceive in her womb and bear a son; and they shall call his name Emmanuel, which means: God-with-us" (Is 7:14). And in another place: "A shoot shall sprout from the stump of Jesse, and from his roots a flower shall blossom" (Is 11:1). In this shoot, undoubtedly, the Blessed Virgin Mary was foretold, who descended from the line of Jesse and of David. Made fertile by the Holy Spirit, she brought forth a new flower of human flesh from her maternal womb, while still remaining a virgin in giving birth.[10]

Commenting on the passage: "Let the earth open, that salvation may sprout forth, and let it cause righteousness to spring up also" (Is 45:8), Leo makes a comparison between the birth of Jesus from the Virgin and the rebirth of Christians from the baptismal font:

> The earth of human nature was already cursed in the first liar. Only in this birth from the Blessed Virgin did it produce a blessed shoot, an exception to the vice of its roots. Its spiritual origin is acquired by anyone who is regenerated. And for every man who is born again, the water of baptism is like the virginal womb. The same Spirit that filled the Virgin now fills the baptismal font; hence, that sin, which was once removed by a holy conception, is now taken away by a mystic ablution.[11]

According to Pope Leo, the birth of Jesus from Mary is a type or model of our spiritual rebirth in baptism. The baptismal font resembles the virginal womb of the Lord's Mother. The Holy Spirit is the efficient cause of the human generation of Christ from Mary and

---

[9] *Sermo* 22, 1; PL 54, 194; CCL 138, 90.

[10] *Sermo* 24, 1; PL 54, 204; CCL 138, 110.

[11] Ibid., 3; PL 54, 206; CCL 138, 112–113.

of the divine regeneration of the Christian in the sacrament of baptism. In these considerations, there is an implicit analogy between the mystery of Mary and the mystery of the Church, the Mystical Body of Christ:

> By the Spirit, Christ is born from the body of his unsullied Mother; by this same Spirit, the Christian is reborn from the womb of holy Church.[12]

Mary's Faith and the Incarnation

Another element relates the mystery of Christ's conception with that of baptismal regeneration; namely, faith. Apart from lauding the mystery of Mary's wondrous virginity, St. Leo does not indulge in much praise of the Lord's Mother; however, he appears genuinely to admire her faith. Inspired by St. Augustine, he notes that Mary "conceived the divine–human offspring in her mind before she conceived him in her body".[13]

In the miraculous motherhood of Elizabeth, he sees, not the cause of Mary's faith, but rather an intervention of God for the purpose of reinforcing it: "The testimony of a previous miracle comes to confirm her faith."[14]

Leo invites us to contemplate Mary's faith, especially in the mystery of the Annunciation:

> Not only our memory but somehow our eyes as well contemplate the conversation between the angel Gabriel and the wondering Mary; likewise the conception by the Holy Spirit is wonderful both in its promise and in the faith that received it.[15]

---

[12] *Sermo* 29, 1; PL 54, 227; CCL 138, 147.
[13] *Sermo* 21, 1; PL 54, 191; CCL 138, 86.
[14] Ibid.
[15] *Sermo* 26, 1; PL 54, 212–13; CCL 138, 125.

READING

WHY CHRIST WAS BORN OF A VIRGIN

He was engendered by a new kind of birth, conceived by a Virgin, born of a Virgin, without a father's carnal concupiscence, without injuring his Mother's integrity. Indeed, such a birth was appropriate for the future Savior of men, who, while sharing the nature of human substance, did not know the contamination of human flesh. The Author of God taking flesh is God himself, as the archangel witnesses to the Blessed Virgin Mary: "The Holy Spirit will come upon you, and the power of the Most High will overshadow you; hence, the holy offspring born of you will be called Son of God" (Lk 1:35). In his origin unlike us; in his [human] nature like us—our common human customs are of no help here. It was decided by God's almighty power that Mary should conceive as a virgin, give birth as a virgin, and remain a virgin. Do not think about the condition of his Mother, but consider the decision of the Son, who wanted in this way to be born a man and so brought it about. If you seek the truth about his nature, then recognize the matter as human; if you want to find the secret of his origin, then acknowledge the divine power. For our Lord Jesus Christ came to take away our infection, not to be infected by it; he did not come to succumb to our vices but to heal them. He came to heal the malady of our corruption and all the wounds of our scarred souls. For this reason he had to be born in a new manner, since he was bringing the new grace of spotless integrity to our human bodies. He had to keep his Mother's original virginity intact, and it was necessary that the power of the holy Spirit should safeguard the defense of her modesty, which he was pleased to call the dwelling place of holiness.

For he had decided to raise up what was fallen and restore what was broken apart and to strengthen purity for overcoming the seductions of the flesh, so that virginity, which in others cannot be preserved after childbirth, might be imitated even by others, in rebirth.

—Leo the Great, *Sermo* 22, 2; PL 54, 195–96

8

SEVERUS OF ANTIOCH
(ca. 465–538)

The life and work of Bishop Severus, patriarch of Antioch, are linked to the history of the Monophysite movement. The spiritual and doctrinal legacy of this movement lives on today in three important Orthodox communities: the Coptic Church of Egypt and Ethiopia,[1] the Jacobite Syriac Church, and the Armenian Church. We have identified the monk Eutyches as the most radical proponent of this teaching about the unity of being in Christ, which went so far as to make him consubstantial with the Father but not with us. In addition to Eutychianism, however, there arose other, more moderate forms of monophysitism, more agreeable with the doctrine proclaimed at Chalcedon. The christological doctrine of Severus of Antioch is one of these more moderate positions.

He was born at Sozopolis, in Pisidia, around 465. He studied at Alexandria in Egypt and at Beritos (the present-day Beirut), which were two of the most prestigious cultural centers of the ancient world. Baptized in 488, he embraced the monastic life and founded a monastery near Gaza, in Palestine. Around 508, he moved to Constantinople, where he managed to obtain the protection of the emperor Anastasius I on behalf of oppressed and persecuted Monophysite monks. In 512, he was consecrated patriarch of Antioch in Syria, but, because of his moderate monophysitism, he appears to have been poorly received both by Catholics and by the more extreme Monophysites. However, due to the example of his

---

[1] Recently, there have been some important convergences between the doctrinal positions of this Church and those of the Catholic Church, especially in Christology (cf. Shenouda III, *Il risveglio spirituale*, ed. by G. Mansour [Cinisello: Edizioni Paoline, 1990], pp. 18–21).

ascetic life and his vast theological erudition and notable talent as an orator, he eventually gained the profound respect of the various groups.

That respect notwithstanding, with the ascension to the throne of the emperor Justinian in 518, Severus was deposed from the patriarchal see of Antioch. In 536, a synod of Constantinople excommunicated him, and his writings were condemned by decree of the emperor Justinian. Severus died in Egypt in 538. Today, the Coptic Church venerates him as a saint and martyr. On the doctrinal level, Severus can be considered very close to the Catholic position.

His Christology is dominated by his preoccupation with safeguarding the unity of the person of Christ against Nestorian diphysitism, but it is also opposed to the definition of Chalcedon, which he considered contaminated by a subtle form of Nestorianism. We have seen that Chalcedon professed faith in the single Person of the incarnate Word, yet existing in two real natures, perfect and distinct, human and divine. According to Severus, this doctrine did not guarantee the unity of subsistence in Christ. Thus, he denied that there were two natures in Christ; he affirmed the existence of only one nature, resulting from the union of divinity and humanity in the mystery of the Incarnation, the humanity having introduced no change in the divinity. In practice, Severus attributes to the term "nature" the meaning that Chalcedon attributed to the term "person", so that his monophysitism is more apparent than real.

Mary Is a Marvelous Mystery

The Mariology of the patriarch of Antioch is plainly dependent on his Christology.[2] It is also easy to show how the emphasis he placed on the unity of the Person of the incarnate Word serves as his basis for maintaining Mary's divine motherhood with even greater vigor.

---

[2] For the Marian thought of Severus of Antioch, see J. Lecuyer, "L'Homélie cathédrale LXVII de Sévère d'Antioche", *De culto mariano saeculis VI-XI*, vol. 3 (Rome, 1972), pp. 1–15; J. M. Sauget, "Une découverte inespérée: l'homélie 2 de Sévère d'Antioche sur l'Annonciation de la Théotokos", in *A Tribute to Arthur Vööbus*, ed. Robert H. Fischer (Chicago: Lutheran School of Theology, 1977), pp. 55–62.

He often applies the title *Theotókos* to Mary, along with the title Ever-Virgin (*Aeipárthenos*). We may conclude that Severus was a strong proponent of the first two Marian dogmas.

Moreover, he was not only a theologian but a skilled poet as well; he often expressed his love and veneration for the Mother of God in lyric compositions.

When he contemplates the figure of Mary in the ineffable light of the incarnate Word, Severus cannot hide his profound wonderment and admiration:

> When a man looks at you, O Mother of God and Virgin, and at the divine mystery that came about in you by a miracle, he closes himself in silence because of the unspeakableness of it and, full of wonder, is moved to offer praises because of the greatness of the One who loved us in such a great way.[3]

In this text, we can already see how the praises addressed to the Mother and those addressed to her Son tend to be combined and equated with each other; everything Severus says in honor of the Mother ultimately refers to the Son, who made Mary a unique participant in his mystery. Thus, Severus compares approaching the image of the Virgin with the appearance of God to Moses on Mount Horeb:

> When I turn my gaze to the Virgin Mother of God and try to sketch a simple thought about her, I immediately seem to hear a voice coming from God and crying loudly in my ears, "Do not come near. Take off the sandals from your feet, for the place where you are standing is holy ground" (Ex 3:5). Truly we must free our minds from every mortal and carnal imagining, as if removing sandals from our feet, when our minds attempt to raise themselves to the contemplation of divine things. But what sort of thing could we contemplate that is more divine or greater than the Mother of God? Drawing near to her is like drawing near to holy ground and reaching heaven.[4]

Severus wishes to teach that approaching the mystery of Mary is the same thing as approaching the mystery of Christ. Hence, the comparison with the burning bush fits perfectly; indeed, Mary had

---

[3] *Ottoeco*, hymn 120; PO 6, 159–60.
[4] *Homily* 67; PO 8, 349–50.

the same function as the burning bush, because the divine omnipotence was hidden in her womb. Within this system of thinking, he loves to picture Mary at the center of a majestic choir of praise, extending from the Old Testament to the New, finding its unanimous convergence in her:

> She is honored by all the saints: by the patriarchs, because it was she who received the glorious blessing they promised; by the prophets, who of old had foretold him many times in divers ways; by the apostles, who preached [him]; by the martyrs, who found in him a teacher amid their struggles, the presenter of their crowns, and the reason for their sufferings. We too praise him; he, for the sake of the salvation and life of our race, wrought and brought everything to completion in wisdom.[5]

In the testimony of Severus, we have a proof that, in the Church of his time, the language of veneration, praise, and devotion was habitually used to characterize the relationship of the faithful with the Mother of God. This kind of relationship is legitimate, precisely because of the Son born of her.

The Miracle of Mary's Virginal Motherhood

Taking as his master Cyril of Alexandria, whom he strongly admired, Severus passionately defended the dogma of Mary's divine motherhood. From one of his homilies, we can extract a typical example of Severus' customary polemic against the Nestorians:

> But the Virgin, the Mother of God, is not at all disposed to tolerate the folly of Nestorius. For how could she not be the *Theotókos*, since she brought into the world, as her child, "the mighty God, the Angel of great counsel, the wonderful Counselor, the Powerful, the Prince of peace, the Father of the age to come" (Is 9:5)?[6]

In the Incarnation, Mary became the true Mother of God; she was made so not by a man, but by God himself working a miracle that, transcending the laws of nature, makes prevail what is better than the

---

[5] *Ottoeco*, hymn 118; PO 6, 157–58.
[6] *Homily* 14, 15; PO 38, 409.

laws of nature. By this expression, Severus is referring to virginity, which he considers superior to marriage:

> And, since there was no union with a husband, the Holy Spirit acted as the initiator and made the conception happen himself. In this way, the very Word of God, when he was conceived and born according to the flesh, made Mary the Mother of God, insofar as she gave birth to the Word, endowed with a body. Thus it is precisely on the basis of that which is better and more admirable that she is called [Mother of God], because the mystery consists in the victory of the best part, in the elevation of our race, which leads to its perfection.[7]

The Antiochene patriarch explains the origin of the custom of calling Mary by the title "Virgin". In the text cited, it is understood that this title has superseded all other titles, such as "spouse" or "wife", because, in the case of two values, the higher value always prevails. In this case virginity prevails over marriage.

But the virginity of the Mother of God places an additional seal on the mystery of Jesus' birth, making it even more impenetrable:

> If you want to know how it happened, your investigations remain blocked by the seal of virginity, which this birth in no wise violated. And that which is sealed is absolutely untouchable; it remains secret, and one cannot speak about it at all. Someone then, struck by this prodigy, will cry out, like Jacob, "How awesome is this place! This is the gate of heaven!" (Gen 28:17).[8]

To illustrate and explain this truth, Severus preferred to use symbols and images, especially those inspired by Sacred Scripture. Thus, he compares the Virgin Mother of God to the burning bush, as we have already seen, to the rock detached from the mountain without the intervention of man (cf. Dan 2:34), a rock that is a figure of Christ.[9] He calls Mary the new Sinai, on which one contemplates, no longer a mere appearance of the divine glory, but God in person,[10] the gate of heaven, from which our first parents were expelled and through which we have been readmitted.[11]

---

[7] Ibid., 16; PO 38, 411.

[8] *Homily* 67; PO 8, 350–51.

[9] Ibid.; PO 8, 354–55.

[10] Ibid.; PO 8, 353.

[11] *Ottoeco*, hymn 121; PO 6, 161–62.

The Blessed Virgin's Role in Salvation

Severus appears to attribute to the Lord's Mother a useful role in the history of salvation. He observes that Jesus was not content to take Mary into the service of the divine economy so that she might give us a phantasm, as many heretics had claimed, but so that she might give birth to a real body, truly like ours.[12] The image of the gate of heaven expresses this idea: by entering through this gate, one gains salvation. But, in the *Homily* 67, the idea is expressed in even more explicit terms:

> She is the leaven of our new creation, the root of the true vine whose branches we have become, by virtue of the germination proper to baptism. She is the point of arrival of the reconciliation of God with men, on which occasion the angels sang: "Glory to God in highest heaven; peace on earth and good will toward men" (Lk 2:14).
>
> For this reason the recollection of the Virgin wakes up our souls, making them consider how, by his intervention, we have been called from such a great irreconcilable enmity, from a situation of war, so to speak, to such a great peace, to divine familiarity, to a marvelous association.[13]

This role of Mary continues even in the time of the Church, seeing that she intercedes before God on our behalf. Our author is certainly convinced of this, since he exhorts his audience to take advantage of her intercession:

> We implore her who is the birthgiver of God and pray her to intercede for us, she who is honored by all the saints.[14]

Indeed, the patriarch of Antioch recognizes that the other saints also share this function of interceding with God on our behalf, so he invites his audience to honor them. But the Mother of God is honored more than all of them, because her power of intercession is much greater:

> More than the other saints, she is able to lift up prayers for us, and we glory to have obtained her as the ornament of our race.[15]

---

[12] *Homily* 14, 12; PO 38, 407–09.
[13] *Homily* 67; PO 8, 364–65.
[14] *Ottoeco*, hymn 118; PO 6, 157.
[15] *Homily* 14, 18; PO 38, 413.

Mary's capacity to intervene with God on our behalf appears to rest on an implicit Pauline analogy. The apostle states that Christ is our mediator as man (cf. 1 Tim 2:5), inasmuch as he is our brother. Severus explains that Mary is our sister. Having noted how, in the Song of Songs, the bridegroom calls his bride "sister", Severus observes:

> But why does the bride, in her turn, not call him brother, but rather son of my sister (cf. Song 1:6)? Because he is the Son of the Mother of God, the Virgin Mary, who is the sister of each one of us, because, genealogically, she too is descended from our common father, Adam.[16]

The Mariology of this notable Monophysite theologian and great devotee of the Virgin presents some very practical aspects. He teaches that Mary ought to be honored, not only by praising her with our lips, but also by the way we live. Christians ought to look to her example and draw lessons to be imitated in their own Christian conduct. Severus particularly proposes her as an example for women to imitate, whether they are virgins or married.[17]

READING

MARY'S INTERVENTION AT THE WEDDING AT CANA

When he wanted to make it plain by deeds and to teach in a clear way that matrimony is also pure and that it does not distance us from God in any way, our Lord and God Jesus Christ, the same who was born of a Virgin according to the flesh and who safeguarded the virginity of her from whom he was born, even after his birth, and who also blessed the world with the way of virginity, took part in the wedding banquet at Cana in Galilee, in the presence of his Virgin Mother and of his disciples. They had been invited out of motives of human friendship or because of family ties, as persons known to the wedding party. And he who "in wisdom has done all things" (Ps 103:24), obe-

---

[16] *Homily* 108; PO 25, 702.
[17] *Homily* 36; PO 36, 471.

dient to the economy, blessed the wedding banquet, where he would also perform his first sign and first miracle.

All this has been recounted by John the Theologian alone, not by any other evangelist, because John lived as a virgin and led his whole life without knowing the carnal relations of matrimony. Also, he was especially dear to Jesus. However, if John had considered marriage abominable, he would have done better to pass over this episode in silence, out of love for those who give up the carnal relations of marriage in order to imitate the angels.

But let us see what sign Jesus performed when he wished to honor the wedding dinner. "When the wine was beginning to run out," says John, "the Mother of Jesus said to him: 'They have no more wine' " (Jn 2:3). This shows that the guests invited to the dinner did not have elevated thoughts, or thoughts worthy of God, on their minds. Indeed, if they had had the kind of concerns they should have had at that moment, they would have begged God to make up for the lack of wine, since anyone who is in need asks to obtain what he needs. But, as I have said, they had invited him to the wedding dinner only because they knew him on a human level, without the slightest consideration of the greatness of his divinity.

When Mary, out of sympathy, puts herself in their shoes and makes a request, Jesus rejects her, lest he seem to be looking for vainglory, or lest it be thought that he wants to share this little glory with his Mother, as if she had feigned making a request and he gladly took the occasion to perform some show of signs. On the one hand, he was trying to keep his audience far away from this false opinion and to show them that he was acting out of concern and practicality rather than for a little glory; on the other hand, he answered [his Mother] in a very harsh tone, to give his audience a lesson, as I have said, and to teach the truth, not because he wanted to displease his Mother: "What is this between you and me, O woman? My hour has not yet come" (Jn 2:4).

His Mother herself makes it clear that these words were not a reproof but an expedient for teaching because of the presence of strangers. She does not distance herself from him or leave, in the manner of a person who has received a reproof; neither is she silent, repenting her eagerness, as happens with a person who has been censured. To the contrary, fully aware in her mind of what was going to happen, she addressed the servants as if Jesus had not said anything at all: "Do whatever he tells you" (Jn 2:5), wishing to show something greater and more befitting God.

Then Jesus, putting himself in harmony with his Mother's thoughts, answered her: "My hour has not yet come." It is as if he had said: You believe that I want to work grand signs all at once; but know that signs come in due course, so that not even the tiniest particle of time escapes from my decisions and actions.

For I manifest my divinity gradually, in relation to my physical maturing; it is in conformity with the true progress of my stature that I appear to grow in wisdom and grace as well (cf. Lk 2:52), through signs and wonders. These I grant according to a criterion pleasing to God; however, I make them known in sequence, as called for by the demands of the divine economy, until a moment beforehand, even an indivisible moment of time. For what depends on divine interventions still takes place, even in the case of the most minuscule and tiny events, even though this may remain completely unknown to us and difficult to discover.

Therefore, immediately after having said to his Mother, for the reasons explained above, the words: "My hour has not yet come", he performed a sign totally beyond the capacity of someone who is subject to the observance of established times. At once he instructs and teaches us, with this action, not to disobey our mothers when they command us to do something inconvenient, even if our refusal seems appropriate and pleases us very much, and to be content immediately with whatever they request by carrying out what they have commanded, or by fulfilling their request in some other way, and never to abandon them totally to sadness.

Examining these words with greater attention, it is found that the Mother of God, after she had conceived and begun to serve the mystery of the economy, was also full of the Holy Spirit and knew what was going to happen in advance. Indeed, she was a prophetess, as Isaiah says: "And I was approached by a prophetess" (Is 8:3). If it was so for her, she might well think that Jesus was able to make wine appear before everyone's eyes spontaneously, either by changing something into wine or by making wine out of nothing.

But just as she knew in advance what was going to happen, and that Jesus was going to order the servants to draw water, so that he might change it into wine, she also thought to give them an order in advance, saying: "Do whatever he tells you" (Jn 2:5). Thus, the foreknowledge of what was going to happen in a certain way was common to Jesus and to her. Jesus had it inasmuch as he was God; she had it in her capacity as a prophetess.

—Severus of Antioch, *Homily* 199; PO 26, 378–84

PART FOUR

The End of the Patristic Period
(Sixth–Eighth Century)

Prologue

The definitions of Ephesus and Chalcedon made a crucial contribution to the clarification of christological doctrine. At the same time, they helped resolve the problem of the personal relation between the Redeemer and his Mother. Since that time, this problem has always been considered basic to a correct development of Marian doctrine. While on the one hand this led to a certain stagnation of theological debate and diverted attention toward less central questions, on the other it gave a powerful impetus to Marian devotion as expressed not only in the personal life of the believer but also in cultural phenomena such as literature, art, and liturgy.

However, one can discern a palpable difference between the way this was played out in Eastern Christianity and in Western Christianity. The Latin authors did not exhibit much originality and fecundity. Usually, they limited themselves to repeating or amplifying elements already worked out by the great Fathers of the fourth and fifth centuries. But we need to remember that this lack of creativity affected almost all sectors of cultural activity at that time; this may be explained in light of the difficult historical circumstances in what had been the Western part of the Roman Empire. The West officially fell in 476 but had been threatened by serious internal problems and barbarian infiltration for some time.

In the East, by contrast, the Marian cult reached its highest manifestations, especially in the liturgy, in homiletics, in poetry, and in art. This achievement was favored by the conditions of relative tranquillity that Eastern Christians enjoyed. The center of the Eastern half of the Roman Empire, with its capital at Constantinople (Byzantium), resisted invaders for centuries, first the Persians, then the Arabs. Many of their territories, however, ultimately fell under the domination of Islam, which at first allowed the Christians a certain amount of religious liberty, allowing them to practice their own faith and to organize in ecclesial communities. A negative outcome of this situation was that the Christian communities of the occupied

323

territories soon lost all contact with the center of the Byzantine Church and, little by little, developed into independent (autocephalic) Churches.

But this did not prevent the Eastern Churches from cultivating various aspects, both personal and communal, of the Christian life. In this quite favorable climate, conspicuous manifestations of Marian devotion continued to flourish. Writers arose who left a profound impression on the history of Marian doctrine and devotion. Some authors of greater significance were Anastasius of Antioch (d. 599), John of Thessalonica (d. 630), Modestus (d. 634) and Sophronius (d. 638), both of Jerusalem, Maximus the Confessor (d. 662), Theodore Syncellus (early seventh century), George the Hymnographer (seventh century), and Anastasius of Sinai (d. beginning of eighth century). A special mention ought to be made of James (Jacob) of Sarugh (d. ca. 520), one of the greatest doctors of the Syrian Church. Until a few decades ago, his poetical works were little known in the West because of the lack of translations from the Syriac. From his verses, much exploited in the liturgies of both East and West, marvelous portraits of Mary arise.

Among the Eastern authors of this period, we have fixed our attention on the great poet Romanos the Melodist; on an anonymous but universally famous composition, the *Akathist* hymn; and, finally, on the last three great Fathers of the Eastern Church: Germanus of Constantinople, Andrew of Crete, and John Damascene.

Among the Westerners, we will concern ourselves with Gregory of Tours, Venantius Fortunatus, Gregory the Great, and Isidore of Seville.

I

ROMANOS THE MELODIST
(d. ca. 560)

John Paul II, in his Marian encyclical *Redemptoris Mater*, looks back upon the Second Vatican Council, delighting in the memory of the Eastern Christians "magnifying Mary ever-Virgin with splendid hymns".[1] The hymns of the Eastern Church have very ancient roots; by the first half of the sixth century, they had already reached great heights of inspiration, art, and lyricism in the poetic genius of Romanos, called "the Melodist".

Born in Syria to a Jewish family around 490, Romanos converted to Christianity and went to Constantinople while still a youth. There he passed his life as a deacon in the Marian shrine called "in the Kyros", the name of the quarter of the city where it was located. He died between 555 and 562 and was buried at the shrine. He was proclaimed a saint, and today the Eastern Church celebrates his feast on October 1.

According to ancient biographical sources, Romanos composed a thousand hymns; the manuscripts, however, contain only eighty-five with his name, and around twenty of these must be considered spurious. Although the majority of his compositions have been lost, what remains is enough to make us admire the greatness of this sacred poet, who left an indelible mark on the liturgical tradition of the Byzantine Church.

Romanos adapted a Syrian poetic genre to create a new Greek language form that came to be called *kontákion*—a sort of homily in verse form. In these compositions, the author shows his sincere poetic inspiration, united to a deep religiosity; this often takes dramatic form, unrestrained by the rather mechanical structure of the

---

[1] *Redemptoris Mater* 331; AAS 79 (1987), 403.

kontákion. His language is agile and lively, a charming reflection of his consistent and clear thinking.

Romanos had a marvelous ability to interpret the mentality of his time as well as the deep religiosity of the Christian people; in doing so he created a new poetry, capable of expressing authentic faith and devotion and, occasionally, of marking the pomp of the Byzantine liturgy with an intense pathos. His hymns had a strong positive influence on the subsequent development of religious poetry, despite some overly weighty oratory arising out of the fog of theological debate or speculation and the occasional use of an exaggerated image or metaphor.

Romanos and the Mother of God

According to tradition, Romanos owed his talent to a special intervention of the Blessed Virgin, whom he faithfully venerated in the shrine of Kyros, near his dwelling, or in the more famous shrine of Blakhernae, which housed a precious relic: the Virgin's mantle.[2] Romanos never misses a chance to express his love and gratitude for the Mother of God; this explains why he names her so frequently in his hymns, especially in their closing invocations. He sometimes dedicated entire compositions to her; these are among his most beautiful works.

Romanos' Marian doctrine follows right in the footsteps of the Fathers who preceded him.[3] He prefers to contemplate the mystery

---

[2] The shrine of Blakhernae was built by the emperor Leo I in 473 to guard the alleged mantle of the Virgin; the origins of this relic and the circumstances under which it was brought to Constantinople are unclear. There are two famous legends about it. One explains that the empress Pulcheria, around 450, received it as a gift from Bishop Juvenal of Jerusalem, where it had been found in Mary's empty tomb. The other legend tells that two noblemen stole the chest containing the precious relic, then brought it to Constantinople. Cf. A. Wenger, *L'Assomption de la très sainte Vierge dans la tradition byzantine du VI au X siècle: Études et documents*, (Paris, 1955), pp. 112ff.; Martin Jugie, *La Mort et l'assomption de la Sainte Vierge: Étude historico-doctrinale*, Studi e testi 114 (Vatican City, 1944), pp. 688–70.

[3] Cf. Romanos the Melodist, *Inni*, ed. G. Gharib (Rome: Edizioni Paoline, 1981). The hymns are prefaced by an important and exhaustive introduction. The complete critical edition of Romanos' hymns is that of P. Maas and C. A.

of the Blessed Virgin in the light of her Son, so it is natural for him to insist on her divine motherhood and her perpetual virginity. He adds that Mary is the best-qualified witness to the Incarnation of the Son of God, the perfect disciple of Christ, the mediatrix and advocate of men.

However, Romanos does more than let himself be caught up in the inexpressible light of this great mystery. He also presents some genuinely human traits and scenes from the life of Mary.

He recalls with interest the Marian prefigurations of the Old Testament, which he interprets along traditional patristic lines: Ezekiel's closed gate represents Mary's perpetual virginity; Daniel's mountain from which a stone was detached without human action is the symbol of her virginal motherhood; she is the root of Jesse, from which sprang Christ the flower; she is the Ark of the Covenant, who carried Christ himself within her. Other examples could be added.

When speaking of the personal relationship between Christians and the Mother of God, Romanos heavily stresses her intercessory role, which derives from the excellence of her role as Mother of God. This qualifies her to be our representative and mediatrix before her Son. In his *Hymn 2 on Christmas*, the poet, in aggrieved tones, describes the sadness of Adam and Eve, who have recourse to the blessed Virgin to obtain solidarity and help for themselves and their descendants; then he puts consoling words into Mary's mouth, as she proclaims herself to be advocate and mediatrix:

> Cease your laments; I will make myself your advocate in my Son's presence. Meanwhile, no more sadness, because I have brought joy to the world. For it is to destroy the kingdom of sorrow that I have come into the world: I, full of grace. . . .
>
> Then curb your tears; accept me as your mediatrix in the presence of him who was born from me, because the author of joy is the God generated before all ages. Remain calm; be troubled no longer: I come from him, full of grace.[4]

Trypanis, *Sancti Romani Melodi Cantica Genuina* (Oxford, 1963); *Cantica Dubia* (Berlin, 1970). For Romanos' Marian doctrine, cf. C. Chevalier, "Mariologie de Romanos (490–550 environ), le roi des mélodes", *Recherches de science religeuse* 28 (1938): 48–71.

[4] *On Christmas 2*, 10–11.

Above all, Romanos the Melodist is the cantor of the mysteries of Christ and Mary, as the Byzantine Church celebrates them during the course of her liturgical year. His hymns introduce a note of freshness and beauty into these celebrations.

The Birth of Mary

Romanos' hymn on the birth of the Virgin may serve as an ancient witness to the introduction of the feast (September 8) in the Church of Constantinople, under the emperor Justinian. The poet sings of this event as a triumph of grace over the weakness and failings of human nature, as revealed in the sterility of Mary's aged parents:

> The prayers of Joachim and Anna and the weeping of sterility reached the ears of God and were well received. Thus they gave a life-giving fruit to the world. For while he [Joachim] was praying on the mountain, she [Anna] hid her mortification in the garden. But the barren woman then joyfully brings to light the Mother of God, the nourisher of our life.[5]

Considering the future mission of Mary, her birth to barren parents is considered a reason for great rejoicing, which the people of Israel already share by anticipation, unwittingly:

> Then the tribes of Israel heard that Anna had conceived the immaculate one. So everyone took part in the rejoicing. Joachim gave a banquet, and great was the merriment in the garden. He invited the priests and Levites to prayer; then he called Mary into the center of the crowd, that she might be magnified.[6]

In this hymn, Romanos recalls two important moments of Mary's infancy and youth: the years she spent in the Temple and her betrothal to Joseph. Apparently Romanos takes his inspiration from the apocrypha, in particular from the *Protoevangelium of James*. Later on, addressing Anna directly, the poet weaves a marvelous praise of her extraordinary little daughter:

---

[5] *On the Birth of Mary* 1.
[6] Ibid., 4.

Your birth is worthy of veneration, O holy woman, because you brought to light the joy of the world, the powerful mediatrix of graces for men. Indeed she is the rampart, the defense, and the haven of whoever trusts in her. Every Christian finds in her, in your fruit, a protector, a defense, and the hope of salvation.[7]

The Annunciation

Romanos' first hymn on the Annunciation[8] begins with an invitation to exalt the Virgin, since Gabriel ought not have a monopoly on this task. Everyone, including the lowly, can turn to her and say:

Hail, untouched Virgin! Hail, chosen spouse of God! Hail, holy one! Hail, delightful and beautiful! Hail, joyful sight! Hail, unseeded earth! Hail, uncontaminate! Hail, Mother who knows not man! Hail, Virgin Bride![9]

In the dialogue between Mary and the angel, Romanos describes him as almost overwhelmed by the shock of having to deliver such an unheard-of message to a simple, lowly maiden:

All of heaven, with its fiery throne, is too small to contain my Lord. And this poor maiden, how will she be able to receive him?[10]

The angel's words appear to produce a mixed reaction on Mary's part, wavering between incomprehension and certitude, hesitation and trust:

This angel here proffers a greeting, but I don't understand the greeting's purpose. And then he adds something else, something terrible to hear, saying, "You will have a Son and give birth to him." But I do not know man. Perhaps he does not know that I am under a seal? Perhaps he is unaware that I am a virgin? No, I do not believe it. If he had not been told, if he had not known it, he would not have come and said to me: Hail, Virgin Bride![11]

---

[7] Ibid., 10.

[8] In Constantinople, the feast of the Annunciation was introduced in the first half of the sixth century.

[9] *On the Annunciation* 1, 1.

[10] Ibid., 2.

[11] Ibid., 5.

Gabriel is troubled in his turn, hearing the Virgin's reaction. However, he refrains from speaking brusque words to her, who is called to give birth to the Lord; therefore, he limits himself to muttering:

> They never believe me. First in the Temple, now in this Virgin's house I find unbelief. The same doubt: there, it was Zechariah's; here, it is Mary's. Nevertheless, I cannot, I dare not give a proof; I do not have the power to obstruct her voice, as I did to the old man. Then, I could reduce him to silence, but now I tremble as I say: Hail, Virgin Bride! [12]

The poet attributes a curious reaction to the angel: he is unsure about the meaning of Mary's words; on the other hand, he is able to see a difference between her reaction and that of Zechariah.

Unable to explain God's hidden design, the angel convinces the Virgin to accept it, explaining to her that it is truly the definitive fulfillment of the symbols and prophetic statements made during the Old Testament time of messianic expectation. By putting the following words into the Virgin's mouth, the poet appears to make her guilty of some hesitation, if not unbelief:

> Truly, you have come from on high. Forgive me; now I recognize you. I was hesitant, out of fear. . . . But since you come from the light, you have made straight all that was crooked. Then let what you have said come to pass in me, because you are truthful. O angel, let your word be fulfilled in me. [13]

In line with a mentality that was fairly widespread among the Eastern Fathers, Romanos attributes some small defects or imperfections to the Virgin, being certain that this does not prejudice Mary's dignity and extreme holiness.

In the verses that follow, the poet touches on the theme of Joseph's reaction to the mysterious pregnancy of his betrothed; he does so by putting it on a level of faith and intense religiosity. Joseph sensed the presence of mystery, so that he feels unable to bear the divine light emanating from the Virgin:

---

[12] Ibid., 7.
[13] Ibid., 11.

O luminous woman, I see a flame, I see an ember glow surrounding you. It frightens me, Mary! Protect me, do not consume me! Your chaste womb has suddenly become a furnace full of fire. Do not let me melt, I beg you, spare me.[14]

Mary, unable to explain the miracle to Joseph, reassures him and enlightens him about the mission that awaits him in the near future:

His greeting, resounding in my ears, made me the luminous woman; it made me a mother. I cannot understand my Child's conception, yet behold, I am great with child, and, as you see, my virginity is intact, since you never knew me. Who will be the witness to these things if not you, my guardian? You must defend me, then, for the sake of your peace of mind.[15]

In these verses we may recognize some common elements of patristic tradition: the conception of the incarnate Word through the ear, a theme that also became part of iconography, and the role of Joseph as witness and guardian of Mary's virginity.

Christ's Birth at Bethlehem

We have three Christmas hymns by Romanos. In the first, he has Mary speak a prayer rich in theology and lyricism:

Tell me, my Child, how were you planted in me, and how were you formed in me? I see you, O my womb, and I am stunned. My bosom is full of milk, and I am not married. I see you wound about with swaddling clothes and perceive that the seal of my virginity is still intact, for it was you that kept it intact, when you deigned to be born, my little Child, God before all ages! High King, what do you have in common with our sorrows? Creator of heaven, why do you come among the inhabitants of earth? Were you taken with desire for a cave? Are you in love with a manger?[16]

In the second hymn, the poet compares Mary to a vine that produces grapes without having been cultivated; he has her address a

---

[14] Ibid., 15.
[15] Ibid., 17.
[16] *On Christmas* 1, 2–3.

prayer to her Son in which the recognition of his divinity is inspired by the knowledge of her own uncorrupt virginity:

> O you, my fruit! O you, my life! Through you, I knew that I am what I am and that you are my God. Because of the inviolate seal of my virginity, I can proclaim that you are the immutable Word become flesh. I knew no seed, but I know that you put an end to my corruption, for I remained pure after you were born from me. You left my womb just as you found it; you kept it whole.[17]

Here, too, we see another very common patristic theme: Mary's virginity as a miraculous proof of the divinity of the Child she bears.

The Sword of Simeon

In the only hymn we have for the Presentation of Jesus in the Temple (Hypapantē), Romanos begins with Origen's interpretation of the sword of Simeon, understood as scandal, infidelity, doubt, but then goes farther, in order to go beyond his somewhat negative exegesis. He writes:

> This mystery will be the object of contradicting ideas, so that doubt will arise in your mind. Yes, when you see your Son nailed to the Cross, Immaculate Virgin, and recall the words of the angel, his divine conception, and his ineffable miracles, at that moment you will doubt: for you, this hesitation will be a sword of pain. But later God will bring ready healing to your heart.[18]

The great mystery he speaks of is the Lord's Passion, in the face of which even Mary's soul will experience crisis. By using the words "doubt" and "hesitation", the Melodist seems to want to mitigate Origen's rather harsh words (scandal, infidelity).[19]

---

[17] *On Christmas* 2, 1.

[18] *On the Presentation* 13.

[19] Cf. G. Segalla, Luigi Gambero, Théodore Koehler, *Maria ai piedi della croce* (Casale Monferrato: Ed. Piemme, 1989), pp. 41–47.

The Virgin Mother on Calvary

Romanos' best-known and most frequently translated hymn is dedicated to the Mother of God at the foot of the Cross. The many collections of liturgical texts that have included it locate it within the
celebration of Holy Saturday. The hymn, a real masterpiece of poetry and doctrine, is woven in the form of a dialogue between
Mother and Son in the most dramatic hour of salvation history. The
Virgin is depicted as the pure and innocent Ewe who follows the
Lamb of God, weighted down by the burden of men's sins. She cannot comprehend how such a tragedy could befall him, just a few days
after his triumphal entry into Jerusalem. Then Jesus explains to his
Mother, broken by sorrow, how all these things are necessary for
emancipating humanity from the slavery of sin; he invites her to accept his self-offering with resignation, since it is a mystery of salvation. Mary appears unable to understand why such a sacrifice is
necessary for the salvation of the world and asks her Son to let her see
him again in the future. Jesus promises that she will be the first to see
him after the Resurrection. Finally, the Blessed Virgin is convinced
by her Son's words and shows him that she is determined to stay
beside him until the supreme moment of death. The hymn concludes with a charming prayer spoken by Christ, in which he invokes
his Mother's intercession.

The image of the Virgin at the foot of the Cross, presented by the
poet using the metaphor of the Ewe, has become an important part
of Byzantine liturgical tradition; it offers a meaningful illustration of
the truth that the remission of sins is tied to expiatory suffering.

READING

MARY AT THE CROSS

Come, let us all celebrate him who was crucified for us: for Mary
looked on him upon the cross and said: "Though you endure crucifixion, yet you are my son, my God."

Worn out with grief, Mary, the ewe, seeing her own lamb taken to
the slaughter, followed with the other women and cried: "Where are

you going, my child? For whose sake are you finishing this swift race? Is there yet another marriage in Cana, and are you hastening there now to change the water into wine for them? Shall I go with you, child, or shall I rather wait for you? Speak to me, O Word; do not pass me by in silence: for you kept me in my purity, my son, my God.

"I never thought that I would see you, my child, in such necessity nor did I ever believe that the lawless would rage so, and unjustly stretch out their hands against you; for still their infants cry "Hosanna" to you; still the road is strewn with palm-branches proclaiming to all how the lawless had sung your praises. And now a worse deed is done, and for whose sake? Alas; how is my light snuffed out, how to a cross is nailed my son, my God.

"You are going to unjust slaughter, my child, and no one is suffering with you. Peter does not go with you, Peter who had said to you: 'Never shall I deny you even though I die.' Thomas deserted you, Thomas who cried, 'Let us all die with him.' The others too, the friends and companions who were to judge the tribes of Israel, where are they now? None of them is here; but one, alone, for the sake of them all, you are dying, my child; because instead of them you have saved all, because instead of them you have loved all, my son, my God."

Mary cried thus, from her heavy grief; and as she wailed and wept in her very deep sorrow, her son turned to her and said: "Why, mother, do you weep? Why do you grieve with the other women? Lest I suffer? Lest I die? How then should I save Adam? Lest I dwell in the tomb? How then should I draw to life those in Hades? And yet, as you know, I am crucified most unjustly. Why do you weep, my mother? Rather cry out thus, that willingly I suffered, your son, your God.

"Put aside your grief, mother, put it aside; mourning is not right for you who have been called the All-favoured. Do not conceal the title with weeping; do not liken yourself, wise maid, to those with no understanding. You are in the centre of my bridal chamber; do not consume your soul as though you were standing outside. Address those within the bridal chamber as your servants; for all, when they rush in terror, will hear you, holy one, when you say: 'Where is my son, my God?'

"Do not make the day of my suffering a bitter day; it is for this day that I, the compassionate, (now) descended from heaven as manna, not upon Mount Sinai but in your womb; for within it I was conceived, David once foretold. Recognize, holy one, the 'mountain God delighted to dwell in'; I now exist, I, the Word, who in you became flesh. This day I suffer and this day I save; do not therefore weep, mother. Rather cry out in joy: 'Willingly he suffered, my son, my God.' "

"See, my child," she said, "I wipe the tears from my eyes, though my heart I wear down still more; but my thoughts cannot be silent. Why, offspring, do you say to me: 'If I do not die, Adam will not be healed'? And yet, without suffering yourself, you have healed many. You made the leper clean and have felt no pain, for so you will it. You bound the paralytic together, yet you yourself were not undone. Again, when by your word you gave sight to the blind, you yourself, good one, remained unharmed, my son, my God.

"You raised the dead but did not yourself die, nor, my son and my life, were you laid within the grave. How then can you say: 'Unless I suffer Adam will not be healed'? Command, my saviour, and he will rise at once and take up his bed. And even if Adam is covered by a tomb, call him forth, as you called Lazarus from the grave; for all things serve you; you are the creator of all. Why then do you hasten, my child? Do not rush to the slaughter, do not embrace death, my son, my God."

"You do not know, mother, you do not know what I say. Therefore open your mind and take in the words you hear, and consider on your own what I say. This miserable Adam, of whom I spoke before, who is sick not only in body but yet more so in his soul, is sick of his own will; for he did not obey me, and is in danger. You know what I say—therefore do not weep, mother; rather cry out: 'Take pity on Adam, and show compassion to Eve, my son, my God.'

"Adam, sick through debauchery, through gluttony, was led down to deepest Hell, and there he weeps for the suffering of his soul; and Eve, who once taught him disobedience, grieves with him and languishes with him, that together they may learn to heed the Healer's word. Now, do you see? Do you understand what I have said? Cry out again, mother: 'If you forgive Adam, forgive also Eve, my son, my God.' "

And when the blameless ewe heard this, she answered to her lamb: "My Lord, if I speak yet once more, do not be angry with me. I shall tell you what is on my mind, so that I may learn from you all I wish to know. If you suffer, if you die, will you come back to me? If you heal Adam, and Eve with him, shall I see you again? For my fear is that from the tomb you may hasten to Heaven, my child; and I, searching to see you, shall weep and cry out: 'Where is my son, my God?'"

When he who knows of all things before their birth heard this, he answered Mary: "Take courage, mother, for you shall be the first to see me (risen) from the tomb; and I shall come to show you from what suffering I liberated Adam and how much I sweated for his sake. I shall reveal it to my friends and show them the tokens in my hands; and then, mother, you shall see Eve living as before, and you shall cry out for joy: 'He saved my parents, my son, my God.'

"Endure a little, mother, and you shall see how I, like a healer, divest myself and come to where they lie, and how I heal their wounds, cutting their calluses and scabs with the lance; and I shall take the vinegar and with it bathe their wounds; I shall open the wound with the chisel (made) of the nails and dress it with the cloak, and my cross I shall use, mother, as a splint, that you may sing with understanding: 'By suffering he freed us from suffering, my son, my God.'

"Put aside your grief, mother, put it aside, and go in joy; for now I hasten to fulfill that for which I came, the will of him who sent me. For from the first this was resolved by me and by my Father, and it was never displeasing to my spirit; that I become man and suffer for him who had fallen. Hasten then, mother, and announce to all that 'By suffering he lays low the hater of Adam, and comes as a conqueror, my son, my God.'"

"I am overcome, my child, overcome by love, and truly I cannot bear it, that I am to be in my room while you are on the cross, I within my house, you within the tomb. Therefore let me go with you, for it heals me to look upon you, I shall look upon the outrageous daring of those who honour Moses: for these blind men, pretending to be his avengers, have come here to kill you. But what Moses said to Israel was this: 'You will see life hanging on the cross.' And what is life? My son and my God."

"If you come with me, mother, do not weep, and do not tremble if you see the elements shaken. For this outrage will make all creation tremble; the sky will be blinded and not open its eyes until I speak; then the earth and the sea together will hasten to disappear, and the temple will rend its veil against the perpetrators of this outrage. The mountains will be shaken, the graves emptied. If, like a woman, you are seized by fear when you see this, cry out to me: 'Spare me, my son, my God.' "

Son of the Virgin, God of the Virgin, and creator of the world: yours is the suffering, yours the depths of wisdom. You know what you were and what you became; because you were willing to suffer, you deigned to come and save mankind. Like a lamb you have lifted our sins from us, and you have abolished them by your sacrifice, my Saviour, and saved every man. You exist both in suffering and in not suffering; by dying you save, and you have given to the holy lady freedom to cry to you: "My son and my God."

—Romanos the Melodist, *Mary at the Cross*,
trans. Constantine A. Trypanis,
in *The Penguin Book of Greek Verse*
(Middlesex: Penguin Books Ltd., 1971)

2

THE "AKATHIST" HYMN
(ca. Fifth/Sixth Century)

The mystery of the Incarnation of the Son of God inspired this celebrated poetic composition, a unique masterpiece of Greek liturgical literature. Undoubtedly the most beautiful, the most profound, and the most ancient Marian hymn in all Christian literature, it sings of the Virgin Mother as the inviolate spouse of God.

To this day, the problem of its authorship has resisted every attempt at a solution. Migne's *Patrologia Graeca*[1] prints it under the name of George of Pisidia (seventh century), while the Latin versions usually ascribe it to Germanus of Constantinople (eighth century). Sergius of Constantinople (seventh century) and the great hymnographer Romanos the Melodist (sixth century), of whom we have already spoken, have also been proposed as authors. These names, however, are only hypotheses and not very important. The manuscript tradition has consistently handed it down to us as an anonymous work, and that is how it entered into the liturgical books.

More recent studies agree in fixing its date of composition either in the second half of the fifth century or in the first years of the sixth century. On the question of authorship, we can accept the conclusion reached by Father Ermanno Toniolo, who is such a profound student of the *Akathist*: "Undoubtedly, its author was a great poet, an outstanding theologian, a consummate contemplative; he was great enough to be able to translate the Church's faith into a prayerful synthesis, yet humble enough to disappear into anonymity. God knows his name; the world does not. It is just as well; in this way, the hymn belongs to everyone, because it belongs to the Church."[2]

---

[1] PG 92, 1335–48.

[2] Ermanno Toniolo, *Acatisto: Canto di lode a Maria, fonte di luce* (Rome, 1976), p. 11. By the same author, cf. "L'Inno Acatisto, monumento di teologia e di culto

Compositional Structure

The *Akathist*, an alphabetical acrostic, received its name because it is sung or listened to while standing, as a sign of respect for the Mother of God. In fact, the Greek word *akáthistos* means "not seated". In the Byzantine Church, this hymn has its own specific feast day, the fifth Saturday of Lent, which therefore is called "*Akathist* Saturday". The hymn, however, is also sung on other dates or during other liturgical celebrations, and in some monastic communities it serves as a little office of the Virgin.

The singing of the *Akathist*, as a celebration of the ecclesial community, begins in the eighth century, when the patriarch St. Germanus of Constantinople had it sung in nocturnal vigils of prayer in thanksgiving to the Mother of the Lord for the liberation of the Byzantine capital from the threat of the barbarians.

The twenty-four stanzas, or strophes, that compose the hymn are acrostic; that is, they begin with the twenty-four letters of the Greek alphabet and form a structure based on the number twelve. The entire composition is divided into two parts of twelve stanzas each. The first part has a primarily narrative structure, while the second part presents a more doctrinal character. Every stanza ends with a refrain: "Alleluia" for the even-numbered stanzas and "Hail, Virgin bride" for the odd-numbered strophes. The literal translation of the second refrain ought to be: "Hail, Virgin and unmarried bride"[3]—one of those expressions in which Byzantine poetry is able to contain theological concepts of penetrating depth.

In essence, the *Akathist* is a hymn in praise of the mystery of the Incarnation of God's Son, who became the Son of the Virgin, who is contemplated and praised in the light of Ephesian theology.

The theme unravels into two threads, which intertwine closely: a christological thread and a Marian thread. The Son of God appears as

---

mariano nella Chiesa bizantina", in *De cultu mariano saeculis VI-XI*, vol. 4 (Rome, 1972), pp. 1–39. An immense bibliography has arisen on the Akathist hymn; here, we recall only the foundational study of G. G. Meersseman, *Der Hymnos Akathistos im Abendland*, 2 vols. (Freiburg, 1958–1960).

[3] The translation by Fr. Vincent McNabb, reproduced at the end of this chapter, attempts to capture the compactness of the original with the phrase HAIL! BRIDE UNBRIDED—trans.

the primary, divine-human cause, who brings about the salvation of humanity; his Mother is the purely human, yet marvelous and efficacious, instrument of this salvation. The poet proclaims his ecstasy and jubilation before this mystery of beauty and grace.

The Narrative Stanzas

The first stanza reports the angelic amazement of Gabriel before the miracle of the Word of God made flesh in Mary's virginal womb. He addresses her in tones of inexpressible joy. In the second and third stanzas, Mary asks the angel for an explanation of how the virginal birth of the child will come about. But Gabriel cannot answer, except with exclamations of amazement. In the fourth stanza, the mystery is stated. The protagonist of the fifth stanza is Elizabeth, who calls Mary, "the whole world's offering of peace, God's goodness unto men, man's trustfulness in God". The sixth stanza is dedicated to Joseph, who, in a troubled state of mind, dreads "hidden wedlock" and finally understands that Mary has become a mother by the working of the Holy Spirit.

In the eighth, ninth, and tenth stanzas, we are presented with the Magi, who, following the light of the star, safely reach the unreachable God, expressing their beatitude in song: "Alleluia!" The praise they offer to the Mother is inspired by their skill as watchers of the stars. After the encounter with Christ, they become his witnesses and proclaimers.

The eleventh stanza is dedicated to the flight and sojourn of the Holy Family in Egypt, an event that offers the poet the chance to recall the marvels wrought by God on behalf of the chosen people during the time of Moses. The last stanza of the first part evokes the inspired reaction of the aged Simeon, who recognizes the Messiah in the infant Jesus.

The Doctrinal Stanzas

The first theological argument treated in the second part is the virginal conception of Christ, a mystery in which his Mother's fruitfulness and physical integrity are united in a single and ineffable mystery (stanza 13). The fruit of this miracle is the human birth of the Son of God, who become man's way to heaven (stanza 14). The fifteenth stanza is a sublime hymn to Mary's divine motherhood.

The sixteenth stanza depicts the amazement of the angels before the mystery of God made man, while the seventeenth stanza observes the human mind's incapacity to penetrate the arcane event of the virginal birth. After mentioning the salvific character of the coming of the Son of God, who has changed from a shepherd into the lamb of expiation (stanza 18), the poet sings with amazement of Mary's collaboration in her Son's mission (stanza 19).

In the twentieth stanza, the poet notes that every one of our songs is inadequate to express Mary's greatness. Nevertheless, the contemplation of her image guides all to the knowledge of God and to the exaltation of Mary (stanza 21). As *Theotókos*, the Virgin is also the source of every blessing for men. And, if her Son came to cancel the debt of sin (stanza 22), then Mary, as Mother, is a living temple of the Son; she is the all-holy and glorious queen. The Lord himself teaches us to praise her (stanza 23).

The hymn concludes with a beautiful prayer in which we, appealing to Mary's divine motherhood, beg of the Virgin a benign hearing and deliverance from evil and punishment (stanza 24).

The amazing beauty of this anonymous poetic work emerges from the ingenious synthesis of two elements: its incredible doctrinal richness and the prayer of praise and invocation that establishes a profound personal relationship with the Mother of the Lord. Therefore, the *Akathist* is a convincing example of how the theology of the Greek Fathers could create titles indicative of fervid admiration for the divine mystery, in which Mary was involved in a unique way. It speaks of the mystery of the incarnate Word, the basis of the extraordinary union she achieved with God. This union is both virginal and spousal. Therefore, our anonymous poet never tires of exalting her as Virgin and spouse.

READING

THE "AKATHIST" HYMN

Tropárion

He who was bodiless, having heard the bidding secretly in his soul,
went with haste to Joseph's dwelling and said to the Unwedded One:

> He who in his condescension boweth the heavens down
> > is housed unchanged and whole within thee.
> I see him take the form of a servant;
> > and wondering I cry to thee:
>
> HAIL! BRIDE UNBRIDED.[4]

Kontákion

To thee, unconquered Queen, I thy city from danger freed an offering of thanks inscribe. O Forth-bringer of God! Yet for thy uncon-
querable might free me from all hurt that I may sing to thee:

> HAIL! BRIDE UNBRIDED.

I

Oîkos   ALPHA

An angel chieftain was sent from Heaven to greet the Forth-bringer
of God with Hail! Then seeing thee, O Lord, take flesh he is won-
der-rapt, and standing crieth out with no lips of flesh to her:

> Hail! by whom true hap had dawned.
> Hail! by whom mishap has waned.
> Hail! sinful Adam's recalling.
> Hail! Eve's tears redeeming.
> Hail! height untrodden by thought of men.
> Hail! depth unscanned by angels' ken.

---

[4] Fr. George Papadeas translates this as "Hail! O Bride Ever Virgin" (*The
Akathist Hymn* [Datona Beach, Fla.: Patmos Press, 1997]).

Hail! for the kingly throne thou art.
Hail! for who beareth all that thou bearest?
Hail! O star that bore the Sun.
Hail! the womb of God enfleshed.
Hail! through whom things made are all new made.
Hail! through whom becomes a Babe their Maker.
Hail! through whom the Maker is adorned.

HAIL! BRIDE UNBRIDED.

II

Kontákion   BETA

The holy one seeing herself in chastity said greatly daring unto Gabriel: Thy dark saying seems hard to my mind. What birth of a seedless begetting dost thou name?

Crying out: ALLELUIA.

III

Oîkos   GAMMA

The Virgin yearning to know the knowledge unknowable made to clamour to the servitor: from a maiden womb how may a Child be born? tell me. To her he said, fearing yet crying out:

Hail! initiated into God's unspeakable counsel.
Hail! keeper of things best kept by silence.
Hail! of Christ's wonders the beginning.
Hail! of his mysteries the head.
Hail! heavenward Ladder by which God came down.
Hail! earthly Bridge carrying the earthborn unto heaven.
Hail! much sung marvel of the angels.
Hail! of the demons much dirged wounding.
Hail! who unspeakably hast the Light forth-brought.
Hail! who the HOW to none hast taught.
Hail! wisdom of the wise outsoaring.
Hail! light on faithful minds outpouring.

HAIL! BRIDE UNBRIDED.

IV

Kontákion   DELTA

Then the power from on high overshadowed unto begetting the
Maid untouched; and he showed her fruitful womb as a meadow
sweet to all who sought to reap salvation, as thus he sang: ALLELUIA.

V

Oîkos   EPSILON

Then the Maid of the God-bearing womb hastened unto Elizabeth;
whose babe, knowing straightway her greeting, rejoiced and with
stirrings as if with song cried out to God's Forth-bringer:

> Hail! vine of an unwithering Shoot.
> Hail! yielder of untainted Fruit.
> Hail! thou whom this man-loving Husbandman has tended.
> Hail! thou who unto life hast brought him
>   who bringeth death to life.
> Hail! field with mercies harvest-rich.
> Hail! board with load of pities spread.
> Hail! flower-strewn meadow.
> Hail! thou who the soul's sage anchorage preparest.
> Hail! grateful incense-cloud of prayer.
> Hail! the whole world's offering of peace.
> Hail! God's goodness unto men.
> Hail! man's trustfulness in God.

> HAIL! BRIDE UNBRIDED.

VI

Kontákion   ZETA

Looking on thee, O Unwedded One, and dreading a hidden wedlock, O Sinless One, the chaste Joseph was riven in mind with a
storm of doubts; but having learned that the begetting was of the
Holy Ghost, said: ALLELUIA.

VII

Oîkos   ETA

The shepherds heard the Angels extolling the Christ coming in the flesh; and running as to a shepherd they see him as a Lamb unspotted being fed on Mary's breast, to whom they carolled, saying:

Hail! Mother both of Lamb and Shepherd.
Hail! fold of rational sheep.
Hail! against unseen foes defending.
Hail! the heavenly gateways opening.
Hail! for the heavens with earth rejoice.
Hail! for things earthly with things heavenly chorus.
Hail! of Apostles never-silent mouthpiece.
Hail! of the Martyrs strength undaunted.
Hail! of Faith the firm foundation.
Hail! of Grace the shining token.
Hail! by whom hell is despoiled.
Hail! by whom we are clothed with glory.

HAIL! BRIDE UNBRIDED.

VIII

Kontákion   THETA

The Magi, having seen the God-heralding star, following its shining, and helped by it as by a lantern sought by its aid the mighty King, and having reached the Unreachable they rejoiced, crying out to thee:
ALLELUIA.

IX

Oîkos   IOTA

The children of the Chaldees seeing in the Virgin's hands him whose hands made men, and knowing him as Lord even though he had taken the form of a servant, hastened to worship with their gifts, and cried out to her who is blessed:

Hail! Mother of the unsetting Star.
Hail! Splendor of the Mystic Day.
Hail! thou who hast quenched the fire of error.
Hail! thou who enlightenest the initiates of the Triune.

Hail! who from his seat has driven the foe of man.
Hail! thou who hast shown to us Christ the merciful
   lover of man.
Hail! thou who hast redeemed us from pagan rites.
Hail! thou who rescuest us from works of mire.
Hail! thou who hast quenched the cult of fire.
Hail! thou who savest us from passion's flame.
Hail! leader of the faithful in ways of self-control.
Hail! Joy of all Generations.

   HAIL! BRIDE UNBRIDED.

X

Kontákion   KAPPA

The Magi being made heralds God-inspired went back to Babylon,
having done thy bidding; unto everyone they preached thee as Christ
and left Herod as if he were raving, unable to sing: ALLELUIA.

XI

Oîkos   LAMBDA

Having shed in Egypt the beams of thy truth thou didst chase the
darkness of untruth; for its idols, O Saviour, unable to meet thy
strength, fell down; and as many as were freed from them cried out to
God's Forth-bringer:

Hail! thou who raisest mankind up.
Hail! thou who castest demons down.
Hail! thou who the cheat of lies hast trodden 'neath thy feet.
Hail! thou who the fraud of idols hast reproved.
Hail! sea the mystic Pharaoh drowning.
Hail! rock refreshing such as for life are athirst.
Hail! pillar of fire in darkness guiding.
Hail! shade of the world wider than a cloud.
Hail! unfailing manna-food.
Hail! server of hallowing delights.
Hail! land of promise.
Hail! from whom flow milk and honey.

   HAIL! BRIDE UNBRIDED.

XII
Kontákion

Unto Simon about to leave this deceitful world wast thou brought as a Babe; but to him wast thou known as the infinite God; wherefore marveling at thy unspeakable wisdom he cried out: ALLELUIA.

XIII
Oîkos

Thus did he show himself as the new Creature when he, the Creator, revealed himself to us who were made by him; and, blossoming from a seedless womb he kept its unsullied purity, so that we the wonder knowing might hymn her and cry out:

Hail! flower unfading.
Hail! crown of chastity.
Hail! flashing token of resurrection.
Hail! mirror of the life of Angels.
Hail! tree of glorious fruit to feed the faithful.
Hail! wood of grateful shade where many shelter.
Hail! womb bearing the Guide of all who stray.
Hail! forth-bringing the Redeemer of all bondsfolk.
Hail! tireless pleader with the just Judge.
Hail! help-bringer to sinners many.
Hail! cloak of those bare of hopes.
Hail! love outrunning all desire.

HAIL! BRIDE UNBRIDED.

XIV
Kontákion

Seeing this Pilgrim Babe let us be pilgrims in this world by fixing our heart in Heaven. To this end did the God of Heaven appear on earth as a lowly man, because he wished to draw heavenward all those who cry to him: ALLELUIA.

XV

Oîkos   OMICRON

Wholly present in the things below yet not wholly absent from the things above was the infinite Word; a divine condescension not a change of place was the child-bearing of this God-filled Virgin who hears these words:

> Hail! thou who didst comprehend the incomprehensible.
> Hail! gate of hallowed mystery.
> Hail! word hidden from unbelievers.
> Hail! chariot most holy of the One above the Cherubim.
> Hail! dwelling-place most glorious of the One
>   above the Seraphim.
> Hail! who hast welded into one things opposite.
> Hail! who hast woven maidenhood with motherhood.
> Hail! by whom was loosed our sin.
> Hail! by whom was opened Paradise.
> Hail! Key of Christ's Kingdom.
> Hail! hope of eternal boons.

> HAIL! BRIDE UNBRIDED.

XVI

Kontákion   PI

All angel-kind marvelled at thy great work of flesh-taking; they saw the inaccessible God accessible to all as a man, dwelling with us and hearing from all: ALLELUIA.

XVII

Oîkos   RHO

Men the most eloquent we see become as dumb as fishes before thee, O Forth-bringer; helpless to say in what way thou, being still a maid, wast able to bring forth. But we, marvelling at the mystery, cry out in faith:

> Hail! casket of God's wisdom.
> Hail! treasury of his providence.
> Hail! confounder of the wisdom of the wise.
> Hail! making babble of men's eloquence.

Hail! for the deep thinkers are made foolish.
Hail! for the makers of myth have failed.
Hail! thou who rendest the word-webs of Athens.
Hail! thou who fillest the nets of the fishers.
Hail! thou who liftest from the deeps of knowing.
Hail! thou who enlightenest many in knowledge.
Hail! barque for those who seek salvation.
Hail! harbour of this life's seafarers.

HAIL! BRIDE UNBRIDED.

XVIII
Kontákion   SIGMA

Being minded to save the world, the Maker of all came willingly into
it and, shepherd because God, to us and for us did he appear a man;
and having called like unto like, as God he hears: ALLELUIA.

XIX
Oîkos   TAU

Unto all maidens and unto all who fly to thee thou art a wall, O
maiden Forth-bringer; the Maker of heaven and earth has prepared
thee unto this, dwelling in thy womb and teaching all to sing unto
Thee:

Hail! pillar of purity.
Hail! gate of safety.
Hail! beginning of spiritual new-making.
Hail! leader of godly living.
Hail! thou who didst bring to a new life those who in sin
     were born.
Hail! thou who healest the minds of the mentally stricken.
Hail! thou who castest down the corrupter of minds.
Hail! thou who didst bring forth the Sower of Holiness.
  Hail! maiden bride-chamber.
  Hail! thou who joinest to their Lord the faithful.
  Hail! fair nursing-mother of virgins.
  Hail! bridesmaid of holy souls.

HAIL! BRIDE UNBRIDED.

XX

Kontákion   UPSILON

No hymn that seeks to weave into one thy many mercies is worthy of
thee; were we to bring thee, O holy King, odes many as the sea sand
we should do nothing worthy of what thou hast given to us who sing
to thee: ALLELUIA.

XXI

Oîkos   PHI

We see the Blessed Virgin as a lamp of living light shining upon those
in darkness; she enkindleth an unearthly light to lead all unto divine
knowledge; she, the Radiance that enlighteneth the mind, is praised
by our cry:

> Hail! ray of the spiritual Sun.
> Hail! ray-flash of never-waning light.
> Hail! lightening-flash illuminating souls.
> Hail! thunder clap frightening foes.
> Hail! thou who sendest forth manifold splendor.
> Hail! who wellest forth a many-streamed river.
> Hail! who imagest Siloam's pool.
> Hail! who cleanest the stain of sin.
> Hail! cleansing-vat that lavest the conscience.
> Hail! loving-cup brimming with gladness.
> Hail! odour of Christ's sweetness.
> Hail! life of the mystic feasting.

HAIL! BRIDE UNBRIDED.

XXII

Kontákion   CHI

When he who payeth all men's debts was minded the ancient debts
to pay, self-exiled he came to them who were exiled from his grace
and, tearing up the bond, he heard from all: ALLELUIA.

XXIII

Oîkos   PSI

All we who psalm thy Son give praise to thee as to the living temple,
O God's Forth-bringer; when within thy womb dwelt the Lord who
holdeth all in his hand, he hallowed, honoured thee, and taught all to
cry to thee:

> Hail! tabernacle of God and the Word.
> Hail! holy beyond all holy ones.
> Hail! ark gilded by the Holy Ghost.
> Hail! unfailing treasure-house of life.
> Hail! precious diadem of godly Sovereigns.
> Hail! worshipful honour of a worthy priesthood.
> Hail! the Church's unassailable tower.
> Hail! indestructible wall of the Kingdom.
> Hail! thou whereby war trophies are set up.
> Hail! whereby foes are stricken.
> Hail! my body's healing.
> Hail! my soul's saving.

HAIL! BRIDE UNBRIDED.

XXIV

Kontákion   OMEGA

O Mother whom all must hymn, O thou who hast brought forth the
Word most holy beyond all the holiest, take our present offering,
keep all from every hurt, and deliver from all wrath to come those
who cry to thee: ALLELUIA.

> —*Ode in Honour of the Holy Immaculate Most Blessed Glorious
> Lady Mother of God and Ever Virgin Mary*, trans. Vincent
> McNabb, O.P. (Ditchling, Sussex: Pepler & Sewell, 1934)

3

GREGORY OF TOURS
(d. 594)

More than a theologian, Gregory was a devoted shepherd of the Church in Gaul. He worked hard to spread devotion to Mary and was the first to collect written accounts of the many miracles attributed to Mary's intercession.

Gregory led the Church of Tours, which, in the fourth century, had already been blessed by the presence of the remarkable and popular bishop St. Martin of Tours. Gregory exercised his ministry during a stormy period of transition, characterized by barbarian invasions.

Born around 538 to a senatorial family in Clermont, Gregory lost his father at a tender age and was raised by his mother and an uncle. While still a youth, he was sent away for classical and ecclesiastical studies. In 562, he was ordained to the diaconate by his great-uncle St. Nicetius, bishop of Lyons. Having fallen ill, he made a pilgrimage to the tomb of St. Martin in Tours, where he was healed.

In 573, while he was at Rheims, the people of Tours requested him as their bishop. Despite the shaky state of his health, he undertook many journeys out of concern for his Church. He restored various sacred buildings and returned the basilica of St. Martin, his illustrious predecessor, to its original splendor. He died at Tours in 594; his cult spread quickly, making him one of the most popular saints in Gaul, together with St. Martin.

His written works are numerous. His principal work, the *Historia Francorum* (History of the Franks), is extremely important because it represents the only literary source for the ancient history of the Franks.

Although he did not leave us very many texts on the Virgin Mary,

Gregory's testimony is precious, especially with regard to questions of history and Church tradition.[1]

Mary's Glorious End

In the West, Gregory is the first writer to witness to the mystery of Mary's Assumption into heaven. He hands down to us information received from an apocryphal Greek text, which he knew in a fifth-century Latin translation, now lost. We give his account:

> Finally, when blessed Mary, having completed the course of her earthly life, was about to be called from this world, all the apostles, coming from their different regions, gathered together in her house. When they heard that she was about to be taken up out of the world, they kept watch together with her.
>
> And behold, the Lord Jesus came with his angels and, taking her soul, handed it over to the archangel Michael and withdrew. At dawn, the apostles lifted up her body on a pallet, laid it in a tomb, and kept watch over it, awaiting the coming of the Lord. And behold, again the Lord presented himself to them and ordered that her holy body be taken and carried up to heaven. There she is now, joined once more to her soul; she exults with the elect, rejoicing in the eternal blessings that will have no end.[2]

Several elements of interest emerge from this narrative. The apostles were miraculously called together around the dying Virgin. Further, her bodily Assumption into heaven is presented as an obvious, accepted fact. For the apostles, after having laid her body in the vault, kept vigil in expectation that the Lord would return to take it away. Thus, in paradise, Mary enjoys eternal happiness in the totality of her human nature.

Even those details of this narrative that are not historically reliable seem to contain some meaningful theological notions. The apostles

---

[1] There are no systematic studies of the Marian thought of Gregory of Tours, no doubt for the reasons indicated. On his narration of miracles, see G.-M. Oury, "Le Miracle dans Grégoire de Tours", in *Histoire des miracles, Actes de la sixième Rencontre d'Histoire Religieuse tenu à Fontevraud les 8 et 9 octobre 1982* (Angers: Presses de l'Université, 1983), pp. 11–28.

[2] *Libri Miraculorum* 1, *De gloria beatorum martyrum* 4; PL 71, 708.

were always considered the most authoritative and best-qualified
eyewitnesses to the mysteries of salvation. They witnessed to everything that Jesus said and did during His entire public life. A certain
logic of faith demanded that these same apostles should become eyewitnesses to the mystery of Mary's Assumption into heaven. This
testifies on behalf of something that Christian tradition has always
emphasized: the intimate connection between the mystery of Christ
and the mystery of his Mother.

Mary's bodily glorification in the eternal life of heaven expresses
the Church's faith in the final glorification of man, saved by Jesus
Christ in the totality of his person. In the flesh of Christ and in the
flesh of Mary, both of whom were taken up into the glory of heaven,
the eschatological humanity of the redeemed is already present. Gregory of Tours offers a crucial historical witness to these truths of the
faith.

Miraculous Interventions of the Mother of God

In his *Libri Miraculorum*, Gregory collects countless stories and popular traditions about miracles attributed to a special intervention of the
Mother of the Lord.

Some cases of miracles occurring in the holy places of Palestine are
noted. For example, Gregory tells that there was a large well at
Bethlehem, from which Mary was said to have drawn water. Anyone
who looked into it often experienced a miracle, as long as he was
pure of heart: he would see the Star that guided the Magi to the place
where the infant Jesus was laid.[3]

Other miracles are recounted in connection with sacred buildings
dedicated to the Blessed Virgin. Gregory recounts a miracle that happened during the construction of a basilica that Constantine ordered
built in honor of the Virgin. There were on hand some columns of
enormous size, intended for the sacred building, but they were so
extremely heavy that it seemed impossible to lift them and set them
up in their proper places. Then the architect had a vision in which
the Virgin herself appeared and reassured him, saying: "Don't worry;

---

[3] Ibid., 1, 1; PL 71, 707.

I will teach you how to lift those columns." And she showed him what machines to use and how to arrange them. Then she added: "Go to the school and fetch three boys. They will help you in this work." The architect did as he had been told; he took three boys and, in less time than it takes to tell, was able to erect the columns. The whole town witnessed the extraordinary deed, which, in Gregory's time, was still celebrated every November.[4]

There is a very dramatic story of the rescue of a Jewish child, the victim of a terrible punishment inflicted by his father, who plied the trade of a glassblower. The boy went to school together with some Christian children; one day, he went with them to Mass in the basilica of the Blessed Virgin. He even went to the eucharistic table along with his companions. Overjoyed because of what had happened to him, he went back home and told his father about it. His father reacted with tremendous rage. He said to his son: "You shared Communion with the other boys, forgetting the religion of your fathers. Therefore, I will severely repay the offense you have committed against the law of Moses." Then, seizing the little boy, he threw him into the fiery furnace of his workshop.

But, the story continues, the Lord did not fail to intervene to help the boy, as he had already helped the three Hebrew boys whom King Nebuchadnezzar had cast into the fiery furnace (cf. Dan 3). And God did not permit this boy to be devoured by the flames either.

The little boy's mother, as soon as she heard what had happened, ran over to free him, but when she realized that the furnace was completely pervaded by the fire, she began to wail in desperation. When the Christians of the city became aware of what was going on, they ran to the glassblower's workshop and, having extinguished the flames, found themselves in the presence of a spellbinding scene: the boy was lying stretched out, as if resting on a featherbed.

They extracted him from the furnace and, full of amazement, found that he was completely unscathed. The news spread rapidly, so that the whole population praised God. But the story does not end here. Obviously, it had to have a conclusion analogous to that of the story of the three boys in Babylon. The glassblower, as the perpetrator of such an inhuman crime, was cast in his turn into the furnace

---

[4] Ibid., 1, 9; PL 71, 713.

and was completely devoured by the flames, until not the smallest trace of his body remained.

Finally, the whole tale ends with a Marian conclusion. The Christians question the boy to find out how he had been saved from the flames. And his response was:

> The woman who sits enthroned in the basilica where I received the bread from the table and who carries a baby in her bosom covered me with her mantle, so that I would not be devoured by the fire.

The boy, then, had a vision of the Blessed Virgin. After he, along with his mother, had been instructed in the Catholic faith, they believed in the Father, the Son, and the Holy Spirit and were reborn in the waters of baptism. Consequently, many Jews of the city converted.[5]

Mary's Concern for Christians

Naturally, narratives of this kind have to be taken for what they are worth, bearing in mind that popular imagination may have elaborated the stories of events that really happened. In any case, these stories reveal the Marian spirit of the Christian people, their devotion to the woman whom the faithful love to associate with Christ, as he opens up the treasury of his grace and mercy. If one considers that these stories were spread virtually everywhere in Christendom, as demonstrated by the multiplication of collections of miracle stories in different languages, one must conclude that Marian piety, as a popular phenomenon, was a prevalent reality throughout the Christian world.

The story of the Jewish boy offers us an interesting detail. The Virgin had put her own mantle on him, as a sign and pledge of protection. The Virgin's mantle became a universal symbol in Christian tradition, used especially in literature, in liturgy, and in Marian iconography.[6] It symbolizes the ideal of a mother's love and concern

---

[5] Ibid., 1, 10; PL 71, 714–15.

[6] For the iconography of Our Lady of the Mantle, see the study of Christa Belting-Ihm, *"Sub matris tutela": Untersuchungen zur Vorgeschichte der Schutzmantelmadonna* (Heidelberg: Winter, 1976).

for her children. Referring to the apostle John, Gregory of Tours wrote:

> From his glorious Cross, the Lord entrusted his Virgin Mother to the blessed apostle John, so that in this way the Lord's command might be fulfilled.[7]

Mary was entrusted to us in the person of the Beloved Disciple; yet, through his stories of the Blessed Virgin's gracious interventions, Gregory wants to say that it is even more important to remember that we have been entrusted to her motherly care. At the end of one story Gregory reflects:

> It is no wonder the Blessed Virgin obtains food for those devoted to her, seeing that she not only conceived without knowing man but also remained a virgin even after giving birth.[8]

In other words, since she received from the Lord the astounding gift of being both Mother and Virgin, it is not surprising that she also receives the gift of obtaining the favors for her own.

READING

MIRACULOUS RELICS OF MARY

Some time ago I saw a man named John, who had left Gaul after contracting leprosy. He had made his dwelling in the very place where, as we have said, the Lord was baptized and stayed there for a whole year. He used to bathe in the river regularly, in order to recover his original health, to the point that his skin was restored, even better than before.

After receiving some relics of blessed Mary in Jerusalem, he set about to return to his homeland, but he wanted to visit Rome first. However, when he was in a lonely region of Italy, he fell in with thieves. Straightway he was despoiled of his garments, and they even robbed him of the purse in which he kept the holy relics. Now his

---

[7] *Historia Francorum* 9, 42; PL 71, 524–25.
[8] *Libri Miraculorum* 1, 11; PL 71, 716.

enemies, thinking that he had some gold coins inside, forced the latch and carefully examined the contents. But because they found no money, they took the relics and threw them into the fire; then, after showering the man with blows, they went off.

But John, though half dead, managed to get up, in order to gather up at least the ashes of the relics. Instead, he saw the relics, unharmed, sitting atop the glowing embers; even the cloth in which they were wrapped was quite unscathed. It did not appear to have been thrown into embers but looked like it had been pulled out of the water.

The man joyfully gathered up all the relics and, resuming the journey he had undertaken, reached Gaul safe and sound.

We have known many others who, after bathing in the Jordan or in the waters of the city of Levi, were purified from this disease.

—Gregory of Tours, *Libri Miraculorum* 1, 19; PL 71, 722

4

VENANTIUS FORTUNATUS
(d. ca. 600)

The Latin poet Venantius Fortunatus had a warm and attractive style; he is also an outstanding witness to the growing Marian devotion in the sixth-century Church. His testimony is truly precious because it comes from a very intuitive writer who reacted immediately to the stimuli of his environment and the situations in which he found himself. For this reason, the content of his poetry is a close reflection of the conditions of his time and his ecclesiastical environment.

Venantius was born near Treviso around 530. He studied at Ravenna and, in 565, made a pilgrimage to the tomb of St. Martin of Tours to thank the saint for the recovery of his sight. He remained for a time at Tours, then moved to the city of Poitiers, where he became bishop. He died around 600.

He has left us a copious collection of hymns, elegies, epigrams, epitaphs, and other kinds of poetic compositions under the title *Carmina Miscellanea*. Some of these have found their way into the Roman breviary. His epic poem on the life of St. Martin of Tours is also well-known. In addition to poetry, he wrote some prose lives of the saints. Truly, Venantius' poetic style does not contradict his name! His verses combine the prevailing classical manner with intuitions and themes foreshadowing the mentality of the Middle Ages.

His verses on the Virgin Mary are attractive, inspired by Scripture, and full of sincere, deep devotion. Everything about her enchanted him: her beauty, her youth, her virginity, her election as Mother of God. In singing the praises of Mary, Venantius was greatly influenced by earlier Fathers of the Church, especially St. Augustine.[1]

---

[9] Bibliographical references: D. Tardi, *Fortunat: Étude sur le dernier représentant de la poésie latine dans la Gaule mérovingienne* (Paris, 1927); H. Düfel, "Die Mariologie des 6. bis 11. Jahrhunderts und ihre Bedeutung für Luthers Stellung zur Marien-

The Vision of the Prophets

Venantius was struck by the sublime mystery of the Virgin Mother of God, which he situates in the center of the awestruck gaze of angels in heaven and men on earth. In various compositions, he appears to be analyzing his almost ecstatic reaction to this drama, which only God's omnipotence could have brought about. In a lengthy song of 360 verses, which bears the title *In laudem sanctae Mariae*,[2] the poet sums up all his feelings and impressions about the mystery of Mary.

He underscores the way this mystery attracted the sentimental interest and the penetrating glance of the ancient prophets. He begins with Isaiah:

> The unanimous voice of men recalls this girl;
> How she, a virgin, bore a man without man's seed.
> In harmony with these glad tidings, Isaiah makes plain
> What God inspires, singing it like a trumpet,
> With eloquence running over, rightly telling of deep things,
> Singing our Emmanuel, given by the Virgin (vv. 3–8).

Next comes Jeremiah, the prophet sanctified in his mother's womb, who foretold that one day the Lord would raise up a shoot from David and that a king would reign wisely. Venantius adds:

> This righteous shoot is the Virgin, and the King is her child,
> The Judge and Ruler of the world (19–20).

The author of Psalm 89 also sang of the Virgin Mary, saying that it was God himself who created her:

> "Mother Zion!" A man will say, and he became man in her;
> This very man born in her is the One who established
>   her (cf. Ps 87:5),
> And the One who established her is the Most High himself.
> This mother Zion was the Virgin Mary (23–26).

---

verehrung unter besondere Berücksichtigung des Venantius Fortunatus und Anselm von Canterbury", in *De cultu mariano saeculis VI-XI*, vol. 2 (Rome, 1972), pp. 137–67; S. Folgado Flores, "Devoción y culto a la Virgen en Venancio Fortunato", in *De cultu mariano saeculis VI-XI*, vol. 3, pp. 87–100.

[2] PL 88, 276–84; MGH *auct. ant.* 4, 1, 371–80.

For the people of the prophets and the just men who longingly awaited the Lord's coming, Mary represented an aspect of hope, because the light to illuminate their darkness was to come from her. The poet affirms this, addressing himself directly to Mary:

> O holy Virgin of God, Mary who bore such a Son!
> Through you the people once in darkness now have light.
> In the land of the shadow of death, light has risen
>   and shines forth (87–89).

Mary's Divine and Saving Motherhood

When Venantius Fortunatus contemplates the mystery of Mary, he is aware that her election and her greatness were planned for the benefit of all men. Reworking the traditional Eve–Mary parallel in metrical form, he sings the contribution that she, as Mother of God the Savior, made to the work of human redemption:

> O remarkable Virgin, our only remedy,
> Whom God filled with the wealth of the world.
> You merited to hold your Maker in your womb
> And give birth to God, conceiving in faith.
> By this new birth, you will wash the world from sin
> And by your sacred offspring, you will give birth to God.
> The Son you bore, O Virgin Mary,
> Cured what Eve bore: the human race's woes (119–26).

It does not escape us that, to illustrate Mary's contribution to the work of human salvation, our poet uses two rather strong theological expressions. He calls her "our only remedy" and states that she washes the world from sin. This kind of language confirms how far the doctrine of Mary's coredemption had developed within Christian reflection.

Farther on, Venantius states that, even though she now dwells in God's glory, the Blessed Virgin continues to be the help of Christians; thus, in heaven, she continues the same mission of salvation that she began in the mystery of the Incarnation:

Happy are you, who became
The ticket, the way, the gate, the vehicle into heaven
For the human race, once fallen under hell's dominion.
Royal splendor of God, beauty of paradise, glory of
   the kingdom,
Receptacle of life, bridge that penetrates into
   the vault of heaven (207–10).

In one passage, Venantius Fortunatus, alluding to the primary and absolutely subordinating salvific action of Christ, attributes something to the Virgin Mother that, properly speaking, ought to be attributed to her Son. He writes:

Destroying hell, you bring back captives to their
   native land;
And restore their freedom, after breaking their yokes
   (329–30).

This way of speaking was fairly widespread among Christian authors and the faithful in general; nor can we consider it incorrect, because it presupposes the implicit view that certain expressions have to be understood as referring only to Christ the Redeemer, in a strict sense, even if they may be applied to Mary indirectly.

The Human Idyll of Mary's Motherhood

In addition to the greatness and divine dignity of Mary's motherhood, Venantius Fortunatus also delights in contemplating the genuinely human episodes of her life, moments of tenderness and poetry, which he exalts in his refined and lyrical style. He stresses that Mary, like every mother, is concerned with giving her Son all the care and attention he needs. This is found in one of his hymns on the Lord's Cross:

And so, when the fullness of sacred time had come,
He was sent from the Father's royal halls: the Creator
   of the world was born.
And, being made flesh, he came forth from a virginal womb.
The Baby cries, laid in the narrow crib;

> The Virgin Mother wraps his limbs round about with
>   swaddling clothes,
> And a tight band enfolds his feet, his hands, his limbs.[3]

Although the incomparable dignity of her divine motherhood elevates Mary above such illustrious women of the Old Testament as Sarah, Rebekah, Rachel, Esther, Judith, Anna, and Naomi, she was nevertheless involved in acts of human service, marvelous in their ordinariness and humility:

> Spotless Mary offers her womb to serve God, her child;
> And she feeds the Bread of Heaven with her milk.[4]

God, the poet observes, is not in the least degraded by having assumed all that is humble in the human condition from Mary; he explains this by a clear and convincing comparison. As the sun or a fire, shining upon a mire, purifies what it touches without becoming contaminated itself, so the Lord of majesty, in taking human flesh, purifies it without being contaminated by its corruption.[5] This comparison has been much exploited in patristic texts on the Incarnation.

The Miracle of Mary's Virginity

Singing the praises of Mary's virginity is part of the earliest Christian tradition. Venantius joins this chorus, offering his tribute of admiration and praise to the unique and unrepeatable miracle of a Virgin who gives birth to God; this miracle, moreover, has borne much fruit in the life of the Church. In fact, it greatly contributed to reviving and spreading among the faithful the ideal of consecrated virginity.

The poet admires Mary's virginity in two specific contexts: in the mystery of the Lord's birth and in the labors of his life, which he lived entirely in virginity. Venantius writes about the Incarnation:

---

[3] *Carmina miscellanea* 2, 2; PL 88, 88; MGH *auct. ant.* 4, 1, 28.
[4] Ibid., 8, 6; PL 88, 269; MGH *auct. ant.* 4, 1, 28.
[5] Cf. ibid., 11, 1; PL 88, 348; MGH *auct. ant.* 4, 1, 255.

Observe: He wanted to be born from a maiden's womb;
See from whose flesh the high Lord's flesh comes forth.
The venerable Spirit, wishing to dwell in a virginal house,
Leaves her womb intact.
God entered her, who did not know man;
The Virgin is known only by the man she bore.[6]

Because of her life of perpetual virginity, Mary stands at the head
of the thousands and thousands of virginal souls who have written a
special chapter of holiness and love in the history of the Church.
Now, they live in glory and happiness:

Then she shines forth, the Mother of God, the Virgin Mary
And she leads the virgin sheep of the Lamb's flock.
She, surrounded by a bevy of maidens,
With the light of her chastity leads on the splendid ranks.
In the banquets of paradise they sing their vows;
One collects violets, another gathers roses;
With their fingers they pick the buds and lilies of the lawns.[7]

In another passage, the poet presents the Virgin Mary as a flower
surrounded by a rosy crown of maidens, of whom she is the first and
preeminent virgin.[8]

The exaltation of Mary, her greatness, her role in the work of salvation, her holiness and her virtues, is a dominant and frequently
recurring motif in Venantius Fortunatus. By way of conclusion, we
cite a brief sequence of verses:

O honored name, Mary blessed forever,
Work of art, giving praise to your noble Artisan.
Sweet maiden, as the angel's precious speech relates,
You possess gifts of beauty beyond those of all men.[9]

On the level of pure theology, the figure of the holy Virgin is
raised up to become a symbol of supernatural beauty, inspiring joy
and trust.

---

[6] Ibid., 8, 6; PL 88, 268; MGH *auct. ant.* 1, 4, 183.

[7] Ibid., PL 88, 267; MGH *auct. ant.* 1, 4, 182.

[8] Ibid., 4, 26; PL 88, 175; MGH *auct. ant.* 1, 4, 97.

[9] *In laudem sanctae Mariae* 229–32; PL 88, 281; MGH *auct. ant.* 1, 4, 377.

READING

HYMN ON THE INCARNATION

The God, whom earth and sea and sky
Adore and laud and magnify,
Whose might they own, whose praise they tell,
In Mary's body deigned to dwell.

O Mother blest! The chosen shrine,
Wherein the Architect divine,
Whose hand contains the earth and sky,
Vouchsafed in hidden guise to lie.

Blest in the message Gabriel brought;
Blest in the work the Spirit wrought;
Most blest, to bring to human birth
The long desired of all the earth.

> —Venantius Fortunatus, *Quem terra, pontus, sidera*;
> PL 88, 265; AH 50, 86–88.
> Trans. John Mason Neale (1818–1866)

5

GREGORY THE GREAT
(ca. 540–604)

This great pope left an indelible mark on the history of Christianity. He guided the Church wisely during extremely difficult times characterized by profound political, social, and religious change. His activity as pope had a deep and long-lasting effect on various areas of the Church's life. He made an important contribution to the growth of the Church's missionary activity. He personally fostered numerous illustrious conversions among the Lombards. He introduced significant reforms in the field of liturgy; in particular, his name is linked to the success of Gregorian chant.

Pope Gregory I was born around 540 in Rome to a patrician family; his family owned a vast palace on the Caelian hill, exactly where the basilica that bears his name now stands. He received the best possible education in letters, grammar, rhetoric, and dialectic. For some time, he held the office of prefect of the city; then he answered the call to the monastic life. He transformed his family's house into a monastery and established other monasteries, using his own funds.

Very soon, however, he was chosen to become a deacon, and Pope Pelagius II sent him to Constantinople as his representative to the imperial court. In 590, he was himself elected supreme pontiff, even though he had made known his extreme reluctance to accept additional responsibilities. He occupied the Chair of Peter until his death in 604. He was the first pope to assume the title "Servant of the Servants of God".

In the works he has left us, Gregory reveals that he was a prolific and inspired writer. He wrote relatively little on the Virgin Mary, always in an occasional way; in this he exemplifies that tradition of sobriety which typifies the Roman pontiffs. Even so, his Marian witness remains worthy of note, both because it comes from a supreme pontiff of the universal Church and because it touches upon themes that are important for the evolution of Marian cult and devotion.[1]

Greatness of the Mother of God

In a homily on the Gospels, Gregory explains Jesus' words: "Who are my mother and my brothers?" (Mt 12:48), identifying the Blessed Virgin with the synagogue:

> The reason it states that his Mother is standing outside as well, as if unrecognized [by him], is that the synagogue was not recognized by its own Founder. For the synagogue, clinging to the observance of the law, lost its spiritual understanding and, holding on to a merely literal understanding, had to remain outside.[2]

Gregory's interpretation does not sound like praise of Mary at all. As was the case with the synagogue, so with Mary: she is not recognized by her Son, because she was preoccupied solely with observing the letter of the law and not the spirit. We should note that this identification is all the more unusual if we consider that, in the Latin tradition ever since St. Ambrose, Mary is usually compared to the Church, not to the synagogue.

In one of his letters, however, Gregory regards the holy Virgin with a more obvious sense of respect and admiration when, along with her condition as handmaid, he underscores her condition as Mother of the Lord:

> Behold, the same Virgin and handmaid of the Lord is also called "Mother". Indeed, she is the Lord's handmaid because the Word, before all ages, was the only begotten Son and equal to the Father; she is truly his Mother because, in her womb, he became man by the work of the Holy Spirit and from her flesh.[3]

---

[1] For the Marian thought of St. Gregory the Great, see R. Brajčić, "Sancti Gregorii Magni 'Hoc ipsum de Spiritu Sancto ex carne Virginis concipi a Sancto Spiritu ungueri fuit' (Reg. XI, 55) ut fundamentum cultus B. V. Mariae in luce interpretationis Deiparogenesis", in De cultu mariano saeculis VI-XI, vol. 3 (Rome, 1972), pp. 100–125; V. Recchia, "Una visione mariana nei dialoghi di Gregorio Magno: Dial. IV, 18," in Virgo Fidelis, ed. F. Bergamelli and M. Cimosa (Rome, 1988), pp. 203–14.

[2] Homiliae in Evangelium 3, 1; PL 76, 1086.

[3] Epist. 11, 67; PL 77, 1207.

In one of his commentaries on the Old Testament, Gregory again emphasizes his esteem and admiration for the holy Virgin when he identifies her with the lofty mountain prophesied by Isaiah (Is 2:2). Indeed, her dignity and greatness surpass that of even the most elect creatures:

> The most blessed and ever Virgin Mary, Mother of God, can be called by this name, "mountain". Yes, she was a mountain, who by the dignity of her election has completely surpassed the height of every elect creature.
>
> Is Mary not the lofty mountain? For God, to achieve the conception of the eternal Word, raised the summit of her merits above the choirs of angels, up to the threshold of the Godhead.[4]

Her superiority to men and angels is based on her elevation to a height that borders on the very throne of the Godhead, because, "in her womb, incorporeal Light assumed a body."[5]

Another reality that evokes amazement and admiration is Mary's virginity. Gregory mentions it at the end of a series of events, listed in ascending order of greatness and importance:

> Consider it carefully, please, and tell me, if you can: How was the Red Sea divided by a staff [of Moses]; how did the hardness of the rock, at the blow of the staff, gush forth a wave of water; how did the dry staff of Aaron flower; how did the Virgin, Aaron's descendant, conceive and remain a virgin, even in giving birth?[6]

We notice the emphasis on virginity *in partu*, a condition that makes the birth of Christ even more marvelous and mysterious. In another passage, he repeats the idea of the supernatural function of the Lord's virginal birth:

> Not with the help of coitus but through the intervention of the Holy Spirit was he conceived. In being born, then, he both showed the fruitfulness of his Mother's womb and preserved it incorrupt.[7]

---

[4] *In I Regum* 1, 5; PL 79, 25.
[5] *Moralia* 33, 8; PL 76, 671.
[6] *In Ezechielem* 2, 8, 9; PL 76, 1033–34.
[7] *Moralia* 24, 3; PL 76, 288.

To demonstrate the absolutely extraordinary character of the event, Gregory adds that the miracle of Jesus entering the upper room through locked doors ought not to astonish us:

> What is so remarkable about the fact that, after his Resurrection, the eternal Conqueror entered through closed doors? After all, when he came to die, did he not come forth without opening the Virgin's womb?[8]

The Virgin Appears to Little Musa

Gregory the Great offers us one of the oldest accounts of a Marian apparition. We have had occasion to recall an even earlier apparition; however, Gregory's account is particularly charming. Very simply and candidly, it reports the experience of a little girl named Musa. The holy pontiff assures us that he received his information from the little girl's own brother, Probus, a true man of God. Here is how the story unfolds.

One night, Musa had a vision in which the holy Mother of God appeared to her, surrounded by a bevy of girls her own age, wearing white dresses. The Virgin insisted that Musa join them. At first Musa did not dare to do so, but the Virgin asked her again if she wanted to join them and enter her service. Then Musa answered that she did want to. Mary ordered her to stop giving herself over to futile and childish things and to prepare herself because, thirty days hence, she would come back to take her into her service, together with the virgins who accompanied her.

After this vision, Musa appeared completely transformed, to the astonishment of her parents, who no longer saw in her a silly and childish little girl but a person full of seriousness and maturity. When questioned about this sudden transformation, Musa explained how the Mother of God had appeared to her and asked her to enter her service, naming also the day on which she was to come back.

Then, twenty-five days after the apparition, Musa fell ill with a fever. On the thirtieth day, when she was about to die, she saw the

---

[8] *Homiliae in Evangelium* 26, 1; PL 76, 1197.

Virgin once more, and the maidens with her. The Mother of God called her. And here is how Gregory's tale ends:

> Musa answered, reverently lowering her eyes, and said in a clear voice: "Here I am, Lady, I come! Here I am, Lady, I come!" In the same breath, she delivered up her spirit and left her virginal body to dwell with the holy virgins.[9]

Prescinding from any judgment about the reliability of this story, we limit ourselves to noting how the faithful at that time already considered it a normal possibility for someone to experience the presence of the Virgin in an apparition and how even a pope found it normal to talk about it.

Marian Cult and Devotion

In other texts, Gregory offers some important testimony about how widespread Marian devotion and piety were in his day. For example, he informs us that some churches were dedicated to the Mother of the Lord. Two explicit cases are reported in his letters.

He speaks of a certain Paul, deacon of the church of Rieti, who had asked the pope for permission to transfer the relics of the holy martyrs Hermas, Jacintus, and Maximus "to the basilica of the Blessed Ever-Virgin Mary, Mother of God and our Lord Jesus Christ, which is located in the city of Rieti".[10]

In a response to John, bishop of Palermo, who had informed Gregory of the completion of a basilica in honor of the Virgin Mary, the Pope grants John the faculty to consecrate it; this delegation was granted as a recognition of John's devotion to Mary.[11]

Another sign of growing devotion to Mary was the proliferation of her images, together with those of the saints. St. Gregory seems to uphold the legitimacy of the specific kind of veneration owed to sacred images.[12] He himself sent an icon of the Virgin to the hermit Secondinus.[13]

---

[9] *Dialogi* 4, 18; PL 77, 348–49.
[10] *Epist.* 9, 49; PL 77, 959–60.
[11] *Epist.* 14, 9; PL 77, 1312.
[12] *Epist.* 9, 52; PL 77, 990–91.
[13] Ibid.

On the doctrinal level, Gregory teaches some principles that legitimate Marian devotion. He acknowledged, for example, that when sins are expiated, it is not only the mediation of Christ that is at work but also the intercession of the saints. Their intercession, while it does not have the same value as true satisfaction, can still cancel or at least mitigate the penalty inflicted because of sin. If this principle is valid in the case of the saints, a fortiori it ought to be applied to the Mother of the Lord; therefore, it justifies and encourages devotion to her.

READING

MARY, THE MOUNTAIN THAT REACHES THE HEIGHTS OF DIVINITY

The most blessed and ever Virgin Mary, Mother of God, can be called by this name, "mountain". Yes, she was a mountain, who by the dignity of her election has completely surpassed the height of every elect creature.

Is Mary not the lofty mountain? For God, to achieve the conception of the eternal Word, raised the summit of her merits above the choirs of angels, up to the threshold of the Godhead.

Isaiah said in a prophecy, "In the last days, the mountain of the LORD's house will be made the highest mountain" (Is 2:2). And this mountain has been made the highest mountain, because Mary's height has shined out above all the saints. For, just as a mountain implies height, so the house signifies a dwelling place. Therefore she is called mountain and house, because she, illuminated by incomparable merits, prepared a holy womb for God's Only-begotten to dwell in.

On the other hand, Mary would not have become a mountain raised above the peaks of the mountains had not the divine fecundity raised her above the angels. Further, she would not have become the Lord's house had not the divinity of the Word assumed humanity and come to dwell in her womb.

Mary is justly called mountain rich in fruits, because the best fruit was born from her, namely, a new man. And the prophet, considering how beautiful she is, adorned in the glory of her fruitfulness, cries out: "There shall come forth a shoot from the stump of Jesse, and a branch shall grow from his roots" (Is 11:1).

David, exulting in the fruits of this mountain, says to God, "Let the peoples praise you, O Lord, let all the peoples praise you. The earth has yielded its fruit" (Ps 67:6–7). Yes, the earth has yielded its fruit, because the Virgin did not conceive her Son by man's doing but because the Holy Spirit stretched out his shadow over her. Therefore the Lord says to David, king and prophet, "I will place the fruit of your womb upon your throne" (Ps 132:11).

So says Isaiah, "And the fruit of the earth shall be exalted" (Is 4:2). For him whom the Virgin bore was not only a holy man but also the mighty God. Elizabeth refers to this fruit when she greets the Virgin and says, "Blessed are you among women, and blessed is the fruit of your womb" (Lk 1:42).

Mary is rightly called mountain of Ephrem because, while she is raised up by the ineffable dignity of the divine birth, the dry branches of the human condition flower again in the fruit of her womb.

—Gregory the Great, *In I Regum* 1, 5;
PL 79, 25–26; CCL 144, 58–59

6

ISIDORE OF SEVILLE
(ca. 560–636)

During the seventh century, Spanish Christianity had one of the leading parts in the choir of Western Marian piety. Its liturgy praised the Virgin Mary, especially in her role as model of the Church. For example, in reference to the baptism of catechumens during the Easter Vigil, it said:

> Today, through a birth as beautiful as the glow of dawn, sons of light are generated by grace from Mother Church, who bears within her the impress of the image of the Virgin Mother, who bore fruit without the intervention of man.[1]

Without a doubt, one of the important and eloquent voices in this choir of Marian piety belongs to Isidore of Seville, an outstanding figure in all literature.

Isidore was born around 560, the youngest of four children of a Spanish-Roman family. His education was greatly influenced by his brother, Leander, who was elected bishop of Seville in 584. Leander had a particular interest in the Virgin Mary. In his writings he called her "Mother of Incorruptibility"; he also acknowledged her role as intercessor with her Son and as Mother and model of virgins.

As for Isidore, he received an excellent classical and Christian education, which helped him acquire a vast and many-faceted erudition. He too was elected bishop of Seville and, as such, presided in 619 at the second regional council held in that city. In 633, he presided at the Fourth Council of Toledo. This important Council not only unified liturgical discipline in Spain but produced one of the most

---

[1] Marius Férotin, *Le Liber Mozarabicus Sacramentorum* (Paris, 1912), 250 n.

precise formulas of trinitarian and christological faith. Isidore experienced the radical political and social transformations that Spain underwent in the seventh century. He died in 636. His encyclopedic writings had an enormous influence on medieval culture.

In his writings, he gives a considerable amount of space to Marian doctrine. Among other things, he justifies the use of various Marian titles and takes a stand in a debate that was starting to garner a certain amount of attention: the problem of the end of Mary's earthly life.[2]

The Meaning of the Name "Mary"

In one of his books of *Etymologies*, Isidore attributes three meanings to the name Mary:

> Mary signifies Light-giver or Star of the Sea; for she gave birth to the Light of the world. In the Syriac tongue, however, Mary means "Lady", and beautifully so, since she gave birth to the Lord.[3]

This triple interpretation had a remarkable and lasting influence; it was a source of inspiration for centuries, especially in homiletic and devotional literature. In another work, Isidore adds to the name "Mary" a whole series of biblically inspired titles, which confer a doctrinal content on his etymological interpretation:

> Mary, which means Lady or Light-giver, illustrious descendant of David, rod of Jesse, closed garden, sealed fountain, Mother of the Lord, temple of God, sanctuary of the Holy Spirit, holy Virgin, pregnant Virgin, Virgin before giving birth, Virgin after giving birth. She received the angel's greeting and knew the mystery of the conception; she asked for details of how the birth would come about; and she did not withhold the obedience of faith, as if it were contrary to the law of nature.[4]

All these Marian symbols and titles were well-known in patristic tradition. But it seems that the formula "sanctuary of the Holy

---

[2] Cf. I. Bengoechea, "Doctrina y culto mariano en san Isidoro de Sevilla (m. 636)", in *De culto mariano saeculis VI-XI*, vol. 3 (Rome, 1972), pp. 161–95.

[3] *Etymologiae* 7, 10,1; PL 82, 289.

[4] *De ortu et obitu Patrum* 111; PL 83, 148.

Spirit" appears for the first time in this text of Isidore. Subsequently it will be much exploited in theological and spiritual literature. Isidore also gives attention to the relationship between the Holy Spirit and the Virgin Mary; a relationship he considers the original source of her fullness of grace and holiness. He defines Mary as the new earth, upon which the torrent of the Spirit poured down:

> Mary, the Virgin Mother of the Lord, is quite properly called "earth". . . . This earth was watered by the Holy Spirit.[5]

The Question of the End of Mary's Earthly Life

Isidore of Seville is one of the authors most often cited by those who confront the problem of the end of Mary's earthly existence and ask whether or not she experienced death. This is his point of view on the question:

> Some say that Mary departed this life by passing through the coarse torments of martyrdom, since the just man Simeon, holding Christ in his arms, was prophesying when he said to his Mother: "A sword will pierce your heart" (Lk 2:35). But it is not certain whether he was speaking of a material sword or if he meant the word of God, which is stronger and more cutting than any two-edged sword. In any case, no particular historical narrative tells us that Mary was killed by the stroke of a sword, since one reads nothing about it, and nothing about her death either. However, some say that her tomb is to be found in the valley of Josaphat.[6]

From this text, it appears that Isidore thought that Mary did indeed die. This is evidenced by the fact that he chose to include this passage in his work that speaks of the birth and death of the Fathers. There is also the reference to Mary's tomb, which, according to tradition, is to be found at Jerusalem, in the valley of Josaphat.

However, the bishop of Seville refrains from offering a hypothesis on how the Blessed Virgin met her death. Following the thought of St. Ambrose, he limits himself to rejecting a literal interpretation of

---

[5] *Quaestiones in Genesim* 2, 18; PL 83, 216.
[6] Cf. I. Bengoechea, "Doctrina", 178.

Simeon's prophecy about the sword. Beyond that point, Isidore aligns himself with the oldest tradition of the Fathers of the Church, choosing not to lift the veil of mystery that covers the end of Mary's earthly life. Nor did Pius XII wish to lift this veil. When he defined the dogma of the Assumption, he left the faithful free to believe as they wished about the question of whether Mary died before she was taken up into heaven, body and soul. Today, as is well known, theologians prefer to accept Isidore's point of view. For, after the original sin, death entered the world and became part of man's eschatological destiny; in addition, Christ himself willed to face death, in order to be like us in all things and to bring about the salvation of the whole human race.

Mary and the Church

The theme of the Church recurs with extreme frequency in the writings of Isidore of Seville, often in the context of his biblical typology. In his book of *Allegories*, numerous pages are dedicated to explaining and developing his doctrine on the Church. He continually uses images and symbols drawn from the Old and New Testaments.

He presents the Virgin Mary as the figure of the Church par excellence; in a certain sense, she is the Church herself. Isidore also notes that Mary possesses certain unique personal characteristics that allow her to assist the Church. Isidore's view of the relationship between Mary and the Church involves a twofold parallel. The first has to do with the birth of the Church. Mary is like a new earth, a virgin earth, from which Christ is born, the founder of the Church. The Church, on the other hand, is born from the pierced side of the Redeemer as he hangs on the Cross.[7]

The second parallelism regards virginal fruitfulness, by which Mary gives birth to Christ, while the Church gives birth to sons of God:

> Mary represents the Church, which, being wedded to Christ, conceived us as a virgin by the Holy Spirit and as a virgin bore us.[8]

---

[7] *Quaestiones in Genesim* 2, 18; PL 83, 216.
[8] *Allegoriae* 139; PL 83, 117.

Mary's maternal action precedes that of the Church; it is proposed to the Church as type and norm for her action of giving birth to Christians sacramentally.

But Isidore also calls Mary the Mother of Christ our Head, who became the prototype for male virgins, while Mary will be the prototype for female virgins:

> In the New Testament, Christ is the head of male virgins, and Mary is the head of female virgins. She is their founder, the Mother of our Head, who is Son of the Virgin and Spouse of virgins.[9]

It may be that, within the idea of Christ, the Head of the Mystical Body, Isidore also includes the members of the Mystical Body. If this is the case, then he could be referring to the concept of the Virgin's spiritual motherhood of Christians.[10]

The Cult of Mary

In reading the works of Isidore of Seville, one senses that he not only possessed a vast and profound knowledge of the mystery of Mary but that he felt intense admiration for her wonderful greatness and personal holiness and for the way she gave her full cooperation in the divine work of human salvation. This admiration is sometimes expressed in sequences of elogies addressed to her and in sentiments of deep affection.

Passing from personal devotion and private feelings to the public worship of the Church, one can conclude that Isidore made an important contribution in this field as well. Let it suffice to recall that Isidore was the founder and institutor of the Visigothic liturgy, which is characterized by its Marian content as much as by any other aspect. *Inter alia,* it is easy to show how the prevalent elements of its Marian contents exactly correspond to the leading themes of St. Isidore's Marian thought, in particular: Mary's virginal motherhood, her cooperation in her Son's saving work, and the Mary–Church

---

[9] *De ecclesiasticis officiis* 2, 18; PL 83, 804.
[10] Cf. Théodore Koehler, "Maria Mater Ecclesiae", *Études mariales* 11 (1953): 144–46.

parallel. Thus it is legitimate to think that the work undertaken by the Fourth Council of Toledo (633) for the purpose of ordering, unifying, inspiring, and compiling the Visigothic liturgy, and thereby introducing its Marian characteristics, was in great part due to the personal contribution of the bishop of Seville, who presided at that Council.

READING

THE WOMAN'S OFFSPRING

"I will put enmity between you and the woman, between your seed and hers" (Gen 3:15). The seed of the devil is a perverse suggestion; the seed of the woman is the fruit of a good work, by which the perverse suggestion of the devil is resisted.

She will tread upon his head, because from the beginning she expels his perverse suggestions from her mind. He will strike at her heel, because until the end he will try to deceive her mind, which he was unable to deceive with his first suggestion. Some have understood the following expression in reference to the Virgin, from whom the Lord was born: "I will put enmity between you and the woman", since it was promised that the Savior was going to be born from her, in order to defeat the enemy and to destroy death, of which the enemy was the author.

For they also understand the following as a reference to the fruit of Mary's womb; namely, Christ: "She will tread upon your head, and you will strike at her heel." This means: You will attack him to kill him, but he (Christ), after you have been defeated, will rise again and tread upon your head, which is death.

—Isidore of Seville, *Quaestiones in Genesim* 5, 5–7;
PL 83, 221

7

THE ICONOCLAST CRISIS
(725–843)

The patristic age, in both East and West, is considered to have ended around the middle of the eighth century. Its conclusion may be called a happy ending, since it put three outstanding Fathers of the Church in the spotlight: Andrew of Crete, Germanus of Constantinople, and John Damascene. Among other achievements, these Fathers wrote wonderfully about the Mother of God; their Marian teaching reaches unprecedented heights.

It was during this same period, however, that doctrine and devotion were caught up in the crucial iconoclast controversy; this led to terrible persecutions and destruction in the Byzantine Church for more than a century (725–843). This catastrophic event strongly conditioned the personal experience of the three Fathers mentioned above.

It is difficult to clarify definitively what the root cause of the iconoclast crisis was. Leaving aside consideration of devotional excesses that sometimes verged on idolatry, one can presume that the imperial government of Byzantium was prompted to persecute the cult of sacred icons by political and personal motives. The Emperor Leo III the Isaurian (717–741), who began the persecution, sought and obtained the support of some bishops but met with the firm opposition of others, including Andrew of Crete, Germanus of Constantinople, and John Damascene, who boldly banded together in a courageous defense of the cult of sacred images. When, in 730, the emperor asked the patriarch Germanus to confirm the imperial decree prohibiting the cult of images, the patriarch refused and was forced to step down.

Then the persecution broke out, which was to take even more violent forms when Leo III was succeeded by his son, Constantine V

Copronymos (741–755). In 753, he forced the bishops, gathered in council in the imperial palace of Hiereia, near Constantinople, to approve the iconoclast doctrine and to prohibit the cult of images. This act provoked a massive revolt among the people, especially among the monks, against whom Constantine unleashed a furious persecution that made many martyrs.

With the successors of Copronymos, the persecution died down until, in 787, new circumstances allowed the calling of the eighth ecumenical council, Nicaea II, in which the iconoclast doctrine was condemned and the cult of icons restored.

There was a resurgence of persecution under the reign of Leo V the Armenian (813–820) and some of his successors. However, in 843, the newly elected patriarch, Methodius I, backed by the empress Theodora, was able to reestablish the cult of images once and for all, appealing to the decisions of Nicaea II. That happened on the first Sunday of Lent, which remains in the Byzantine liturgical calendar as a feast of the Triumph of Orthodoxy.

The three final Fathers of the Eastern Church will carry out their teaching and pastoral activity within the context of these historical and religious events.[1]

---

[1] For the history of iconoclasm, see the foundational studies by Georg Ostro-gorsky, *Studien zur Geschichte des byzantinischen Bilderstreites* (Breslau, 1929); and his *Storia dell'impero bizantino* (Turin: Einaudi, 1970). Cf. also André Grabar, *L'Iconoclasme byzantin: Dossier archéologique* (Paris, 1957); J. Meyendorff, *Byzantine Theology: Historical Trends and Doctrinal Themes* (New York: Fordham University Press, 1974).

8

GERMANUS OF CONSTANTINOPLE
(d. ca. 733)

In addition to being one of the greatest Marian theologians of the eighth century, Germanus left a body of doctrinal work that still has exceptional value. The most important and most recent Marian documents of the Church mention him; for example, the dogmatic bulls defining the Immaculate Conception and the Assumption, chapter 8 of *Lumen Gentium*, and John Paul II's encyclical *Redemptoris Mater*.

Germanus was born in Constantinople, sometime between 631 and 649. After joining the clergy of the cathedral of Hagia Sophia, he was consecrated metropolitan bishop of Cyzicus in 705. In 715, he was called to rule the patriarchal see of Constantinople.

A strong and confident defender of the cult of images (as we have already seen), he came into conflict with the iconoclast Emperor Leo the Isaurian around 727, when Leo intensified his campaign of persecution. Forced to resign his office as patriarch in 730, Germanus died some years later, around 733, at a great age.

He was excommunicated posthumously in 754 by the iconoclast Council of Hiereia; however, the ecumenical Council of Nicaea II definitively rehabilitated him in 787.

He composed homilies celebrating Marian feasts—Presentation in the Temple, Annunciation, Dormition, the feast of Mary's Cincture (preserved in the church of the *Chalkoprateia* in Constantinople)—and commemorating events such as Mary intervening to liberate Constantinople from the Arab siege of 718. Obviously, Germanus also had occasion to speak of the Blessed Virgin in his writings that defend the cult of images, for, in his day, icons of Mary outnumbered those of any other saint.

Even though his style betrays (to a substantial degree) that prolix-
ity typical of Byzantine rhetoric, Germanus has left us a precious
theological legacy concerning the Blessed Virgin. His writings appear to be backed up by a vast and profound knowledge of the tradition and doctrine of earlier Church Fathers. He also shows a keen
sensitivity in interpreting the Marian sentiments and piety of the
Christian people.[1]

Exaltation of the Blessed Virgin

The Marian homilies of Germanus are totally infused with an unbounded admiration for Mary's greatness, virtues, and holiness. Following the tradition of the Eastern Church, he gives her the titles
Theotókos (Mother of God), *Aeipárthenos* (Ever-Virgin), and *Panagía*
(All-Holy). He tirelessly proclaims her praises in his writings.

We find an example of his interior attitude toward Mary in his
homily on the Presentation. Our author contemplates how, according to the account found in the apocrypha, Mary entered the Temple
of Jerusalem at three years of age to consecrate her life to the Lord.
Germanus invites the faithful to exalt this sublime creature:

> Hail, God's holy throne, divine offering, house of glory, all-beautiful
> ornament, and chosen jewel, and universal propitiatory, the heaven
> that tells the glory of God, dawn shining with light inaccessible. . . .
>
> Hail, Mary, full of grace, holier than the saints, higher than the
> heavens, more glorious than the cherubim, more honorable than the
> seraphim, more venerable and lofty than all creation; in your glorious

---

[1] The Marian doctrine of our author has been relentlessly studied. We limit
ourselves to some of the most essential bibliographical indications: I. Carli, *La
dottrina sull'Assunzione di Maria di S. Germano di Costantinopoli* (Rome, 1944);
Melchior a S. Maria, "Doctrina S. Germani C. de morte et assumptione
B.V.M.", *Marianum* 15 (1963): 195–213; E. Perniola, *La Mariologia di S. Germano*
(Rome, 1954); T. Horvath, "Germanus of Constantinople and the Cult of the
Virgin Mary, Mother of God, Mediatrix of All Men", *De cultu mariano saeculis VI-
XI*, vol. 4 (Rome, 1972), pp. 285–99; V. Fazzo, "Agli inizi dell'Iconoclasmo.
Argomentazione scritturistica e difesa delle icone presso il patriarca Germano di
Costantinopoli", in *Parola e Spirito: Studi in onore di S. Cipriani*, (Brescia, 1981), pp.
809–32.

and splendid Presentation, you bring us the liberating olive branch of the spiritual Flood; Hail, dove: you bring us the glad tidings of the birth of salvation . . . all-golden urn, you contain the sweetness of our souls, Christ our manna.[2]

Germanus' deeply-held convictions about Mary clearly emerge from the poetic rhythm of the discourse and from his heartfelt allegories and metaphors. He considers Mary's divine motherhood to be the root and foundation of her exceptional holiness. Being the "throne of God", the "house of glory", the golden vessel that contains "Christ our manna", Mary is also "full of grace" and the creature who is "holier than the saints".

The effects of Mary's divine motherhood are not limited to her person. She receives this unique prerogative for the benefit of all men, for whose sake God became Mary's Son. Therefore, the Blessed Virgin holds out to all men "the liberating olive branch"; she brings to everyone "the glad tidings of the birth of salvation".

Mary Assumed into Heaven

The testimony of Germanus confirms that the truth of Mary's Assumption into heaven, body and soul, was readily accepted in the eighth-century Eastern Church. Pius XII cites our doctor in the apostolic constitution *Munificentissimus Deus*, which defined the Assumption as a dogma of the faith.

While Germanus draws on numerous legendary details from John of Thessalonica (d. ca. 630),[3] his teaching on the Assumption contains some original aspects. He takes it for granted that the Blessed Virgin had to ascend to heaven in her own body, because this was demanded by compelling reasons:

---

[2] *Homily 1 on the Presentation*, 17–18; PG 98, 308 A–C.

[3] See this author's lengthy homily on the Dormition (PO 19, pp. 375–438), which offers firsthand information on the origin of this feast and its development. As the title itself indicates, the subject of the homily is the death of the Blessed Virgin, which (the author says) was accompanied by many marvels. Even though it does not speak directly about the mystery of the Assumption, its theme is of extreme importance for the history of the dogma.

[Her body], being human, was adapted and conformed to the supreme life of immortality; however, it remained whole and glorious, gifted with perfect vitality and not subject to the sleep [of death], precisely because it was not possible that the vessel that had contained God, the living Temple of the most holy Divinity of the Only-begotten, should be held by a tomb made for the dead.[4]

He considers Mary's Assumption into heaven to be a privilege with which Jesus intended to repay his Mother, as it were, for all he had received from her during his earthly life:

Hasten to meet the One born from you. In my filial duty, I want to make you happy; I want to offer payment for the hospitality of the maternal womb, wages for nursing me, recompense for my upbringing; I want to give surety to your heart. O Mother, who had me as your only begotten Son, choose to dwell with me![5]

In other words, this singular privilege appears to be due to the demands of Jesus' filial piety toward his Mother; that is, to something more than mere motives of fittingness:

Indeed, as a son looks for and desires his own mother, and the mother delights to live with her son, thus it was right that you also, whose heart was full of motherly love for your Son and God, should return to him; likewise it was altogether fitting that God, who for his part had the kind of feelings of love toward you that a son has for a mother, should make you a sharer in his community of life.[6]

One could not more strongly emphasize the notion of the demands of Jesus' filial love for his own Mother. But the patriarch of Constantinople gives a couple of other reasons that justify Mary's privilege. There is the reason of the Virgin's purity and complete integrity:

You are, as it is written, "all-beautiful" (Song 2:13), and your virginal body is all-holy, all-chaste, all the dwelling place of God, so that dissolving into dust is foreign to it.[7]

---

[4] *Homily 1 on the Dormition*, PG 98, 345 B.
[5] *Homily 3 on the Dormition*, PG 98, 361 C.
[6] *Homily 1 on the Dormition*, PG 98, 348 A.
[7] Ibid., 345 B

The other reason is the mediation and intercession that Mary carries out in God's presence on behalf of men:

I will build you up as a rampart for the world, as a bridge for those tossed about by the tides, as an ark for those who are saved, as a staff for those who are led by the hand, as the intercessor for sinners, and as the ladder that can conduct men to heaven.[8]

Regarding the question of Mary's death, Germanus of Constantinople considers it normal that Mary would have had to face this human experience before her glorious Assumption:

Even though you experienced death, which human nature cannot avoid, yet your eye, keeping watch over us, neither slumbers nor sleeps.[9]

A first reason is based on the universal jurisdiction of the law of death, from which no creature can be excused:

Indeed, you shared in our bodily condition, so that you could not avoid meeting with death (which is common to all men), just as your own Son, the God of all, also tasted death.[10]

From this comes a second reason for Mary's death: her earthly destiny could not differ from that of her Son, who also willed to face death and the tomb. But the experience of the tomb had to come to a glorious conclusion for Mary as well, just as had happened in the case of Christ:

Having hurried [to the tomb] and found the wrappings and the shroud, Peter and John believed that Christ was risen. And when we, the disciples of the Lord, gathered with the throng in your presence, O Gethsemane, for the funeral of the Ever–Virgin Mary, we all saw that she was laid in the tomb and then transferred elsewhere. She passed beyond our sight, beyond any dispute, before the tomb was sealed with the stone. . . . While she was being praised with hymns, and was about to be lowered into the tomb, she left the tomb empty.[11]

---

[8] *Homily 3 on the Dormition*, PG 98, 361 D.
[9] *Homily 2 on the Dormition*, PG 98, 357 B.
[10] *Homily 1 on the Dormition*, PG 98, 345 D.
[11] *Homily 3 on the Dormition*, PG 98, 372 A–B.

The patriarch of Constantinople does not fail to notice a third reason that explains the death of Mary. Her death had to happen in order to confirm the reality of the mystery of the Incarnation. Let us follow his reasoning:

> How could the dissolution of the body have reduced you to dust and ashes, since you, through the Incarnation of your Son, have freed man from the corruption of death? Thus you separated yourself from earthly things, so that the mystery of the tremendous Incarnation might truly be confirmed. Indeed, you endured being removed from temporal things, so that it would be believed that the God born of you was also a complete man, the Son of a true Mother, and that his Mother was herself subjected to the laws of physical necessity. This was the consequence of a divine decision and of the norms that govern the proper seasons of life.[12]

Further, the mystery of Mary's death and Assumption into heaven was witnessed by the apostles, who could confirm the truth with authority:

> Your departure did not lack witnesses, nor was your Dormition false. Heaven tells the glory of those who ran to meet you then; earth presents the truth about it; the clouds cry out the honor they paid you, and the angels tell of the offering of gifts that was made to you then, when the apostles were at your side [as you passed away] above Jerusalem.[13]

On the other hand, Germanus strongly underscores the fact that the Assumption did not interrupt Mary's spiritual presence among us:

> Even though you departed, you did not separate yourself from the Christian people. You, the way leading to incorruptibility, did not distance yourself from this corruptible world; on the contrary, you remain close to those who call upon you. They who seek you faithfully do not fail to find you.[14]

---

[12] *Homily 1 on the Dormition*, PG 98, 345 C–D.
[13] *Homily 2 on the Dormition*, PG 98, 357 B.
[14] *Homily 1 on the Dormition*, PG 98, 345 B–C.

Some characteristics of Mary's spiritual presence in our world are analogous to the presence of her Son. Our author places these significant words on Christ's lips:

> Just as I, though I am not in the world, look far and wide, looking out for those who are in the world, so your protection will not be taken away from the world, until the end.[15]

Mary's Mediation

From her place in the glory of heaven, Mary acts as Mediatrix on behalf of men. This is a theme on which Germanus offers abundant citations. We offer a well-known passage, taken from the famous homily he preached after the liberation of Constantinople from the siege of the Arabs:

> May the Ever-Virgin—radiant with divine light and full of grace, mediatrix first through her supernatural birth and now because of the intercession of her maternal assistance—be crowned with never-ending blessings . . . seeking balance and fittingness in all things, we should make our way honestly, as sons of light.[16]

While Mary's mediation is not a matter of absolute necessity, Germanus makes a daring observation: We do "not need any other mediator in God's presence".[17] Germanus never tires of exhorting the faithful to appeal to the Blessed Virgin, because her assistance, her protection, and her prayer of intercession are very efficacious in the order of eternal salvation. He does not hesitate to make a very strong-sounding statement:

> No one is saved except through you, O All-Holy. No one is delivered from evils except through you, O All-Chaste. No one obtains the grace of mercy except through you, O All-Honorable.[18]

---

[15] *Homily 3 on the Dormition*, PG 98, 360 D.

[16] *Homily for the Liberation of Constantinople* 23, ed. V. Grumel in *Revue des études Byzantines* 16 (1958): 198.

[17] *Homily on the Cincture*, PG 98, 380 B.

[18] Ibid.

A little farther on he explains:

> For, just as in your Son's presence you have a mother's boldness and strength, do you with your prayers and intercessions save and rescue us from eternal punishment, for we have been condemned by our sins and do not dare even to lift our eyes to heaven above.[19]

The Cult of Icons

In his homilies, Germanus alludes only a couple of times to icons of the Mother of God. He considers them useful and effective as symbols that can make God's presence and action come alive in the minds of believers. We read in one homily:

> The material colors of your icons, O *Theotókos*, cause the lavishing of your blessings on us to shine forth.[20]

Not only on the level of meaning but also on the moral level of practical living, icons can exercise a profound influence on the faithful who contemplate them:

> Who, looking at your image, does not immediately forget all his troubles?[21]

We have three letters that Germanus wrote to the three bishops of Asia Minor in response to the first manifestations of the iconoclast crisis. Germanus defends the cult of images of Christ, of the Virgin Mother of God, and of the saints, explaining that it is not intended as a substitute for the worship of the one true God. The cult of images has to do with those human beings who had a privileged relationship with God. Icons depict only their physical appearance, through which the cult reaches the person himself, not stopping at the painted image.[22]

St. Germanus also reports the case of a miraculous icon of the Virgin, venerated at Sozopolis in Pisidia, which emitted oil from the palm of the Virgin's hand. This miraculous occurrence remained famous in the tradition of the Byzantine Church.[23]

---

[19] Ibid., PG 98, 380 D–381 A.
[20] *Homily 2 on the Dormition*, PG 98, 356 C.
[21] *Homily on the Cincture*, PG 98, 381 B–C.
[22] *Letter to John of Sinada*, PG 98, 160.
[23] *Letter to Thomas of Claudiopolis*, PG 98, 185.

READING

MARY'S SPIRITUAL PRESENCE AMONG THE FAITHFUL

O most holy Mother of God, after heaven and earth were honored by your presence, how is it possible to accept that your departure has left men deprived of your protection? Let it never occur to us to think in this way. For just as you, when living in this world, never felt estranged from a heavenly life, even so, after your departure, you are not spiritually separated from the [earthly] existence of men. If, on the one hand, you were consecrated as the heavenly tabernacle of God, because you held the Son of the Most High within you, your womb being capable of carrying his weight; on the other hand, you have been called the spiritual earth, because you received his body within you. Thus it is right to think that, since you were intimately united with God during all of your earthly sojourn, you never abandoned those who continue to live in this world, when you left this world's life.

We however, accustomed to venerate you faithfully, uselessly say: Why were we not considered worthy to have you stay with us in your bodily presence? Therefore we call thrice blessed those who delighted in the contemplation of your earthly existence, those who helped you, O Mother of life, as your companions in life. In any case, still desiring that you might dwell bodily in our midst, the eyes of our souls are compelled to look toward you daily.

Indeed, as you were a fellow citizen of our ancestors, even so you dwell with us spiritually, and your ample protection in our regard is like a sign that you are with us. We all hear your voice, and all our voices reach your ears. Through the protection you offer us, we are known by you. We, in our turn, recognize your ever-wonderful assistance. Nothing, not even death, can come between you and your servants.

You did not abandon those who greeted you, nor have you abandoned those whom you gathered together, because your spirit lives forever and your flesh did not have to bear the corruption of the grave. You see everyone, and your vigilance, O Mother of God, extends to all. Yes, our eyes are prevented from seeing you, O Most

Holy One, but still you delight to remain in our midst, manifesting yourself in various ways to those who are worthy. Truly, the flesh cannot impede the power and ability of your spirit, because your spirit blows where it wills, being a spirit pure and immaterial, incorruptible and immaculate, a companion spirit of the Holy Spirit, the favorite spirit of the Godhead of the Only-begotten.

—Germanus of Constantinople, *Homily I on the Dormition*,
PG 98, 344 B–345 A

9

ANDREW OF CRETE
(d. ca. 740)

A contemporary of Germanus of Constantinople and John Damascene, this great hymn writer made his own important contribution
to Marian theology, especially with regard to the Blessed Virgin's
personal holiness and her intercessory role. Woman without stain,
assumed into heaven, queen who cares and prays for those devoted
to her—these are some of the ideas Bishop Andrew stresses in presenting Mary to the people of God. His witness to the faith and
Marian piety of his time is particularly abundant and eloquent.

Andrew was born at Damascus around 660. Unable to speak until
the age of seven, he acquired the ability to speak after receiving his
First Holy Communion. It is possible, however, that this traditional
story was only a means of giving a supernatural explanation for his
amazing oratorical abilities.

Having become a monk in Jerusalem, he later became a deacon of
the cathedral of Hagia Sophia in Constantinople. Around 717, he
was consecrated metropolitan archbishop of the island of Crete. He
also experienced the first phase of the iconoclast controversy, during
which he firmly opposed the persecutory policies of Leo the
Isaurian.

He was a zealous pastor of the Church in Crete, building many
churches, developing works of social concern and assistance, concerning himself with the education of youth, and promoting the
monastic life. The likely year of his death is 740. The Eastern Church
venerates him as a saint.

Andrew has always been recognized as one of the most skilled orators of the Byzantine church and as a deeply inspired hymn writer.
His "Great Canon", which is still sung today in the East during Lent,
is subdivided into nine series of odes, each of which ends with a

so-called *theotókion*, or verset in honor of the Mother of God, that usually invokes her compassion and aid.

He also composed three liturgical canons specifically devoted to the Mother of the Lord: for the Conception of Anna, the Nativity of Mary, and the Annunciation. He dedicated different homilies to her: one on her Conception, four on her Nativity, five on her Presentation in the Temple, two on the Annunciation, one on the Purification, five on the Dormition, one short homily on the cult of sacred images, and one homily on the *Akathist* hymn. Some of these homilies have never been published, and this makes the reconstruction of his complete Marian thought more difficult. But some themes emerge with efficient clarity even from the known writings. The bishop of Crete does not neglect to touch upon the traditional Marian questions: the prophetic pre-announcement of Mary in the inspired Scriptures, her divine motherhood, her triple virginity before, during, and after giving birth, her unsullied personal holiness. His doctrine has solid christological foundations, so that it fits neatly into the bigger picture of salvation history.[1]

Mary, Spotless Creature

Andrew's witness to the Church's faith in the exceptional holiness of the Mother of the Lord is absolutely remarkable. He affirms more than once that the Blessed Virgin lived her whole life without being contaminated by any moral stain. The insistence with which the bishop of Crete returns to this point is so strong that some have seen him as an exponent of the Immaculate Conception. Even if we cannot accept this thesis without hesitation, we must at least recognize that Andrew had a highly elevated concept of the Virgin's sinlessness and holiness. We cite one of the numerous texts:

---

[1] For the Marian thought of Andrew of Crete, see: Martin Jugie, "Saint André de Crète et l'Immaculée Conception", *Echos d'Orient* 13 (1910): 129–33; G. Grecu, *Doctrina marialis iuxta S. Andream Cretensem (saec. VII-VIII)* (thesis, Propaganda Fide University, Rome, 1938); C. Conci, "La mariologia di S. Andrea di Creta" (thesis, Gregorian University, Rome, 1950); R. García, "Andrés de Creta, doctor de la Immaculada Concepción y teólogo clásico de la Asunción de Maria a los cielos", *Studium* 10 (1970): 3–52.

It was right, then, that the admirable Joachim and his spouse, Anna, inspired by divine thoughts, did obtain her as the fruit of their prayer; her, I say, the queen of nature, the firstfruits of our race, whose birth-day we celebrate, whose swaddling clothes we honor, and whom we venerate as the source of the restoration of our fallen race.[2]

This text presents Mary as the firstfruits of the human race; that is, the first creature who received the gift of salvation. But Andrew ex-plains it even more clearly:

This is Mary the *Theotókos*, the common refuge of all Christians, the first to be liberated from the original fall of our first parents.[3]

We could present many more passages in which Andrew expresses this concept. However, when our author speaks of Mary as the first person to be redeemed, or as the first to be liberated from original sin, he does not define the nature of the intervention God wrought in her. Hence we would not be justified to attribute to him the con-cept of preservation from original sin as we understand the concept today, precisely as the solemn Magisterium of the Church has de-fined it. It is true that Andrew is mentioned in the bull *Ineffabilis Deus* as being among the witnesses to the Immaculate Conception. More than anything else, however, his testimony witnesses to the develop-ment of the faith of the Christian people, on their journey toward a light that would illuminate the mystery ever more clearly.

Also, we have to keep in mind that the bishop of Crete did not share the notion of original sin that the Latin theologians had already formed. Therefore, it is understandable that he could speak in these terms without considering the problem of the presence or absence of original sin in Mary.

Instead, Andrew appears to have believed that God prepared the holy Virgin in advance, on both the moral and the personal level, to make her worthy and capable of being God's Mother:

A place had to be prepared before the King's arrival. The royal gar-ments had to be woven before they could receive the royal Child at his birth. Finally, the clay had to be prepared before the Potter's arrival.[4]

---

[2] *Homily 3 on Mary's Nativity*, PG 97, 860 B–C.
[3] *Homily 4 on Mary's Nativity*, PG 97, 880 C.
[4] *Homily 3 on the Nativity*, PG 97, 860 B.

We have already seen, in more than one place, how this concept of Mary's purification at the moment of the Annunciation was shared by other Fathers of the Church in preceding centuries.

What our author certainly meant to say is that the most holy soul of the Mother of God had to be free from any shadow of imperfection or personal sin. The conception of this beautiful and holy creature was such an extraordinary event that it deserves to be celebrated with all due solemnity. Therefore, Andrew wrote a canon celebrating Mary's conception by her mother, Anna:

> Let all creation dance; let David dance as well, for from his line and his seed arose the branch that will bear the Flower, the Lord and Redeemer of all. . . .
>
> Anna was sterile and barren, but not childless in God's eyes. For, from all eternity, she was predestined to be the mother of the chaste Virgin, from whom the Creator was to come forth in the form of a servant.
>
> Unsullied Lamb, who alone, from your womb, gave Christ the wool of our nature, we all celebrate your birth from Anna with songs.[5]

The last words of this text might be evidence that a feast of Mary's Conception by Anna was already being celebrated at that time in the Eastern Church. The feast would be justified as the celebration of the birth of a creature of exceptional spiritual beauty and holiness.

Andrew compares Mary to virgin soil, soil not contaminated by the hand of man, from which the Creator brought forth the new Adam:

> Today that [human] nature, which was first brought forth from the earth, receives divinity for the first time; the dust, having been raised up, hastens with festive tread toward the highest peak of glory. Today, from us and for us, Adam offers Mary to God as firstfruits, and, with the unpoisoned parts of the muddy dough, is formed a bread for the rebuilding of the human race. . . .
>
> Today pure human nature receives from God the gift of the original creation and reverts to its original purity. By giving our inherited splendor, which had been hidden by the deformity of vice, to the Mother of him who is beautiful, human nature receives a magnificent and most divine renovation, which becomes a complete restoration.

---

[5] *Canon on the Nativity*, PG 97, 1316 C–1320 A.

The restoration, in turn, becomes deification, and this becomes a new formation, like its pristine state.[6]

And so there is no doubt that the bishop of Crete affirms Mary's extraordinary initial sanctity, even leaving aside any question of her preservation from original sin. This holiness is considered something positive, an interior richness, a treasure of virtue, a special act of God's love.

Mary's Death and Assumption

In his homilies on the Dormition, Andrew expounds a rather nuanced and slightly uncertain doctrine on this matter. He has no doubts that the Virgin really did die. Since not even Christ escaped the death sentence promulgated by God for all humanity, this is all the more reason that Mary could not avoid it. Other considerations aside, she had to resemble her Son in her death as well. This is the same reasoning that we found in the writings of St. Germanus of Constantinople.

Andrew, however, poses a problem that no one had thought of before: Was it possible that an all-holy creature, such as Mary, could have been subjected to that death which was clearly introduced as punishment for Adam's falsehood? In other words: Could Mary receive the punishment for sin?[7]

Yes and no. The Virgin was subject to the law of death; however, for her, it was not a punishment for sin. Since she differed from all other creatures, in that she was free from the faults of sin and gifted with a unique holiness, her death did not imply a condemnation and a curse. To the contrary, this condemnation and curse were conquered, precisely in the mystery of Mary's death:

> Death, natural to men, also reached her; not, however, to imprison her, as happens to us, or to vanquish her. God forbid! It was only to secure for her the experience of that sleep which comes from on high, leading us up to the object of our hope. . . .

---

[6] *Homily 1 on the Nativity*, PG 87, 809 D–812 A.

[7] Cf. *Homily 1 on the Dormition*, PG 97, 1953; *Homily 2 on the Dormition*, PG 97, 1081.

No man lives, says Scripture, who will not see death. But even though the human creature we celebrate today must obey the law of nature, as we do, she is superior to other humans. Therefore, death does not come to her in the same way that it comes to us. Instead, it comes in a superior way, and for a reason higher than the reason that obliges us to surrender totally to death.[8]

After her death, Mary was called to enjoy heavenly glory, and yet, our author reveals some uncertainty about the nature of her Assumption. He tries to explain it in a long passage from his *Second Homily on the Dormition*, which, frankly, does not win any points for clarity:

The [Lord's] birth escaped corruption, nor did her tomb allow corruption, which does not touch what is holy. You want me to tell you what the proof is. Let none of you for your part overlook her empty tomb, for I ask you: Why is no body visible? And why are the burial wrappings missing from the tomb, if not because what had been entombed there escaped destruction, and because the treasure was transferred to another place?

If this is how things stand, why should not the transfer have truly happened, since the other circumstances agree with it: the separation of the soul from the body, the laying of the body in the tomb, the division of the human remains, the separation into parts, dissolution, union, reconnection, the disappearance into the invisible? Indeed, the tomb remains empty to this day, as confirmed by witnesses; indeed, the tomb itself witnesses to the transfer.

I do not know if the elements were recomposed into a unity, as a consequence of the reunification of the parts. Therefore I will reason about these things for a moment. Perhaps the Creator of all things, according to his hidden pleasure, decided in this way to honor her who had given birth to him. Or perhaps one of the two parts prevailed upon the other so that, after a mutual separation, the one [the body] was fated to remain within the confines of earth, while the other [the soul] had to stay away from earth. Or perhaps an unknown and uncommon occurrence of a supernatural character took place in her case, in which all her essential characteristics were made anew, because she had received the supreme Word in a way beyond all telling or knowing.[9]

---

[8] *Homily 1 on the Dormition*, PG 97, 1052 C–1053 A.
[9] *Homily 2 on the Dormition*, PG 97, 1081 D–1084 B.

From this rather laborious text one gathers that Mary's soul definitely rose to heaven, while the fate of her body is not clear. It may have been reunited with her soul in the glory of heaven, or it may have been transferred to some suitable place on earth, a sort of earthly paradise. Only one thing is clear: her tomb remains empty.

Andrew responds to the difficulty that might arise because of the silence of the Sacred Scriptures and the earliest Fathers of the Church on this topic. He holds that the explanation for their silence lies in the fact that the Mother of the Lord died rather late; that is, some time after the books of the New Testaments had been completed.[10]

Mary's Queenship and Mediation

Andrew willingly attributes royal dignity and corresponding titles to the Blessed Virgin. In his homilies, we repeatedly meet expressions such as: Queen of the human race, Immaculate Queen, New Queen, Queen of all men. He sees Mary's queenship foretold in the words of the Psalm: "The queen stands at your right hand, arrayed in gold" (Ps 45:9); he considers the feast of the Nativity of Mary as a festive banquet offered by the Queen of heaven for her subjects: "Royal is this banquet of the Queen, a descendant of royal seed."[11]

Speaking of the Dormition of Mary, the bishop of Crete expresses himself thus:

> Today, Jesus transports the Queen of the human race outside of her earthly dwelling: his Ever-Virgin Mother, in whose womb he took human form without ceasing to be God.[12]

Elsewhere he addresses an extraordinary elegy to Mary, showing what great progress Marian devotion had made:

> Queen of the whole human race, truly faithful to the meaning of your name, you are above all things—except God![13]

---

[10] *Homily 1 on the Dormition*, PG 97, 1060 B–C.
[11] *Homily 3 on Mary's Nativity*, PG 97, 844 C.
[12] *Homily 2 on the Dormition*, PG 97, 1080 B.
[13] *Homily 3 on the Dormition*, PG 97, 1100 A.

In Andrew's writings, there is also some emphasis on Mary's role as mediatrix on our behalf. Exalting the marvel of the Incarnation that took place in her womb, establishing a kind of familial relationship between God and humanity, our doctor exclaims:

> O, how marvelous it is! She acts as mediatrix between the loftiness of God and the lowliness of the flesh, and becomes Mother of the Creator.[14]

In another homily, he greets her as "mediatrix between law and grace",[15] considering her as a meeting point between the Old and New Testaments. Hence he invokes her assistance:

> Chaste Mother of God and Virgin, never cease to intercede for us, that we . . . may be saved from all misfortune.[16]

However, Andrew does not make Mary's mediation into a duplicate of Christ's mediation. Her mediation is based on her role as Mother of God; thus, it remains subordinate to her Son's mediation.

READING

THE CULT OF SACRED ICONS

Christianity contains nothing untried or abnormal. The very use of sacred images belongs to an ancient tradition, as worthy examples of faith have testified.

The first example is that of the image of our Lord Jesus Christ, sent to King Abgar; this image on a wooden tablet showed the outlines of his bodily form, similar to images painted with colors.

The second example is that of the image not painted by human hands (*acheropita*) of her who gave birth without seed: it is found at Lidda, a city also called Diospolis. The image is painted in very bright colors and shows the body of the Mother of God, three cubits in

---

[14] *Homily 1 on Mary's Nativity*, PG 97, 808 C.
[15] *Homily 4 on Mary's Nativity*, PG 97, 865 A.
[16] *Penitential Canon for the First Thursday of Lent*, PG 97, 1425.

height. It was venerated in the time of the apostles on the western wall of the temple that they built. It is so finely done that it appears to have been produced by the hand of a painter. It clearly shows her purple habit, her hands, her face, and all of her outward form, as can still be affirmed today. They say that when Julian, that apostate and enemy of Christ, heard about the painting, he wanted to know more about it. So he sent some Jewish painters [to examine it], who informed him that it was genuine; Julian, dumbfounded, had no desire to investigate further.

It is told that the temple was constructed when the Mother of God was still living. Going up to Zion, where she lived, the apostles said to her, "Where were you, Lady? We have built you a house at Lidda." Mary answered them, "I was with you, and I am still with you." Returning to Lidda and entering the temple, they found her complete image painted there, as she had told them. This is what an ancient local tradition has testified from the beginning, and the tradition lives today.

Third example. Everyone witnesses to the fact that Luke, apostle and evangelist, painted the incarnate Christ and his immaculate Mother with his own hands and that these images are conserved in Rome with fitting honor. Others assert that these images are kept at Jerusalem. Even the Jew Josephus tells that the Lord looked just like the picture: eyebrows meeting in the middle, beautiful eyes, long face, somewhat oval, of a fair height. This was undoubtedly his appearance when he dwelt among men. Josephus describes the appearance of the Mother of God in the same way, as it appears today in the image that some call "the Roman woman".

—Andrew of Crete, *On the Veneration of Sacred Images*,
PG 97, 1301–4

10

JOHN DAMASCENE
(d. ca. 750)

St. John Damascene is generally considered the last and one of the most outstanding Fathers of the Greek Church. Reading his writings, one gets the impression that all the marvelous theology that was to be developed in the Middle Ages had already been outlined by him and, in some cases, brought to a remarkable level of development. In his writings, he sums up the whole tradition of the Eastern Fathers; he understands and interprets it with a keen intellect and a remarkable synthetic ability. He considerably influenced Western thought as well, especially Scholasticism.

His Marian doctrine may be considered a complete and substantial synthesis of patristic faith and teaching about the mystery of the Mother of God. His love for Mary inspired him to participate with indomitable courage in the battle to defend the cult of sacred images. Unfortunately, we know very little about the life of this great Father and Doctor of the Church, despite the research carried out by capable scholars; in addition, the few pieces of information that have survived are not always completely reliable.

John was born in Damascus to a noble Christian family of Arab origin, around 650. Like his father, he was in the service of the caliphs at various times; then, at a relatively mature age, he entered the monastery of St. Saba, near Jerusalem, as a monk. There he was ordained a priest and continued his mission of teaching, preaching, and writing. He died around 750, at a very advanced age.

He wrote numerous works, which embrace nearly all areas of theology. He was also a poet and composed hymns, some of which became part of the Byzantine liturgy. He wrote frequently and extensively about the Blessed Virgin. His four Marian homilies (one on the Nativity and three on the Dormition) are of particular importance. He also wrote a canon and some hymns on the Dormition. In addition, his theological masterpiece, the *Treatise on the Orthodox Faith*, discusses Marian themes. John treats, more or less, all the mariological questions that were current in his day: Mary's predestination, the Old Testament figures and prophecies that were usually applied to her, her divine maternity, her perpetual virginity, and the meaning of the name Mary, which he interprets as "Lady", according to Syriac etymology. He was the first author to speak of consecration to Mary. In our rather panoramic exposition, we confine ourselves to certain aspects of mariological doctrine that are most original and most important to him, aspects for which the Church's Magisterium still invokes him today as an authority. Along with Germanus of Constantinople and Andrew of Crete, he is cited in *Munificentissimus Deus*, the document in which Pius XII proclaimed the dogma of the Assumption; his name appears in chapter 8 of *Lumen Gentium* as well as in John Paul II's encyclical *Redemptoris Mater*. His Marian thought has been the object of various studies and research, which have emphasized its value and depth.[1]

John Damascene often speaks of Mary as a sublime creature, filled with spiritual treasures. Accordingly, his homily on the Nativity, for example, goes so far as to make clear and explicit allusions—unprecedented in previous centuries—to the mystery of the Immaculate

---

[1] The Marian doctrine of John Damascene has been studied from various points of view. We give here the principal references: M. Schumpp, "Zur Mariologie des hl. Johannes Damascenus", *Divus Thomas* 2 (1924): 222–34; C. Chevalier, "La Mariologie de saint Jean Damascène", *Orientalia Christiana Analecta* 109 (Rome, 1936); Valentine Albert Mitchel, *The Mariology of Saint John Damascene* (Turnhout: Proost et Co., 1930); V. Grumel, "La Mariologie de saint Jean Damascène", *Echos d'Orient* 40 (1937): 318–46; J. M. Canal, "San Juan Damasceno, doctor de la muerte y de la Asunción de Maria", *Estudios Marianos* 12 (1952): 270–330; L. Ferroni, "La Vergine, nuova Eva, cooperatrice della divina economia e mediatrice secondo il Damasceno", *Marianum* 17 (1955): 1–36; B. M. Garrido, "Lugar de la Virgen en la Iglesia, según san Juan Damasceno", *Estudios Marianos* 28 (1966): 333–53; D. Dimitrijevic, "Die Entwicklung der liturgischen Verehrung der Mutter Gottes nach dem Ephesinum bis zum 12. Jahrhundert", in *De culto mariano saec. VI-XI*, vol. 4 (Rome, 1972), pp. 101–10; Frederick M. Jelly, "Mary's Mediation in the Distribution of Grace according to St. John Damascene's Homilies on her Dormition", *De culto mariano*, pp. 301–12.

Conception. Naturally, it is necessary to keep in mind the different view of original sin that already divided Byzantine theology from Western thought.

For John, both the Virgin Mary's conception and her birth took place completely under the influence of divine grace. These two events also shaped the role played by her parents, Joachim and Anna. Their previous sterility is explained thus:

> Because it would come to pass that the Virgin *Theotókos* would be born of Anna, nature did not dare anticipate the seed of grace but remained unfruitful until grace bore fruit.[2]

Anna's sterility was, therefore, a condition previously arranged in the divine plan, so that the role of grace would appear fully predominant. This is why Damascene always names the Virgin's parents with profound respect: they would offer themselves as the passive instruments of God's miraculous intervention:

> O blessed loins of Joachim, whence the all-pure seed was poured out! O glorious womb of Anna, in which the most holy fetus grew and was formed, silently increasing! O womb in which was conceived the living heaven, wider than the wideness of the heavens.[3]

In these considerations (not devoid of realism), the author wants us to notice that even the physiological process of Mary's conception and birth unfolded in a sinless fashion, under the mysterious guidance of the Almighty. The very seed of which Mary was born was utterly perfect (*panámōmos*). This concept of perfection, then, is decidedly positive: it goes beyond a simple absence of sin and corruption to include an exceptional richness of grace.

Now one can understand why the Damascene gave himself over to the praise of Mary, seeing her as a new heaven:

> This heaven is clearly much more divine and awesome than the first. Indeed he who created the sun in the first heaven would himself be born of this second heaven, as the Sun of Justice.[4]

---

[2] *Homily on the Nativity* 2; PG 96, 664 A.
[3] Ibid., 2; PG 96, 664 B.
[4] Ibid., 3; PG 96, 664 D.

Mary also appears as a lofty ladder, planted between heaven and earth, a kind of means of communication between God and man:

> Today [Christ] . . . built himself a living ladder, whose base is planted in the earth and whose tip reaches heaven. God rests upon it. Jacob saw a figure of it. God, unchanged, came down it. . . . He was made manifest on the earth and lived among men.[5]

The author emphasizes the fact that Mary's spiritual beauty derives from her special relationship with God:

> She is all beautiful, all near to God. For she, surpassing the cherubim, exalted beyond the seraphim, is placed near to God.[6]

All these texts come from the homily on the Nativity of the Virgin. It is understandable that the author should treat the theme of Mary's exceptional purity and sanctity in this context, since he considers it a condition that belongs to the very beginning of her earthly existence.

Mary Assumed into Heaven

The three homilies on the Dormition reveal the exceptional importance of Damascene's teaching for the development of doctrine on the Assumption. John explicitly teaches the truth of Mary's bodily Assumption into heaven. In conformity with the teaching of his two famous contemporaries, Germanus of Constantinople and Andrew of Crete, our doctor accepts the thesis that Mary's death is a premise of her imminent glorification:

> O how could the Font of life be led to life through death? O how could she, who in giving birth surpassed the limits of nature, now yield to nature's laws and have her immaculate body undergo death? She had to put aside what was mortal and put on incorruptibility, seeing that even the Lord of nature did not excuse himself from facing death. He truly died in the flesh to destroy death by means of death; in place of corruption he gave incorruptibility; he made death into a font of resurrection.[7]

---

[5] Ibid., 3; PG 96, 665 A
[6] Ibid., 9; PG 96, 676 D.
[7] *Homily 1 on the Dormition* 10; PG 96, 713 D.

Even though she must pass through death before being glorified, nevertheless the personal destiny of the Mother of God had an unusual outcome:

> Even though your most holy and blessed soul was separated from your most happy and immaculate body, according to the usual course of nature, and even though it was carried to a proper burial place, nevertheless it did not remain under the dominion of death, nor was it destroyed by corruption.
>
> Indeed, just as her virginity remained intact when she gave birth, so her body, even after death, was preserved from decay and transferred to a better and more divine dwelling place. There it is no longer subject to death but abides for all ages.[8]

In his second homily on the Dormition, Damascene uses biblical typology to present a whole series of reasons why it was fitting that Mary's body was not consumed by decay in the tomb. In this text, as in the passage cited above, one notes the homilist's tendency to explain the privilege of the Assumption by referring to the mystery of Mary's virginity in giving birth. Although this might seem to be an argument from fittingness, in Damascene's eyes it has the character of most strict necessity, because of the indispensable role played by Mary in the mystery of the Incarnation:

> It was necessary that the body of the one who preserved her virginity intact in giving birth should also be kept incorrupt after death. It was necessary that she, who carried the Creator in her womb when he was a baby, should dwell among the tabernacles of heaven. . . .
>
> It was necessary that the Mother of God share what belongs to her Son and that she be celebrated by all creation. An inheritance is normally passed down from parents to children; now, however, to use the expression of a wise man, the sources of the sacred rivers flow back toward their origin, now that the Son has made all created things his Mother's slaves.[9]

With regard to the external details of the event, Damascene does not offer anything new, limiting himself to reporting those details

---

[8] Ibid. 10; PG 96, 716 A–B.
[9] *Homily 2 on the Dormition* 14; PG 96, 741 B.

that are known through apocryphal descriptions. But he does not dwell excessively on the curious details or astounding contents of the apocryphal writings; rather, his attention is clearly focused on the theological and spiritual aspects of the mystery.

Mary, Mediatrix between Earth and Heaven

John introduces the concept of Mary's mediation with the Old Testament image of Jacob's ladder. As we said earlier, he loves to use this image for Mary:

> That man [Jacob] contemplated heaven joined to earth by the two ends of a ladder and saw angels going up and down upon it and saw himself symbolically wrestling with the Strong One, the Invincible. So you have assumed the role of a mediatrix, having become the ladder by which God comes down to us, assuming the weakness of our nature, embracing it and uniting himself to it, and thus making man into a mind that can see God. Thus [O Mary] you have reunited what had been divided.[10]

He attributes great efficacy to the holy Virgin's mediation in the plan of salvation. Mary has a very active part in causing the fruits of the Incarnation to be applied. Accordingly, he ascribes the benefits of salvation to her and to her divine Son, almost without distinction:

> Through her, the long warfare waged with the Creator has been ended. Through her, the reconciliation between us and him was ratified. Grace and peace were granted us, so that men and angels are united in the same choir, and we, who had been deserving of disdain, have become sons of God. From her we have harvested the grape of life; from her we have cultivated the seed of immortality. For our sake she became Mediatrix of all blessings; in her God became man, and man became God.[11]

Damascene does speak of Mary's compassion on Calvary, without, however, including her among the causes of our redemption.

---

[10] *Homily 1 on the Dormition* 8; PG 96, 713 A.
[11] *Homily 2 on the Dormition* 16; PG 96, 744 C–D.

Instead, this sorrowful experience of Mary is linked to Simeon's prophecy:

> It was necessary that she who contemplated her own Son on the Cross, and who had been pierced through the heart by the sword she had avoided while giving birth, should contemplate him reigning with the Father.[12]

Speaking of the divine favors that the Mother of the Lord distributes to Christians in copious measure throughout the world, our doctor exhorts his audience to acquire the dispositions that will render them open to Mary's mediation:

> If we firmly abstain, then, from past vices and love the virtues with all our heart, taking them as our companions in life, the Virgin will frequently visit her servants, bringing all manner of blessings. She will be accompanied by Christ her Son, the King and Lord of all, who will dwell in our hearts.[13]

In this passage, the author sums up the ways in which Mary exercises her power on our behalf: In giving us the incarnate Word to be our Redeemer, she has obtained for us all the graces we need for salvation, and, like an inexhaustible spring, she continues to pour them out upon us.

Devotion to Mary

With regard to Marian devotion, a very practical part of Christian life, it is particularly interesting to revisit the thought of St. John Damascene. He introduces the fine distinction between the cult of adoration, or *latria*, owed to God alone, and the honor or veneration that ought to be given to the holy Virgin. Later on the term *dulia* was introduced for this, but it was unknown to our doctor. Here is a text:

> But we, who consider God the object of adoration—a God not made out of anything, but existing from all eternity, beyond every cause, word, or concept of time and nature—we honor and venerate the mother of God.[14]

---

[12] Ibid., 14; PG 96, 741 B.
[13] Ibid., 19; PG 96, 752 D.
[14] Ibid.,15; PG 96, 744 A.

The cult of Mary, even though inferior to that owed to God, is superior to the honor paid to the other saints and to the angels in heaven. Because she is queen and mistress of all things, she merits the veneration suited to her greatness and unique dignity:

> If the memory of all the saints is celebrated with panegyrics, who will refuse to praise the font of justice and the treasury of holiness? This is not done to glorify her but so that God might be glorified with an eternal glory.[15]

Such veneration can also be extended to images of Mary. In his discourses in defense of sacred icons, Damascene makes some extremely clear distinctions about this form of veneration.

God cannot be represented by any image because he is an absolutely pure spirit; to the contrary, the incarnate Word, the Virgin, and the saints can be depicted. Angels, too, can be represented by means of images since, although they are pure spirits, they have sometimes appeared in human guise.

The cult paid to images is legitimate, because it is not directly addressed to the material substance of which the images are made but to the person they represent. This is a way of acknowledging that God works through the creatures he has made.

As for icons of the Mother of God, they merit a special veneration because of Mary's unique personal position in the economy of salvation.

In addition to the extreme theological clarity with which our doctor resolves the objective question of Marian devotion, he is not held back by any inhibition or timidity when he wants to express his personal feelings toward her. Let us choose two texts from among the most expressive:

> O daughter of Joachim and Anna, O Lady, receive the word of a sinful servant, who nevertheless burns with love and places in you his only hope of joy; in you he finds the guardian of his life, not only a Mediatrix in your Son's presence, but also a sure pledge of salvation.[16]

And again:

---

[15] *Homily 1 on the Dormition* 1; PG 96, 700 A.
[16] *Homily on the Nativity* 12; PG 96, 680 B.

What is sweeter than the Mother of my God? She has taken my mind captive; she has taken possession of my tongue; she is on my mind, day and night.[17]

St. John Damascene proposed a practice of Marian devotion that seems to come very close to the concept of consecration to the Blessed Virgin as understood and practiced in Marian devotion today. He explains it in a passage from a homily on the Dormition:

> We today also remain near you, O Lady. Yes, I repeat, O Lady, Mother of God and Virgin. We bind our souls to your hope, as to a most firm and totally unbreakable anchor, consecrating to you (*anathémenoi*) mind, soul, body, and all our being and honoring you, as much as we can, with psalms, hymns, and spiritual canticles.[18]

The Greek word used by Damascene, *anatíthēmi*, means (*inter alia*) to dedicate, consecrate, offer in a religious sense. Damascene's text, therefore, is a good description of the act of a servant and devotee of Mary, who offers his whole self to her as his sovereign and lady. Thus, a consecration.

READING

MARY'S TOMB, PLACE OF GRACE

Your holy and all-virginal body was consigned to a holy tomb, while the angels went before it, accompanied it, and followed it; for what would they not do to serve the Mother of their Lord?

Meanwhile, the apostles and the whole assembly of the Church sang divine hymns and struck the lyre of the Spirit: "We shall be filled with the blessings of your house; your temple is holy; wondrous in justice" (Ps 65:4). And again: "The Most High has sanctified his dwelling" (Ps 46:5); "God's mountain, rich mountain, the mountain in which God has been pleased to dwell" (Ps 68:16–17).

---

[17] *Homily 3 on the Dormition* 1; PG 96, 753 B–C.
[18] *Homily 1 on the Dormition* 14; PG 96, 720 C–D.

The assembly of apostles carried you, the Lord God's true Ark, as once the priests carried the symbolic ark, on their shoulders. They laid you in the tomb, through which, as if through the Jordan, they will conduct you to the promised land, that is to say, the Jerusalem above, mother of all the faithful, whose architect and builder is God. Your soul did not descend to Hades, neither did your flesh see corruption. Your virginal and uncontaminated body was not abandoned in the earth, but you are transferred into the royal dwelling of heaven, you, the Queen, the sovereign, the Lady, God's Mother, the true God-bearer.

O, how did heaven receive her, who surpasses the wideness of the heavens? How is it possible that the tomb should contain the dwelling place of God? And yet it received and held it. For she was not wider than heaven in her bodily dimensions; indeed, how could a body three cubits long, which is always growing thinner, be compared with the breadth and length of the sky? Rather it is through grace that she surpassed the limits of every height and depth. The Divinity does not admit of comparison.

O holy tomb, awesome, venerable, and adorable! Even now the angels continue to venerate you, standing by with great respect and fear, while the devils shrink in horror. With faith, men make haste to render you honor, to adore you, to salute you with their eyes, with their lips, and with the affection of their souls, in order to obtain an abundance of blessings.

A precious ointment, when it is poured out upon the garments or in any place and then taken away, leaves traces of its fragrance even after evaporating. In the same way your body, holy and perfect, impregnated with divine perfume and abundant spring of grace, this body which had been laid in the tomb, when it was taken out and transferred to a better and more elevated place, did not leave the tomb bereft of honor but left behind a divine fragrance and grace, making it a wellspring of healing and a source of every blessing for those who approach it with faith.

—John Damascene, *Homily 1 on the Dormition* 12–13;
PG 96, 717 D–720 C

Select Bibliography*

Alvarez Campos, Sergio. *Corpus Marianum Patristicum*, 6 vols. Burgos: Ediciones Aldecoa, 1970–1981. Indices (1985).

de Aldama, José Antonio. *María en la patrística de los siglos I y II.* Biblioteca de los Autores Cristianos. Madrid, 1970.

———. *Virgo Mater: Estudios de Teología patrística.* Granada: Facultad de Teología, 1963.

Bäumer, Remigius, and Leo Scheffczyk, eds. *Marienlexikon.* St. Ottilien: EOS Verlag, 1988– .

Besutti, Giuseppe Maria. *Bibliografia mariana* (1948–1983), 7 vols. Rome: Marianum, 1948–1987.

Burghardt, Walter. "Mary in Western Patristic Thought", in *Mariology.* Ed. Juniper Carol, vol. 1, pp. 109–155. Milwaukee, 1955.

———. "Mary in Eastern Patristic Thought", in *Mariology.* Ed. Juniper Carol, vol. 2, pp. 88–153. Milwaukee, 1957.

Casagrande, D. *Enchiridion Marianum Biblicum Patristicum.* Rome, 1974.

De Fiores, Stefano, and S. Meo, eds. *Nuovo dizionario di mariologia.* Milan: Edizioni Paoline, 1985.

Delius, W. *Geschichte der Marienverehrung.* Munich-Basel: E. Reinhardt, 1963.

Fernandez, D. "Doctrina mariologica antiquorum Patrum occidentalium". In Pontificia Academia Mariana Internationalis. *De Mariologia et Oecumenismo.* Rome, 1962.

———. "Mariología patrística postconciliar". *Ephemerides Mariologicae* 27 (1977): 49–80.

Gharib, G., E. Toniolo, L. Gambero, G. Di Nola, eds. *Testi mariani del primo millennio.* 4 vols. Rome: Città Nuova, 1988– .

Graef, Hilda. *Mary: A History of Doctrine and Devotion.* New York: Sheed and Ward, 1964.

---

* As we have already given specific bibliographical references throughout the book, we limit ourselves here to some references of a general character.

Jouassard, G. "Maria à travers la Patristique: Maternité divine, virginité, sainteté". In *Maria: Études sur la sainte Vierge*. Ed. H. Du Manoir, vol. 1, pp. 69–157. Paris, 1949.

Koehler, Theodore. *Storia della Mariologia*. 5 vols. Vercelli: Centro Mariano Chaminade, 1971–1976.

O'Carroll, Michael. *Theotokos: A Theological Encyclopedia of the Blessed Virgin Mary*. Wilmington, Del.: M. Glazier, 1982.

Ortiz de Urbina, I. "La Mariologia nei Padri siriaci". *Orientalia Christiana Periodica* 1 (1935): 100–113.

————. "Lo sviluppo della Mariologia nella Patrologia Orientale". *Orientalia Christiana Periodica* 6 (1940): 40–82.

Peretto, E. "Mariologia Patristica". In *Complementi Interdisciplinari di Patrologia*. Ed. A. Quacquarelli, pp. 697–756. Rome, 1989.

Roschini, G. *Maria Santissima nella storia della salvezza*, 4 vols. Isola del Liri, 1969.

Söll, Georg. *Storia dei dogmi mariani*. Rome, 1981.

Spedalieri, F. *Maria nella Scrittura e nella tradizione della Chiesa primitiva*, 2 vols. Messina: La Sicilia, 1961–1964.

Acknowledgments

Quotations from *Ephrem the Syrian*, translated and introduced by Kathleen E. McVey, copyright 1989 by Kathleen E. McVey; used by permission of Paulist Press Inc.

Quotations from *The Apocryphal Old Testament*, ed. H. F. D. Sparks, copyright 1984 by Oxford University Press; used by permission of Oxford University Press.

Quotations from *The Apocryphal New Testament*, ed. J. K. Elliott, copyright 1993 by Oxford University Press; used by permission of Oxford University Press.

Index of Scripture References

Index of Names and Subjects

Page numbers with "n." indicate footnotes and are followed by the note number.

Bover, J. M., "La mediacíon universal de María según san Ambrosio", 190 n. 1

Boyer, C., "La controverse sur l'opinion de Saint Augustin", 226 n. 25

Brajčić, R., "Sancti Gregorii Magni", 367 n. 1

Byzantine Theology (Meyendorff), 380 n. 1

Caesaro-papism, 92

Callixtus I, St. (pope), 86

Camelot, T., "Marie la nouvelle Eve", 124 n. 12

Campos, Sergio Alvarez, *Corpus Marianum Patristicum*, 217 n. 2

Canal, J. N., "San Juan Damasceno, doctor de la muerte y de la Asunción de Maria", 401 n. 1

Candall, M., "La Virgen Santísima prepurificado en su Anunciación", 264 n. 9

Capanaga, Victorino, *La Virgen María según San Augustin*, 218 n. 2

Capelle, B., "La Pensée de saint Augustin sur 'Immaculée Conception", 226 n. 25

Cappodocia, Christianity in, 141–42, 141 n. 1

Carli, I., *La dottrina sull'Assunzione di Maria di S. Germano di Costantinopoli*, 381 n. 1

Carmen Paschale (Sedulius), 283, 284

Carmina Miscellanea (Fortunatus), 359

Caro, R.: *La Homilética Mariana Griega en el Siglo V*, 152 n. 5,

250 n. 2, 260 n. 1, 261 n. 2; "Proclo de Costantinopla", 250 n. 2

Casagrande, D., *Enchiridion Marianum Biblicum Patristicum*, 217 n. 2

catacombs, Marian art of, 83–85

Catechesis IV (Cyril of Jerusalem), 132

Catechesis XII (Cyril of Jerusalem), 133, 138, 139–40

Celestine I (pope), 236, 237, 241

celibacy. See virginity; virginity of Mary

Chevalier, C.: "La Mariologie de saint Jean Damascène", 401 n. 1; "Mariologie de Romanos", 326–27 n. 3

Christ: hypostatic union theology, 137, 153, 247, 251, 306; as Lamb, 283–84, 333, 336, 337; Mary and predestination of, 218–19; as spouse of Mary, 117, 118, 167, 296–97, 300–301, 338. *See also* Adam–Christ parallel; genealogy of Christ; Incarnation

Christian conduct. *See* women, Mary as model of

Church–Mary parallel. *See* Mary–Church parallel

Cicero, *Hortensius*, 216

Clement I, St. (pope), 27, 82

Clement of Alexandria, St.: on Mary–Church parallel, 71; on virginity of Mary, 70–71

communicatio idiomatum principle, 235

Conci, C., "La mariologia di S. Andrea di Creta", 392 n. 1

Confessions (Augustine), 216

Constantine I, the Great (Roman emperor), 92, 99, 354